THE STUDIA PHILONICA ANNUAL
Studies in Hellenistic Judaism

Society of Biblical Literature

THE STUDIA PHILONICA ANNUAL
Studies in Hellenistic Judaism

Editors
David T. Runia
Gregory E. Sterling

THE STUDIA PHILONICA ANNUAL
Studies in Hellenistic Judaism

Volume XXVI

2014

EDITORS
David T. Runia
Gregory E. Sterling

ASSOCIATE EDITOR
Sarah J. K. Pearce

BOOK REVIEW EDITOR
Ronald Cox

SBL Press
Atlanta

THE STUDIA PHILONICA ANNUAL
Studies in Hellenistic Judaism

The financial support of

C. J. de Vogel Foundation, Utrecht
Queen's College, University of Melbourne
Yale University
Pepperdine University

is gratefully acknowledged

ISBN: 9781628370188 (hardcover: alk. paper)
ISBN: 9781628370195 (electronic book)
ISSN : 1052-4533

The cover photo, *Ezra Reads the Law*, is from a wall painting in the Dura Europos synagogue and used with permission from Zev Radovan (www.BibleLandPictures.com).

Printed on acid-free, recycled paper conforming to ANSI/ NISO Z39.48-1992 (R1997) and ISO 9706:1994 standards for paper permanence.

∞

THE STUDIA PHILONICA ANNUAL
STUDIES IN HELLENISTIC JUDAISM

Contributions should be sent to the Editor, Prof. G. E. Sterling, 409 Prospect Street, New Haven, CT 06511, USA; email: gregory.sterling@yale.edu. Please send books for review to the Book Review Editor, Prof. Ronald Cox, Religion Division, Pepperdine University, 24255 Pacific Coast Highway, Malibu, CA 90263-4352; email: rcox@pepperdine.edu.

Contributors are requested to observe the "Instructions to Contributors" located at the end of the volume. These can also be consulted on the Annual's website: http://www.nd.edu/~philojud. Articles which do not conform to these instructions cannot be accepted for inclusion.

The Studia Philonica Monograph series accepts monographs in the area of Hellenistic Judaism, with special emphasis on Philo and his *Umwelt*. Proposals for books in this series should be sent to the Editor, Prof. Thomas H. Tobin, S.J., Theology Department, Loyola University Chicago, 1032 West Sheridan Road, Chicago, IL 60660-1537, U.S.A.; email: ttobin@luc.edu.

CONTENTS

NOTE. The editors wish to thank the typesetter Gonni Runia once again for her tireless work on this volume. They wish to express their thanks to Sami Yli-Karjanmaa for his assistance with the bibliography, and also to Dr Lisa Marie Belz, OSU, Ph.D., Jonathan Hatter and Cory Louie, for meticulously proof-reading the final manuscript. As in previous years we are deeply grateful to our publisher, The SBL Press, and to its staff. In particular we wish to express our heartfelt thanks to Leigh Andersen for all her assistance and support during the past nine years. It has been a true delight to work together with her to ensure that every year the Annual has been ready and available at the Annual meeting of the Society in November. We shall miss her greatly. All the members of *The Studia Philonica Annual* team extend to her our very best wishes as she moves to a new and exciting phase of her life.

ABBREVIATIONS

The abbreviations used for the citation of ancient texts and modern scholarly literature generally follow the guidelines of the Society of Biblical Literature as published in *The SBL Handbook of Style* (Hendrickson: Peabody Mass. 1999) §8.4. In addition to the abbreviations listed in the Notes to contributors at the back of the volume, please note the following:

CAF	*Comicorum Atticorum fragmenta*
CJAS	Christianity and Judaism in Antiquity Series
FHG	*Fragmenta historicorum Graecorum,* ed K. Müller, Paris: Didot, 1841–1870; reprint, Frankfurt-Main: Minerva, 1975
ITRL	The I Tatti Renaissance Library
JETS	*Journal of the Evangelical Theological Society*
JPT	*The International Journal of the Platonic Tradition*
PCG	*Poetae comici graeci*
RGRW	Religions in the Greco-Roman World

The Studia Philonica Annual 26 (2014) 1–27

THE DEIFICATION OF MOSES IN
PHILO OF ALEXANDRIA

M. DAVID LITWA

Introduction

Crispin Fletcher-Louis once remarked that "It is well known that in the second Temple period Philo deified Moses."[1] In fact, Moses's deification in Philo is a deeply contested issue. Depending on which passages one highlights, Philo seems to both clearly assert and strongly deny Moses's deification. In his *Questions on Exodus*, for instance, Philo says that Moses was "divinized" (2.40), "changed into the divine," and thus became "truly divine" (2.29). Moreover, ten times Philo calls Moses "(a) god" (θεός) in accordance with Exod 7:1: "I [God] have made you a god to Pharaoh." In *On the Sacrifices*, for instance, Philo says that God appointed Moses as god, "placing all the bodily region and the mind which rules it in subjection and slavery to him" (§9).[2] In an influential study, Wayne Meeks stated that "the analogy between Moses and God implied by this title θεός is taken so seriously in this passage [*Sacr.* 9] that it approaches consubstantiality."[3]

At loggerheads with these passages are those wherein Philo presents God as utterly unique (*Leg.* 2.1; *Sacr.* 92), and where he strongly attacks polytheism, idolatry (*Decal.* 65; *Spec.* 1.28), and the self-deification of rulers.[4] In *The Worse Is Wont to Attack the Better*, Philo writes that God, as Being

---

[1] "4Q374: A Discourse on the Sinai Tradition: The Deification of Moses and Early Christology," *Dead Sea Discoveries* 3 (1996): 236–52 (242).

[2] Cf. *Leg.* 1.40; *Migr.* 84; *Somn.* 2.189; *Mos.* 1.158.

[3] *The Prophet-King: Moses Traditions and the Johannine Christology* (Leiden: Brill, 1967) 104–5. For Moses exalted in the Bible and other Jewish works, see George W. Coats, *Moses: Heroic Man, Man of God* (JSOTSup 57; Sheffield: JSOT Press, 1988), esp. 155–78; Larry Hurtado, *One Lord, One God: Early Christian Devotion and Ancient Jewish Monotheism* (Philadelphia: Fortress, 1988), 56–59; Jan Willem van Henten, "Moses as Heavenly Messenger in *Assumptio Mosis* 10:2 and Qumran passages," *JJS* 54 (2003): 216–27; A. Graupner and M. Wolter (eds.), *Moses in Biblical and Extra-Biblical Traditions* (BZAW 372; Berlin: de Gruyter, 2007).

[4] E.g., *Legat.* 75–76, 93, 114–15, 118, 143, 162.

itself, IS in truth (§161). The very fact that Moses *is made* a god in Exod 7:1 shows that he is fixed in the realm of becoming. Moses is thus not a god in truth (πρὸς ἀλήθειαν δὲ οὐκ ἔστι θεός, §162)—nor technically "IS" he *anything* in truth since he is an entity in the sphere of *becoming*. The apparent nail in the coffin of Moses's—or anyone's—deification in Philo is the oft-quoted passage in *Embassy to Gaius* 118: "Sooner could God transform into a human than a human into God."[5]

Is Philo simply inconsistent on the question of Moses's deification? According to Meeks, Philo "wavers," "now elevating him [Moses] virtually to a 'second god,' again restricting him to the sphere of the human."[6] In this judgment, Meeks followed E. R. Goodenough who saw Philo's presentation of Moses in both human and divine terms as a "vacillation."[7] Goodenough proffered a solution for the irresolution. Philo, he says, was essentially a monotheist. Thus, if carefully cross-examined, Philo would without question assert that Moses was "essentially a man," and not a god. Philo *called* Moses a god, said Goodenough, because he followed the "popular tendency" which deified "great figures and heroes." Nevertheless, Philo did not follow this "popular tendency" logically, but only "under the stress of his emotions."[8] Goodenough himself preferred the compromise position that Philo's Moses was part of a τρίτον γένος, a Pythagorean third type of being between humanity and deity.[9]

Since the time of Goodenough, scholars have attempted to resolve the inconsistencies of Philo on the question of Moses's deification with mixed results. Howard Teeple delicately (or irresolutely) concluded that Philo

---

[5] Θᾶττον γὰρ ἂν εἰς ἄνθρωπον θεὸν ἢ εἰς θεὸν ἄνθρωπον μεταβαλεῖν. Louis Feldman, among others, employs this passage to deny the deity of Moses ("The Death of Moses, According to Philo," *Estudios Bíblicos* 60 [2002]: 225–254 [234]). Cf. his more recent (slightly expanded) remarks in *Philo's Portrayal of Moses in the Context of Ancient Judaism* (Notre Dame: University of Notre Dame Press, 2007), 342. It is important to note that what Philo means by "God" in this passage is the "ingenerate and incorruptible" (ἀγένητον καὶ ἄφθαρτον) God. For a human to become ingenerate and incorruptible is indeed impossible, but it is not what Philonic deification means. Colson obscures this point in the Loeb translation by rendering θεοπλαστῆσαι in *Legat.* 118 as "deification." Θεοπλαστέω is not an ancient term for deification. Elsewhere Philo uses it to refer to idolatry (and it is indeed idolatry to become the high God). In *Legat.*, Philo's standard term for deification is ἐκθέωσις.

[6] *Prophet-King*, 105.

[7] *By Light, Light: The Mystic Gospel of Hellenistic Judaism* (New Haven: Yale University Press, 1935), 223.

[8] *Ibid.* 224.

[9] Here Goodenough himself seems to vacillate, for but a few pages before this comment he speaks of Moses's union with Deity "so complete" that he can take God's place with Sophia. "Here one becomes identical with God." This "mystic intercourse as male with Sophia as female is the sweet token of one's ultimate deification" (*ibid.*, 202).

"did not *fully* deify Moses."[10] Donald Hagner stated that "Philo remains too much under the control of the monotheism of the Old Testament to allow more than a nominal apotheosis of Moses."[11] After duly quoting the two main anti-deification texts (*Det.* 162 and *Legat.* 118), he continued: "Similarly, even in the height of ecstasy, the soul, while drawing near to the Existent, never merges with it nor is absorbed into it."[12] Here Hagner betrays his assumption that deification means mystical fusion with the Godhead. Oddly, he never inquires into what deification might have meant to Philo. In his study on the θεῖος ἀνήρ in Hellenistic Judaism, Carl Holladay argued that Moses's being made a "god" in Exod 7:1 is explained by Philo's desire to make Moses a Platonic sage.[13] Such a sage is, according to Plato's *Republic*, a philosopher king. Philo, Holladay thought, had no direct proof-text for calling Moses a king. He did, however, have a clear text in which Moses was called "god" (θεός) (Exod 7:1). Θεός in Philo could become a metaphor for Moses's kingship in a culture where kings had long been viewed as gods. Moses's godhood is thus a metaphor for his rule in various senses—over his body, over fools, over other human beings, and over the natural elements.[14] The capstone of Holladay's argument is again *Det.* 160-62, where Philo disallows the literal interpretation of θεός as applied to Moses. Moses is passive and does not really exist. The Existent is active and truly existing. Thus Moses can never be θεός in the truest sense, namely Being itself.

Scholarship after Holladay has been heavily influenced by him, resulting in a scholarly trend to deny the deification of Moses in Philo.[15] The most

[10] *The Mosaic Eschatological Prophet* (Philadelphia: Society of Biblical Literature, 1957), 38, emphasis mine.

[11] Donald A. Hagner, "The Vision of God in Philo and John: A Comparative Study," *Journal of the Evangelical Theological Society* 14 (1971): 81–93 (90).

[12] *Ibid.*, 90.

[13] *Theios Aner in Hellenistic-Judaism: A Critique of the Use of This Category in New Testament Christology* (Missoula, MT: Scholars Press, 1977), 196–97.

[14] *Ibid.* 148–52.

[15] Hurtado, *One Lord, One God*, 61. Hurtado duly quotes *Det.* 161–62 to indicate that Moses was not a "real" god (62). Philo's deification language is applied "only in an ethicized sense" and thus Moses is only an "ideal man" (63). Wendy Helleman calls Philo's version of deification a form of assimilation to God ("Philo of Alexandria on Deification and Assimilation to God," *SPhA* 2 [1990]: 51–71). Assimilation, she argues, is not a direct participation in "the divine nature as such," but an imitation of divine qualities or virtues (63). She questionably assumes that in the ancient world divine qualities or virtues cannot express divine nature (cf. 2 Pet 1:4). Barry Blackburn thinks it "quite misleading" to speak of Moses's "apotheosis" since this same apotheosis will "be experienced by the soul of every wise man" (*Theios Anēr and the Markan Miracle Traditions* [WUNT 2.40; Tübingen: Mohr Siebeck, 1991], 66). Moses is a creature who cannot belong to the ontological

M. David Litwa

recent denial has come from the pen of Richard Bauckham.[16] After a study of the ten uses of θεός applied to Moses, Bauckham agrees with Holladay that Moses was only a θεός in the sense of being a philosopher king. Even though many kings in the ancient world were considered to be gods, Bauckham assumes that Moses the king is definitely a human figure.[17] Yet Bauckham goes even further than Holladay by reducing Moses's kingship to a mere ethical rule over his moral inferiors and his own passions.[18] The only rule Moses has is "figurative-ethical … It does not refer to literal participation in God's rule over the cosmos or to literal government on earth."[19] Bauckham concludes that Philo's use of θεός in reference to Moses is "entirely out of line with his own usage of θεός" in other passages.[20] Moses the θεός is not god (or a god), and thus not deified.

In the present essay, I will question Bauckham's conclusions. Even more pointedly than in other studies, Bauckham's overly narrow selection of evidence guides his results. By focusing merely on the use of the word "god" as applied to Moses, he misses an important side of Philo's thought regarding Moses's deification, not to mention the entire theological and philosophical context that makes a Philonic form of deification possible.

---

category of Philo's high God, the Existent (67). Holladay's conclusion is restated in Ian W. Scott's "Is Philo's Moses a Divine Man?" *SPhA* 14 (2002): 87–111. With Holladay, Scott rightly points out that the "divine man" (θεῖος ἀνήρ) is a dubious and ill-defined category, ill-suited to careful historical research. If the very category of "divine man" is incoherent, then Moses was certainly not a divine man, and we must proceed to a more fruitful question, namely "Is Philo's Moses a *deified* man?"

[16] "Moses as 'God' in Philo of Alexandria: A Precedent for Christology?" in *The Spirit and Christ in the New Testament and Christian Theology: Essays in Honor of Max Turner* (ed. I. Howard Marshall; Grand Rapids: Eerdmans, 2012), 246–65.

[17] Bauckham also notes—in tension with his argument—that, in Philo, θεός in Exod 7:1 is "usually connected with rule," but not in the passages in which *"Moses stands for God himself (Somn.* 2.189; *Mut.* 19; *Migr.* 84)" (*ibid.* 254, my emphasis).

[18] *Ibid.*, 255. In making this argument, Bauckham does not sufficiently appreciate that ancient Platonists made no hard and fast distinction between ethics and ontology. One can be deified by virtue, and this is just as realistic as somatic transformation. On deification by virtue, see M. David Litwa, *We Are Being Transformed: Deification in Paul's Soteriology* (BZNW 187; Berlin: de Gruyter, 2012), 193–225.

[19] "Moses as God," 263.

[20] *Ibid.* 262–63.

The Deification of Moses in Philo

The Theological Rationale

Many scholars—even those distrustful of Moses's deification in Philo—remain open to the notion of Moses's deifying transformation *with the caveat* that the deified Moses does not threaten the position of Philo's high God, or the "Existent." David Runia, for example, denied Moses's deification if it meant that he had the same nature as the Existent. Nevertheless, he admitted on the basis of passages in *Questions on Exodus* (2.29, 40, and 46) that Moses attained a "derived divinity."[21] Even though Moses is not literally "god" (*Det.* 161-62; cf. *Mut.* 128-129), says John Lierman, he remains "a divine figure" in the sense that he has been elevated to the "divine office" of "god" (one of the twin powers of the Existent; *Mut.* 19-22). Moses is god because of his divine function, a criterion which Lierman thinks makes a person divine.[22] Thus Lierman accepts the deification of Moses, provided that it is understood as a "delegated" rather than an "essential" divinity.[23]

The idea of "derived" (Runia) or "delegated" divinity (Lierman) is an important advance because it allows us to transcend disjunctive thinking about the divine. In later Christian theology, the doctrine of *creatio ex nihilo* constructed an impermeable barrier between the essence of God and that of every creature. In this theology, a creature cannot strictly speaking be a god at the same time.[24]

Theologians in the first century c.e., I believe, did not think in these terms. As we can see from a variety of sources, divinity constituted a great

---

[21] "God and Man in Philo of Alexandria," *JTS* 39 (1988): 48–75 (69, cf. 60). Cf. Runia's earlier study where he writes that the "logical outcome of Philo's adoption of Greek intellectualism is the affirmation of man's potential apotheosis, that the mind can gain a place in the noetic world on the level of the divine" (*Philo of Alexandria and the* Timaeus *of Plato* [Amsterdam: VU Boekhandel, 1983], 439).

[22] *The New Testament Moses: Christian Perceptions of Moses and Israel in the Setting of Jewish Religion* (WUNT 2.173; Tübingen: Mohr Siebeck, 2004), 231.

[23] *Ibid.* 246.

[24] Gerhard May argued that the doctrine of *creatio ex nihilo* appeared among proto-orthodox writers in the late second century c.e. in response to Gnostic thought (*Creatio ex Nihilo: The Doctrine of 'Creation Out of Nothing' in Early Christian Thought* [trans. A. S. Worrall; Edinburgh: T&T Clark, 1994]. See also David Runia, "Plato's *Timaeus*, First Principle(s), and Creation in Philo and Early Christian Thought," in *Plato's Timaeus as Cultural Icon* (ed. Gretchen Reydams-Schils; Notre Dame: University of Notre Dame Press, 2003), 133–51. *Creatio ex nihilo* is often viewed as a uniquely Christian doctrine. It was, however, a logical deduction drawn from Plato's distinction between Being (or reality) and becoming (what does not truly exist).

chain of being, a chain in which the divine and human worlds were intimately interlinked. Philosophers and theologians in the ancient Mediterranean world acknowledged many levels of divinity from Zeus to Pan or (more philosophically stated) from the one invisible and unknowable God to the most insignificant daimon.[25]

Like his philosophical contemporaries, Philo too recognized several different tiers of divinity.[26] At the top of the pyramid is the supreme God, whom Philo calls "the Existent" (ὁ ὤν), a designation he borrows from Exod 3:14 (see, e.g., *Abr.* 121). Since the high God is Being itself (*Fug.* 89), Philo does not think that a human can become or even share the Existent's nature. To think so would, for Philo, be tantamount to blasphemy. Though a person who worships the Existent alone is no longer human but god, the Existent remains "God of gods," or "King of the gods."[27] "No existing thing is of equal honor to God ... there is only one sovereign and ruler and king" (*Conf.* 170); he is the "Primal God, the Begetter of the Universe" (*Mos.* 2.205). Numerous other passages can be piled up to show that Philo's Existent is divine in an ultimate, unshareable sense.[28]

Nonetheless, for the Alexandrian exegete there exists an entire divine world dependent on the Existent in the world of becoming. Philo repeatedly assumes and asserts that divinity can be and is shared by lesser (including created) beings. First among these is the Logos, God's Mind and "second God" (*QG* 2.62).[29] Below the Logos are the Existent's two "powers" (δυνάμεις), namely the "Beneficent" and "Punishing" Powers (whom Philo

---

[25] Those who would argue that deification contradicts monotheism must state carefully what they mean by monotheism. Typically ancient monotheism amounts to the idea of the high God's absolute power, not to the idea that there was a numerically singular divine being. See further Peter Hayman, "Monotheism—a Misused Word in Jewish Studies?" *JJS* 42 (1991): 1–15; Polymnia Athanassiadi and Michael Frede, eds., *Pagan Monotheism in Late Antiquity* (Oxford: Clarendon, 1999); John J. Collins, "Powers in Heaven: God, Gods, and Angels in the Dead Sea Scrolls", in *Religion in the Dead Sea Scrolls* (eds. John J. Collins and Robert A. Kugler; Grand Rapids: Eerdmans, 2000), 9–28; Mark S. Smith, *The Origins of Biblical Monotheism* (Oxford: Oxford University Press, 2000); Nathan MacDonald, *Deuteronomy and the Meaning of "Monotheism"* (Tübingen: Mohr Siebeck, 2003); Stephen Mitchell and Peter van Nuffelen, eds., *One God: Pagan Monotheism in the Roman Empire* (Cambridge: Cambridge University Press, 2010); Beate Pongratz-Leisten, ed. *Reconsidering the Concept of Revolutionary Monotheism* (Winona Lake, IN: Eisenbrauns, 2011); Litwa, *We Are Being Transformed*, 229–57.

[26] Cf. Runia, "God and Man," 56; Peter van Nuffelen, *Rethinking the Gods: Philosophical Readings of Religion in the Post-Hellenistic Period* (Cambridge: Cambridge University Press, 2011), 205–12.

[27] *Prob.* 43; cf. *Mos.* 2.206, 238.

[28] E.g., *Leg.* 1.36; 2.1; *Sacr.* 91–92; *Mut.* 27; *Virt.* 65; *Legat.* 115.

[29] Cf. *Leg.* 3.207–208; *Somn.* 1.229–230.

names "God" and "Lord," respectively).[30] The stars, including the sun and moon (*Prov.* 2.50), for Philo, are also divine.[31] Under these cosmic divinities were the "heroes" and "daimones" of the Greeks, whom Philo calls "angels," in accordance with his scriptures (*Somn.* 1.140-41).[32] In this cosmology, divinity was not a quality of the Uncreated alone. It was shared by a hierarchy of beings existing on a broad scale.[33]

To understand this theology, we can say that Philo distinguishes between at least two fundamental types of deity, what I will call "primal deity" and "mediate deity." Primal deity is "true God" and unshareable. This deity is Philo's high God, the reality of true Being, whom he calls the "Existent" (*Somn.* 1.229). Mediate deity, on the other hand, is deity in the realm of becoming, and thus shareable. A key human example of mediate deity is Moses himself, whom Philo repeatedly calls θεός ("god" or "a god"). For Louis Feldman, Moses as θεός is a theologically "troublesome" idea and a "problem" which Philo must solve.[34] Yet it is only a problem, I suggest, for those who do not distinguish multiple grades of divinity in Philo's thought. Moses is a θεός as a "participant" or "partner" (κοινωνός) in God's possessions (*Mos.* 1.155). He is not θεός "in truth" (πρὸς ἀλήθειαν) (*Det.* 162). On this score, however, neither are the two Powers of the Existent properly called "God" (*Abr.* 119-21).[35] This is because both Moses

---

[30] *Abr.* 119–22; *Mut.* 28–29; *Conf.* 137; *Mos.* 2.99; *Somn.* 1.162–63.

[31] Six times Philo calls the stars "(sensible) gods" (*Opif.* 27; *Spec.* 1.19; *Aet.* 46, 112; *QG* 1.42, 4.157), and often attributes to them a divine nature (*Opif.* 84, 143–44; *Gig.* 8; *Prov.* 2.50; *QG* 4.188). Cf. Plato, *Apol.* 26d1–3: "Do I [Socrates] not believe that the sun and moon are gods, just as other people?" See further Alan Scott, *Origen and the Life of the Stars: A History of an Idea* (Oxford: Clarendon Press; New York: Oxford University Press, 1991), 69–75; David T. Runia, "Worshipping the Visible Gods: Conflict and Accommodation in Hellenism, Hellenistic Judaism and Early Christianity," in *Empsychoi Logoi—Religious Innovations in Antiquity: Studies in Honour of Pieter Willem van der Horst* (ed. Alberdina Houtman, et al.; Leiden: Brill, 2008), 47–64.

[32] Even angels, it is important to note, qualify as "sacred and divine natures" (ἱεραὶ καὶ θεῖαι φύσεις) (*Abr.* 115).

[33] On the many levels of deity in Philo, see further David Winston, "Philo's Conception of the Divine Nature," in *Neoplatonism and Jewish Thought* (ed. Lenn E. Goodman; Albany: SUNY Press, 1992), 21–23; David T. Runia, "The Beginnings of the End: Philo of Alexandria and Hellenistic Theology," in *Traditions of Theology: Studies in Hellenistic Theology, Its Background and Aftermath* (ed. Dorothea Frede and André Laks; Leiden: Brill, 2002), 281–312 (esp. 289–99); Ronald Cox, *By the Same Word: Creation and Salvation in Hellenistic Judaism and Early Christianity* (BZNW 145; Berlin: de Gruyter, 2007), 87–140; Roberto Radice, "Philo's Theology and Theory of Creation," in *The Cambridge Companion to Philo* (ed. Adam Kamesar; Cambridge: Cambridge University Press, 2009), 128–29.

[34] "The Death of Moses," 239; cf. Feldman, *Philo's Portrayal*, 342–43.

[35] This is true even though the proper name of one of the powers is θεός! (*Somn.* 1.229–230).

and the Powers exist in the world of becoming, and so do not have the essence of primal Godhood, namely pure Being. Nonetheless, the inferiority of reality in the world of becoming (what I will call "generate reality") does not exclude it from sharing in divinity as it exists in this world. Philo may periodically modify and restrict his idea of graded divinity (by declaring that the extracosmic and primal God is the only God), yet he always slides back into what appears to have been the default philosophical and cultural presupposition of his day: generate beings in our cosmos can become participants in divinity.[36] Admittedly, then, there *is* an unbridgeable gap in Philo's onto-theology—but it is the gap between *Being and becoming*, not between divinity and generate reality.

Consequently, *if* Moses is deified in Philo, he never becomes or threatens to become the primal God. The importance of this point cannot be overstressed for avoiding misunderstandings about the Philonic form of deification. In a recent article, for instance, Feldman repeatedly emphasizes that the exalted and glorified Moses does not become God in any sense.[37] In Feldman's universe, there are two clear, straightforward and totally separate categories: (1) human and (2) God. Deity has no levels—thus Moses is either God or not divine at all. In my view, this typology results in an overly simplistic reading of Philonic monotheism. From Philo's perspective, there is a world of theological difference between becoming divine and being (the primal) God. Feldman neglects this difference and thus refuses to accept Philo's clear statement that Moses is divinized (*QE* 2.40).[38] Given the hierarchy of divinity in Philo's world, however, a strong ontological differentiation between the primal God and deified humans is compatible with a Philonic theory of deification. Contrary to what some Jewish apologists claimed (including Philo himself), the deification of a human being was not typically a hubristic attempt to replace the primal God.[39] Self-deifying megalomaniacs like Gaius Caligula may have pretended to be Zeus, but Roman emperors were in fact typically viewed as Zeus's servants and viceregents who were after death made immortal by the gods themselves.[40] In the vast majority of cases, then, deification was not construed as a threat to the primal God or God's monarchy since the deified human never

---

[36] See further Litwa, *We Are Being Transformed*, 258–82.

[37] "The Death of Moses," *passim*.

[38] *Ibid.*, 242.

[39] Philo, the great enemy of Gaius Caligula's self-deifying pretensions, showed himself open to other legitimate forms of ruler cult. (Note well: the difference between cult and bestowing honor in this period is fluid.) See Litwa, *We Are Being Transformed*, 92–94.

[40] See especially on this point J. R. Fears, "Jupiter and Roman Imperial Ideology," *ANRW* 2.17.1:3–141.

replaced the primal God but rather shared God's rule and—after death—became part of God's divine *familia*.

The Mode of Deification: Participation

The mode of deification in Philo is participation. As true Being (τὸ ὄν, *Fug.* 89), Philo's primal God is divine in and of himself. Other divine beings, by contrast, need to participate in the divinity of the Existent to gain the name of θεός. In Philo's thought, there were both shareable and unshareable attributes of divinity. Absolute Being and eternality are unshareable qualities enjoyed by the Existent alone, whereas immortality and ruling power can be shared. A human could become divine by participating in these shareable divine qualities among which we might also add other attributes—for example repose, passionlessness, or immutability.

For Philo, a human being cannot participate directly in the Existent. Nevertheless, he allows humans to participate in the highest manifestation of shareable divinity—what one might call Philo's "Prime Mediate divinity"—the Logos. Although Philo's presentation of the Logos varies, we can safely say that the Logos is the Mind of the Existent.[41] The Logos is a noetic being who typically represents the fullness of divinity as far as it can be known to human beings. Sounding like a Stoic, Philo calls the human mind (νοῦς) a fragment of the Logos (*Opif.* 146). Thus simply by virtue of being human (i.e., having νοῦς), one already has a share in divine reality. The νοῦς is not the reality of the Existent (who exists—or subsists—beyond the categories of generate being), but the reality of what Philo calls the "second God" (δεύτερος θεός) or the Logos (*QG* 2.62). Those who participate in the divine Logos can be called divine and "θεός" as well. Philonic deification, I contend, is the process of becoming wholly and purely νοῦς. This "noetification" is what happened to Moses when he ascended Mount Sinai and when he was finally translated to heaven after death.

Preliminaries: Moses as Philosopher-King

For Philo, Moses's ascent to the intelligible world on Sinai was the culmination of his philosophical vocation. To understand his ascent, then, one must first understand Moses as a (Platonic) philosopher. The necessary equipment of a philosopher is a philosophic soul. For Philo, there are a host of "mighty" and "bodiless souls," invisibly flitting around in the lower

---

[41] For God the Logos as pure creative Intellect, see *Opif.* 8; *Fug.* 10. For the Logos as the νοῦς ὑπὲρ ἡμᾶς, see *Her.* 236.

atmosphere (*Conf.* 176-77).[42] Rational, immortal, sinless, and ever happy, some of these souls never deigned to be involved with earthly affairs. Others, however, descended into bodies (*Gig.* 12). Moses was one of these latter souls "loaned" (χρήσας) to the earth (*Sacr.* 9) to perform an appointed task: to model the ascent back to divinity.[43] Thus incarnated, Moses's philosophical soul renounced bodily pleasures and desires. The Jewish sage spent his life, like Socrates, meditating on dying to bodily life. The purpose for this death was to obtain a higher life which Philo conceives of as an "immortal" (ἀφθάρτου) and "bodiless" (ἀσωμάτου) existence alongside the unbegotten and incorruptible God (παρὰ τῷ ἀγενήτῳ καὶ ἀφθάρτῳ) (*Gig.* 14).

This meditation on death is the practice of deification since it is the only way to attain the divine, incorporeal image.[44] In his work *On the Creation*, Philo posits an iconic affinity between God and human beings (§69). The image of God, for Philo, was not the Existent but the Logos (*Plant.* 17-20).[45] The human made according to the Image (Gen 1:26-27) conforms to the Logos in that both are purely incorporeal and noetic (*Opif.* 134-35; cf. *QG* 2.56).[46] For an embodied human to be conformed to God's Image, then, requires a "noetification" in which the human becomes purely and wholly νοῦς—the immortal, intellectual reality that is the same "stuff" as the Logos.[47]

Philo's Moses is the model of what it means to noetically participate in the divine reality of the Logos. Even when he was an infant, the beauty of Moses's νοῦς could be seen in his very noble (ἀστειοτέραν) appearance (*Mos.* 1.9).[48] As a young boy, Moses's mind naturally conformed to the cosmic Mind—the Logos pervading the universe—a Mind which Philo calls

---

[42] Cf. *Plant.* 14; *Gig.* 16 and *Abr.* 115.

[43] The pseudepigraphical *Assumption of Moses* (first century c.e.), also presents Moses as a pre-existent being (1.14). Cf. Quintus Curtius' comment about Alexander the Great: "… those who consider the greatness of what he accomplished may well believe that so great a man was merely loaned (*accommodasse*) to humankind by the gods, in order that, when his allotted service to humanity was completed, they might quickly take him back into their own family" (*sorte completa, cito repeterent eum suae stirpi*) (*Hist. Alex.* 10.6.6–7, trans. John C. Rolfe, LCL).

[44] For Moses as the image of God see Jarl E. Fossum, *The Name of God and the Angel of the Lord* (WUNT 36; Tübingen: Mohr Siebeck, 1985), 93–94.

[45] Cf. *Spec.* 1.81; 3.83; *QG* 2.62.

[46] Philo can call the Logos himself the "Human according to the Image" (*Conf.* 146).

[47] Cf. *Fug.* 167; *Mut.* 33. Runia put it this way: "If man is part of the Logos (part-whole relation), and the Logos is only nominally separated from God, then (part of) man is part of God" ("God and Man," 72).

[48] Josephus writes that soon after his Egyptian foster mother adopted Moses, she testified to Pharaoh that Moses was "in form divine and noble in mind" (μορφῇ τε θεῖον καὶ φρονήματι γενναῖον) (*Ant.* 2.232).

the "right Reason of nature." As a result, people did not know whether Moses's mind within him was human, divine, or something in between (ἀνθρώπειος ἢ θεῖος ἢ μικτὸς ἀμφοῖν) (*Mos.* 1.27; cf. Aesch., *Prom.* 114-16).[49]

Although he barely needed it, Moses was trained in the full Platonic curriculum. He learned the various kinds of math, music, and astronomy before proceeding to the higher arts.[50] His education in philosophy taught him virtues, both intellectual (e.g., honesty, or a sense for truth) and practical (e.g., how to govern). These virtues he ably and zealously put into practice. With God's help, Moses soon reached "the very summits of philosophy" (*Opif.* 8). But he had not yet undergone training to be king.

After his (just) killing of the Egyptian, Moses fled the country, and became a shepherd. Although it was a lowly and dirty task, Philo insists that God ordained Moses to lead sheep in order to learn how to lead people (*Mos.* 1.60-62). As a shepherd, Moses learned all the virtues befitting a king: "self-restraint," "continence," "good sense," "patience under evil," "endurance of toil and hardships," "justice," "advocacy of excellence," and "censure … of wrongdoers" (*Mos.* 1.54). When his wilderness training was complete, Moses obtained the office of king over Israel.

As king, Moses ruled not only over human beings, but over nature. Philo explains this point in his *Life of Moses* as an introduction to Moses the miracle-worker (1.155-57). Since Moses renounced the riches of kingship, God rewarded him by making Moses his "friend" (Exod 33:11). "Friendship" in the ancient world was a privileged status that kings and emperors often bestowed on lesser rulers and representatives.[51] According to the Stoics, friends shared all their possessions (κοινὰ τὰ φιλῶν) (*SVF* 3.618). As God's friend, Moses became co-regent or partner (κοινωνός) in the governance of God's possessions. Since God owned the entire cosmos, Moses obtained control of cosmic forces. Earth, air, fire, and water changed their natural properties in submission to Moses's will (hence the parting of the Red Sea, the water from the rock, etc.).[52]

---

[49] According to Artapanus (*ap.* Eusebius *Praep. ev.* 9.27.6), Moses was deemed worthy of divine (ἰσόθεον) honor and was called "Hermes" because of his ability to interpret sacred writings.

[50] Cf. Plato, *Resp.* 522b-531c.

[51] See further Peder Borgen, *Philo of Alexandria: An Exegete for His Time* (Leiden: Brill, 1997), 201. Philo mentions that Tiberius Gemellus was κοινωνός (i.e., full partner in rule) with his older cousin the emperor Gaius Caligula (*Legat.* 23, 25, 28; cf. 268; *Flacc.* 40).

[52] Cf. Bauckham's anti-cosmic interpretation of Moses's rule in *Mos.* 1.155–58 ("Moses as God," 257–59). Oddly, Bauckham concludes that Moses's rule over the cosmos likely does not refer to Moses's "literal kingship" since enjoying rule over the "whole cosmos" is the "privilege of the sage, not a unique gift to Moses" (*ibid.* 257). Yet why should Moses's cosmic kingship be denied simply because it is not unique? On the divinity of the Stoic

Moses as Lawgiver

Philo's Moses not only controls the universe and its order; he embodies it. This view accords with the philosophy of law in Philo's day. Hellenistic philosophers, with the exception of the Epicureans, generally assumed that there were two kinds of order in the universe: human and natural. Human order was the order of states and cities. Natural order was the order of the cosmos, best illustrated by the stars harmoniously circling above. Earthly order (or justice), philosophers insisted, was meant to correspond to heavenly order (or justice). The focal point of correspondence, in Philo's time, was the person of the king. The king was the mediator of heavenly order to the world. He was called to conform the earthly commonwealth to the heavenly city of the cosmos. No ordinary person could be expected to achieve this feat. The king had to be, in some sense, the image of God and a god himself. A treatise attributed to Diotogenes expands on this point:[53]

> So just as God is the best of those things which are most honorable by nature, likewise the king is best in the earthly and human realm. Now the king bears the same relation to the state as God to the world; and the state is in the same ratio to the world as the king is to God. For the state, made as it is by a harmonizing together of many different elements, is an imitation of the order and harmony of the world, while the king who has an absolute rulership, and is himself Animate Law (νόμος ἔμψυχος), has been metamorphosed into a deity among men (θεὸς ἐν ἀνθρώποις παρεσχαμάτισται). (*ap.* Stobaeus, *Anth.* 4.7.61)[54]

Philo calls Moses the king a νόμος ἔμψυχος (*Mos.* 1.162; cf. 2.4). But the law lived out naturally by Moses had to be distributed to the nation. Moses gave benefaction to his people by writing them a code (the Torah) that conformed to his own nature, which in turn conformed to the law of the cosmos. Moses was thus the perfect lawgiver. As Diotogenes indicates, the perfect lawgiver is no average citizen, or mere human being. As "Animate Law," the king is "metamorphosed into a god." That Moses underwent such a metamorphosis can be deduced from Philo's treatment of Moses as prophet and priest.

---

sage, and of Moses in particular, see David Winston, *The Ancestral Philosophy: Hellenistic Philosophy in Second Temple Judaism* (ed. Gregory E. Sterling; BJS 331/SPhM 4; Providence, RI: Brown Judaic Studies, 2001), 176–80.

[53] The treatise is best dated to the third or second century B.C.E. See the discussion in Glenn F. Chesnut, "The Ruler and the Logos in Neopythagorean, Middle Platonic, and Late Stoic Political Philosophy," *ANRW* 2.16.2:1313–1315.

[54] Trans. Erwin R. Goodenough, "The Political Philosophy of Hellenistic Kingship," *YCS* 1 (1928): 68–77 (68).

Moses as Prophet and Priest

Plato did not speak of the ideal philosopher as a prophet or priest. Nevertheless, the Platonic philosopher, in Philo's mind, accomplished both a priestly and a prophetic task. Philo reminds his readers that "early kings were at the same time high priests who by their acts showed that those who rule over others should themselves be servants in ministering to God" (*QE* 2.105). For Philo, the perfect king and law-giver ought not only to know human things. He must know divine things as well (*Mos.* 2.5). To know these, he must be initiated into spiritual mysteries beyond the ken of normal human perception. He is called to escape this world of shadows in order to behold and internalize the very forms of the virtues (in particular the love of humanity, the love of justice and good, and the hatred of evil). Upon his return to earth, the ruler is fit to mediate these virtues as a prophet declaring the law.

For Moses, the path from Plato's cave to the vision of the Good was the trail up Mount Sinai. There Moses underwent his priestly initiation. He entered into the "darkness where God was" (Exod 20.21). For Philo, this was not to enter a visible mass of condensed smoke. Rather Moses's trip up Sinai's slopes was "an ethereal and heavenly journey" (*QE* 2.44) to enter the intelligible realm (*Mut.* 7; *Post.* 14). He beheld the forms which are the truly real, though unseen, models and archetypes of earthly things.[55] "See," God says to Moses, "that you make according to the pattern (τὸν τύπον) displayed to you on the mountain!" is a common refrain in Exodus (e.g., Exod 25:40 LXX). The τύπος for Philo is the model of all existing things: the Logos or Mind of God.[56]

To enter God's Mind, God's Mind entered Moses—that is, Moses underwent prophetic ecstasy. Philo's theory of ecstasy, in tune with many of his contemporaries, involved divine possession of the human mind.[57] The prophet is "inspired" (ἐπιθειάσας) (*Mos.* 2.259, cf. 263, 272), "carried by

---

[55] Philo also discourses on Moses's philosophic ascent in his exposition of the book of Leviticus, where it says that God "called Moses up above" (Lev. 1:1). "Above" is the incorporeal realm where Moses clearly beheld the forms, in a "radiant vision, as though in unclouded sunshine" (*Plant.* 27).

[56] Philo associates Moses's reception of the name "god" with his entrance into the intelligible world (*Mos.* 1.158). The connection is difficult to understand, unless the intelligible world is the place where Moses was first promoted to godhead.

[57] For ecstatic prophecy, see Christopher Mount, "1 Corinthians 11:3–13: Spirit-Possession and Authority in a Non-Pauline Interpolation," *JBL* 124 (2005): 313–40 (esp. 316–25); and in Philo specifically, Gerhard Sellin, *Der Streit um die Auferstehung der Toten: Eine religionsgeschichtliche und exegetische Untersuchung von 1 Korinther 15* (FRLANT 138; Göttingen: Vandenhoeck & Ruprecht, 1986), 143–55.

God" (θεοφορεῖται) (*Mos* 2.250, cf. 264, 273), or "possessed" (κατασχεθείς) (*Mos.* 2.288). Becoming a prophet thus entails a metamorphosis (μεταμορ-φούμενος, *Mos.* 1.57; cf. 2.280; Mark 9:2) where he "is transformed into a prophet" (μεταβαλὼν εἰς προφήτην), involving a change in both appearance and mind (*Mos* 2.272). Moses's mind was even said to be "ensouled by God" (ἐψυχῶσθαι ὑπὸ θεοῦ) (*Leg.* 1.40). Consequently, the inspired Moses was "no longer in himself" (οὐκέτ' ὢν ἐν ἑαυτῷ) (*Mos.* 2.250). This theory of prophetic ecstasy already assumes a kind of deification in which God's Mind enters and inhabits the prophet. In the midst of this possession, God transforms the mind and makes it more like himself. Philo explains this point in *Questions on Exodus*:

> For when the prophetic mind becomes divinely inspired and filled with God, it becomes like the monad, not being at all mixed with any of those things associated with duality. But he who is resolved into the nature of unity is said to come near to God in a kind of family relation, for having given up and left behind all mortal kinds, he is changed into the divine, so that such men become kin to God and truly divine. (2.29)

Commenting on this passage, Feldman writes: "That he [Moses] is *truly* divine indicates that he is not *actually* divine [*sic*], since he is only *akin* to G-d."[58] But Feldman works with a false opposition. To be akin to God—part of God's family—is to be divine, although not identical with the primal God. Note the realism of Philo's language. Moses the inspired prophet truly was "resolved into the nature of unity." His nature was temporarily made one like the simple—or monadic—nature of God. Moses's "monadification" does not replace the primal God—he only comes *near* to the Existent. Nevertheless, leaving behind "all mortal kinds" implies a true transformation that—if only for a moment—makes Moses "truly" (i.e., not just metaphorically) divine.[59]

Moses's Ascent[60]

Philo presents Moses's ascent on Sinai as a proleptic experience of deification. The divine Spirit purged Moses in preparation for his priestly

---

[58] "Death of Moses," 242; repeated in Feldman, *Philo's Portrayal*, 344.

[59] Commenting on *QE* 2.29, Christian Noack speaks of a "mystical participation [of the human νοῦς] in the divine reality and thus a new quality of consciousness. … In the process of dividing from the lower parts of the soul during inspiration, the *nous*—consciousness itself—is also transformed, and obtains a transcendent, divine character" (*Gottesbewußtsein: Exegetische Studien zur Soteriologie und Mystik bei Philo von Alexandria* (WUNT 2.116; Tübingen: Mohr Siebeck, 2000], 157).

[60] For Mosaic ascent traditions, see Fossum, *Name of God*, 129–44.

initiation in heaven. For his initiation, Moses had to be clean in body and soul. That is, he had to cut away all passions, and sanctify himself "from all the things that characterize mortal nature," including eating, drinking, and sexual intercourse (*Mos.* 2.68). Moses had to transcend the limits of his mortal nature in order to come into his true, divine (i.e., purely noetic) nature.

Moses's divinization was thus his metamorphosis into divine reality, which for the Platonically-minded Philo is νοῦς.[61] The noetic transformation Moses underwent is described in an important passage in *Questions on Exodus* (2.46). Here Philo calls Moses's upward call to Sinai "a second birth better than the first." Moses's first birth, Philo says, was "mixed with a body and had corruptible parents." In Moses's second birth, the lawgiver becomes—in a phrase unfortunately garbled in the Armenian—"an unmixed and simple soul of the sovereign." In the Loeb edition to Philo, Ralph Marcus rightly understood the phrase to mean "an unmixed and simple sovereign part of the soul," meaning "mind."[62] In other words, Moses—elsewhere called ὁ καθαρώτατος νοῦς (*Congr.* 132)—became pure mind.[63] This interpretation is borne out by the context of QE 2.46. As mind, Philo says, Moses did not have a mother (a material progenitor), but only a father (an intellectual progenitor), whom Philo indentifies with God.[64] This "God" is probably the divine Mind, or Logos, although Philo does not specify (cf. *Mos.* 2.209-210; *Her.* 62). Moses's second birth was a coming into being "without a body"—i.e., his coming into being as pure, divine mind.[65] Moses's kinship with the divine (*QE* 2.29) is not just metaphorical, but ontological. When he is "changed into the divine" he is changed into the

[61] For Plato on the divinity of νοῦς see *Phaed.* 80a4; *Resp.* 589d2; *Tim.* 41c7; 45a1; 51e5–6; 69d6; 73a7; 88b2; 90a2–b1; *Alc. maj.* 1.133c1–6. Cf. Aristotle *De an.* 1.4 408b29; *Part. an.* 4.10 686a29; *Gen. an.* 2.3 736a28; *Eth. nic.* 10.7 1177a16, b28–30; *Eth. eud.* 8.2 1248a27; Ps. Aristotle, *Mund.* 1. 391a15; Iamblichus, *Protr.* 8; Cicero, *Tusc.* 1.65; Porphyry, *Vit. Plot.* 2.

[62] Note *g. ad loc.* For the mind as the "sovereign and ruling element" (τὸ ἀρχηγετικὸν καὶ τὸ ἡγεμονικόν), see *QG* 1.45; cf. 2.54: "the mind is the sovereign and ruling part of the soul."

[63] Cf. *QE* 2.44.

[64] For "father" as mind (νοῦς) and "mother" as "the matter of the body" (ἡ τοῦ σώματος ὕλη), see *Leg.* 2.51; 3.225.

[65] The Armenian of this passage reads that Moses's coming into being was "from the aether and without a body." The Greek fragment, however, reads only ἄνευ σώματος. Cf. *Somn.* 1.36: Μωυσῆν ἀσώματον γενόμενον. Philo also finds Moses's bodilessness signified in his pitching the Tent of Meeting "outside the camp" (Exod 33:7, *Gig.* 54; cf. *Leg.* 2.54–55; 3.46–48; *Det.* 160; *Ebr.* 100, 124).

divine nature, namely pure νοῦς. In this respect, Moses conformed to the reality of the Logos, the divine Mind (*QE* 2.46).[66]

Philo is rather forthright about Moses's deification on Sinai. God's command to Moses, "Come up to Me to the mountain and be there" (Exod 24:12) signifies that Moses was *"divinized* by ascending not to the air or to the ether or to heaven higher than all but to (a region) above the heavens—and beyond the heavens there is no place but God" (*QE* 2.40, my emphasis). It is impossible to escape the candor of this passage. Feldman's claim that in this text Philo speaks "of the divinization of the soul, not of Moses himself" is a theory born of desperation and not true to Philo's language.[67] *QE* 2.40 is not a general statement about the soul, but about Moses. The very distinction between soul and self fails to note their identification in Platonist (and Philonic) thinking (*Alc. maj.* I.130c).[68] If Philo is speaking of the divinization of Moses's soul, he is speaking of the divinization of Moses himself.

There were two consequences to Moses's deification: Moses, like the Logos, became simple and immutable. "Simple," in this context means not having multiple parts. By becoming pure mind, Moses became absolutely one. "For when the prophetic mind becomes divinely inspired and filled with God," Philo explains, "it becomes like the monad" (*QE* 2.29). In this respect, Moses conformed to the purely noetic nature of the Logos, which is absolutely one (*QE* 2.46). The Logos is not a body compounded of matter—which always involves multiplicity. It is pure, monadic mind.[69] On Sinai, then, Moses abandoned the world of multiplicity, and was "resolved into the nature of unity." In this way he was "changed into the divine" (*QE* 2.29).

---

[66] Cf. Noack, *Gottesbewußtsein*, 141. For Moses as the (prophetic) logos, see *Leg.* 3.43; *Migr.* 23, 151; *Her.* 182–85, 205–06; *Congr.* 170.

[67] *Philo's Portrayal*, 345.

[68] Philo, *Opif.* 69; cf. Cicero, *Leg.* 1.22,59; Seneca, *Ep.*, 31.11.

[69] For Philo, the monad is associated with what is intelligible and unmixed (*Spec.* 1.66), undivided (1.180), and what truly exists (*Deus* 11). God is himself a monad (*Her.* 183). The monad is an image of the singular, complete God since the monad does not receive addition or subtraction (*Her.* 187). It is "an incorporeal image of God (ἀσώματος θεοῦ εἰκών)," assimilated to God because it stands alone (*Spec.* 2.176). Moreover, it is the image of the original cause (*Spec.* 3.180), and is associated with the maker of the universe (*Somn.* 2.70). The Logos, significantly, does not differ at all from the monad (ἀδιαφορῶν μονάδος) (*Deus* 83). Noack identifies the "cosmic monad" with the divine Logos based on *QE* 2.37 (*Gottesbewußtsein*, 134). Similarly for Eudorus of Alexandria, the monad is the second-tier principle after the One, and is—like the Logos—a thinking intellect (Robert M. Berchman, "The Categories of Being in Middle Platonism: Philo, Clement, and Origen of Alexandria," in *The School of Moses: Studies in Philo and Hellenistic Religion* [ed. John Peter Kenney; BJS 304/SPhM 1; Atlanta: Scholars Press, 1995], 98–140).

Moses's immutability is indicated by Deut 5:31 where God says to Moses: "But you, stand here with me!" Philo considers this verse to be "an oracle vouchsafed to the prophet: true stability and immutable repose (ἠρεμία) is that which we experience at the side of the immutable ever standing God" (*Gig.* 49).[70] Repose is not only a moral quality (control of the passions) but an ontological state like that of "the immutable and ever standing God." God "makes the worthy man sharer of his own *nature* (τῆς ἑαυτοῦ φύσεως)," we read in another passage, "which is repose (ἠρεμίας)" (*Post.* 28, my emphasis).[71]

The vision of God

Perhaps the clearest indication of Moses's deification is his vision of (the second) God and its results. While on Sinai Moses—with far-reaching intellectual penetration—craved "for wisdom and knowledge with insatiable persistence" (*Plant.* 23-27). He "searched everywhere and into everything in his desire to see clearly and plainly" God, "who alone is good" (*Mut.* 8-10). So "unceasingly" did Moses "yearn to see God … that he implored God to reveal clearly his own nature" (*Post.* 13-16). "Manifest yourself to me," Moses begs, "that I may see you knowingly!" (Exod 33:13, LXX). The Existent granted Moses's request. He did not, however, reveal his essence to Moses. Rather, he revealed his Image, the Logos. Moses apprehended God from God's own perfect noetic representation (*Leg.* 3.97-103). In terms of Philo's scriptural exposition, Moses beheld the "Place" (a name for the Logos) where God stands (Exod 24:10) (*Conf.* 95-97).[72] By gazing at the Logos, the Existent's splendor reached Moses in order that through the secondary splendor, Moses beheld "the more splendid (splendor of the Existent)."[73]

---

[70] Philo also bases Moses's immutability on an allegorical interpretation of Num 14:44, which reads, "Moses and the ark were not moved." For Philo, Moses signifies the "wise man," and the ark signifies "virtue." Neither the wise man nor virtue, says Philo, are subject to change because both "are stayed on the firm foundation of right reason" (*Gig.* 48).

[71] On Moses's immutability, see further *Conf.* 30; Goodenough, *By Light, Light*, 228; Michael Williams, *The Immovable Race: A Gnostic Designation and the Theme of Stability in Late Antiquity* (NHS 29; Leiden: Brill, 1985), 14–15, 27, 43–45; Hywel Clifford, "Moses as Philosopher-Sage in Philo," in *Moses in Biblical and Extra-Biblical Traditions*, 151–68 (157–59).

[72] Compare the use of מקום as a circumlocution for God in rabbinic literature.

[73] On Philo's notion of the vision of God in general, see the recent article by Scott D. Mackie, "Seeing God in Philo of Alexandria: The Logos, the Powers, or the Existent One?" *SPhA* 21 (2009): 25–47. Mackie argues that, despite inconsistencies, Philo asserts that a vision of the Existent is possible. In the case of Moses, however, I believe that Winston's

When Moses beheld the Good (through the Logos), his priestly initiation was complete (*Mos.* 2.71). At this point Moses came down out of the divine world, as Plato bids in the *Republic* (519d-520c), to help his fellow human beings. In Philo's framework, Moses the divinized mind reentered his body to continue to lead the Israelites on the road to virtue.

The body of Moses bore the marks of his divinized mind.[74] In Exodus, Moses descends Mt. Sinai with a radiant face (Exod 34:29-35). Philo interprets this radiance in terms of beauty:[75] Moses was "far more beautiful (πολὺ καλλίων) with respect to his appearance [or face, ὄψιν] than when he had gone up [Mount Sinai]." Beauty was one of the trademarks of divinity. Diotima asks Socrates in Plato's *Symposium*, "Don't you say that all the gods are ... beautiful (κάλους)?" (202c)? The historian Charax says of Io that she was considered a goddess on account of her beauty (θεός ἐνομίσθη δία τὸ κάλλος).[76]

Brilliance and beauty, furthermore, are often revealed in a divine epiphany. In a nighttime epiphany of Heracles, for example, the house is flooded with light, and his parents "can see the walls as clearly as if it was bright dawn" (Theocritus, *Id.* 24.22, 38). In a dream epiphany to Aeneas, the divine Penates are "manifest in brilliant light" (*multo manifesti lumine*) (Virgil, *Aen.* 3.151). Aeneas later tells Dido that he saw Mercury come to him *manifesto in lumine* ("in brilliant light") (4.358). Venus subsequently appears to Aeneas "bright white amidst ethereal clouds" (*aetherios inter ... candida nimbos*) (8.608).[77] When Aphrodite reveals herself to Anchises in a Homeric hymn, "from her cheeks immortal beauty (κάλλος ἄμβροτον) shone forth" (*Hymn. Aphr.* 5.173-75). Similarly, as Demeter reveals herself to

---

position still holds: in the vision of God, one can only behold the Logos or the Powers (God and Lord)—not the Existent (*The Logos and Mystical Theology in Philo of Alexandria* [Cincinnati: Hebrew Union College Press, 1985], 54). Cf. Ellen Birnbaum, *The Place of Judaism in Philo's Thought* (BJS 290; SPhM 2; Atlanta: Scholars Press, 1996), 77–90.

[74] Moses's body, Philo explains, dramatically increased in strength (ἰσχύς) and vigorous condition (εὐεξία) (*Mos.* 2.69). In his *Opponents of Paul in 2 Corinthians* (Philadelphia: Fortress, 1986), 255, Dieter Georgi asserted that such strength and vigor are not simply human qualities, but belong to the reality of the divine sphere. This conclusion is not immediately apparent, since Philo often depreciates external εὐεξία gained by athletes in favor of an internal εὐεξία gained by philosophers (Philo's allegorical athletes). Nonetheless, on at least two occasions, Philo speaks of an inward transformation of the mind resulting in an outward εὐεξία. Compare the divine inspiration of Isaac in *Det.* 29 and Abraham in *Virt.* 217. Moses—whose prophetic ecstasy is a kind of metamorphosis (μεταμορφούμενος; *Mos.* 1.57)—is similarly inspired. Inspiration is a true transformation because it assumes the (if only temporary) deification of the mind.

[75] Note the explanatory γάρ introducing *Mos.* 2.70.

[76] *FGrH* 103 frg. 13, end. Cf. also Dionysius of Halicarnassus *Ant. rom.* 6.13.1.

[77] Cf. Ovid, *Fast.* 1.94; Apollonius Rhodius, *Argon.* 4.1701–1717.

Metaneira, "Beauty (κάλλος) breathed about her … a light beamed far out from the goddess's immortal skin … The well-built house flooded with radiance like lightning" (*Hymn. Dem.* 276, 278, 280).[78] Here beauty and light are combined, as in the case of Moses.[79] Like Demeter's beauty, the beauty of Moses was concentrated in a "sun-like splendor flashing like lightning" from his face (*Mos.* 2.70). Philo also uses the verb that describes the lightning shining from Moses's face (ἀπαστράπτω) to describe the divine light emerging from the burning bush (*Mos.* 1.66), the pillar of fire (2.254), and the Powers of God (*Deus* 78).[80] The fact that Moses's splendor is "sun-like" also recalls Jewish and Christian texts in which God or the divine Christ has "the appearance of the sun" (1 En 14:20; cf. Rev 1:16).

As also occurs in divine epiphanies, the brilliance of Moses causes a shock of consternation. Moses's kinsmen, when they catch sight of their ruler, are "amazed and panic-stricken and were not able to withstand with their eyes for any length of time the assault" of the rays launched from Moses's face (*Mos.* 2.69). Similarly, Metaneira before the unveiled Demeter is seized with "reverence, awe and pale terror" (*Hymn Dem.* 2.188-190).[81] Enoch before "the Great Glory" lies "prostrate and trembling" (1 En 14:24). When Anchises sees Aphrodite in her unveiled beauty, "He turns his gaze away in terror, hides his face under the covers, and begs for mercy" (*Hymn Aph.* 181-90). John falls as though dead before the divine Christ, whose face shines like the sun (Rev 1:17). Before the god Janus, Ovid feels his hair "stiffen with fear," and his chest freeze with a sudden chill (*Fast.* 1.97-98; cf. Virgil, *Aen.* 4.279-80). The "bright burst of Phoebus" in the Homeric *Hymn to Apollo* throws "great awe (μέγα … δέος) into all" (446-447). The comment of Jean-Pierre Vernant applies to both Jewish and Greek sources: "the body of the gods shines with such an intense brilliance that no human eye can bear it."[82]

---

[78] See further Nicholas J. Richardson, *Homeric Hymn to Demeter* (Oxford: Clarendon and Oxford University Press, 1974), 252–54. In the *Hymn to Demeter* by Callimachus, Demeter is again metamorphosed into her "goddess shape." "Her steps touched the earth, but her head reached to Olympus." Those who see her become "half-dead" and rush suddenly away (*Hymn Cer.* 57–60; cf. *Gos. Pet.* 10.40).

[79] Cf. also *Hymn Aphr.* 174–75; T. *Job* 46.7–9.

[80] Cf. *Det.* 118; *Fug.* 139; *Cher.* 62. Maximus of Tyre notes that the daimonic Hector can be still seen "sweeping over the plain [of Troy], flashing like lightning (ἀστράπτων)" (*Diss.* 9.7).

[81] Richardson, *Hymn to Demeter*, 208–210; cf. Richard Buxton, *Forms of Astonishment: Greek Myths of Metamorphosis* (Oxford: Oxford University Press, 2009), 164–65.

[82] *Mortals and Immortals: Collected Essays* (Princeton: Princeton University Press, 1991), 44. For further responses to an epiphany, see Marco Frenschkowski, *Offenbarung und*

Philo uses the language of overpowering light specifically to describe God. In *On Flight and Finding*, he writes that the person who tries to gaze on the Supreme Essence "will be blinded by the rays that beam forth all around him" (§165). Humans cannot bear the rays that burst from God, even as their human eyes cannot directly view the sun.[83] The parallel between Moses's sun-like appearance and that of "the Supreme Essence" is striking. Scott Hafemann concluded from comparing these texts that Moses, when he descended from Sinai, mediated the divine presence.[84] Philo's language, I think, allows for a stronger conclusion. The Alexandrian depicts Moses descending from Sinai with all the trademarks of a divine epiphany (beauty, light, the shock of awe)—indeed a theophany. If Moses mediated divine reality on Sinai, it is because he was himself deified.

Moses was deified on Sinai not because he was a god in and of himself, but because he participated, however temporarily, in divine reality. In *On Dreams* 2.228, Philo affirms that "that which draws near to God enters into affinity (οἰκειοῦται) with that which IS." The "affinity" Moses shares with God the Logos is noetic. This noetic participation is symbolized by the presence of divine light beaming from Moses's face.

Moses's Final Deification at Death

Over a century ago, Wilhelm Bousset wrote that the experience of ascent was a foretaste of the experience of death.[85] Similarly, the deification that Moses experienced on Sinai was only a foretaste of his permanent deification at the end of his life. According to Philo, Moses did not die like other people. In fact, he *could* not die like them, because he was immutable. This is Philo's interpretation of the fact that Moses could not be "added" to his people (a stock phrase used to speak of the death of the patriarchs, e.g., Gen 25:8). Thus he had to be willingly and consciously "translated," (μετανίστημι, cf. Deut. 34:5-6) back to the divine realm (*Sacr.* 7-10).

Moses's translation was his final pilgrimage to the heavenly realm in which all the transformations he experienced at Sinai became permanent

---

Epiphanie: Die verborgene Epiphanie in Spätantike und frühem Christentum (2 vols.; WUNT 2.80; Tübingen: Mohr Siebeck, 1997), 2:91–93.

[83] *Abr.* 76; *Praem.* 36–40; *Fug.* 165.

[84] *Paul, Moses, and the History of Israel: The Letter-Spirit Contrast and the Argument from Scripture in 2 Corinthians 3* (WUNT 2.81; Tübingen: Mohr Siebeck, 1995; repr. Bletchley: Paternoster, 2005), 292–93.

[85] "Die Himmelsreise der Seele," *AR* 4 (1901): 136–169, 229–73 (136).

(*Mos.* 2.288).[86] Just as in *Questions on Exodus* 2.29, the departing Moses is resolved "into the nature of unity" and "changed into the divine." His "migration" from this world was an "exaltation," in which he "noticed that he was gradually being disengaged from the [bodily] elements with which he had been mixed" (*Virt.* 76). When Moses shed his mortal encasing, God resolved Moses's body and soul into a single unity, "transforming [him] wholly and entirely into most sun-like νοῦς" (ὅλον δι' ὅλων μεθαρμοζόμενος εἰς νοῦν ἡλιοειδέστατον) (*Mos* 2.288; cf. *Virt.* 72-79).

It is important to note the brilliant light imagery here, since it connects Moses to divine Glory traditions. At Sinai, Moses saw the divine Glory (the Logos), and participated in it. Philo translated these scriptural ideas into philosophical terms. Moses, who once saw God's glorious Logos (or Mind), is now permanently transformed into the brilliant reality of νοῦς.[87] Philosophically, Philo views νοῦς as a fiery substance. In *Flight and Finding* (§133), for instance, he describes νοῦς as a "hot and fiery pneuma" (ἔνθερμον καὶ πεπυρωμένον πνεῦμα), and in *On Dreams* (1.30-33), the mind itself is *pneuma*, bodiless and imperceptible.[88] This pneuma was widely considered to be a divine substance in the ancient world, which the Stoics called "creative fire" (πῦρ τεχνικόν).[89] This noetic or pneumatic reality, it appears, is what Moses was turned into. This is what it meant for Moses to be "changed into the divine." Philo calls this process "immortalization" (ἀπαθανατίζεσθαι) (*Mos.* 2.288; cf. *Virt.* 72-79), a word frequently used in the ancient world to refer to deification.[90]

---

[86] Meeks points out that the "striking thing about Philo's descriptions of Moses's translation is that they parallel exactly his descriptions of the ascent on Sinai." In both cases, Moses leaves the mortal, bodily realm to enter the "incorporeal and intelligible" (*Mos.* 2.288; *Virt.* 76; *QG* 1.86), and comes by the "summons" of God (*Mos.* 2.288) (*Prophet-King*, 124).

[87] Bauckham is perhaps right to chastise Meeks and Borgen for seeing a heavenly enthronement behind Philo's description of Moses's transformation on Sinai. But his assertion that the "only kind of transformation" Philo recognizes for Moses is "an ethical assimilation to the divine virtues" is mistaken ("Moses as God," 260–61).

[88] David Winston and John M. Dillon, *Two Treatise of Philo of Alexandria: A Commentary on De Gigantibus and Quod Deus Sit Immutabilis* (BJS 25; Chico, CA: Scholars Press, 1983), 202–03. Dillon notes that pneuma can be called a "bodiless" and "immaterial" substance insofar as it is free from mortal, changeable material.

[89] Litwa, *We Are Being Transformed*, 158–161.

[90] E.g., Diodorus Siculus, *Bibl.* 1.94.2 (the deification of Zalmoxis); 2.20.2 (the deification of Semiramis). Cf. Lucian, *Deor. conc.* 9; *Scyth.* 1. (On Zalmoxis, see Ivan Linforth, "ΟΙ ΑΘΑΝΑΤΙΖΟΝΤΕΣ," *CP* 13 [1918]: 23–33.) Philo often uses ἀπαθανατίζω to speak of deification through philosophy (*Opif.* 77) or virtue (*Det.* 111; *Conf.* 149; *Virt.* 14; *QG* 1.51; cf. *Post.* 123; *Somn.* 1.36; *Spec.* 4.14). Justin Martyr uses ἀπαθανατίζω to speak of the deifying transformation of Roman emperors after their death (*1 Apol.* 21.3). Cf. Tatian *Or.* 10.3; 16.2; 25.2.

Yet is it appropriate to view Moses's immortalization and noetic trans-formation as a form of deification? If Philo truly viewed immortalization as a transformation into divine reality, then I believe that we are justified in calling it deification. Becoming divine reality, or νοῦς, is also a sharing in the reality of the divine Logos.[91] Transformation into mind is thus an assimilation to a divine being. Again, the Logos is God's Mind. For Moses to be transformed into mind (μεθαρμοζόμενος εἰς νοῦν, *Mos.* 2.288) is an assimilation to the Divine Mind himself, or the Logos (*Her.* 236). But assimilation to the Logos is assimilation to a divine being, Philo's "second God" (*QG* 2.62). Because Moses's transformation into divine reality is simultaneously an assimilation to a divine being, we can, I think, call the immortalization and noetification of Moses a Philonic form of deification.[92]

Burial and Deification

Recently Ian Scott argued against Moses's deification because Moses pro-phesied his own burial (*Mos.* 2.291). If Moses is buried, the argument runs, he cannot make his ascent to the divine world mentioned in the *Life of Moses* 2.288.[93] In view of Philo's anthropology and cosmology, however, a future burial does not negate the reality of Moses's deification. What is buried is the *body*, what ascends is the true Moses—his sun-like νοῦς. It is Moses's νοῦς that participates in the divine Logos, and is progressively deified. At the end of his life, Moses's "most sun-like mind" is ready to leave the body and ascend to the divine region (*Mos.* 2.888). This is made explicit in *On the Virtues* 76, where Moses leaves his body behind as a mere oyster shell (ὄστρεον) (cf. Plato, *Phaedr.* 250c). It is only this "oyster shell" that is buried. The real—deified—Moses has already taken flight to the divine world.

Admittedly, Philo is not perfectly consistent in his language (he rarely is). The idea that Moses's twofold nature of soul and body was "resolved"

---

[91] Cf. Sellin: "When the sage like Moses ascends and stands near the Logos (*QE* 2.39; cf. *Somn.* 165f; 2.227f) on the level of God's 'powers' (*Somn.* 2.254), then he is on account of his equal rank, identical (*identisch*) with the Logos" (*Streit*, 168; cf. 142; 164–67). Impor-tantly, Cleanthes had identified the sovereign mind of the universe (or Logos) with the sun (Winston, *Logos and Mystical Theology*, 33). Moses's identification with "most sun-like Mind" may indicate his union with the Logos.

[92] For further commentary on *Mos.* 2.288, see Fred W. Burnett, "Philo on Immortality: A Thematic Study of Philo's Concept of Παλινγενεσία," *CBQ* (1984): 447–70 (esp. 453–56).

[93] This argument is used more recently by Walter Wilson (*Philo of Alexandria: On Virtues* [PACS 3; Leiden: Brill, 2011], 195), and ultimately goes back to Charles Talbert ("The Concept of the Immortals in Mediterranean Antiquity," *JBL* 94 [1975]: 419–36 [424, cf. 430]).

into a single unity (*Mos.* 2.288) seems to contradict the idea that Moses experienced a "disjunction" (διάζευξις) of mind and body (*Virt.* 76). But the contradiction is more apparent than real. The fact that "the Father" "resolved" (literally "elementized," ἀναστοιχεόω) Moses—previously soul and body—into a monadic νοῦς (*Mos.* 2.288) does not necessarily imply that there was no bodily remainder left behind to be buried. The "elementized" Moses was broken into his basic elements—as if spun in a gigantic centrifuge. The real Moses was refined into νοῦς, allowing him to make his ascent to the divine realm. The oyster shell body was left behind in a heap of matter unable to ascend.[94] Consequently, Moses's corpse—which was not the true Moses at all—could still be buried (though mysteriously no one knows his grave).[95]

Classical sources confirm that a corporeal remainder speaks nothing against the deification of one's true self, which is soul or mind. In Quintus Curtius's *History of Alexander* (first century C.E.), the character Perdiccas comments that, when Alexander died, there was nothing left of him except that which was "separated from his immortality." "Let us," he exhorts, "pay as soon as possible the rites due to his body (*corpori*)" (10.6.7). Alexander became a staple example of royal deification in later times, even though his body was obviously buried and was in fact on display at Alexandria during Philo's lifetime. Moreover, Cassius Dio reports that at Augustus's funeral, Tiberius remarked, "It is fitting that we should not mourn for him, but while now *giving his body back to nature* (τὸ μὲν σῶμα αὐτοῦ τῇ φύσει), should *forever glorify his soul as a god* (τὴν δὲ ψυχὴν ὡς θεοῦ)" (56.41.9, my emphasis). Five days after his ritual burning, Augustus's bones were placed in his mausoleum (*Rom. hist.* 56.42.4). James Tabor comments: "Here we have a clear recognition of bodily mortality, the idea of the immortal soul, and the notion of the apotheosis of an extraordinary individual—all lumped together."[96] I conclude that Moses's deifying ascent in *Mos.* 2.288 and Moses's prophecy of his own burial (2.291), do not cancel each other out. The true—deified—Moses made his ascent to the divine world.[97]

---

[94] Note that the body left behind at death is deprived of the divine image (*Spec.* 3.207).

[95] Elsewhere Philo interprets the missing grave to mean that (1) Moses was transferred "from a sensible and visible place to an incorporeal and intelligible form" (*QG* 1.86) or (2) that no one "could perceive the passing of a perfect soul to Him that IS" (*Sacr.* 9).

[96] "'Returning to the Divinity': Josephus's Portrayal of the Disappearances of Enoch, Elijah, and Moses," *JBL* 108 (1989): 225–38 (231).

[97] Josephus's account of Moses's death is worth comparing to Philo's. At the end of Moses's life, says Josephus, a "cloud of a sudden descended upon him and he disappeared

The idea that Philo is in *The Life of Moses* 2.288 employing Platonic imagery—as Scott rightly points out—says nothing against Moses's deification. As Scott himself remarks: "in this [Platonic] tradition the goal for every soul, the aim of the philosophical life, was to return to or merge back into the one divine being."[98] I take issue with Scott's interpretation that philosophical deification always implies absorption into primal divinity (why not assimilation to a mediate deity?). It is at any rate a misunderstanding of Platonism—and I would add ancient cosmology—when Scott claims that the return to the divine source "is not a matter of one's becoming a god oneself, but rather the fulfillment of the human creature's yearning for eternal communion with its origin."[99] How can "merging back into one divine being" now be reduced to the fulfillment of creaturely yearning and "communion" (a relational soteriology in which one presumably remains human in the divine sphere)? Ancient sources, including Philo, show that to be in the divine realm is to be divine oneself. The fact that Moses was part of a *class* of souls who in good Platonic fashion experienced or would experience deification does not speak against Moses's deification. (The point is *not* that Moses is *uniquely* deified, but that *he is deified*!) One cannot avoid the ontological implications of Philo's remark that the ascended Moses—as one who became most sun-like νοῦς (*Mos.* 2.288)—was "changed into the divine" (*QE* 2.29).

I am happy to admit with Scott that even in Moses's deified state there was "a radical contrast" between his immortal, ascended mind and the ultimate source of deity—the Existent. But to conclude from this that the immortalization and ascent of Moses described in *The Life of Moses* 2.288 is not a deification is a *non sequitur*. Moses's mind participating in the deity of the Logos does not threaten or replace the divinity of the Existent. Philo's

---

in a ravine" (*Ant.* 4.326). Moses, instead of dying, mysteriously disappeared. The parallel to Romulus's miraculous end and apotheosis is clear (Livy, *Hist.* 1:16; Cicero, *Resp.* 2.10; 6.21; Plutarch, *Rom.* 27), but Josephus's account boldly contradicts the biblical report that Moses died (Deut 34:5). The Jewish historian explains the contradiction by claiming that Moses had written in Deuteronomy an account of his own death for fear lest people say that "by reason of his surpassing virtue he had gone back to the divine" (πρὸς τὸ θεῖον αὐτὸν ἀναχωρῆσαι) (*Ant.* 4.326). Moses's "return to the divine" appears to be a Josephan euphemism for "deification." Thus by his report on Moses's translation, Josephus accomplishes two ends: (1) he backhandedly refers to Moses's death—thus nodding to Deut 34—but since the account of his death was only a "decoy" report, he (2) subtly implies that Moses's end was in reality no less grand than that of the other deified heroes of Greece and Rome. See further Feldman, "Death of Moses," 252–53.

98 "Moses a Divine Man," 104.

99 *Ibid.*, 105.

Moses occupies a fairly low rank on the divine hierarchy, seemingly on par with angelic beings.[100]

Speaking more personally, Scott confesses his concern to preserve the "vast chasm between Creator and creature."[101] I concur that this is a Philonic concern (especially in anti-idolatry discourse). Yet (as stated above) Philo's primary philosophic concern is to distinguish Being (the Existent) from becoming, rather than to keep apart the sphere of the divine and the sphere of generate beings. The distance between the Existent and generate reality is absolute. The distance between the divine Logos and human beings is not. They exist in a part-to-whole relationship, since humans are a fragment of the divine Mind.[102] Even a generate being can be deified (i.e., share in deity) by participating in a mediate God, such as the Logos.

Opponents of Moses's deification in Philo often resort to understanding deification in some sort of metaphorical sense. Scott refuses to let Moses be "ontologically divine" because Moses as "god" (Exod 7:1) and "deiform" (θεοειδές) (*Mos.* 1.158-59) only means that Moses is a mediator.[103] Similarly, Holladay and Bauckham try to reduce Moses's godhood to a statement about his (solely human) kingship. Neither attempt to make Moses's deity in Philo figurative (i.e., symbolizing some exalted *human* role) is successful. Moses's proleptic transformation on Sinai and his final metamorphosis into divine νοῦς at death indicate that Philo could think of Moses's deification in quite realistic (i.e., "ontological") terms. These transformations indicate that Moses is not a god purely because he functions as a human mediator or a

---

[100] In *Spec.* 1.66, Philo describes angels in a way similar to his description of the transformed Moses in *Mos.* 2.288. Angels are "all mind through and through (ὅλας δι' ὅλων νοεράς), pure intelligences (λογισμοὺς ἀκραιφνεῖς), assimilated to the Monad (μονάδι ὁμοιουμένας)." In light of this parallel we should perhaps call Moses's final transformation a kind of angelification where he becomes, to use the language of Luke, ἰσάγγελος—"like" or "equal to angels" (20:36). To speak of Moses as "angelified" is probably fair and helpfully underscores the fact that Moses transformed is not equal to the Logos—let alone the Existent. Nevertheless, the fact that Philonic angels are (1) purely noetic beings like the divine Logos and (2) assimilated to the monad indicates that they also participate in the divinity of the Logos, and are part of the divine world. Accordingly, Moses "angelified" is also Moses deified. Angelification, in other words, is a form of deification because becoming noetic reality still involves, for Philo, a "change into the divine" (*QE* 2.29).

[101] "Moses a Divine Man," 110.

[102] Runia may well be correct that Philo shows a preference for the copy-to-model relation of humans to the Logos (e.g., *Opif.* 69), rather than their part-to-whole relation (e.g., *Det.* 90). Yet as he points out, both relations are interpretations of scripture (model/copy from Gen 1:26–27; part/whole from Gen 2:7)—scriptures which "Philo tends to reconcile … and thus puts the two kinds of relation on a par" ("God and Man," 68). In my view, the model/copy model and the part/whole model work together to express a common idea of participation in the divine.

[103] "Moses a Divine Man," 106–107.

king. Philo the Platonist exegete did not share our apprehension of metaphysics.[104] If mediating divine reality or functioning as a king involves participation in God, it can qualify as a form of "real" deification.[105] Scott's conclusion that Moses's divinity is merely "metaphorical" or "allegorical" is thus inadequate.[106]

Equally unjustified is Scott's assertion that "the basis of Moses' greatness is *entirely unlike* that of the divinized heroes of the Hellenistic world."[107] This statement finds no support in Scott's article, where traditions of deification in the Greco-Roman world are never discussed. Here I believe Scott's theological categories have dictated the results of his research. In his desire to deny any realistic ("ontological") implications of Moses's divinity, Scott is concerned to (in his language) break the bridge between the "Church" and "the pagan temple."[108] With the use of such an expression, the author situates himself in a trajectory of apologetics inappropriate for scholarly inquiry. The truth, it seems to me, is that Philo shared a good deal of theological assumptions with his non-Jewish philosophical contemporaries (e.g., the distinction between Being and becoming, levels of deity, the notion of participating in the divine, etc.). Philo's exaltation of the Existent as the sole source of the divine and alone worthy of worship made his theology distinctive (indeed, distinctively Jewish). These ideas, however, do not disallow a Philonic form of deification.[109]

---

[104] The idea that Moses is "ontologically" divine does not, as Scott implies, mean that Moses is "divine in an independent … sense" (*ibid.*, 108), since the one who shares God's divinity remains dependent upon God.

[105] See especially on this point Manfred Clauss, *Kaiser und Gott: Herrscherkult im römischen Reich* (Stuttgart: Teubner, 1999).

[106] "Moses a Divine Man," 108. Bauckham makes a similar conclusion in "Moses as 'God,'" 254–55. Contrast Meeks, who argued—based on Philo's insight that Moses as "god" cannot be added or subtracted (*Sacr.* 10)—that "Moses thus shares God's nature, and is accorded the title 'God' in the proper sense" (*Prophet-King*, 105).

[107] "Moses a Divine Man," 109, emphasis mine. Cf. Hurtado, *One Lord, One God*, 63.

[108] *Ibid.*, 111. Note the continued tradition of Christianizing Philo.

[109] Theological biases are also at play, I think, in the work of Bauckham, who explicitly frames Moses's deification as a potential precedent for Christ's divinity ("Moses as God," 246). (Note especially his subtitle: "A Precedent for Christology?") Christian piety demands that real godhood belong to Christ and to Christ alone. The deity of other would-be precedents in Jewish tradition must therefore be "metaphorical." The way Bauckham phrases his conclusion shows his real concerns: "Philo's use of the word 'god' with reference to Moses provides no precedent for the attribution of divine nature or status to Jesus" (*ibid.*, 264).

Conclusion

The question of Moses's deification in Philo has not been fully resolved here. Philo is too complex a thinker for one essay to unravel all the issues surrounding this topic. By focusing on Moses's deification in his ascent and death, I hardly wish to reduce a complex issue to something simple and clear-cut. There is little doubt in my mind that in many places Philo could and did think of Moses's godhood in metaphorical terms. The point is that he can *also* think in ontological ways about Moses's participation in divinity. The different ways that Philo can speak about Moses's deification do not represent a vacillation, in my judgment. Rather, they represent the complexity of his theological thought, as well as his ability to modify his teachings to suit the occasion or the text that he is interpreting.

Although it might seem strange to us, Philo can assert both a strong doctrine of monotheism and a realistic form of deification without contradiction. In this article I have tried to indicate how this assertion makes theological sense in Philo's thought world. The three fundamental theological ideas that I have proposed are: (1) the recognition of different levels of deity, (2) the ability to participate in deity, and (3) the notion of shareable and unshareable deity. Given these ideas, Philo could (and I argue *did*) present a form of deification that posed no threat to his primal God (the Existent). In fact, Philo presented a form of deification in which Moses *did not even directly participate in the Existent at all*. In short, my argument is that Moses is deified by participating in the *Logos*, the Mind of God, and Philo's "second God." In his pre-mortem ascent to heaven, Moses's νοῦς—having temporarily left his body behind—was purified and deified by fuller participation in the Logos. At his death, Moses was permanently resolved into pure νοῦς, the reality of the Logos, and made his enduring ascent to the divine realm. In this way, Moses assimilated to and identified with a divine being (the Logos) and became divine himself.

University of Virginia
Charlottesville, Virginia

The Studia Philonica Annual 26 (2014) 29–55

PHILO'S DOCTRINE OF *APOKATASTASIS*:
Philosophical Sources, Exegetical Strategies, and Patristic Aftermath[*]

ILARIA RAMELLI

Introduction: The Notion of Apokatastasis *and the Focus of This Essay*

The term ἀποκατάστασις means essentially restoration, re-establishment, reconstitution into an original condition that was later lost. In medical language, for instance, it referred to the restoration of someone, or someone's limbs, to health after illness, a distortion, and the like. In astronomical and cosmological language, *apokatastasis* referred to the return of the planets and/or the stars to their original positions after many revolutions at the end of a "great year." In political language it referred especially to the return of an exiled person to his or her homeland. Greek philosophers such as the Stoics, as I shall indicate, privileged the cosmological meaning. In Philo the *apokatastasis* of the soul is essentially its restoration to virtue, as will be detailed here. Patristic authors—chiefly Origen of Alexandria in the early third century and Gregory of Nyssa in the late fourth—will take over this meaning, but will particularly develop the idea of *apokatastasis* as universal restoration, that is, the return of all human beings and all rational creatures to God, the supreme Good, after abandoning evil and being entirely purified. This also implies the ultimate salvation of all rational creatures.[1]

[*] This essay is the expanded and revised version of the paper I delivered at the SBL Annual Meeting, Baltimore, 25 Nov. 2013, Philo-Midrash session. I am deeply grateful to the organizers and the colleagues and friends who commented on my work at the session (especially David T. Runia and Teun Tieleman) and at various stages, as well as to the anonymous readers of the journal. Special thanks to David T. Runia and Gregory E. Sterling for their observations and the invitation to publish my study in their prestigious journal.
    [1] See my *The Christian Doctrine of Apokatastasis. A Critical Assessment from the New Testament to Eriugena* (Leiden: Brill, 2013), reviewed by Mark J. Edwards, *JTS* 65.2 (2014) doi: 10.1093/jts/flu075: jts.oxfordjournals.org/content/early/2014/06/30/jts.flu075.full; Johannes van Oort, *VC* 64 (2014): 352–353; Anthony Meredith, *JPT* 8.2 (2014): 255–257.

I shall here investigate Philo's notion of the restoration of the soul and its possible roots in Greek philosophy, in the light of research I am carrying on into Greek philosophical notions of *apokatastasis*, as well as in the light of the theme of the illness, death, and restoration of the soul in early imperial philosophy (including Roman philosophy). The LXX foundation of this doctrine has to be taken into account as well, but through Philo's allegorical-philosophical filter. This also seems to be applicable to Philo's notion of the restoration of Israel (although in this case the terminology of *apokatastasis* is not used). It will emerge from this examination that Philo, unlike his patristic followers, is far removed from an eschatological orientation as well as from universalism: his concept of *apokatastasis* bears no relation to the doctrine of the eventual universal salvation, nor to the resurrection of the body, as it does in Origen. Nevertheless, Philo must be credited with being one of the main inspirers of Origen's thought and exegesis in general, and of his doctrine of *apokatastasis* in particular.

Philo's Possible Philosophical Sources concerning the Concept of Apokatastasis

Philo, as David Runia remarks, "a une très bonne connaissance des doctrines des différentes *haireseis* ou écoles de pensée à l'intérieur de la philosophie grecque. Non seulement il est bien informé, mais il est probable qu'il connaissait directement ou indirectement les écoles philosophiques à Alexandrie."[2] This, even though Philo did not profess an affiliation to any of the Greek philosophical schools, not even Platonism. Indeed, according to Peder Borgen's description, he was a "philosophically minded exegete, and a philosopher imbued with the Bible."[3] What Philo mainly wished to do was to "explain and defend the traditions of his people, showing that if properly understood they were in fact superior to the cultures of the other ethnic groups in the city, including Greeks and Romans."[4] The philosophy he professes is the Mosaic philosophy,[5] just as Justin, one century later,

---

[2] David T. Runia, "Philon d'Alexandrie," in *Dictionnaire des Philosophes Antiques* (ed. Richard Goulet; Paris: CNR, 2011), 5A:362–90, esp. 380–81.

[3] Peder Borgen, "Philo of Alexandria," in *Jewish Writings of the Second Temple Period* (ed. Michael E. Stone; Assen: Van Gorcum; Philadelphia: Fortress, 1984), 252–64, esp. 264.

[4] David T. Runia, "Philo and the Gentiles," in *Attitudes to Gentiles in Ancient Judaism and Early Christianity* (ed. David Sim and James McLaren; London: T&T Clark, 2013), 28–45, esp. 29.

[5] Philo often describes "us" as "the disciples of Moses" (e.g. *Spec.* 1.345; *Det.* 86). On Philo's commitment to revealing the universal philosophical message of the Bible to the Gentiles, and especially learned Greeks, see Valentin Nikiprowetzky, *Le commentaire de*

professed his adhesion to the "divine philosophy" (φιλοσοφία θεία), that is, Christianity, albeit he, like Philo, received a good philosophical formation, especially in Platonism and Stoicism. Philo too shows the greatest affinities with Platonism, and a good deal of familiarity with Stoicism and Pythagoreanism.[6] He praises Plato himself as "the great Plato" (ὁ μέγας Πλάτων, *Aet.* 52) and, if the variant in the manuscript tradition is correct, "the most sacred Plato" (τὸν ἱερώτατον Πλάτωνα, *Prob.* 13, which introduces a quotation from *Phaedr.* 247A7). His selective use of Plato—focussing on the *Phaedrus, Phaedo, Symposium, Timaeus, Republic,* and *Laws*—corresponds to that which was widespread in Middle Platonism.[7] In Daniel Boyarin's words, "Philo's Judaism is simply an important variety of Middle Platonism."[8] He has also a good knowledge of Pythagoreanism, Aristotelianism,[9] and Stoicism. He could not receive Stoic immanence because of the transcendence of the biblical God,[10] but Stoic ethics and physics had a large

---

l'écriture chez Philon d'Alexandrie (Leiden: Brill, 1977), 117–55; Peder Borgen, *Philo of Alexandria: An Exegete for His Time* (Leiden: Brill, 1997), 140–57, 206–260.

[6] See David T. Runia, "The Rehabilitation of the Jackdaw. Philo of Alexandria and Ancient Philosophy," in *Greek and Roman Philosophy 100 BC-200 AD* (ed. Richard Sorabji and Robert W. Sharples; London: Institute of Classical Studies, University of London, 2007), 483–500. Ekaterina Matsuova, "Allegorical Interpretation of the Pentateuch in Alexandria: Inscribing Aristobulus and Philo in a Wider Literary Context," *SPhA* 22 (2010): 1–51, rejects the widespread hypothesis of the influence of Stoic allegoresis on Philo's allegorical method, rather pointing to Pythagorean allegorical criticism (21). She regards the Derveni papyrus as an example of Pythagorean interpretation, even though one could point to analogies between the Derveni allegorical technique and Stoic allegoresis.

[7] According to David Lincicum, "A Preliminary Index to Philo's Non-Biblical Citations and Allusions," *SPhA* 25 (2013): 139–67, and "Philo's Library," paper at the SBL Annual Meeting, Baltimore 25 Nov. 2013, Philo session, Plato is quoted eighteen times by Philo, and alluded to 315 times. Among his works, the *Apology* is alluded to twice, the *Cratylus* eleven times, the *Crito, Letters,* and *Eryxias* once, the *Gorgias* twelve times, the *Ion* thrice, the *Laws* twenty-two times, the *Meno* twice, the *Menexenus* is quoted once and alluded to once, the *Phaedo* is alluded to sixteen times, the *Phaedrus* is quoted twice and alluded to sixty-one times, the *Philebus* is alluded to seven times, the *Politicus, Parmenides,* and *Protagoras* are alluded to once, the *Republic* is alluded to twenty-five times, the *Symposium* is quoted once and alluded to nine times, the *Sophist* is quoted once and alluded to thrice, the *Theaetetus* is quoted thrice and alluded to sixteen times, and the *Timaeus* is quoted eleven times and alluded to 120 times (!).

[8] Daniel Boyarin, *Border Lines. The Partition of Judaeo-Christianity* (Philadelphia: University of Pennsylvania Press, 2004), 115.

[9] Lincicum, "Philo's Library," lists no direct quotation, but thirty-six allusions to Aristotle in Philo's corpus.

[10] This is emphasized, e.g., in *QG* 2.54; *Abr.* 79–80; *Leg.* 3.36, where for this reason God is called ἄποιος; *Somn.* 1.67, where God is declared ineffable; *Mut.* 9–10, where God is said to be incomprehensible, ἀκατάληπτος, cf. *Post.* 15. See my "The Divine as Inaccessible Object of Knowledge in Ancient Platonism: A Common Philosophical Pattern across Religious Traditions," *JHI* 75 (2014) 167–188.

impact on his philosophical ideas. Now Stoic cosmology was a core part of Stoic physics, and a main feature of Stoic cosmology was the doctrine of *apokatastasis*. It is very probable, and virtually certain, that Philo was acquainted with this doctrine. However, as I shall point out, Philo's notion of *apokatastasis* is not cosmological, but spiritual, and is based, not on the astronomical-cosmological meaning of ἀποκατάστασις and ἀποκαθίστημι, but on its medical meaning, as far as the restoration of the soul is concerned (as I shall show, Philo also postulates the restoration of Israel, but does not use the terminology of *apokatastasis* in this connection).

In Stoicism, the doctrine of *apokatastasis* was the cosmological theory of the cyclical return of the universe to its original condition at the end of every great year. Eusebius ascribes the very term ἀποκατάστασις to this Stoic doctrine: "The common logos, that is, the common nature, becomes more and more abundant, and in the end dries up everything and resolves everything into itself. It returns to the first logos and the famous 'resurrection' [ἀνάστασις] that makes the great year, when the universal restoration [ἀποκατάστασις] takes place" (*Praep. ev.* 15.19.1-3 = *SVF* 2.599). Eusebius describes the Stoic doctrine as a universal *apokatastasis*—this was especially interesting to him, who was in turn a supporter of universal *apokatastasis*, though not in the Stoic cosmological sense, but in the Christian (Origenian) sense.[11] The Stoics' cosmological doctrine of *apokatastasis* was linked to the astronomical meaning of ἀποκατάστασις. This is especially evident from *SVF* 2.625, preserved by Nemesius, *NH* 38: "The Stoics maintain that the planets will return [ἀποκαθισταμένους] into the same constellation [...] Universal restoration [ἀποκατάστασις] takes place not only once, but many times, or better the same things will continue to be repeated [ἀποκαθίστασθαι] indefinitely, without end." Indeed, Stoic *apokatastasis* is the infinite repetitions of a cosmic cycle (see also *SVF* 2.599): aeons or "great years" succeed to one another, identical to one another,[12] with the same persons making the same choices. In periodical conflagrations, all beings return to fire / aether / Logos / pneuma / Zeus, the

---

[11] See my "Origen, Eusebius, and the Doctrine of Apokatastasis," in *Eusebius of Caesarea: Traditions and Innovations* (ed. Aaron Johnson and Jeremy Schott; Cambridge, MA: Center for Hellenic Studies, Harvard University Press, 2013), 307–23.

[12] "Identical" and "almost identical": see Jonathan Barnes, "La doctrine du retour éternel," in *Les Stoïciens et leur logique* (ed. Jacques Brunschwig; Paris: Vrin, 1978), 3–20, esp. 9–12; Anthony Long, "The Stoics on World-Conflagration and Everlasting Recurrence," *Southern Journal of Philosophy* 23 suppl. (1985): 13–38, esp. 26–31; Ricardo Salles, "Tiempos, objetos, y sucesos en la metafísica estoica," *Diánoia* 47–49 (2002): 3–22; Marcelo Boeri, "Incorpóreos, tiempo, e individuación en el estoicismo," *Diánoia* 48–51 (2003): 181–93.

supreme but immanent divinity. After that, this immanent principle constitutes again another universe (πᾶν) or "whole" (ὅλον).

The noun ἀποκατάστασις and the verb ἀποκαθίστημι in reference to the Stoic doctrine of *apokatastasis* are attested by Christian sources alone, as I have shown in the cases of Eusebius and Nemesius. Marcus Aurelius (*Ad seips.* 11.1.3), Alexander of Aphrodisias (*In Ar. Gen. et corr.* 314.13-15), and Simplicius (*In Ar. Phys.* 886.12-13) present, instead, παλιγγενεσία and πάλιν γίγνομαι, which signify a rebirth or renewal. Either ἀποκαθίστημι or καθίστημι is attested in a Greek fragment from Chrysippus's *On Providence* on *apokatastasis* and preserved by another Christian author, Lactantius (*in libros quod de providentia scripsit, cum de innovatione mundi loqueretur, Inst.* 7.23 = *SVF* 2.623, where *innovatio* seems to render παλιγγενεσία): "This being the situation, it is clear that it is not at all impossible [οὐδὲν ἀδύνατον] that we too, after our death [μετὰ τὸ τελευτῆσαι], once given cycles of time have elapsed [περιόδων τινῶν εἰλημμένων χρόνου or περιόδῳ τινὶ χρόνου], are restored/reconstituted [καταστήσασθαι or ἀποκαταστῆναι[13]] into the structure [σχῆμα] that we presently have."[14] Lactantius speaks of *innovatio mundi* in his introductory words, even though in this specific fragment the question seems to be the restoration of human beings after their death—and Lactantius quotes it because he is dealing with the resurrection[15]: "Since not only the prophets, but also 'pagan' poets and philosophers agree that there will be the resurrection of the dead [*anastasim mortuorum*], let nobody ask us how this will be possible, since it is impossible to account for the works of God: but if God in the beginning created the human being in an ineffable way I do not know, let us believe that a human being can be restored [*restitui*] by the same God who created it from scratch" (*Inst.* 7.23.5). Note the use of *restitui*, which corresponds to the passive of ἀποκαθίστημι. However, the Stoic restoration was quite different from the Christian resurrection, the restoration of human beings after death, was understood by the Stoics in the context of their cosmic *apokatastasis* theory. Within this framework, human beings will be restored to live again on earth the same life they had lived before, in the previous cosmic cycles, and they will live after, in the following cycles, without end.

---

[13] Depending on the manuscript tradition: see Stefan Freund, "Chrysipp und die ἀποκατάστασις. Beobachtungen zu Text, Zusammenhang, Überlieferungsgeschichte, und Rezeption von SVF II 623," *Rheinisches Museum* 149 (2006): 51–64, esp. 53.

[14] On this fragment see Freund, "Chrysipp," 51–64. On Stoic *apokatastasis* see also Richard Sorabji, *Time, Creation and the Continuum* (London: Institute of Classical Studies, University of London, 1983), 183–90.

[15] See Jaap Mansfeld, "Resurrection Added. The *Interpretatio Christiana* of a Stoic Doctrine," *VC* 37 (1983): 218–33.

The Stoics seem to have been inspired by Heraclitus[16] especially with regard to the role of fire and conflagrations in Stoic cosmology, and by the Pythagoreans in relation to the "Great Year," but they drew inspiration from Empedocles as well, especially as for the cosmic cycles determined by the alternate prevailing of Friendship—the principle that unites—and Enmity, the principle that divides. Now, Philo also knew doxographic literature,[17] which could easily include the opinions of Heraclitus and Empedocles, and, remarkably enough, there is evidence, studied by Lucia Saudelli, that Philo knew Heraclitus's ideas.[18] More specifically, David Lincicum records three quotations of, and three allusions to, Empedocles in Philo's works, and even 26 quotations of, and 20 allusions to, Heraclitus.[19] Origen, too, another supporter of the doctrine of *apokatastasis*, knew Empedocles, like Clement of Alexandria.[20] Origen cites Empedocles as both a philosopher and a poet several times, in his polemic against the Middle Platonist Celsus (*Cels.* 1.32; 7.41; 8.53). In *Cels.* 8.53 Origen also quotes a verse by Empedocles, and proves familiar with his theory of the reincarnation and cycles of purification. Origen then refutes Empedocles' doctrine of *apokatastasis ante litteram*, just as he refuted the Stoic doctrine of *apokatastasis* (*Cels.* 4.12; 4.67-68; 5.20; *Princ.* 2.3), because he wanted to show that his own, *Christian* doctrine of *apokatastasis* was very different from the philosophical theories of *apokatastasis* that had been propounded so far, especially for two reasons. One is that, while the Stoics (and apparently also Empedocles before them) posited an infinite sequence of aeons, Origen thought that there will come an end to this sequence at the eventual *apokatastasis*; after that, no aeon will begin again, but there will be pure

---

[16] Jean-Baptiste Gourinat, "Éternel retour et temps périodique dans la philosophie stoïcienne," *Revue philosophique de la France et de l'étranger* 127 (2002): 213–27. On the Stoic doctrine of *apokatastasis* as presented by Dio Chrysostom see Ilaria Ramelli, "Stoic Cosmo-Theology Disguised as Zoroastrianism in Dio's *Borystheniticus*? The Philosophical Role of Allegoresis as a Mediator between Physikē and Theologia," *Jahrbuch für Religionsphilosophie* 12 (2013): 9–26.

[17] Runia, "Philon d'Alexandrie," 387.

[18] Lucia Saudelli, *Eraclito ad Alessandria* (Turnhout: Brepols, 2012). See also Erich Gruen, "Hebraism and Hellenism," in *The Oxford Handbook of Hellenic Studies* (Oxford: Oxford University Press, 2009; online ed. 2012 DOI: 10.1093/oxfordhb/9780199286140.013. 0011), 1–6, esp. 4: Philo "traces the impact of Jewish learning back to the Presocratic thinker Heraclitus and sees its effect in the verses of Hesiod, the teachings of Socrates, and the Stoic doctrines of Zeno."

[19] Lincicum, "Philo's Library."

[20] For an analysis of Clement's knowledge of, and attitude towards, Empedocles see Ilaria Ramelli, "Vie diverse all'unico mistero," *Rendiconti dell'Istituto Lombardo, Accademia di Scienze e Lettere* 139 (2005): 455–83; *Empedocle* (ed. Alessandro Tonelli and Ilaria Ramelli; Milan: Bompiani, 2002).

eternity. Thus, for example, in *Princ.* 3.1 Origen foresees "a stage in which there will be no aeon any more," and in 2.3.5 he stresses that there will come the end of all aeons, and this will be the eventual *apokatastasis* itself, "when all will be no more in an aeon, but God will be 'all in all'." Instead of being in an aeon of history, rational creatures will finally come to be in God, and God will represent all goods for all of them, no one excluded. The same final state, after all aeons, is described by Origen in *Comm. Jo.* 13.3: after life in the next aeon (ζωὴ αἰώνιος), in Christ, there will come the eventual restoration, which will surpass and supersede all aeons; then all will be in the Father and God will be "all in all" (again 1 Cor 15:28, Origen's favourite Scriptural passage in support of the *apokatastasis* doctrine[21]).

The second reason why Origen criticised the Stoic doctrine of *apokatastasis* is that, according to the Stoics, each aeon will be the theatre of the same people, the same events, and the same moral choices, repeated *ad infinitum*. Origen, on the contrary, postulated not only a limited number of aeons, but also aeons that are all different from one another, in that they aim at the moral and spiritual development of rational creatures and mark an overall advancement in the history of their salvation. This is why Origen accuses the Stoic theory of *apokatastasis* of denying human free will: "If this is the case, our *freedom of will* is over. For, if during given cycles, out of necessity, the same things have happened, happen, and will happen […] it is clear that out of necessity Socrates will *always* devote himself to philosophy, and will be accused of introducing new divinities and of corrupting the youths; and that Anitus and Meletus will *always* be his accusers, and that the Areopagus judges will condemn him to death […] If one accepts this idea, I do not quite know how *our freedom* will be saved and how *praises and blames* will possibly be justified" (*Cels.* 4.67-68). Likewise Origen attacks the Stoic notion of *apokatastasis* in *Princ.* 2.3.4 because it denies human free will. The argument here is the same as in the previous passage from *Contra Celsum*, though the examples differ: in the polemic against the "pagan" Middle Platonist, the examples are taken from philosophy, Socrates and his accusers; in his treatise of systematic theology, Origen draws his examples from the Bible: Adam and Eve, Jesus, Judas, and Paul: "I do not quite know what arguments can be adduced by those who maintain that the aeons follow each other being *perfectly identical to one another*." He explained, "For, if one aeon will be perfectly identical to another, Adam and Eve will do for the second time the same things that they already did […] Judas will betray the Lord again, and Paul will keep again the mantels of those who were stoning Stephen, and all that has

---

[21] See my "Christian Soteriology and Christian Platonism," *VC* 61 (2007): 313–56.

happened in this life will happen again." He then objected, "But this theory can be supported by no argument, since the souls are pushed by their free will, and their progresses and regresses depend on the faculty of their will. Indeed, the souls are not induced to do or wish this or that by the circular movement of the heavenly bodies that after many aeons accomplish the same cycle, but wherever the freedom of their inclination has pushed them, there they orient the course of their actions" (*Princ.* 2.3.4).

Interestingly enough, Origen attributes the Stoic doctrine of an infinite sequence of cyclical aeons to Platonists and Pythagoreans as well (*Cels.* 5.20). He thus tended to distinguish his own doctrine of *apokatastasis* from "pagan" philosophical cosmologies in general. His doctrine is instead a biblical doctrine, in that it is grounded in Scripture, just as Philo's doctrine of *apokatastasis* was grounded in Scripture—but while the Septuagint was common to Philo and Origen, the New Testament was available to Origen alone, and this, as I shall show, will make a big difference. As I shall point out, Philo was also a main source of Origen's *apokatastasis* doctrine, though there are also pivotal points of divergence between their two doctrines, which I shall indicate and endeavour to account for. Philo, like Origen after him, certainly knew the Stoic doctrine of *apokatastasis*, but he seems to have drawn the main inspiration for his own doctrine of the restoration of the soul and of Israel from Scripture, and from Hellenistic and Imperial philosophical motifs related to the illness, death, and recovery of the soul, as I shall point out.

Biblical Roots of Philo's Doctrine of Apokatastasis

Philo's doctrine of the *apokatastasis* of the soul, which I shall analyse in the next section, was grounded not only in philosophy, but certainly also in Scripture, Philo's authoritative text, as was also his idea of the restoration of Israel. In the LXX, the biblical text regularly used by Philo, the agent of restoration is always God, and the verb expressing this restoration is ἀποκαθίστημι or ἀποκαθιστάνω (in the LXX only the verb occurs, while the corresponding noun, ἀποκατάστασις, is absent: its sole appearance in the Bible is in the New Testament, in Acts 3:21: χρόνοι ἀποκαταστάσεως πάντων, with a strong eschatological connotation).[22] For instance, in Exod 14:26-27

---

[22] When it is not necessarily God who restores, it is in trivial meanings of the verb such as the restitution of money, possessions, a position, an earthly kingdom, and the like (Gen 23:16; 29:3; 40:13 and 21; 41:13; 2 Kgs 9:7; 1 Esd 1:29 and 33; 5:2; 6:25; 1 Macc 15:3; 2 Macc 12:25; 12:39). On Acts 3:21 as referring to the eschatological restoration see, e.g., Lutz

God restores the water, that is, causes it to flow again, after immobilising it for the passage of the Hebrews, and to submerge the Egyptians: "Let the water be restored [ἀποκαταστήτω] and let it cover the Egyptians [...] the water was restored [ἀπεκατέστη]" by God. The salvific implications of this action of restoration on the part of God are clear. In Lev 13:16 God heals the leper's skin, and the meaning of the verb is therapeutic: "the skin is restored [ἀποκαταστῇ] to health" by God. This is why the diagnosis and therapy of leprosy depended on the priests, as agents of God. Again, the salvific implications of this action of restoration to health on the part of God are clear. In Job 5:18 God is said to punish somebody, but also to restore this person again: πάλιν ἀποκαθίστησιν. Origen will make the most of this verse, taking it as a support of his doctrine of *apokatastasis*.[23] Certainly Philo, too, could see in it a confirmation of his doctrine of the *apokatastasis* of the soul, and the same is the case with the following three biblical passages. In Job 8:6 and 22:28, God is presented as the one who will restore (ἀποκαταστήσει) the life of the suffering just; in Job 33:25 God is said to be going to restore (again ἀποκαταστήσει) the suffering man, and his tormented flesh, to his youth. Likewise, in Ps 34:17 God is invoked to restore the soul of the anguished: "restore / save [ἀποκατάστησον] my soul / life from their evildoing." The connection between restoration and salvation is particularly clear in this passage, which explicitly speaks of the restoration of the soul. In other cases, Philo had to apply an allegorical exegesis in order to evince from Scripture the concept of the *apokatastasis* of the soul. This is true of the following passages as well.

In Isa 23:17 God is said to be going to restore Tyre to its old prosperity: Tyre "will be restored (by God) to its ancient state" (ἀποκαταστήσεται εἰς τὸ ἀρχαῖον). This expression will be picked up by the main Christian theorisers of *apokatastasis*, Origen and Gregory of Nyssa. It emphasises in particular that *apokatastasis* will be a restoration to one's original state, the ἀρχαῖον. This will also be a basis for their notion of *apokatastasis* as *oikeiōsis* (that is, both a return of rational creatures to the state that is proper and familiar to them, namely their original condition without sin, and a re-appropriation

Doering, "*Urzeit–Endzeit* Correlations in the Dead Sea Scrolls and Pseudepigrapha," in *Eschatologie–Eschatology. The Sixth Durham-Tübingen Research Symposium: Eschatology in Old Testament, Ancient Judaism, and Early Christianity, Tübingen, September 2009* (ed. Hans-Joachim Eckstein, Christof Landmesser, and Hermann Lichtenberger; Tübingen: Mohr Siebeck, 2011), 19–58, esp. 20, and my *The Christian Doctrine of Apokatastasis*, 13–18.

[23] See Ilaria Ramelli, "Origen's Exegesis of Jeremiah: Resurrection Announced throughout the Bible and its Twofold Conception," *Aug* 48 (2008): 59–78.

by the Godhead of all of its creatures, alienated from itself by evil).[24] Philo too adapted the notion of *oikeiōsis* to his transcendent worldview and used it in the context of the relationship between humans and the divinity (*Opif.* 145-146), but he did not apply it to the specific notion of *apokatastasis*, as Origen and Gregory of Nyssa would. Again in the Septuagint, in Jer 15:19 God is said to be going to restore Israel, if the people return to God by repenting: "if you return [ἐπιστρέψῃ], I shall restore [ἀποκαταστήσω] you." Origen will interpret this verse as a reference to his own doctrine of *apokatastasis*, and I shall point out that Philo, too, developed a notion of the restoration of Israel, even though he did not use the terminology of *apokatastasis* in this connection. In Jer 16:15 it is again God who restores Israel: "I shall restore [ἀποκαταστήσω] them to their land, which I gave to their forefathers;" as well as in Jer 23:8, "The Lord is alive, who gathered the whole offspring of Israel [...] and restored [ἀποκατέστησε] them into their land;" and in Jer 27:19, "and I shall restore [ἀποκαταστήσω] Israel into its meadow." In Ezek 16:55 God will restore Sodom and Samaria, as well as Jerusalem, to their original condition: "Your sister Sodom and her daughters *will be restored* [ἀποκατασταθήσονται] as they were from the beginning, and Samaria and her daughters will be restored [ἀποκατασταθήσονται] as they were from the beginning, and you and your daughters *will be restored* [ἀποκατασταθήσεσθε] as you were from the beginning." All of these occurrences were liable to allegoresis as references to the *apokatastasis* of the soul. In Dan 4:36 (A) God is said to have restored Nebuchadnezzar's kingdom: after hearing a voice from heavens, "my kingdom was restored [ἀποκατεστάθη] to me (by God) and my glory was returned to me (by God)." In Hos 2:5 God will restore (ἀποκαταστήσω) Israel to the condition it had the day of its birth: "I shall *restore* her as she was in the day of her birth." In Tob(BA) 10:13, God is said to restore Tobit in the sense that God will let him return safe home: "May the Lord of heaven bring you back safe [ἀποκαταστήσαι] home."

In some of the passages I have quoted from the Septuagint, such as Jer 15:19, restoration also implies a sense of reconciliation between creatures and God. Later on, in the Midrash as well, an equation appears between restoration and reconciliation between humans and God: "Let not a man, after sinning, say: 'There is no restoration for me,' but rather let him trust in

---

[24] See my "The Stoic Doctrine of *Oikeiōsis* and its Transformation in Christian Platonism," *Apeiron* 47 (2014): 116–40.

the Lord and repent, and God will receive him" (Midrash on Psalms 40.4).[25] In Philo's doctrine of the *apokatastasis* of the soul, which will be examined next, the concept of reconciliation with God is also present; this is essentially effected through virtue.

Apokatastasis *of the Soul in Philo. Souls' Illness, Death, and Restoration*

While the Stoics took up the astronomical-cosmological meaning of ἀποκατάστασις, as noted above, Philo, for his part, took up mainly the medical meaning of the term, related to the notion of the illness of the soul and its recovery, within the framework of his focus on spiritual pedagogy or psychagogy: the guidance of souls toward God through the Logos,[26] who performs an action of spiritual illumination. This is a mystical work as a spiritual pedagogue and exemplar at the same time,[27] as spelled out especially in *Sacr.* 8 and *Conf.* 145-147. In the former passage in particular, Philo remarks that, "by the same Logos with which God has made the universe, God also leads the perfect person from earthly things up [ἀνάγει] to Himself."[28] Indeed, Philo uses the very term ἀποκατάστασις, which in the LXX is unattested, as mentioned above, whereas the corresponding verb ἀποκαθίστημι / ἀποκαθιστάνω is abundantly attested. The noun ἀποκατάστασις occurs in Philo at *Her.* 293, where it is applied to the restoration of the soul to perfection. The noun ἀποκατάστασις was not unknown in Hellenistic Judaism. It is attested in the *Letter of Aristeas* (§123), but not in the sense of restoration of the soul that it bears in Philo. In the *Letter* it is rather taken in its political meaning: the restoration of someone after an exile or reconstitution of someone into his or her original condition.[29] Philo also has more trivial meanings of ἀποκατάστασις. He uses this noun in

---

[25] Claude G. Montefiore and Herbert Loewe, *A Rabbinic Anthology* (London: Macmillan, 1938), 321. Cf. L. Newman, "The Quality of Mercy: On the Duty to Forgive in the Judaic Tradition," *JRE* 15 (1987): 155–72, esp. 163.

[26] This emphasis on spiritual pedagogy is singled out by Paul Blowers as one of the most characteristic features of Philo's thought (*Drama of the Divine Economy*, Oxford: Oxford University Press, 2012), 47.

[27] David Winston, *Logos and Mystical Theology in Philo of Alexandria* (Cincinnati: Hebrew Union College Press, 1985), 15–18, 43–58.

[28] On this passage, see Ronald Cox, *By the Same Word: Creation and Salvation in Hellenistic Judaism and Early Christianity* (Berlin: De Gruyter, 2007), 87–94.

[29] Indeed, in the lexical work *De adfinium vocabulorum differentia*, probably due to Ammonius the grammarian, at entry 71 a lexical distinction is drawn between the rendering of an object, which is indicated with ἀπόδοσις, and the reintegration or restoration of a person into his or her previous state, which is indicated by ἀποκατάστασις.

Decal. 164 to indicate the sabbatical restoration of portions of land to their original owners (τῶν κληρουχιῶν ἀποκατάστασις εἰς τοὺς ἐξ ἀρχῆς λαχόντας οἴκους) according to the Law. He depicts this initiative as inspired by principles of justice and philanthropy. Actually, Philo constantly argues that the whole of the Mosaic Law conforms to the principles of justice and love for humanity. Shortly after Philo, Josephus in *A.J.* 11.63 will refer to the restoration of the Jewish people to their land, the promised Land: τῆς τῶν Ἰουδαίων ἀποκαταστάσεως. This concept, albeit without the lexicon of *apokatastasis*, is found in Philo as well, as I shall show in a moment. Josephus also uses ἀποκατάστασις in the sense of "restoration" in reference to a city in *A.J.* 11.98: "the restoration [ἀποκατάστασις] of Jerusalem."

But Philo uses the noun ἀποκατάστασις in a much less trivial way, with reference to the *apokatastasis* of the soul, meaning its restoration to health or recovery. In *Her.* 293 he interprets Gen 15:16 according to the Septuagint's text: "at the fourth generation they will return here" (τετάρτῃ δὲ γενεᾷ ἀποστραφήσονται ὧδε). He reads this verse allegorically and thus remarks that this return was mentioned "not only in order to point to the time in which they will inhabit the holy Land, but also to indicate the perfect restoration of the soul [ὑπὲρ τοῦ τελείαν ἀποκατάστασιν ψυχῆς παραστῆσαι]." In this way Philo joins the concept of the restoration of Israel—on which more below in the next section—to that of the restoration of the soul, which is its allegorical counterpart. The perfect restoration of the soul is its restoration to its original perfection, that is, when it was untainted by sins. In fact, as Philo explains in §§293-299, at the beginning it is like a wax tablet without any mark, but soon it begins to acquire evils (κακά), sins (ἁμαρτήματα), and passions (πάθη). Here Philo cites Gen 8:21 in support of his argument: "the imagination of man's heart is evil from his youth" (RSV). The superimposition of πάθη, that is, evil passions—Philo uses Stoic terminology[30]—onto the soul demands the therapeutic action of philosophy (ἰατρικὴ φιλοσοφία). This unfolds itself into *logoi* (arguments, reasoning) that bring about health and salvation (λόγοις ὑγιεινοῖς καὶ σωτηρίοις). As a result of the action of philosophy, vigour and strength grow in the soul, and the latter will therefore remain stable "in all virtues." This is Philo's account of the restoration or *apokatastasis* of the soul, when it turns away from sin (ἀποστραφεῖσα τοῦ διαμαρτάνειν) and recovers its original purity and "inherits wisdom" (κληρονόμος ἀποδείκνυται σοφίας). The *apokatastasis*

---

[30] On Stoic *pathe, eupatheiai* and *propatheiai* see Margaret Graver, *Stoicism and Emotion* (Chicago: University of Chicago, 2007); Ilaria Ramelli and David Konstan, "The Use of ΧΑΡΑ in the New Testament and its Background in Hellenistic Moral Philosophy," *Exemplaria Classica* 14 (2010): 185–204.

of the soul is also described by Philo as a restoration of the soul to health (ὑγίεια) after it has repudiated evil (ἀποστρεφόμενοι τὰ φαῦλα). The notion of ἀποκατάστασις as the restoration of the soul, also implying its attainment of perfection and beatitude, as I have demonstrated elsewhere,[31] will influence Clement of Alexandria, who was very well acquainted with Philo, and, even more deeply, Origen of Alexandria, who was also profoundly familiar with Philo's ideas and elaborated the most complete and consistent conception of the *apokatastasis* of souls, or better, of rational creatures.[32]

Another theory in Philo is closely related to the concept of *apokatastasis* of the soul understood as a return of the soul to its proper health. It is an important theory in Philo, which derives directly from his exegesis of Scripture in both the literal and the spiritual sense, and also owes much to his (Middle) Platonist frame of mind: the notion of the death of the rational soul, as a parallel to that of the body.[33] The motif of the death of the soul is found not only in Philo (e.g. *Det.* 47-51; *Post.* 39; *Congr.* 54-57: see below), but in early Imperial philosophy as well as in the New Testament,[34] and later in Origen and Gregory of Nyssa, who both were thoroughly acquainted with Philo's thinking. John Conroy in a recent essay is correct to view Philo's notion of the death of the soul as ontological and not just meta-phorical,[35] though he does not take into account the close parallels that are to be found in ancient philosophy, especially Roman Stoicism, and the New Testament (Paul and the Pastoral Epistles, but also Luke), as well as in Origen, who after Philo probably made the most of the notions of the illness and death of the soul.[36]

---

[31] See my *The Christian Doctrine of Apokatastasis*, Ch. 1, the section on Clement.

[32] See Ilaria Ramelli, *Gregorio di Nissa sull'anima e la resurrezione* (Milan: Bompiani–Catholic University, 2007), 833, 843, 849, 883–900.

[33] See Dieter Zeller, "The Life and Death of the Soul in Philo of Alexandria," *SPhA* 7 (1995): 19–56.

[34] See Emma Wasserman, *The Death of the Soul in Romans 7* (WUNT 2.256; Tübingen: Mohr Siebeck, 2008), and my "1 Tim 5:6 and the Notion and Terminology of Spiritual Death: Hellenistic Moral Philosophy in the Pastoral Epistles," *Aev* 84 (2010): 3–16. On the death of the soul in 1 Cor 11:30 see my "Spiritual Weakness, Illness, and Death in 1 Cor 11:30," *JBL* 130 (2011): 145–163. On the issue of the death of the soul underlying Luke 22:45 see my "ΚΟΙΜΩΜΕΝΟΥΣ ΑΠΟ ΤΗΣ ΛΥΠΗΣ (Luke 22,45): A Deliberate Change," *ZNW* 102 (2011): 59–76.

[35] John T. Conroy, "Philo's Death of the Soul: Is This Only a Metaphor?" *SPhA* 23 (2011): 23–40, who insists on the specific notion of the death of the *rational* soul in Philo, with the corollary that impious and vicious people descend to the level of animals, having only their vital soul left but not their rational soul. This idea was later developed by Origen.

[36] These parallels are pointed out in my articles indicated in note 34 above.

Even if in *Aet.* 5 Philo sets forth, or reports, the principle that "just as nothing comes into existence from nothing [ἐκ τοῦ μὴ ὄντος], so nothing perishes / is destroyed [φθείρεσθαι] so to be reduced to non-being [εἰς τὸ μὴ ὄν],"[37] he seems to have really postulated a substantial death of the rational soul: when the soul dies because it adheres to vice rather than virtue, and especially rejects piety, which makes it immortal (*QG* 1.10; *Opif.* 154), it disappears ontologically. The impious are "really dead in their souls" (ὄντως ... τὰς ψυχὰς τεθνᾶσι, *Spec.* 1.345); this is "the real death" (*Leg.* 1.105-108), of which Origen was obviously mindful when describing the death of the soul as "the real death" (ὁ ὄντως θάνατος, see below). After the death of the body, neither does the soul exist any longer, because with the rejection of virtue it has gravitated to matter rather than to the Logos of immortality (*QG* 3.1). This is consistent with Philo's statement in *Spec.* 4.187 that God's creation consists in bringing non-being into existence, essentially by means of an ordering action: "God called into existence what did not exist [τὰ μὴ ὄντα] by bestowing order [τάξιν] out of disorder [ἐξ ἀταξίας] ... union and harmony from what was dispersed and discordant." Therefore, if one chooses evil, which is non-being, disorder, and conflict, one necessarily regresses into non-being, and therefore becomes non-existent. This is essentially the death of the soul according to Philo. He often uses θάνατος and related terms to indicate spiritual death, that is, the death of the soul brought about by sin. In *Leg.* 2.77-78 Philo draws a clear distinction between the death of the body and that of the soul. He explains that pleasures bring about death (ἡδοναῖς ... θάνατον ἐπαγούσαις), not physical death, which is the separation of the soul from the body (οὐ χωρισμὸν ψυχῆς ἀπὸ σώματος), but the death of the soul, namely, the destruction of the soul by sin / evil (ὑπὸ κακίας φθοράν). In this connection, Philo interprets Num 21:6 allegorically and takes the "death-giving serpents" there (τοὺς ὄφεις τοὺς θανατοῦντας) to mean immoderate passions. Thence he explains: "For really there is nothing that brings about death to the soul so much as immoderate passions" (ὄντως γὰρ οὐδὲν οὕτως θάνατον ἐπάγει ψυχῇ, ὡς ἀμετρία τῶν ἡδονῶν). Also, in *Congr.* 57 Philo remarks: "The true Hades— that is to say, the true death—is the life of the wicked man." A life led in vice is tantamount to death. Consistently, in *Fug.* 58 he describes virtuous life as a good (ἀγαθόν) and death produced by wickedness (κακία) as evil (κακόν). Here, again, the context is exegetical: Philo is commenting on Deut 30:15: "I have set before your face life and death [τὴν ζωὴν καὶ τὸν θάνατον],

---

[37] Blowers, *Drama of the Divine Economy*, 59, takes this principle as endorsed by Philo himself; those critics who attribute to Philo a doctrine of *creatio ex nihilo* or a theory close to that do not think, consistently, that the principle at stake was subscribed by Philo himself.

good and evil [τὸ ἀγαθὸν καὶ τὸ κακόν]." Philo interprets this verse by identifying life with the good and virtue (τὸ μὲν ἀγαθὸν καὶ ἡ ἀρετή ἐστιν ἡ ζωή) and death with evil and vice (τὸ δὲ κακὸν καὶ ἡ κακία ὁ θάνατος). The second verse that Philo interprets in this passage, relating it to the previous verse, is Deut 30:20: "This is your life and length of days: to love the Lord your God." Again Philo comments on this identifying life with virtue, in this case the love of God, as per the Biblical verse at stake: "The most beautiful definition of immortal life is this: to be taken by unfleshly and incorporeal passion and love of God" (ὅρος ἀθανάτου βίου κάλλιστος οὗτος, ἔρωτι καὶ φιλίᾳ θεοῦ ἀσάρκῳ καὶ ἀσωμάτῳ κατεσχῆσθαι).

Origen and Gregory of Nyssa will take over Philo's line in this respect. They often speak of death in both senses: the death of the body and that of the soul. By "death," they often mean the state of being far from God—who is the Good—in sin and darkness. It is certainly very meaningful that precisely in connection with the interpretation of death as spiritual death produced by sin, Origen refers to Philo as the initiation of this interpretive tradition: *quidam ex his qui ante nos interpretati sunt locum hunc* (*Hom. Num.* 9.5: the reference is anonymous since in the homilies, which addressed the church, Origen never cites non-Christian authors as authorities, but Annewies van den Hoek rightly considers this to be from Philo[38]). Indeed, in *Her.* 201 Philo already interpreted the "dead" as impious and foolish people.

A series of passages in Philo consistently admit that some people who are alive physically, in their bodies, can be dead spiritually, in their souls—a concept that also appears in 1 Tim 5:6 and other early imperial texts, both philosophical and non-philosophical.[39] In *Det.* 49, the life of the vicious and foolish man is declared to be in fact a death: "the wise person seems to be dead [τεθνηκέναι] to corruptible life, but she lives the incorruptible one; the fool, instead [ὁ δὲ φαῦλος], is alive to the life according to vice, but is dead [τέθνηκε] to the happy life." The resultative perfect (τέθνηκε, the same as in 1 Tim 5:6) describes the state of spiritual death of the depraved person, and again one finds here the opposition with an apparent life. Philo is here appropriating the Stoic distinction between the wise person (σοφός) and the fool (φαῦλος). Likewise in *Her.* 293, Philo refers again to this distinction and claims that the fool, even if he is living in his body, is in fact already dead spiritually, since he is not leading a life of virtue: "According to the Legislator, only the wise enjoys a good old age and a very long life, whereas the

---

[38] Annewies van den Hoek, "Philo and Origen: A Descriptive Catalogue of their Relationship," *SPhA* 12 (2000): 44–121, esp. 98.

[39] See my "The Pastoral Epistles and Hellenistic Philosophy: 1 Tim 5:1–2, Hierocles, and the 'Contraction of Circles,'" *CBQ* 73 (2011): 562–81.

fool [τὸν φαῦλον] has an extremely short life and is always learning to die [ἀποθνήσκειν ἀεὶ μανθάνοντα], or rather is already dead [τετελευτηκότα] to the life according to virtue." In *Praem.* 79, Philo explains that a man may endure for a long time in spiritual death, even as long as his earthly life: "People think that death is the culmination of punishments, but at the tribunal of God this is only the very beginning. Since the crime is extra-ordinary, it was necessary that an extraordinary punishment be found for it. Which? To be always dying while living [ζῆν ἀποθνήσκοντα ἀεί] and, in a way, to suffer an immortal, unending death [θάνατον ἀθάνατον]." He explained: "For the kinds of death are two: the first is to be dead [τεθνάναι, *sc.* physical death], which is good or indifferent [ἀγαθὸν ἢ ἀδιάφορον]; the other is to die [ἀποθνήσκειν, *sc.* spiritual death], which is an evil, absolutely [κακὸν πάντως], and the more enduring, the heavier: and consider how this kind of death can endure together [συνδιαιωνίζει] with the sinner for an entire life." Similarly, in *Fug.* 55, Philo maintains that a man can be physically alive—that is, apparently alive—but spiritually dead. For foolish people, even if they live long, are spiritually dead, while the wise and virtuous live forever, even if their life in the body may be short: "Some are dead [τεθνήκασι] even if they are living, and live although they are dead [τεθνηκότες]. The fools, he said, even if they keep living into the most advanced old age, are dead [νεκρούς], in that they are deprived of the life according to virtue. The virtuous, instead, even though they are separated from the company of the body, keep living forever, in that they have attained immortality." The phrase ζῶντες τεθνήκασι in this passage by Philo corresponds to the singular ζῶσα τέθνηκε in 1 Tim 5:6. Both passages are describing a person who is physically alive but spiritually dead because leading a life of sin.

Both Philo's conception of the illness and death of the soul and that—which I have investigated earlier—of the restoration of the soul had a considerable impact on Origen and, more indirectly, on Gregory of Nyssa. Philo's eschatological ideas, or virtual lack thereof, however, diverge considerably from those of Origen and Gregory, both of whom were strong supporters of the theory of *apokatastasis* in the sense not only of the restoration of individual souls, but also of the restoration of all rational creatures. In their view, universal *apokatastasis* entailed both universal resurrection (of all human beings, in all of their components: body, soul, and intellect) and universal salvation, that is, the salvation of all rational creatures or *logika*: angels, humans, and demons. As I shall point out in a moment, Origen denied that any soul can ever perish ontologically (*substantialiter*); souls can be morally dead, but they will certainly rise again because their substance never vanishes, since it was created by God and as such it is good. Philo, instead, seems to believe that eternal life is a privilege granted by God only to virtuous souls, whereas the others seem to be doomed to perish altogether. Indeed, in Philo's view, the rational soul alone is immortal and incorruptible, and only those who have exercised it will survive; the others, having renounced their own rational soul, will perish like irrational beings: "The soul quits its residence in its mortal body and returns to its homeland, which it had abandoned to come to this place ... another life without a body, which *the soul of the wise alone will live*" (*QG* 3.11).[40] This is because only a purified soul, meaning its rational element, is really incorruptible and therefore immortal: "The kind of soul that is perfectly purified is inextinguishable and immortal, and destined to travel from here up to heaven, and not to the dissolution and corruption that death brings about" (*Her.* 276). Such a soul alone will escape death.

As I shall indicate in more detail in the next paragraph, Origen also claimed that the soul of a man who lives in vice perishes, because in his opinion the soul experiences mortality through the real death (ὁ ὄντως θάνατος), that is, spiritual death, brought about by sin and vice, as he declares in his *Dialogue with Heraclides* and elsewhere. However, Origen did not regard this perdition and state of "being lost" (ἀπόλεια) as eternal. For Jesus has come to find and save the lost sheep, and Scripture proclaims everywhere the resurrection of those who have died: "Don't you see in Scriptures the announcement of the resurrection of the dead?" (*Hom. Jer.* 11.16). Indeed, in his *Homilies on Jeremiah* Origen especially develops his twofold conception of resurrection, both of the body and of the soul (and within the soul one could further distinguish the irrational faculties and the rational soul or intellect).[41] This multi-layered conception is common to both Philo and Origen, but the latter did not admit of an ontological death of the soul, while the former did.

It is necessary to account for this remarkable difference in eschatology and soteriology, which is all the more striking in that Philo's anthropology, theology, protology, and Scriptural allegoresis are very similar to those of

---

[40] Cf. *Spec.* 3.206–207; *Cher.* 144; *Sacr.* 6; *Prob.* 117–118. See also Lester Grabbe, "Eschatology in Philo and Josephus," in *Judaism in Late Antiquity* (ed. Alan Avery-Peck and Jacob Neusner; Leiden: Brill, 2000), 4:163–185; Wilfried Eisele, *Ein unterschütterliches Reich: Die Mittelplatonische Umformung des Parusiegedankens im Hebräerbrief* (Berlin: De Gruyter, 2003), 160–240, according to whom Philo can be said to have an eschatology only to a limited extent: it is better to speak of human destiny in terms of aretalogy, in that, as I have demonstrated above, immortality for Philo depends on virtue. See also Christian Noack, *Gottesbewußtsein. Exegetische Studie zur Soteriologie und Mystik bei Philon* (Tübingen: Mohr Siebeck, 2000).

[41] See Ilaria Ramelli, "Origen's Exegesis of Jeremiah: Resurrection Announced throughout the Bible and Its Twofold Conception," *Aug* 48 (2008): 59–78.

Origen and, more indirectly, Gregory of Nyssa. Even the extremely close relation between philosophy and allegorical exegesis is the same in Philo and in Origen, as I have argued elsewhere:[42] philosophy (especially Middle- and Neoplatonism) and allegorical exegesis of Scripture are deeply inter- woven in Philo as well as in Origen and Gregory, and many theological and philosophical notions passed on from Philo to Origen and Gregory through allegory. I have also demonstrated that Origen tends to refer to Philo ex- pressly as a predecessor precisely in points that are crucial to his Scriptural allegorical method.[43] Now it is again Scripture and its exegesis, more than Platonist philosophy—which was the same philosophical background for both Philo and Origen, in the form of Middle Platonism—that very probably made the difference between Philo's and Origen's eschatological and soteriological views. For what grounded Origen's and other Fathers' doctrine of universal restoration and salvation is to be found mainly in the New Testament and its proclamation of Christ's incarnation, sacrificial death, and resurrection. It is on these that universal *apokatastasis* depends according to Origen.[44] Everything rests on Scripture and its interpretation. Even if in the Septuagint too one could find many verbal references to the restoration of the soul (all the more so if one wanted to read the Bible allegorically), it is in Paul that Origen, and later Gregory of Nyssa, could come across the strongest passages to buttress their theory of *apokatastasis* understood as universal restoration and salvation, and not just as the restoration of single souls. This ruled out the ontological destruction of any soul and affirmed that every single rational creature will be restored to God–the Good in the end. But Philo, even though he might perhaps have learnt something of the earliest Christian preaching,[45] nevertheless could

---

[42] In "Philosophical Allegoresis of Scripture in Philo and Its Legacy in Gregory of Nyssa," *SPhA* 20 (2008): 55–99.

[43] In "Philosophical Allegoresis" and further in "Philo as Origen's Declared Model. Allegorical and Historical Exegesis of Scripture," *Studies in Christian-Jewish Relations* 7 (2012): 1–17.

[44] As argued in Ilaria Ramelli, "Origen and Apokatastasis: A Reassessment," in *Origeniana Decima* (ed. Sylwya Kaczmarek and Henryk Pietras; Leuven: Peeters 2011), 649– 70.

[45] Notwithstanding Eusebius's account of Philo's acquaintance with the apostle Peter and his identification of the ascetics described in Philo's *De vita contemplativa* with the first Egyptian Christians (see my "The Birth of the Rome-Alexandria Connection: The Early Sources on Mark and Philo, and the Petrine Tradition," *SPhA* 23 [2011]: 69–95), in Philo's corpus there is no reliable hint of acquaintance with early Christian ideas. *Legat.*, 118 may suggest that Philo at least heard of the first Christian preaching: that God became a human being. Blaming Caligula for demanding to be worshipped like a deity, Philo remarks: "This was not an insignificant fact, but the most serious of all: to make a human being, a created and perishable thing, into the image of the uncreated and eternal Being! The Jews (in

not have read Paul's letters, or the rest of what became the New Testament, or, for instance, the *Apocalypse of Peter*, which Clement and Origen considered to be inspired.[46] In all of these texts, and most of all in Paul, Origen, and later Gregory of Nyssa, as well as other Patristic authors, saw important elements in support of the doctrine of *apokatastasis* understood as universal restoration and salvation.[47]

The Restoration of Israel in Philo and in the Jewish Eschatological Expectations of His Day

In the final part of *De praemiis et poenis* Philo also speaks of the restoration of Israel, which is primarily grounded in the OT passages I have already highlighted in the second section above.[48] However, Philo does not use the lexicon of *apokatastasis* here, but only the concept. In *Praem.* 162-172, he is speaking of those Jews who have adopted polytheism, forgetting their ancestral faith in the One and supreme God. If these people "change their ways" and purify their souls and minds, then God, who is the merciful Saviour, will forgive them. For the relationship of human beings to God's Logos is a work of God: the human mind was formed after God's Logos,

---

Rome) deemed this the height of profanation. *God would more easily become a human being than a human being God*" (θᾶττον γὰρ ἂν εἰς ἄνθρωπον θεὸν ἢ εἰς θεὸν ἄνθρωπον μεταβαλεῖν). Eusebius reported that the *Legatio* was read in the Senate under Claudius (*Hist. eccl.* 2.18.9), when the Christians were already preaching in Rome and Alexandria. Paul's letters, too, were already proclaiming the divinity of Christ, e.g. Phil 2:6 ("he was in the form of God, but did not count equality with God a thing to be grasped"). Gregory E. Sterling, "The Place of Philo of Alexandria in the Study of Christian Origins," in *Philon und das Neue Testament* (Tübingen: Mohr Siebeck, 2004), 21–52, thinks that Philo and the NT shared common traditions, such as the creative role of the Logos. Folker Siegert, "Der Logos, 'älterer Sohn' des Schöpfers und 'zweiter Gott'," in *Kontexte der Johannesevangelium* (ed Jörg Frey and Udo Schnelle; Tübingen: Mohr Siebeck, 2004), 277–94, underlines the closeness between Philo's Logos and the Logos in John. Another passage in Philo was liable to a Christian interpretation by Christian readers: Philo is allegorizing Sarah as virtue, which bears virtues such as justice, temperance, wisdom (*Congr.* 2). He then adds that Sarah/virtue "has the habit of bearing to God alone, giving back with gratitude the first fruits of the goods that she has received to God, who *had opened her perpetually virginal womb*" (τῷ τὴν ἀειπάρθενον μήτραν ... ἀνοίξαντι, *Congr.* 7). Philo is alluding to Gen 29:31, which, however, says that God opened Leah's womb, with no mention of virginity, let alone perpetual. In Luke, Jesus's birth is already presented as a virginal birth, and the early Gospel of James attests to the widespread belief concerning Mary's perpetual virginity.

[46] See my "Origen, Bardaisan, and the Origin of Universal Salvation," *HTR* 102 (2009): 135–68.

[47] As is pointed out in Ramelli, *The Christian Doctrine of* Apokatastasis.

[48] On Philo's eschatological expectations about Israel see Runia, "Philo and the Gentiles," 36–38.

which is its archetype (§163). At §164 Philo goes on to foresee the restoration of all these Israelites to freedom through virtue, after their enslavement to vice: "even though they may be at the very extremities of the earth, acting as slaves to those enemies who have led them away in captivity, still they shall all be restored to freedom [ἐλευθερωθήσονται] in one day, as at a given signal; their sudden and universal change to virtue causing a panic among their masters; for they will let them go, because they are ashamed to govern those who are better than themselves" (trans. Yonge[49]). As is evident, the notion of restoration is explicit in the translation, but not in the text, which literally reads: "they will all be liberated." This is clearly a reminiscence of the liberation of the Jews from captivity in Egypt, which Philo allegorized as vice. Here, however, this new liberation configures itself as a gathering of Israelites from all places and is explicitly identified by Philo with their salvation (§165): "But when they have received this unexpected liberty, those who but a short time before were scattered about in Greece, and in the countries of the barbarians, in the islands, and over the continents, rising up with one impulse, and coming from all the different quarters imaginable, all hasten to one place pointed out to them, being guided on their way by some vision, more divine than is compatible with its being of the nature of humanity, invisible indeed to everyone else, but apparent only to those who were saved, having their separate inducements and intercessions, by whose intervention they might obtain a reconciliation with the Father." This restoration, Philo explains, will be made possible by the merciful nature of God and by the intercessory prayers of the holy founders of the nation of Israel. The gathering and restoration of the Israelites will result in an enormous prosperity of the Land of Israel: "And when they come, cities will be rebuilt which but a short time ago were in complete ruins, and the desert will be filled with inhabitants, and the barren land will change and become fertile, and the good fortune of their fathers and ancestors will be looked upon as a matter of but small importance, on account of the abundance of wealth of all kinds which they will have at the present moment" (§168). When, in §§169-170, Philo warns the enemies of Israel that God has permitted them to take hold of Israel only "for the sake of giving an admonition" to the Israelites who "had forsaken their national and hereditary customs," Philo's words are impressively similar to Paul's, when he warns the nations that God has hardened Israel only for a while, for the sake of their own salvation, but will finally

---

[49] *The Works of Philo, Complete and Unabridged* (trans. Charles Duke Yonge; New Updated Edition, Peabody: Hedrickson, 1995).

restore Israel, so that, once "the totality [πλήρωμα][50] of the nations has entered," then "all [πᾶς] of Israel will be saved" (Rom 11:23–26). For, "if their trespass means riches for the world, and if their failure means riches for the Gentiles, how much more will their full inclusion mean! ... If their rejection means the reconciliation of the world, what will their acceptance mean but life from the dead?" (Rom 11:12, 15). Though, while Paul, here and elsewhere, impresses a universalistic tone to his eschatological soteriology, this is not the case with Philo. At any rate, the parallels look impressive, and even include the simile of the tree that is cut away but can revive again, which is the same in both Philo and Paul. Philo has in *Praem.* 172: "For as, when the trunk of a tree is cut down, if the roots are not taken away, new shoots spring up, by which the old trunk is again restored to life as it were; in the very same manner, if there be only left in the soul ever so small a seed of virtue, when everything else is destroyed, still, nevertheless, from that little seed there spring up the most honourable and beautiful qualities among humans; by means of which, cities, which were formerly populous and flourishing, are again inhabited, and nations are led to become wealthy and powerful." Paul likewise speaks of the trunk from which some of the Jews have been broken off, but God will graft them in again (Rom 11:16-24).

For Paul, the restoration of Israel will take place at the end of times and will follow the salvation of all nations. As for Philo, it is doubtful how eschatological and universal the restoration of Israel described by him is, and whether it applies to Israel ethnically understood or to philosophical souls, as especially the last quotation suggests.[51] This motif of the restoration of Israel interestingly also appears, with overtly eschatological and ethnic overtones, in some "intertestamentary" literature, which is broadly contemporary to Philo, and later in Origen, according to whom the restoration of Israel is eschatological and refers to all Jews, who will be all restored and saved eventually, as all Gentiles will. The very announcement of universal *apokatastasis* in Acts 3:20–21 (the only passage in all of Scripture where the noun ἀποκατάστασις occurs, in the syntagm χρόνοι ἀποκαταστάσεως πάντων) should probably be understood in the framework of

---

[50] Πλήρωμα in the LXX means "totality," and not simply "fullness," e.g., Ps 23:1, where it corresponds to πάντες; 49:12; 88:12; 95:11, where it corresponds to πάντα; 97:7; Jer 8:16; 29:2; Ezek 12:19, where it corresponds again to πάντες; 19:7; 30:12.

[51] In *Leg.* 2.9.34, too, when he mentions the offspring of Israel, from the context he seems to mean the philosophical soul: "God will not permit the offspring of the seeing Israel to be changed in such a manner as to be stricken down by the change, but will compel it to emerge and rise again like one who rises from the deep, and so will cause it to be saved."

Jewish eschatological expectations between the second century B.C.E. and the first half of the first C.E. These expectations—which Philo is likely to have known, even if it is unclear to what extent he shared them—embraced the coming of the Messiah and the restoration of Israel, and often also entailed the turning of the "nations" to the God of Israel[52] and the remission of sins.[53] As I shall show in the following section, Origen will make the most of this concept of the eschatological restoration of Israel joined with a universalistic soteriology. Philo never explicitly speaks of a restoration of Israel; however, he does invest Israel with universalistic features,[54] especially in his esoteric, allegorical works, where Israel is constituted by all those who see God. Philo seems to hope that this category—which Christians such as Origen would apply to the *verus Israel*—will expand. Origen would be confident that the *verus Israel* will expand until it embraces all humanity.

The Impact of Philo's Apokatastasis Notion onto the Christian Doctrine of Apokatastasis

Philo seems to be far from an eschatological orientation and his concept of *apokatastasis* of the soul bears no relation to the doctrine of universal salvation. Nevertheless, he must be credited with being one of the main inspirers of Origen's thought and exegesis in general, and of his doctrine of *apokatastasis* in particular. Clement of Alexandria and Origen were certainly influenced by Philo's idea of the restoration of the soul.

Clement frequently speaks of the restoration of the soul in basically the same terms as Philo does, and often describes salvation as the soul's health, like Philo, such as in *Strom.* 7.7.48 or *Paed.* 1.8.65.2 and 1.11.96.3. In *Strom.* 7.10.57.1-4, Clement depicts the perfection of the soul endowed with knowledge or gnosis as an *"apokatastasis* or restoration to the highest place of rest" (εἰς τὸν κορυφαῖον ἀποκαταστήσῃ τῆς ἀναπαύσεως τόπον). This will mean to see God "face to face," with a pure heart. For Clement, just as for Philo, the *apokatastasis* of the soul is effected through purification, but while Philo thought of philosophy as the exclusive agent of this purification,

---

[52] E.g. Tob 14:6; 1 *En.* 91:14.

[53] Full documentation in my *The Christian Doctrine of Apokatastasis*, 35–36, to which I add now Lutz Doering, "*Urzeit–Endzeit* Correlations in the Dead Sea Scrolls and Pseudepigrapha," in *Eschatologie–Eschatology. The Sixth Durham-Tübingen Research Symposium: Eschatology in Old Testament, Ancient Judaism, and Early Christianity, Tübingen, September 2009* (ed. Hans-Joachim Eckstein, Christof Landmesser, and Hermann Lichtenberger; Tübingen: Mohr Siebeck, 2011), 19–58.

[54] Runia, "Philo and the Gentiles," 42.

Clement also individuates the biblical otherworldly fire as a powerful means of purification. Thus, Clement ascribes to this "otherworldly fire" (πῦρ αἰώνιον)[55] a purifying and educative function; this is also why he says it is wise and endowed with discernment: "The fire sanctifies, not the flesh of sacrificial offerings, but the sinners' souls, and I mean a fire that is not a fire that devours everything and tests, but the fire that is endowed with discernment [φρόνιμον], which spreads in the soul that passes through that fire" (*Strom.* 7.6.34.1-3).

Origen likewise expresses the concept of the restoration of the soul in a number of passages. For instance, in *Cels.* 7.4 ἀποκατάστασις indicates the restoration of a soul to God (ἀποκατάστασις πρὸς τὸν θεόν) thanks to virtue. The restoration of the soul cannot take place without virtue, which is also what Philo maintained. Origen adds that virtue, and the restoration effected by it, is prevented by demons but helped by God.

But Clement and Origen, and especially the latter, added to Philo's notion of the *apokatastasis* of the soul an eschatological and universal dimension, which it did not possess in Philo. For Origen, not only some souls, but all souls will be restored, and this not merely in this world, but more perfectly in the ultimate end, the *telos*.[56] Moreover, Clement, Origen, Gregory of Nyssa, and other supporters of the Christian doctrine of *apokatastasis* included the resurrection of the body into their holistic notion of restoration.[57] This is a point that Philo did not contemplate; for him, restoration can affect the soul and the soul alone; the body is doomed to perish and never to rise again. Both Origen and Gregory of Nyssa, instead, devoted whole works to the resurrection as part and parcel of the restoration of the whole human being (body, soul, and spirit or intellect) and of all human beings. Origen wrote a lost *De resurrectione* and Gregory a preserved dialogue *De anima et resurrectione*.[58] For them, there is no restoration of the soul without the resurrection of the body, and vice versa there can be no resurrection of the body without the perspective of a full

---

[55] For the translation of αἰώνιον as "otherworldly" or "pertaining to the world to come" instead of "eternal," see the analysis of the biblical and patristic meanings of αἰώνιος in Ilaria Ramelli and David Konstan, *Terms for Eternity:* Αἰώνιος *and* ἀίδιος *in Classical and Christian Authors* (Piscataway: Gorgias Press, 2007; new ed. Gorgias and Logos Bible Software, 2013), with the reviews by Carl O'Brien *CR* 60.2 (2010): 390–91; Danilo Ghira *Maia* 61 (2009): 732–34.

[56] Ramelli, *The Christian Doctrine of Apokatastasis*, chapter on Origen.

[57] See my "Apokatastasis in Coptic Gnostic Texts from Nag Hammadi and Clement's and Origen's Apokatastasis: Toward an Assessment of the Origin of the Doctrine of Universal Restoration," *Journal of Coptic Studies* 14 (2012): 33–45.

[58] On Origen's *De resurrectione* see my *Apokatastasis*, the chapters on Origen and Methodius, and on Gregory's *De anima et resurrectione* see my full commentary *Gregorio di Nissa sull'Anima e la Resurrezione*.

restoration of the soul in all of its components, rational soul and inferior faculties. The latter will be elevated to the former. This is a holistic notion of resurrection that opens the door to universal salvation, which indeed both Origen and Gregory supported. Other Christian thinkers, who were unacquainted with Philo's (and Origen's) notion of the restoration of the soul, only maintained the resurrection of the body, without any renovation of the soul, which is the path to eternal damnation. Against this view, a contemporary of Augustine, Theodore of Mopsuestia, reacted, deeming it impossible that the resurrection may not imply the correction and restoration of the soul as well: "Non enim ... tamquam magnum quiddam resurrectionis collaturus est praemium, si eos suppliciis quibusdam sine fine et sine correctione tradiderit. Ubi iam loco muneris *resurrectio* putabitur, si *poena sine correctione* resurgentibus inferatur? Quis ita demens ut tantum bonum credat materiam fieri resurgentibus infiniti supplicii? Quibus utilius erat omnino non surgere, quam tantorum et talium malorum, post resurrectionem, sub infinitis poenis experientiam sustinere" (*ap.* Mercator, PL 48.232).

It seems that already Pantaenus, the teacher of Clement of Alexandria and very probably acquainted with Philo's ideas, applied the notion of *apokatastasis* to universal restoration. He also characterized restoration as unity, as Origen will do later on: "All those who come from the same race and have chosen the same faith and justice will be one and the same body, in that they will be restored [ἀποκαταστησόμενοι] to the same unity" (*ap.* Clement, *Ecl.* 56.2-3). Pantaenus is likely to have used the terminology of *apokatastasis*—it is probably not the case that Clement simply attributed it to him—due to his Stoic philosophical competence, and also because of his acquaintance with the Bible, where he could find the very term ἀποκατάστασις applied to eschatology in Acts 3:21, in Peter's aforementioned prophecy of "the times of universal restoration." The notion of *apokatastasis* as the final return of all to unity will be developed especially by Origen and John the Scot Eriugena, while it was absent from Philo's concept of *apokatatasis* of the soul, probably also because this was a strictly individualistic notion. His concept of the gathering and restoration of Israel is somewhat closer to that of restoration as a return to unity, though both the eschatological orientation and the universalistic perspective seem to be absent. Pantaenus, in the passage I have quoted above, based himself on two New Testament passages that could not have been known to Philo: 1 Cor 12:12, with the idea of becoming "one and the same body;" and Eph 4:13, "until we all attain to the unity of the faith and of the knowledge of the Son of God."

In addition to the issues of the resurrection of the body, eschatological orientation, and the universality of the restoration, one more fundamental difference between Philo's and Origen's (and Gregory of Nyssa's) notion of *apokatastasis* concerns—as I have mentioned in the previous section— their understanding of the death of the soul: for Philo, this is an ontological destruction, for Origen (and his followers, *in primis* Gregory of Nyssa) there can be no ontological or substantial destruction of any soul, since rational creatures were created by God in order for them to exist, and whatever God has created is good. This is why they cannot be destroyed ontologically. This would be a defeat for God the Creator. This is why Origen explicitly rejected Philo's thesis of the substantial annihilation of the soul that chooses evil. On the one hand, he maintains that if one chooses evil, which is non-being, one ends up with non being, and therefore dies, but this death is moral and not ontological. In *Comm. Jo.* 2.133, Origen is clear that "the One who is Good, therefore, coincides with the One who Is. On the contrary, evil and meanness are opposed to the Good and non-being to Being. As a consequence, meanness and evil are non-being [οὐκ ὄν]." This is why choosing evil means becoming "non-being," but for Origen this cannot mean a substantial annihilation of God's creatures: *Donec adhaeremus Deo et inhaeremus ei qui vere est, etiam nos sumus. Sin autem abscesserimus a Deo [...] vitio in contrarium decidimus. Non ergo per hoc substantialis animae designatur interitus* (*Hom. Ps.* 2.38.12). If one adheres to God, who Is, one remains in being; if, on the contrary, one rejects God, one falls into non-being. But Origen is careful to add that this does not mean that the soul is destroyed or perishes ontologically (*substantialis interitus*). I deem it extremely probable that Origen here was polemicizing with Philo, who was convinced that a soul that does evil perishes ontologically: it simply ceases to exist as a substance—this is really what Origen is referring to by *substantialis interitus*. (An alternative to annihilation would have been metensomatosis or reincarnation, but Origen rejected it outright, denouncing this theory as impious in several passages.)

Origen hammers home that the annihilation of the wicked is not ontological, but spiritual, also in *Hom. Ps.* 2.38.1: *peccatores ad nihilum redigit: haec est ergo imago terreni id est peccatorum, quam ad nihilum redigit Deus in civitate sua.* Sinners will actually perish in the other world, but not ontologically: they will perish as sinners to live as saints, once purified by sins. This is rather a transformation of sinners into saints. What will perish ontologically, according to Origen, is rather evil itself, sin, which was not created by God. Souls, or better rational creatures, who were created by God, and as such are good, will never perish ontologically, will never undergo a *substantialis interitus*. The same set of ideas underlies another homiletic passage by Origen: *"Cum pereunt peccatores videbis." Fortassis hoc prius erit ut peccatores et impios iusti videant condemnatos.* [...] *Postea enim quam viderint quomodo pereunt peccatores, tunc ipsi exaltabuntur* [...] *"Et ecce non erat* [sc. *impius]." In die iudicii omnino non esse. Qui enim non est particeps Illius qui semper est, iste neque esse dicitur* (*Hom. Ps.* 5.36.5). The impious will no longer exist, because he has chosen not to participate in God, who always is, and is Good itself. But, again, the destruction of the sinner in the next world to which Origen refers will be, properly speaking, the destruction of his sin, of evil, so that the sinner will be no longer a sinner, but a righteous person: *Hoc enim etiam Dominus pollicetur, ut exterminet romphaeam, id est peccatum, ita ut ultra iam non sit peccator.* For evil, when it is no longer chosen by anyone, will vanish according to its very ontological non-subsistence: *Non enim decidentia de homine vitia ad aliam aliquam substantiam congregantur, sed sibi abeunt, et in semet ipsa resoluta evanescunt atque in nihilum rediguntur* (*Comm. Cant.* 4.1.13). For evil, according to Origen (*Cels.* 4.63), just as to Plato (*Resp.* 445C6), is indefinite: it is something ἀόριστον, like non-being, but virtue is one and simple, and therefore definite, like the Good, i.e. God, the One. What will be burnt away by the "otherworldly fire" (πῦρ αἰώνιον) will be not sinners, who will not undergo a *substantialis interitus*, but their "bad beliefs" (φαῦλα δόγματα), their "evil thoughts" (μοχθηροὶ λόγοι, *Comm. Matt.* 5.10.2). Thus, the death and destruction that Philo attached to the soul itself as a consequence of its life of vice, Origen transferred onto the destruction of evil and sin, which results into the purification of the sinner and his ultimate salvation.

The impossibility of an ontological destruction of the soul directly bears on the possibility of universal salvation. In Philo's perspective, only souls— and not bodies—will be saved, and only *some* souls: actually, a scanty minority, it seems: the souls of those who have led a philosophical and pious life (which from Philo's viewpoint is much the same thing). Origen took over Philo's notion of the restoration of the soul, just as Clement had done, but according to Origen *all* souls, and not only few, will be restored and saved, and they will have back their bodies as well, transformed and glorified as souls themselves will be. In this way they will be able to participate in the divine life and to be "deified."[59]

I have already noted that Philo, like some intertestamentary literature, envisages the restoration of Israel, although without applying to it the very terminology of *apokatastasis*, and I have pointed out both the similarities and the differences between this notion of his and Paul's. Origen seems to

---

[59] On deification in Clement, Origen, Gregory of Nyssa and other Fathers see my *The Christian Doctrine of* Apokatastasis.

have definitely followed Paul rather than Philo in the idea of an eschatological restoration of Israel within the framework of a universalistic soteriology (since in Philo, as I have remarked in the previous section, both the
eschatological and the universalistic perspective seem to be lacking, not
only in the case of the restoration of the soul, but also in the case of the
restoration of Israel). Thus, in *Comm. Rom.* 7.13, after noting that Paul
offered himself as anathema—that is, as a cursed person— for the salvation
of Israel, Origen declares that Paul's prayer was received by the Lord and
will be fulfilled in the very end, when "the totality of the nations will enter"
and "all of Israel will be saved." This prophecy of Paul's is particularly
important for Origen, who highlights it by means of its reiteration in many
other places of his commentary as well.[60] In *Comm. Cant.* 2.1.45 it is
particularly evident that *plenitudo gentium* for Origen means the totality of
the nations which will enter the Kingdom just before the salvation of all
Israel, because he adds *omnis*, "all": *Posteaquam intraverit omnis plenitudo
gentium* [...] *venient etiam ipsi, et tunc omnis Israhel salvabitur.* The salvation
of "all of Israel" is likewise evoked in a number of other passages in
Origen's commentaries and homilies.

In conclusion, it seems that the absence of universalism and eschatological orientation are the two main elements that distinguish Philo's
doctrine of the restoration of the soul and of Israel from the *apokatastasis*
doctrine of his greatest admirer among Patristic thinkers, Origen of Alexandria. I have endeavoured to account for this divergence, drawing reasons
from Scripture and its exegesis, as well as from Origen's refusal—I suspect
in a specific polemic against Philo—to admit of an ontological destruction
of any soul.

Catholic University of the Sacred Heart
Milan, Italy

---

[60] For instance in 8.1.1160: *in nouissimis, cum omnis Israhel saluus fiet*, or in 8.9.1185:
*illorum enim uel in fine saeculi conuersio erit, tunc cum plenitudo gentium subintrauerit et omnis
Israhel saluus fiet*; or again in 8.12.1196: *si ergo pro eo ut introiuerit gentium plenitudo caecitas
facta est in Israhel pro omnibus quae fecerunt, sine dubio, cum ingressa fuerit gentium plenitudo,
caecitas cessat, and in 8.9.1184: uelum capiant etiam ipsi [sc. Israhel] in nouissimis saltem
temporibus [...] gentium fides et conuersatio Israheli aemulationem conuersionis conferat et salutis.*

The Studia Philonica Annual 26 (2014) 57–77

THE PHILONIC AND THE PAULINE:
HAGAR AND SARAH IN THE EXEGESIS OF
DIDYMUS THE BLIND

JUSTIN M. ROGERS

Throughout the history of biblical exegesis, Hagar and Sarah have stood as symbols. The simple narrative of Gen 16 has been read as suggesting much more than an arranged sexual engagement. Even in modern times, feminist scholars seek to highlight the nature of oppression and injustice by investigating the ancient accounts of the two women.[1] Similarly, ancient Christian interpreters were inclined to see Hagar and Sarah as symbols of greater truths.

In the early church, there are two primary strands of symbolic interpretation applied to Hagar and Sarah. The first is located initially in Paul's letter to the Galatians, in which Hagar and Sarah are allegorized as two covenants, the Jewish and the Christian (Gal 4:21–31). Later Christian authors follow this scheme, understanding the women to symbolize the fruitful church (Sarah) and the barren synagogue (Hagar).[2]

The second interpretation seems to have been limited to Alexandrian interpreters of the Bible. Philo is the first to understand Hagar as preliminary studies (the ἐγκύκλιος παιδεία) and Sarah as virtue (ἀρετή) or wisdom (σοφία).[3] It is striking that both Clement of Alexandria and Origen almost always follow the Philonic interpretation, and not the Pauline.[4] The first author on record who attempts to harmonize the Philonic and Pauline

---

[1] Hagar has received more attention from postcolonial and feminist scholars; see the essays in Phyllis Trible and Letty M. Russel, eds., *Hagar, Sarah and Their Children: Jewish, Christian and Muslim Perspectives* (Louisville: Westminster John Knox, 2006).

[2] E.g., John Chrysostom, *Hom. Gal.* 4.27; Jerome, *Comm. Gal.* 4.27.

[3] *Congr.* is the Philonic tractate in which the interpretation is most common (*Congr.* 11, 20, 23–24, 121–122, 180), but the allegory is found elsewhere in the Philonic corpus (e.g., *Mut.* 255; *Somn.* 1.240; *QG* 3.19, 21).

[4] See Johan Leemans, "After Philo and Paul: Hagar in the Writings of the Church Fathers," in *Abraham, the Nations and the Hagarites* (ed. Martin Goodman, George H. van Kooten & Jacques T. A. G. M. van Ruiten; *Themes in Biblical Narrative: Jewish and Christian Traditions* 13; Leiden: Brill, 2010), 435–47, 437–38.

interpretations is Didymus the Blind (ca. 313–398 C.E.). In this study, we will attempt to show how Didymus draws from the work of his Alexandrian predecessors as he seeks to combine their Philonic interpretations with the Pauline allegory. In doing so, it seems that Didymus juxtaposes the two primary interpretations of Hagar and Sarah for the first time in the history of biblical interpretation.[5]

Didymus's interpretation of Hagar and Sarah has received little attention in scholarship.[6] But it provides one of the most fertile areas for investigating Philo's influence on Didymus.[7] On virtually every exegetical point, Didymus follows Philonic interpretations. He agrees with Philo that the literal interpretation of the relationship between Abraham and Sarah implies sexual abstinence. Didymus also agrees with Philo's allegorical interpretation that Hagar represents preliminary studies and Sarah wisdom or virtue. But it is the way in which Didymus weaves the Philonic interpretation with the Pauline that makes his exegesis of Hagar and Sarah unique.

Hagar and Sarah: The Literal Interpretation

The Greek text of Gen 16:1–2 seems straightforward: Sarah offers an Egyptian slave girl to her husband so that he (or she) might obtain a child.[8]

---

[5] Modern interpreters generally believe that Philo did not influence Paul's allegory directly; e.g., C. K. Barrett, "The Allegory of Abraham, Sarah, and Hagar in the Argument of Galatians" in *Rechtfertigung: Festschrift für Ernst Käsemann zum 70. Geburtstag* (ed. Johannes Friedrich, Wolfgang Pöhlmann & Peter Stuhlmacher; Tübingen: Mohr Siebeck, 1976), 1–16; Steven Di Mattei, "Paul's Allegory of the Two Covenants (Gal 4.21–31) in Light of First-Century Hellenistic Rhetoric and Jewish Hermeneutics," *NTS* 52 (2006): 102–22. Nevertheless, it is possible that Philo and Paul depend on the same exegetical tradition; see Peder Borgen, "Some Hebrew and Pagan Features in Philo's and Paul's Interpretation of Hagar and Ishmael," in *The New Testament and Hellenistic Judaism* (ed. Peder Borgen & Søren Giversen; Aarhaus: Aushaus UP, 1995), 151–64.

[6] The first publication on the subject to my knowledge is that of Alfred Henrichs, "Philosophy, the Handmaiden of Theology," *GRBS* 9 (1968): 437–50; see also the brief discussion based on Henrichs in David T. Runia, *Philo in Early Christian Literature* (CRINT 3.3; Assen: Van Gorcum; Minneapolis: Fortress, 1993), 199–200, 203, and Leemans, "After Philo and Paul."

[7] Philo's influence on Didymus served as the basis of my doctoral dissertation; "Didymus the Blind and His Use of Philo of Alexandria in the *Tura Commentary on Genesis*," (Ph.D. diss., Hebrew Union College-Jewish Institute of Religion, 2012). For a brief survey see Albert C. Geljon, "Philo's Influence on Didymus the Blind," in *Philon D'Alexandrie: un penseur à l'intersection des cultures Greco-Romaine, Orientale, Juive et Chretienne* (Monothéismes et Philosophie 12; ed. Sabrina Inowlocki & Baudouin Decharneux; Turnhout: Brepols, 2011), 357–72.

[8] The Greek text that Didymus cites reflects the notion that the child of Hagar will

One might expect both Philo and Didymus to reject the literal sense of the biblical text altogether since it seems so explicitly sexual. For Didymus in particular, the apparent reference to digamy would be unseemly.[9] Indeed, some early Christians argued on the basis of Abraham's behavior in the passage that polygamy was valid.[10] Despite the potential moral implications, however, both Philo and Didymus, among others, retain the literal, "plain sense" of the text.[11]

In his treatment of Gen 16:1–2, Philo usually prefers to offer an allegorical understanding, but does not deny the text its literal meaning.[12] Likewise, Didymus insists that the literal sense (τὸ ῥητόν) in these verses is "worthy of investigation" (ἄξιον θεωρῆσαι) and "useful" (χρήσιμος), but spends the majority of his energy expounding the allegorical sense. Philo and Didymus interpret this passage literally because they believe a practical ethical lesson can be derived from it. Both Philo and Didymus argue that sexual activity must be motivated solely by the desire to produce offspring.[13]

---

actually belong to Sarah and not to Abraham (τεκνοποιήσω rather than τεκνοποιήσῃς), a reading not attested in the manuscript tradition before his time; see John W. Wevers, *Genesis. Septuaginta: Vetus Testamentum Graecum auctoritate academiae scientiarum Gottingensis* (Göttingen: Vandenhoeck & Ruprecht, 1974), 172.

[9] Aristotle, in his *Poetics* 1460b–1461b, had formulated "five categories from which critical objections are drawn": (1) ἀδύνατα ("impossibilities"); (2) ἄλογα ("absurdities"); (3) βλαβερά ("morally harmful things"); (4) ὑπεναντία ("contradictions"); and (5) [τὰ] παρὰ τὴν ὀρθότητα τὴν κατὰ τέχνην ("things contrary to artistic correctness"). The above text could have fit into number (3) above, and therefore, could have been justified for allegorical interpretation (on the whole issue of προβλήματα in ancient texts, see A. Gudeman, "Λύσεις," *PW* 13.2 [1927]: cols 2511–2529, and especially cols. 216–17 on Aristotle).

[10] See Tertullian, *Mon.* 6 and Theodoret, *Quaest. Gen.* 68. Tertullian takes up the argument of the Apostle Paul from Rom 4 and Gal 3 that Abraham was justified by faith *before* circumcision (arguing the point from Gen 15:6 prior to the institution of circumcision in Gen 17:10ff). Since the digamy of the patriarch (Gen 16:2ff) was also posterior to his justification by faith, then anyone who wishes to follow Abraham in digamy must also admit circumcision.

[11] It is misleading to say, as Henrichs does, "To Jews and Christians alike, monogamy was the only acceptable relationship between man and woman. To accept this passage in its literal sense was beyond their capacity" ("Philosophy," 439). Polygamy, at least for men, was not banned by the rabbis; see B. Z. Schereschewsky & M. Elon, "Bigamy and Polygamy," *EncJud* (2nd ed.; 3:691–94), 691.

[12] See *Abr.* 248–54; *QG* 3.20.

[13] For Philo's position on the issue, see Richard A. Baer, *Philo's Use of the Categories Male and Female* (Leiden: Brill, 1970) and esp. Kathy L. Gaca, "Philo's Principles of Sexual Conduct and their Influence on Christian Platonist Sexual Principles," *SPhA* 8 (1996): 21–39, who argues that Philo derives the idea from Pythagorean sources.

Philo

In discussing when men ought to have sexual relations with women, Philo gives his opinion as follows:[14]

> They too must be reproached who plough a hard and stony land. And who should they be but those who unite with barren women? For on the prowl for licentious pleasure, like the most lustful of men they destroy the generative seeds with deliberate intent. For what other reason do they have such women plighted to them? It cannot be in the hope of offspring, a hope they know must inevitably fail of accomplishment; it can only be through exceeding frenzy and an incontinence that is incurable. (*Spec.* 3.34)[15]

The preceding passage represents two pillars of Philo's general position on sexuality: (1) sexual relations (within a marriage) should always aim at procreation; (2) sexual relations must never be motivated by pleasure.[16]

A number of sex acts are then illicit according to Philo. Homosexuality is "unnatural" for these two reasons (*Abr.* 137; *Spec.* 2.50). Adultery is ruled out by the second consideration (*Det.* 102). Therefore, for Philo, Abraham's obvious sex act with Hagar could not have been motivated by pleasure (*Congr.* 12). It must be that both Abraham and Sarah understood that procreative sex alone was acceptable.

In Sarah's "speech" recorded in *De Abrahamo* 248–52, Philo describes Sarah's motivation behind the Hagar proposal.[17] She is made to claim that the marriage is not "due to an irrational lust [δι᾽ ἐπιθυμίαν ἄλογον], but because of the necessity of fulfilling the law of nature" (*Abr.* 249).[18] Apparently the law of nature in this context refers to the procreative principle. Since Sarah was incapable of fulfilling the natural law of procreation, she proposed a surrogate. Philo goes on to state that Abraham kept Hagar "only till she became pregnant," and afterwards "abstained

---

[14] Philo cites no scripture for this opinion in contrast to his previous discussion regarding sexual abstinence during the woman's menstrual cycle.

[15] Trans. David Winston, *Philo of Alexandria: The Contemplative Life, The Giants, and Selections* (CWS; Ramsey, NJ: Paulist, 1981), 200.

[16] Philo seems to allow one exception to these two reasons: the consummation of the marriage (see *Virt.* 112 discussing marriage to a prisoner of war, Deut 21:10–13). Philo's sexual ethics are discussed at length in Isaac Heinemann, *Philons griechische und jüdische Bildung* (Breslau: M. & H. Marcus, 1932; repr. Hildesheim: G. Olms, 1962), 231–329, esp. 267–68. See also Gaca, "Philo's Principles."

[17] Josephus also retains the literal sense of the biblical text, but finds it necessary to censor Sarah's proposal of Hagar as being commanded by God (*Ant.* 1.187). Philo, by contrast, mentions no divine command, but allows Sarah to speak in favor of his own sexual ethics; see Maren R. Niehoff, "Mother and Maiden, Sister and Spouse: Sarah in Philonic Midrash," *HTR* 97 (2004): 413–44, 421–22.

[18] Cf. Tob 8:7.

from her through his natural continence" (*Abr.* 253). It seems clear that Philo sees in the story of Abraham and Sarah proof of his position on procreative intercourse.

Didymus

Didymus agrees exactly with Philo's literal interpretation of Hagar and Sarah. In his comments to Gen 16:1–2,[19] Didymus introduces the discussion as follows: "The apostle anagogically interprets these women as referring to the two covenants by the law of allegory [Gal 4:24].[20] But since the literal meaning is also present, it is itself worthy of investigation" (*In Gen.* 234.31–235.2, trans. mine).[21] Suspending the allegorical discussion, Didymus launches into a literal understanding of the sexual relationships the patriarchs had with their wives.

Didymus does not cite Philo by name at this point in his exegesis,[22] preferring rather to cite a certain παράδοσις in confirmation of procreative sex. Evidence in favor of this "tradition" can be found already in the patriarchal example. Didymus writes:

> The saints cohabit not as though hunting after pleasure, but for the sake of procreation. For a certain tradition is handed down concerning them that they would go in to their wives only when it was time for conception. They would come together neither when she was nursing or feeding her child nor when she was pregnant. For in none of these times did they esteem intercourse appropriate. (*In Gen.* 235.2–8, trans. mine)[23]

---

[19] The Greek text of Didymus reads, Σάρα δὲ ἡ γυνὴ Ἀβρὰμ οὐκ ἔτικτεν αὐτῷ. Ἦν δὲ αὐτῇ παιδίσκη Αἰγυπτία, ᾗ ὄνομα Ἁγάρ. Εἶπεν δὲ Σάρα πρὸς Ἀβράμ· Ἰδοὺ δὴ συνέκλεισέν με Κύριος τοῦ μὴ τίκτειν· εἴσελθε οὖν πρὸς τὴν παιδίσκην μου, ἵνα τεκνοποιήσω ἐξ αὐτῆς. Ὑπήκουσεν δὲ Ἀβρὰμ τῆς φωνῆς Σάρας.

[20] Ἀναγωγή is Didymus' favorite term for allegorical interpretation. In Neo-Platonism, the term carries the notion of "leading up" one's soul to God; see Robert M. Grant, *The Letter and the Spirit* (London: S.P.C.K., 1957), 124. Wolfgang Bienert has examined the term in Didymus, arguing that Origen is his primary source, and that Origen employed the term because ἀλληγορία was associated with secular exegesis (principally of Homer); *Allegoria und Anagoge bei Didymos dem Blinden von Alexandria* (Berlin: de Gruyter, 1972), 64.

[21] Ἀνήγαγεν ταύτας ἀπόστολος εἰς τὰς δύο διαθήκας ἀλληγορίας νόμῳ· ἐπειδὴ δὲ καὶ τὸ ῥητὸν γεγένηται, καὶ αὐτὸ ἄξιον θεωρῆσαι.

[22] Didymus cites Philo's name twice in the midst of his allegorical discussion (see below).

[23] Οἱ ἅγιοι οὕτως συνεβίουν ὡς μὴ ἡδονὰς θηρᾶν ἀλλὰ τέκνων χάριν. Καὶ γὰρ παράδοσις τοιαύτη περὶ αὐτῶν φέρεται, ὅτι τότε μόνον συνῇεσαν ταῖς γυναιξίν, ὅτε καιρὸν εἶχον συλλήψεως· οὔτε δὲ θηλαζούσῃ οὔτε τρεφούσῃ τὸ βρέφος συνῇεσαν οὔτε κυοφορούσῃ· ἐν οὐδενὶ γὰρ τούτων τῶν καιρῶν οἰκείαν ἡγοῦντο τὴν σύνοδον.

Didymus goes on to illustrate his interpretation, suggesting that Jacob abstained from intercourse with Rachel once he discovered that she was barren (*In Gen.* 235.8–15), and Abraham did the same with Sarah (*In Gen.* 235.16–20). One can see that Didymus agrees with both of Philo's principles. The patriarchs had intercourse only for procreation (τέκνων χάριν) and never for pleasure (ἡδονή). Consequently, the barrenness of their wives led the patriarchs to abandon intercourse with those women altogether.

Didymus agrees with Philo more explicitly when he attributes Sarah's proposition to reflect her knowledge that Abraham was capable of reproduction when she was not.[24] Sarah says to Abraham in Philo's *De Abrahamo* 148–49, "But the purpose for which we ourselves came together … has not been fulfilled, nor is there any future hope of it, through me at least who am now past the age. But do not let the trouble of my barrenness extend to you, or kind feeling to me keep you from becoming what you can become, a father …" (trans. Colson, PLCL).

Didymus ascribes to Sarah a similar notion when he comments:

> Therefore, Sarah, being a wise and holy woman, abstained from copulation with him [Abraham], since she had known for a long time that if she lay with him she would not become pregnant. But since she knew that he was able to have children, she gave her own slave girl to him to be his concubine. Both temperance [σωφροσύνη] and absence of envy [ἀφθονία] are demonstrated in the case of Sarah, and freedom from passion [ἡδονή] is demonstrated in the case of Abraham, who chose this course at the instigation of his wife and not because of his own desire. Rather he yielded for the birth of children (*In Gen.* 235.16–24, trans. mine).[25]

Didymus again emphasizes the lack of passion in Abraham and the presence of virtue in Sarah, who understood the procreative purpose of marriage. Philo also is careful to mention that Sarah never displays "jealousy" (ζηλοτυπία),[26] but is motivated by the noble desire to see the purpose of marriage fulfilled.[27] In both Philo and in Didymus Abraham is presented as a subject obedient to Sarah's noble will.

---

[24] It is possible to read the biblical text as Sarah's experiment to determine whether she was barren or he was sterile.

[25] Καὶ ἡ Σάρα οὖν, σοφὴ καὶ ἁγία οὖσα, πολλῷ χρόνῳ εἰδυῖα ὅτι συνευναζομένη οὐκ ἔλαβεν κατὰ γαστρός, ἀπέσχετο τῆς πρὸς αὐτὸν κοινωνίας καί, ἐπειδὴ ἐγίγνωσκεν ἀκόλουθον εἶναι ἔχειν ἐκεῖνον τέκνα, τὴν παιδίσκην ἑαυτῆς ἔδωκεν αὐτῷ εἰς γυναῖκα παλλακίδα. Σωφροσύνη ἅμα καὶ ἀφθονία τῆς Σάρας καὶ τοῦ Ἀβρὰμ <δείκνυται> ἀπάθεια το<ῦ> πρὸς τῆς γυναικὸς καὶ οὐκ ἀπὸ ἰδίας ὁρμῆς ἑλομένου τοῦτο ἀλλ᾽ εἴκοντος διὰ τέκνων γένεσιν.

[26] *Abr.* 249, 251.

[27] *Abr.* 248; *QG* 3.20.

Didymus does not cite Philo for his literal interpretation, although he certainly agrees with him. The source for Didymus' comments is "tradition." It is possible that Didymus is simply referring to the tradition implicit in scripture,[28] but limiting intercourse to procreation is the standard Hellenistic Jewish and early Christian position.[29] Josephus and Philo agree on the subject,[30] as do virtually all of the early Fathers.[31] The same attitude is attributed to the Essenes as well.[32] The ubiquity of the position in Hellenistic Judaism and in early Christianity leads me to view the position of Philo and Didymus on procreative sex as representing the standard teaching of the Hellenistic synagogue, which was later incorporated into the church.[33] Didymus may well be aware of Philo's literal interpretation, but he does not need to single out Philo as the authority on the position, since it is standard in the church of his time.

Hagar and Sarah: The Allegorical Interpretation

Both Philo and Didymus spend the majority of their efforts explaining the allegorical sense of the Hagar-Sarah episode. Philo famously asserts that

---

[28] Didymus uses the term παράδοσις in this sense in at least one other context (*Comm. Zach.* 142.3, citing Rom 1:22, 24; and *Comm. Zach.* 142.7, referring to a chain of scripture citations).

[29] The rabbinic position is that marriage was for the purpose of procreation. But marital sex in the rabbinic sources is not limited to procreation (*b. Yebam.* 65a). A man who has been married for ten years without having any children is not permitted to abstain from intercourse with his wife, but he is required to take another wife so that he can fulfill the command to "be fruitful and multiply" (*m. Yebam.* 6:6). The rule is based on the case of Abraham, as the Talmud makes clear (Gen 16:6; *b. Yebam.* 64a).

[30] For Josephus, note *C. Ap.* 2.199: "The Law knows only natural intercourse, that is, with a woman, and natural intercourse only when it is intended for procreation," μῖξιν μόνην οἶδεν ὁ νόμος τὴν κατὰ φύσιν τὴν πρὸς γυναῖκα καὶ ταύτην, εἰ μέλλοι τέκνων ἕνεκα γίνεσθαι (trans. mine).

[31] Clement of Alexandria is the most relevant for Didymus (see all of *Paed.* 2.10). On the sexual principles of Clement, see Gaca, "Philo's Principles," 34–39, who argues that he, just as Philo, depends on the Pythagorean tradition.

[32] Josephus states of the Essenes in *B.J.* 2.161: "They do not have intercourse with their pregnant wives, demonstrating that they do not marry for pleasure [ἡδονή] but for procreation," ταῖς δ' ἐγκύμοσιν οὐχ ὁμιλοῦσιν, ἐνδεικνύμενοι τὸ μὴ δι' ἡδονὴν ἀλλὰ τέκνων χρείαν γαμεῖν (trans. mine).

[33] Gaca may well be correct that Philo's *articulation* of his position comes from Pythagorean sources ("Philo's Principles"), but it seems to me that the position itself was a traditional synagogal doctrine. Of the Stoic moralists, Musonius Rufus upholds the doctrine and Seneca can be understood similarly. In general see David Winston, "Philo and the Rabbis on Sex and the Body," *Poetics Today* 19 (1998): 41–62.

Hagar represents preliminary or encyclical studies (προπαιδεία or ἐγκύκλιος παιδεία) and Sarah represents virtue (ἀρετή). This doctrine is among the most common themes in the works of Philo, and serves as the foundation for an entire allegorical treatise (the *De congressu eruditionis gratia*). The interpretation also enables Philo to explain Abraham as a man who reaches virtue through "learning" (διδασκαλία).[34] He first consorts with the encyclical studies, represented by Hagar, and then progresses to philosophy or virtue, represented by Sarah.

The Philonic interpretation of Hagar and Sarah sets the stage for the Fathers in the Alexandrian tradition to propose secular (Hellenic) education as a preparatory exercise for Christian virtue.[35] Clement is perhaps the strongest proponent of this view,[36] but Origen and Didymus also are in agreement.[37] We shall discuss several aspects of Philo's allegory of Sarah and Hagar before moving into the reception of the Philonic interpretation in Didymus the Blind.

Penelope and Her Handmaids

The groundwork for Philo's interpretation had already been laid in the Homeric scholarship of Hellenistic times. The inspiration for Philo's allegory of Hagar and Sarah can be traced to the interpretation of Penelope and her slave girls.[38] Several ancient critics are credited with comparing the suitors of Penelope with students who fail to advance beyond the preliminary studies to philosophy. Penelope's handmaidens represent the encyclical disciplines while the mistress herself represents philosophy. Stobaeus

---

[34] Isaac reaches virtue by φύσις and Jacob by ἄσκησις (see *Abr*. 52–53).

[35] See Edgar Früchtel, "Philon und die Vorbereitung der christlichen Paideia und Seelenleitung," in *Frühchristentum und Kultur* (ed. Ferdinand R. Prostmeier; Kommentar zu frühchristlichen Apologeten 2; Freiburg: Herder, 2007), 19–33.

[36] Annewies van den Hoek has established this theme as one of four major blocks of Philonic influence on Clement. See *Clement of Alexandria and His Use of Philo in the Stromateis* (Leiden: Brill, 1988), 23–47.

[37] The most interesting passage from Origen on this theme comes from the *Ep. Greg.* 1. See the general discussion of Alberto C. Capboscq, "Aspekte der Paideia bei Gregor dem Wundertäter," in *Frühchristentum und Kultur*, 279–91.

[38] See F. H. Colson, "Philo on Education," *JTS* 18 (1917): 151–62, followed by many others. Philo's interpretation does not match the Hellenistic allegory exactly, as Conley points out; see Thomas Conley, *"General Education" in Philo of Alexandria* (ed. Wilhelm Wuellner; Center for Hermeneutical Studies in Hellenistic and Modern Culture. Protocol of the Fifteenth Colloquy: 9 March 1975; Berkeley: CHSHMC, 1975), 6–7. Perhaps a pre-Philonic adaptation of the Odysseus allegory is responsible for the Philonic material, as Pearce proposes; see Sarah J. K. Pearce, *The Land of the Body: Studies in Philo's Representation of Egypt* (WUNT 208; Tübingen: Mohr Siebeck, 2007), 171.

preserves a fragment attributed to Ariston of Chios (ca. 250 BCE): "Ariston of Chios used to say that those who labor with the preliminary studies but neglect philosophy are like the suitors of Penelope who, when they failed to win her over, became involved with the handmaidens" (trans. mine).[39] Against this background it is clear that for Philo, Penelope was, *mutatis mutandis*, equivalent to Sarah and the handmaidens to Hagar.[40]

But a second consideration may have drawn Philo to the allegorical understanding of the *Odyssey*. In Homer's epic, Calypso holds Odysseus captive for seven years before he is permitted to leave Ogygia.[41] In Hellenistic interpretation, Calypso represents the sage's struggle to linger in the sciences of astronomy and astrology.[42] Odysseus is able to break away from these preliminary studies and advance to philosophy, or Penelope. Abraham, being from "Ur of the Chaldeans," was steeped in the astral sciences. But he moved beyond these to a contemplation of God.[43] Hence Abraham could be viewed as a proto-Odysseus, representing the journey of the soul from the encyclical disciplines to philosophy.[44]

Philo

Philo can derive great benefit from the literal interpretation of Gen 16:1–3, as we have seen. Philo's usual procedure, however, is to dispose of the blatantly sexual surface understanding in favor of the allegorical meaning. Rather than proposing a sexual relationship between Hagar and Abraham, Sarah is insisting that the student must mate with preliminary studies before he can advance to virtue (*Congr.* 9–12).[45] It was not only advisable, but necessary, for Abraham to consort with "Hagar" so that he could

[39] Ἀρίστων ὁ Χῖος τοὺς περὶ τὰ ἐγκύκλια μαθήματα πονουμένους, ἀμελοῦντας δὲ φιλοσοφίας, ἔλεγεν ὁμοίους εἶναι τοῖς μνηστῆρσι τῆς Πηνελόπης, οἳ ἀποτυγχάνοντες ἐκείνης περὶ τὰς θεραπαίνας ἐγίνοντο (*SVF* 1.350). Von Arnim also lists different versions of a similar statement, which are attributed to Aristotle, Aristippus and Bion, respectively.

[40] On Philo's adaptation of the allegory see Yehoshua Amir, "The Transference of Greek Allegories to Biblical Motifs in Philo," in *Nourished with Peace: Studies in Hellenistic Judaism in Memory of Samuel Sandmel* (ed. Frederick E. Greenspahn, Earle Hilgert and Burton L. Mack; Chico: Scholars Press, 1984), 15–25.

[41] *Od.* 7.259–60.

[42] See the discussion of Felix Buffière, *Les mythes d'Homère et la pensée grecque* (Paris: Les Belles Lettres, 1956), 388–91.

[43] See *Migr.* 177ff; *Congr.* 49–50; *Ebr.* 94; *Somn.* 1.53.

[44] Philo quotes *Od.* 4.392 in *Migr.* 195, possibly reflecting a knowledge of the Hellenistic allegory.

[45] Note especially the way Philo summarizes the paragraph: νοῦ γὰρ πρὸς ἀρετήν ἐστι σύνοδος ἐξ αὐτῆς ἐφιεμένου παιδοποιεῖσθαι, εἰ δὲ μὴ δύναιτο εὐθύς, ἀλλά τοι τὴν θεραπαινίδα αὐτῆς, τὴν μέσην παιδείαν, ἐγγυᾶσθαι διδασκομένου (*Congr.* 12).

receive the educational preparation to enter into philosophy.[46] In general terms, Philo represents the dominant position of his time on the subject of secular education and philosophy.[47]

It was well-established at the time of Philo that the encyclical studies are necessary for philosophy.[48] Seneca's *Epistle* 88 is written from a perspective similar to Philo's; it seems certain that Philo and Seneca stood in a similar intellectual milieu. In *Ep.* 88.20 Seneca asks, "What then? Do liberal studies contribute nothing to us? To other things much; to virtue, nothing …. So why do we educate children in liberal studies? Not because they can grant virtue, but because they prepare the mind to accept virtue" (trans. mine).[49] The words of Seneca seem to represent the majority opinion at the turn of the Common Era: the encyclical studies are necessary but not sufficient for virtue.[50]

It is apparent that Philo concurs with the philosophical consensus. The *encyclia* must be applied as a necessary step in the student's pursuit of σοφία or ἀρετή. Since "wisdom" and "virtue" are the ultimate result of a secular Greek education, the encyclical studies were for Philo a spiritual endeavor, for they prepared the mind for the contemplation of the divine.[51]

---

[46] The bibliography on secular education in Philo is extensive; see, e.g., Colson, "Philo on Education;" Monique Alexandre, *De congressu eruditionis gratia* (PAPM 16; Paris: Cerf, 1967); Alan Mendelson, *Secular Education in Philo of Alexandria* (Cincinnati: Hebrew Union College Press, 1982); Pearce, *The Land of the Body*, 170–77; Karl O. Sandnes, *The Challenge of Homer* (Edinburgh: T&T Clark, 2009), 68–78; Manuel Alexandre, Jr., "Philo of Alexandria and Hellenic Paideia," *Euphrosune* n.s. 37 (2009): 121–30; and see esp. for our subject, Abraham O. Bos, "Hagar and the *Enkyklios Paideia* in Philo of Alexandria," in *Abraham, the Nations and the Hagarites*, 163–75.

[47] The standard work on education in antiquity is still Henri-Irénée Marrou, *Histoire de l'éducation dans l'Antiquité* (6th ed.; 2 vols.; Paris: Seuil, 1981); on the ἐγκύκλιος παιδεία more specifically see Harald Fuchs, "Enkyklios Paideia," *RAC* 5:365–98; Marrou, "Les arts libéraux dans l'Antiquité classique," in *Arts libéraux et philosophie au Moyen Âge* (Actes du IVe Congrès international de Philosophie médiévale, 27 août-2 sept, 1967; Montreal: Institut d'Études Médiévales, 1965), 5–33; Ilsetraut Hadot, *Arts libéraux et philosophie dans la pensée antique* (Paris: Études Augustiniennes, 1984).

[48] See Colson, "Philo on Education"; Monique Alexandre, "La culture profane chez Philon," in *PAL* 105–30; Peder Borgen, "Greek Encyclical Education, Philosophy and the Synagogue: Observations from Philo of Alexandria's Writings," in *Libens Merito: Festskrift til Stig Strømholm på sjuttioårsdagen 16 sept. 2001* (ed. Olle Matsson; Acta Academiæ Regiæ Scientiarum Upsaliensis 21; Uppsala: Kungl. Vetenskapssamhället, 2001), 61–71.

[49] *Quid ergo? nihil nobis liberalia conferunt studia? Ad alia multum, ad virtutem nihil…. Quare ergo liberalibus studiis filios erudimus? Non quia virtutem dare possunt; sed quia animum ad accipiendam virtutem praeparant* (cf. *Ep.* 88.2).

[50] Other sources make a similar point (e.g., Quintilian, *Inst.* 1.10; Ps-Plutarch, *Lib. ed.* 7d).

[51] Moses is portrayed in Philo's *De vita mosis* as the ideal sage-in-training, who passes through the encyclical disciplines as well as other forms of propaideuctic instruction; see

As Alan Mendelson writes, "He [Philo] endows the encyclia with inherent spiritual value; this position represents a significant shift in the history of liberal studies."[52]

Philo cites as confirmation of his allegorical interpretation the etymologies of the names of Sarah and Hagar. The former means "sovereignty of me."[53] According to Philo, the only "sovereignty" to which the text can refer is virtue herself, since she alone is truly sovereign over the mind.[54] Hagar, on the other hand, means "sojourning."[55] This indicates to Philo that one must not linger with Hagar, the μέση παιδεία, but only sojourn therein. Another helpful element is Philo's consistent allegorization of Egypt as "the body."[56] Since Hagar is from Egypt, we learn that the body (along with its senses) is involved in accessing the preliminary studies.[57] Once the student has progressed (προκόπτω) through the circuit of intermediate studies, only then is he prepared to leave the body and prepare the mind for virtue and philosophy.[58] Abraham is the living embodiment of the student's journey to philosophy.

Didymus

When we turn to Didymus the Blind, we find Philo's name mentioned twice as a source for the allegorical interpretation. Because the text is quite lengthy, we shall discuss it in two parts. The first section introduces the juxtaposition of the Pauline and Philonic interpretations, focusing on Sarah.

David Winston, "Sage and Super-Sage in Philo of Alexandria," in *Pomegranates and Golden Bells: Studies in Biblical, Jewish and Near Eastern Ritual, Law and Literature in Honor of Jacob Milgrom* (ed. David P. Wright, David Noel Freedman & Avi Hurvitz; Winona Lake, IN: Eisenbraun's, 1995), 815–24.

[52] *Secular Education*, xxiv.

[53] This is Colson's translation of ἀρχή μου; in the context of *Congr.* 2 this translation is the best one (see also *Cher.* 7; *Mut.* 77).

[54] Philo apparently inherited the connection between Sarah and virtue from certain φυσικοὶ ἄνδρες (*Abr.* 99). In context, it appears that Philo claims to have inherited the entire Sarah-Hagar allegory from Hellenistic Jewish predecessors, and not just the etymologies of their names; on the latter point see Lester L. Grabbe, *Etymology in Early Jewish Interpretation* (BJS 115; Atlanta: Scholars Press, 1988), 10.

[55] The Greek is παροίκησις (*Congr.* 20).

[56] E.g., *Leg.* 2.77; *Sacr.* 48; *Post.* 62; on this subject, see Pearce, *The Land of the Body*, 81–127.

[57] *Congr.* 20–21.

[58] Posidonius in Seneca, *Ep.* 88.21–23, divided education into four "arts": (1) *artes vulgares* (= manual labor); (2) *artes ludicrae* (= entertainment); (3) *artes pueriles* (= *artes liberales*/ἐγκύκλιοι τέχναι); (4) *artes liberae* (= for those concerned with ἀρετή); see Alfred Stückelberger, *Senecas 88. Brief über Wert und Unwert der freien Künste* (Heidelberg: C. Winter, 1965), 52–55. Philo is concerned only with the third and fourth stages.

The second section, quoted below, delves further into Hagar. Didymus begins his allegorical discussion as follows: [59]

> The literal sense is useful, as we have discussed in detail. But the anagogical interpretation can be explained [ἐξομαλίζομαι] as follows: the blessed Paul, using typology, interpreted the two woman anagogically as the two covenants. Philo also, by employing typology in a different way, interpreted Sarah anagogically as perfect virtue and philosophy, since she was a free and noble-born wife and cohabited with her husband according to the laws. And virtue indeed cohabits with the sage according to the laws in order that divine offspring might be produced from it, for "Wisdom gives birth to prudence for a man" (Prov 10:23). And it is said to the pious and holy man, "Your wife flourishing like a vine ... your sons as newly-planted olive trees around your table. In this way a man who fears the Lord shall be blessed." (Ps 127:3–4) (*In Gen* 235.25–236.5, trans. mine)[60]

Didymus mentions both Philo and Paul as differing in their interpretations, although both utilize the same exegetical method. A greater measure of authority is assigned to Paul initially, who is provided the epithet ὁ μακάριος.[61] As the passage goes on to show, however, Didymus regards the two as exegetical equals, at least on this particular subject.

The first feature Didymus cites as Philonic is that Sarah refers to "perfect virtue and philosophy" (ἡ τέλεια ἀρετὴ καὶ φιλοσοφία). Philo characteristically identifies Sarah with "virtue," and less commonly with "perfect virtue."[62] For the Stoics, virtue was perfect and hence incapable of

---

[59] The Genesis commentary of Didymus consistently follows a tripartite structure: (1) Citation of the biblical lemma; (2) Explanation of the literal meaning; (3) Explanation of the allegorical meaning. In this sense, it is tempting to think that Didymus is patterning himself after Philo's *Quaestiones*. It may be, however, that Origen too structured his lost Alexandrian Genesis commentary in the Philonic fashion. Ronald Heine has linked the structure of Origen's great Genesis commentary with that of Philo's *Quaestiones* based on extant fragments; "Origen's Alexandrian *Commentary on Genesis*," in *Origeniana Octava* (2 vols.; ed. L. Perrone; Leuven: Peeters 2003), 1:63–73, esp. 64.

[60] Χρήσιμον μὲν οὖν καὶ τὸ ῥητόν, καθὰ διεξεληλύθαμεν. Ὁ δὲ τῆς ἀναγωγῆς λόγος οὕτως ἂν ἐξομαλισθείη, ὡς τύπῳ ὁ μακάριος Παῦλος εἰς τὰς δύο διαθήκας ἀνήγαγεν τὰς δύο γυναῖκας· τούτῳ καὶ Φίλων χρώμενος ἐν ἑτέροις πράγμασιν ἀνήγαγεν τὴν μὲν Σάραν εἰς τὴν τελείαν ἀρετὴν καὶ φιλοσοφίαν, αὐτὴν οὖσαν γαμετὴν ἐλευθέραν τε καὶ εὐγενίδα καὶ κατὰ νόμους σύνοικον· συνοικεῖ δὲ ἡ ἀρετὴ τῷ σοφῷ κατὰ νόμους, ἵνα θεῖα γεννήματα ἐξ αὐτῆς ἀπογεννήσῃ· «Ἡ σοφία» γὰρ «τίκτει ἀνδρὶ φρόνησιν», καὶ πρὸς τὸν εὐλαβῆ καὶ ὅσιον λέγεται· «Ἡ γυνή σου ὡς ἄμπελος εὐθηνοῦσα ***, οἱ υἱοί σου ὡς νεόφυτα ἐλαιῶν κύκλῳ τῆς τραπέζης σου. Οὕτως εὐλογηθήσεται ἄνθρωπος ὁ φοβούμενος τὸν Κύριον».

[61] Philo is never given an epithet in the cases in which his name occurs in the Tura commentaries of Didymus (*In Gen.* 118.24; 119.2, 19; 139.10–12; 147.17; 235.27; 236.7; *Comm. Eccl.* 279.16; 300.15–16?). This point is made by David T. Runia, "Philonic Nomenclature," *SPhA* 6 (1994): 1–27, esp. 5.

[62] See *Leg.* 3.244; *Post.* 130.

being perfected further.[63] For the Peripatetics and Academics "progress" is not an entirely negative state, provided one is continuing to develop.[64] But for Philo and for the Alexandrian Fathers one could be proclaimed virtuous while still progressing.[65] Hence, Didymus specifies that Sarah represents virtue in its perfected state. The point is almost certainly borrowed directly from Philo. Origen, for example, submits that Abraham continued to progress after Sarah's death. His allegorization of Keturah suggests that she, and not Sarah, was the final stage in Abraham's ethical progress (*Hom. Gen.* 11:1–2). Philo discusses Keturah rarely,[66] but apparently regarded her also as a symbol of secular education.[67] Didymus does not discuss Keturah in the Genesis commentary, but since Sarah was "perfect virtue," his interpretation presumably would agree with that of Philo and not with Origen.

Even though it seems that Didymus borrows his description of Sarah from Philo, his scheme is different from that of Philo. "Perfect virtue" should not be equivalent to φιλοσοφία, as Didymus has it, but rather to σοφία. "Wisdom" is the ethical summit of progress in both Philo (see *Congr.* 77–79, and esp. §79) and in Clement (*Strom.* 1.28–32).[68] Didymus seems to be imprecise with his terminology.

Second, Didymus calls attention to Sarah as "the free and noble-born wife" (γαμετὴ ἐλευθέρα τε καὶ εὐγενίς). The Stoics regarded the wise man

---

[63] In other words, one was in vice until he attained virtue. Plutarch is representative: "'Yes,' they [the Stoics] say, 'but just as in the sea the man an arm's length from the surface is drowning no less than the one who has sunk five hundred fathoms, so even those who are getting close [οἱ πελάζοντες] to virtue are no less in a state of vice than those who are far from it. And just as the blind are blind even if they are going to recover their sight a little later, so those progressing [οἱ προκόπτοντες] remain foolish and vicious right up to their attainment of virtue'" (trans. Anthony A. Long and David N. Sedley, *The Hellenistic Philosophers* [Cambridge: Cambridge University Press, 1987], 61.T).

[64] See Geert Roskam, *On the Path to Virtue: The Stoic Doctrine of Moral Progress and its Reception in (Middle) Platonism* (Ancient and Medieval Philosophy Series 1; Leuven: Leuven University Press, 2005), esp. 152–219 on Philo.

[65] E.g., *Agr.* 160; *Abr.* 34; *Virt.* 67. John Dillon writes, "Philo's innovation here [scil. *Leg.* 3.125ff] (if it *is* his) is thoroughly un-Stoic, as the Stoics would not recognize the *prokopton* as possessing virtue at all (at best he would possess 'sparks' or adumbrations of virtues)." John Dillon, "Plotinus, Philo and Origen on the Grades of Virtue," in *Platonismus und Christentum: Festschrift für Heinrich Dörrie* (ed. Horst-Dieter Blume and Friedhelm Mann; JAC 10; Münster: Aschendorff, 1983), 85–105, esp. 103.

[66] She is mentioned only twice in the extant corpus (*Sacr.* 43; *QG* 4.147). The latter passage allegorizes all three of Abraham's wives as the highest sensory δυνάμεις: hearing, sight and smell.

[67] *Sacr.* 43–44.

[68] See the helpful diagram of Van den Hoek, *Clement*, 46.

alone as free and well-born.[69] Philo adopts and develops the Stoic doctrine, even writing a youthful tractate on the subject, the *Quod omnis probus liber sit*. In addition, the pair εὐγένεια and ἐλευθερία and their cognates occur together fourteen times in the extant writings of Philo,[70] and occur regularly in Clement as well.[71] Neither Philo nor Clement applies these descriptions explicitly to Sarah. Perhaps this is because the Stoics generally regarded the wise *man* as free, and did not speak consistently of the female sage. Nevertheless, the general terminology and exegetical rationale for regarding Sarah as "free" and "of noble birth" can be traced through Clement to Philo.

Third, the idea of virtue "living in the house" (συνοικέω) with the sage is Philonic.[72] Clement too recognizes this Philonic theme, and applies it to Abraham.[73] The term "house" can be allegorized in Philo as "virtue."[74] The "soul" can also be interpreted as a "house" or "tent" for virtue.[75] Didymus suggests that the sage (Abraham) lives with virtue (Sarah) in order to produce "divine offspring" (θεῖα γεννήματα). This point is based on the literal interpretation of both Philo and Didymus, reviewed above, that a couple can come together only for the purpose of producing offspring. The same applies allegorically. The soul's "mating" with virtue can produce either the offspring of virtue or repel the soul to produce the offspring of pleasure.[76] While the exact phrase θεῖα γεννήματα is not used in Philo, the equivalent phrase θεῖα σπέρματα does occur.[77] Only when Abraham had finished the circuit of preliminary studies was he able to produce "divine offspring" with Sarah.

Didymus closes this segment of his exegesis with two scriptural citations, one from Prov 10:23 and the other from Ps 127:3–4 (LXX). Citations

---

[69] See *SVF* 3.365; 3.594; 3.619 (= Clement, *Strom.* 2.19). "Freedom" for the Stoics was only a theoretical possibility; see Anthony A. Long, *Hellenistic Philosophy: Stoics, Epicureans, Sceptics* (2nd ed.; Berkeley: University of California Press, 1986), 204–208.

[70] E.g., *Agr.* 59; *Ebr.* 58; *Migr.* 67; on εὐγένεια in Philo see Walter T. Wilson, *On Virtues: Introduction, Translation, and Commentary* (PACS 3; Leiden: Brill, 2011), 381–418.

[71] E.g., *Strom.* 2.19; 3.30, 78; on Clement's use of Philo's *Virt.* in *Strom.* 2.78–100 see Van den Hoek, *Clement*, 69–115.

[72] E.g., *Prob.* 107: "For having inured the soul from the first to hold aloof through love of knowledge from association with the passions, and to cleave to culture and wisdom, they set it wandering away from the body and brought it to make its home [συνοικέω] with wisdom and courage and the other virtues." Cf. also *Det.* 59.

[73] *Strom.* 1.30; Van den Hoek does not address this particular phrase in Clement.

[74] See *Leg.* 3.2; *Cher.* 49.

[75] E.g., *Leg.* 2.61; 3.239; *Det.* 59; in Didymus, the "tent" itself is a symbol for ethical progress (see Geljon, "Philo's Influence on Didymus," 366).

[76] *Leg.* 2.48; cf. *Congr.* 6.

[77] *Cher.* 46; cf. *QG* 3.18.

from non-Pentateuchal books, and especially citations from Proverbs, remind us of Clement's *modus operandi*. Van den Hoek has rightly noted the importance of Proverbs in Clement's discussion of the Hagar-Sarah narrative.[78] While we cannot say that Didymus has followed Clement directly here, his turn to extra-Pentateuchal citations is certainly reminiscent of Clement's hermeneutical procedure. So while it seems clear that Didymus received much of his material directly from Philo, his method of applying the Philonic material reminds us more of Clement.[79]

In the second part of his "anagogical" interpretation, Didymus attempts to explain further his understanding of Hagar. He writes:

> Therefore, Sarah is interpreted anagogically as perfect and spiritual virtue, but Hagar, the Egyptian slave-girl, is said by Philo to mean "the preliminary studies," but by Paul the "shadow" [σκιά]. For it is impossible to understand any of the spiritual or lofty concepts apart from the "shadow" present in the literal sense [τὸ γράμμα] or apart from the introductory aspects of the *propaideia*. For it is necessary to produce offspring from the more inferior things first. Hence they offered sacrifices according to the "shadow," they observed the Passover in a sensory fashion and circumcised in a bodily way, being led along by these things to sacrifice "a sacrifice of praise to God" (Ps 49:23; Heb 13:15), which belongs to the free woman. Therefore, since diligence [σπουδή] orders the sage to go on to greater things, virtue subjects him to the divine "shadow" for the purpose of utilizing the introductory matters first and producing offspring from them. For since he who is in the process of approaching virtue cannot reach perfection so as to produce offspring from it, it is advisable for him first to practice in the *propaideia* in order that he might advance to it completely, if he is able (*In. Gen.* 236.6–21, trans. mine).[80]

In the first section of exegesis analyzed above, Didymus sets aside the Pauline understanding of Sarah in favor of the Philonic interpretation. For

---

[78] She notes eight such cases in which Clement turns to Proverbs for proofs (*Clement*, 26).

[79] Philo, of course, tends to focus primarily on the Pentateuchal text in his exegesis. The extent to which other biblical literature influenced Philo has been discussed by Naomi G. Cohen, *Philo's Scriptures: Citations from the Prophets and Writings* (JSJSup 123; Leiden: Brill, 2007).

[80] Εἰς μὲν οὖν τὴν τελείαν ἀρετὴν καὶ πνευματικὴν ἡ Σάρα ἀνάγεται, ἡ δὲ Ἄγὰρ ἡ παιδίσκη ἡ Αἰγυπτία παρὰ μὲν Φίλωνος τὰ προγυμνάσματα σημαίνειν εἴρηται, παρὰ δὲ Παύλῳ τὴν σκίαν. Ἀδύνατον γάρ τι τῶν πνευματικῶν ἢ ὑψηλῶν νοημάτων χωρὶς τῆς κατὰ τὸ γράμμα σκιᾶς ἢ τῶν εἰσαγωγικῶν προπαιδεύσεως καταλαβεῖν· δεῖ γὰρ ἐκ τῶν ὑποδεεστέρων πρότερον τεκνοῦν. Κατὰ γοῦν τὴν σκιὰν ἐβουθύτουν, πάσχα ἐπετέλουν αἰσθητῶς καὶ περιετέμνοντο σωματικῶς, διὰ τούτων χειραγωγούμενοι ἐπὶ τὸ θύειν «τῷ Θεῷ θυσίαν αἰνέσεως», ὅπερ ἐστὶν τῆς ἐλευθέρας ἴδιον. Ἐπεὶ οὖν σπουδὴ τῷ σοφῷ τάξει χωρεῖν ἐπὶ τὰ μείζονα, ὑποβάλλει ἡ ἀρετὴ σκοπῷ θείῳ τοῖς εἰσαγωγικοῖς πρότερον χρῆσθαι καὶ ἐξ αὐτῶν τεκνοποιεῖν. Ἐπεὶ γὰρ ἄρτι προσιὼν τῇ ἀρετῇ τελειότητος ἐφάψασθαι οὐχ οἷός τε ἐστιν ὥστε καὶ ἐξ αὐτῆς τεκνῶσαι, ὑποτίθεται αὐτῷ πρότερον ἐγγυμνάσασθαι τοῖς προπαιδεύμασιν, ἵν᾽ οὕτω καὶ αὐτὴν τελείως χωρῇ, εἰ δυνηθῇ.

Didymus, Sarah refers to "perfect virtue and philosophy," that is, to the highest spiritual goal. In the second section, Didymus attempts to harmonize the two interpreters by identifying Hagar as a "shadow."[81] Although this identification is ascribed to Paul, Paul nowhere refers to Hagar as a shadow. The identification is made by Didymus, but he was certainly influenced by Origen, as we shall see.

The identification of Hagar as a shadow serves three purposes. First, the New Testament uses the term σκιά to refer to the Law and worship under the Law in contrast with the "new covenant."[82] This enables Didymus to incorporate the Pauline understanding of Hagar as a "covenant" (Gal 4:24). Second, as a shadow, Hagar both leads to and is a reflection of an object greater than herself. The student can follow the "shadow" and locate the true object that casts the shadow. This allows Didymus to incorporate the Philonic theme of progressing through education (the shadow) in preparation for virtue (the substance). Yet a third purpose of the "shadow" concept is to subject literalism (τὸ γράμμα) both in biblical interpretation and in legal observance to the "spiritual or lofty concepts." This theme is derived primarily from Origen, for whom σκιά is a favorite term for literalism.

Didymus inherited the term "shadow" from the Alexandrian tradition as a derogatory way of referring to literalism. Even Philo himself refers to literal interpretation as a "shadow" in *De Confusione* 190, but the description is not common in the Philonic corpus.[83] Neither is the term common in Clement of Alexandria.[84] But in Origen the term occurs dozens of times in reference to literalism, especially characteristic of the Jews.[85] Philo, of course, was not a representative of Jewish interpretation since he understood the Bible, in Origen's vocabulary, "spiritually."[86] Although Didymus,

---

[81] Manlio Simonetti surveys the allegory and argues that Didymus abandons the Pauline in favor of the Philonic; see "Lettera e allegoria nell'esegesi veterotestamentaria di Didimo," *Vetera Christianorum* 20 (1983): 341–89, esp. 355. In my view, Runia is more correct when he suggests that Didymus rejects neither the Philonic nor the Pauline reading, but coalesces them into a single interpretation (*Philo in Early Christian Literature*, 202).

[82] See esp. Heb 8:5; 10:1; cf. Col 2:17.

[83] After encouraging expositors not to stop at the literal meaning of Gen 11, Philo advises "to press on to allegorical interpretations and to recognize that the letter is to the oracle but as the shadow to the substance and that the higher values therein revealed are what really and truly exist" (trans. PLCL).

[84] See Leemans, "After Philo and Paul," 440.

[85] E.g., *Cels.* 2.2.15ff; *Comm. Joh.* 1.6.34; *Philoc.* 1.6. The term "shadow" does not play prominently in the vocabulary of Clement of Alexandria, but it is used in reference to a literal worship according to the Law in Athanasius (*Exp. Ps.* 27.360.41). Didymus uses the term some 239 times.

[86] In Alexandrian Christianity Philo is understood to be *ethnically* Jewish, but not *exegetically* Jewish. In other words, to interpret the Bible ἰουδαϊκῶς meant to interpret in a

like Origen, assigns value to the literal interpretation of the biblical text, he never stops at the surface level. Like the preliminary studies, the literal meaning is only minimally beneficial. Every biblical passage has a deeper meaning. To reap the full value of the scriptural text one must access the anagogical understanding.

In the Tura commentary on Ecclesiastes, in his discussion of Ecclesiastes 9:9a, Didymus interprets the "wife of your youth" as "true and ethical virtue," but states that it is necessary to remain with another woman before reaching that state. He writes:

> And according to this Philo understood …[87] to give birth before perfect virtue. For if one does not beget from these lesser women, he cannot become a father of undefiled works and of the contemplations of wisdom. The same thing the Apostle calls 'letter' and 'spirit' (2 Cor 3:6). And it is impossible to understand the things belonging to the anagogical sense [ἀναγωγή] without meticulously investigating the things belonging to the literal sense [ἱστορία] (*Comm. Eccl.* 276. 20–23, trans. mine).[88]

Here Didymus sets forth his understanding of biblical interpretation. The literal meaning provides an access point for the deeper, spiritual sense.[89] The metaphor of two women expressing the two senses of scripture fits well with Didymus's Hagar-Sarah exegesis. But there is a further connection between Didymus's understanding of the Bible and the Philonic theme of progress.

In Philo, the education which Hagar represents is "secular" in nature. One attended the school of the γραμματίστης (primary school), and then advanced to that of the γραμματικός (secondary school). Finally one was educated under a ῥήτωρ or σοφιστής. And, for a lucky few, an education in

---

"slavishly literal fashion" (see Clement, *Strom.* 6.5.41; *Paed.* 1.6.34; Origen, *Comm. Jo.* 10.42.291; 32.5.63; *Fr. Ps.* 75:3). It was thus no scandal to use Philo against literal, "Jewish" interpretation, as Didymus does here.

[87] The Greek is illegible. Gronewald hypothesizes Ἀγα<ρ> in his apparatus criticus, but has . .αν in the text (see note below). Henrichs attempts to tentatively substitute the term ταμίαν ("Philosophy," 449), but there is no space for it in the papyrus, as Gronewald states; Michael Gronewald, ed., *Didymos der Blinde, Kommentar zum Ekklesiastes V. Kap. 9.8–10.20* (Papyrologische Texte und Abhandlungen 24; Bonn: R. Habelt, 1979), 16.

[88] καὶ κατὰ τοῦτο ὁ Φίλων ἐξέλαβεν τὴ[ν] ..αν προτίκτει[ν] τῆς ἀρετῆς τῆς τελείας· εἰ μὴ γάρ τις τέκῃ ἐκ τούτων τῶ[ν μ]ικρῶν, οὐ δ[ύ]ν[ατ]αι πατὴρ τῶν ἔργων τῶν ἀμιάντων καὶ τῶν θεωρημάτων τῆς σοφίας γενέσθαι. τὸ δὲ αὐτὸ τοῦτο ὁ ἀπόστολος γράμμα καὶ πνεῦμα λέγ[ει· κ]αὶ ἀδύνατόν ἐστιν τὰ τῆς ἀναγωγῆς νοῆσαι μὴ ἀκριβώσαντα τὰ τῆς ἱστ[ορία]ς.

[89] This view was for Origen a natural result of his theory of inspiration; see Blossom Stefaniw, *Mind, Text, and Commentary: Noetic Exegesis in Origen of Alexandria, Didymus the Blind and Evagrius Ponticus* (Early Christianity in the Context of Antiquity 6; Frankfurt am Main: Peter Lang, 2010), 107–110. The same probably was true for Didymus.

philosophy might be obtained.[90] Philo must have assumed that most, if not all, of these teachers would have been non-Jews. Scriptural education in the house of prayer or under a Jewish teacher is rarely alluded to in Philo, and is not accounted for in Philo's general educational system of progress and perfection.[91] Despite the fact that Philo stood in a tradition of Jewish exegetes,[92] the θεῖα παιδεύσις, as Didymus was to call it, did not figure into his interpretation of Hagar as education. In Clement and Origen as well, education remained "secular."[93]

By the time of Didymus, however, catechetical schools were the norm, and Didymus himself was a teacher in this educational institution (Rufinus, *Hist.* 11.7).[94] So one's ethical progress could be viewed increasingly through an examination of the biblical text in an ecclesiastical environment.[95] Just as Philo in his Allegorical Commentary attempts to assist students in their pursuit of perfection, so also Didymus believes that his lectures aid his

---

[90] Greg Sterling reminds me that those who were eligible for Alexandrian citizenship also had available the ephebate, which, by the time of Philo, had ceased to be a military education alone.

[91] If Philo operated a "school of sacred laws" on his own, as some have argued, then he leaves no special place for the education in his system of progress and virtue; see Gregory E. Sterling, "The School of Sacred Laws: the Social Setting of Philo's Treatises," *VC* 53 (1999): 148–64, who summarizes earlier research, and concludes that Philo did indeed operate a school.

[92] Philo's exegetical predecessors occupied much research on Philo in the 1970s; see Robert G. Hamerton-Kelly, "Sources and Traditions in Philo Judaeus: Prologomena to an Analysis of His Writings," *SPh* 1 (1972): 3–26; Burton L. Mack, "Exegetical Traditions in Alexandrian Judaism: A Program for the Analysis of the Philonic Corpus," *SPh* 3 (1974–75): 71–112. On the direct references to other scholars in Philo see Montgomery J. Shroyer, "Alexandrian Jewish Literalists," *JBL* 55 (1936): 261–84, and David Hay, "References to Other Exegetes," in *Both Literal and Allegorical: Studies in Philo of Alexandria's Questions and Answers on Genesis and Exodus* (ed. D. H. Hay; Atlanta: Scholars Press, 1991), 81–97. For a reconstruction of the traditions Philo inherited on the creation account see Thomas Tobin, *The Creation of Man: Philo and the History of Interpretation* (CBQMS 14; Washington, D.C.: The Catholic Biblical Association of America, 1983), and less plausibly, Robert Goulet, *La philosophie de Moïse: Essai de reconstitution d'un commentaire philosophique préphilonien de Pentateuque* (Histoire des Doctrines de l'Antiquité Classique 11; Paris: J. Vrin, 1987).

[93] For Clement see, e.g., *Strom.* 1.32.1–4; for Origen see *Hom. Gen.* 11.2 and *Sel. Gen.* 16:14 (PG 12:116A).

[94] On Didymus in a scholastic setting, see Ann Browning Nelson, "The Classroom of Didymus the Blind" (Ph.D. diss., University of Michigan, 1995) and Layton, *Didymus*.

[95] Layton concludes of Didymus's own education, "The profile of Didymus' knowledge suggests a schooling that imitated the traditional curriculum but was directed at forming a Christian identity, rather than preparing the student for one of the standard professions ... His philosophical training came to him already imprinted with a Christian ideology" (*Didymus*, 143).

students in their ethical progress.[96] The Tura Commentary on Psalms in particular is a guidebook for the προκόπτων.[97] So essentially Didymus has taken the theme of ethical progress via secular education from Philo and applied it exclusively to scriptural learning.

We can see the shift in attitude clearly in Didymus's interpretation of the command to "grow and multiply" (Gen 1:28). He comments, "Since divine instruction [θεία παίδευσις] involves an introduction [εἰσαγωγή], a progression [προκοπή] and a perfection [τέλος], we must understand the command to 'grow' in this sense" (*In Gen.* 69.8–9).[98] The Philonic scheme is present, as we can see. But the subject must undergo specifically *divine* instruction before advancing to perfection. In other words, biblical exegesis has taken the place of secular studies. And where would one obtain such an education in "divine instruction" but in Didymus's own classroom?

The same scheme applies also to the procedure of exegesis. One must begin by investigating the literal meaning (τὸ γράμμα), represented by Hagar.[99] Having completed this preliminary stage, he is now prepared to access the anagogical meaning, represented by Sarah. To access the literal meaning prepares the student for the eventual "sacrifice of praise" (Ps 49:23 LXX).[100] Didymus often uses this biblical catch-phrase to express Christian worship in contrast to the literal sacrifices of the Mosaic Law.[101] The Jews ("they" of the passage above) are to be blamed because they linger in preliminary studies, and refuse to progress to the deeper (i.e., Christian) understanding of the Law.[102] They are no better than the Greeks who linger

---

[96] Hay writes that Philo's primary purpose is "the means of turning to God, the barriers people encounter when they try to grow closer to God, and the stages of spiritual progress;" see "Philo of Alexandria," in *Justification and Variegated Nomism* (2 vols.; ed. D. A. Carson, Peter T. O'Brien and Mark A. Siefrid. Tübingen: Mohr Siebeck; Grand Rapids: Baker, 2001–2004), 1:357–80, esp. 365.

[97] On Didymus's interpretation of the Psalms in general, see Layton, *Didymus*, 36–55. On Psalm 24 (23 LXX) specifically, see Albert Geljon, "Didymus the Blind: Commentary on Psalm 24 (23 LXX): Introduction, Translation and Commentary," *VC* 65 (2011): 50–73.

[98] Καὶ ἐπεὶ ἡ θεία [παίδε]υσις καὶ εἰσαγωγὴν ἔχει καὶ προκοπὴν καὶ τέλος, κατὰ τ[αύτην τὸ] «αὐξάνεσθε» νοητέον.

[99] This is Origen's argument for the "flesh" of scripture (i.e., the most obvious meaning) in *Princ.* 4.2.4.

[100] On the notion of progress as the key element in Origen's exegesis, see Karen Jo Torjesen, *Hermeneutical Procedure and Theological Method in Origen's Exegesis* (PTS 28; Berlin/New York: De Gruyter, 1986).

[101] Didymus refers to the "sacrifice of praise" 33 times, almost always referring to the worship of the "spiritual covenant" (e.g. *Comm. Ps.* 285.15; *Fr. Ps.* 521.3).

[102] Note the comments of Origen regarding Sarah's entrance into the harem of Abimelech: "If anyone wishes to hear and understand these words literally he ought to gather with the Jews rather than with the Christians" (*Hom. Gen.* 6.1; trans. Ronald E. Heine [FC 71; Washington, DC: Catholic University Press of America, 1982]).

in secular education. As mere "sophists" (to use Clement's Philonic characterization), they are indicted for their failure to progress to more advanced learning.[103]

In addition, just as Abraham could not by-pass Hagar, the literal sense represents a necessary foundation for the deeper, spiritual sense of scripture. The literalism of the Jewish system is therefore a legitimate, but merely preparatory stage, in one's ethical progress.[104] This applied both in the practice and in the exegesis of the Law.[105] Just as Paul identified the Mosaic Law as a παιδαγωγός for the Jews (Gal 3:24–25), so also Philo identified "philosophy" as such for the Greeks (*Virt.* 65). Clement follows Philo in identifying "philosophy" as preparatory instruction for the Greeks.[106] Didymus includes both the "Jewish" interpretive system and the Greek educational curriculum as foundational for Christian virtue.

Viewed in this light Didymus' commentaries become more than biblical expositions. They represent the journey of the soul. The "journey" is both aided by and patterned after the progressive layers of meaning in the biblical text. So Didymus understands ethical progress to be an inherently spiritual endeavor bound up entirely with one's scriptural education. In this, he reinterprets the Philonic model.[107] Studying the literal meaning of Scripture prepares one for deeper understandings the way secular education prepares one for philosophy, and finally, for virtue.

Didymus's anagogical interpretation of the two women allows him to accomplish three goals. First, he is able to justify his own procedure of interpretation, that is, of explaining the literal meaning first and then advancing to the spiritual meaning. Second, Didymus is able to assign to

---

[103] Compare *Strom.* 1.28.4 with Philo's *Cher.* 8–10; see the comments of Van den Hoek, *Clement*, 27.

[104] On Origen's characterization of the Jews as literalists, see Peter W. Martens, "Why Does Origen Accuse the Jews of 'Literalism?' A Case Study of Christian Identity and Biblical Exegesis in Antiquity," *Adamantius* 13 (2007): 218–30.

[105] The practical application of the Mosaic Law was, to Philo, an act of φιλοσοφία; see Valentin Nikiprowetzky, *Le Commentaire de l'Écriture chez Philon d'Alexandrie: Son Caractère et sa Portée* (ALGHJ 11; Leiden: Brill, 1977), 100–102.

[106] Whereas for Philo the preparatory nature of "secular education" in general is a more common theme than "philos phy," for Clement the two are reversed, "philosophy" being more prominent in his scheme (*Strom.* 1.28.3). But the difference of emphasis is not significant. As Clement says, philosophy and secular education "cooperate [συνέργω] for the acquisition of wisdom" (*Strom.* 1.30.1).

[107] Nikiprowetzky comments, "La Pentateuque est «une école de prêtrise,» c'est-à-dire que par l'intermédiaire de symboles divers, par l'intelligence et la pratique des Lois, il enseigne au progressant à suivre les pas de Moïse et à réaliser sous sa conduite l'Exode spirituel. Tout le «système» de Philon consiste à reconnaître inlassablement cet enseignement au fond des textes et derrière les symboles de l'Écriture" (*Le Commentaire*, 239).

his scriptural interpretation ethical significance for the "journey of the soul" each of his students must make. Biblical interpretation assists them in reaching this philosophical goal. Third, Didymus can incorporate, with some measure of difficulty, the Pauline contrast of Hagar and Sarah as Jew and Christian, respectively. He is assisted in this goal by the Origenian contrast of literal versus spiritual, often cast as Jewish versus Christian, exegesis.

To accomplish his exegetical goals Didymus relies more heavily on Philo than on Paul. In fact, it is not Philo who is understood to align with Paul, but rather it is Paul who is reinterpreted to square with Philo! The result is something that neither Paul nor Philo would have recognized as their own. Hagar and Sarah represent stages not only of scriptural meaning, but also of ethical progress. The covenantal model of Paul fits only slightly as Didymus could contrast Jewish and Christian approaches to Scripture. Ultimately, Didymus follows Philo in asserting that the sage must abandon the maid and advance to the spiritual heights of the mistress.

Conclusion

Didymus the Blind mentions Philo more than any other non-biblical source. Philo's expositions, being allegorical in nature, must have seemed more Christian than Jewish to a fourth-century Alexandrian author, and his presentation of the Mosaic legislation as a philosophy appealed to the desire to elevate the intellectual status of the Christian faith. As we can see from the example above, Philo could be cited by name with no hint of scandal. This detail alone is telling. Beyond that, we can see that Philo's allegorical interpretation of Hagar and Sarah had become so central for Didymus that even Paul required a reassessment in light of the Philonic material.

It is not simply the Philonic allegory that Didymus recognizes as beneficial. Philo's literal interpretation also contains important lessons for the behavior of the Christian student. Didymus's Philonic application of this literal interpretation proves that he had read Philo directly on the point of Hagar and Sarah. As a thinker, no exegete was more influential on Alexandrian Christianity than Philo, and no Alexandrian Christian specifically cites Philo more than Didymus the Blind. The Hagar-Sarah narrative is simply one rich example of the exegetical points Didymus the Blind incorporates from Philo of Alexandria.

Freed-Hardeman University
Henderson, Tennessee, USA

The Studia Philonica Annual 26 (2014) 79–92

PHILO AND PLUTARCH ON THE NATURE OF GOD

FREDERICK E. BRENK

Philo and Plutarch came out of similar Platonic backgrounds, but not all persons with similar backgrounds arrive at the same conclusions. The purpose here is to locate their positions within the context of religious monotheism. Many studies have appeared recently on "pagan monotheism."[1] A major question has been whether it ever existed. The opponents point to no worship of such a God.[2] At the time of Philo and Plutarch, outside of Judaism, were prayers, sacrifices, or libations ever made simply to God and not to a particular god? Possibly this existed in the cult of Theos Hypsistos, treated intensively by Stephen Mitchell.[3] Unfortunately, its nature is rather murky. Nicole Belayche has been particularly biting in her contestation of Mitchell.[4] For example, she agrees that the term θεὸς ὕψιστος

---

[1] The starting point for many has been Michael Frede, "Monotheism and Pagan Philosophy in Later Antiquity," in *Pagan Monotheism in Late Antiquity* (eds. Polymnia Athanassiadi and Michael Frede; Oxford: Oxford University Press, 1999), 69–80. See the comments on this by John A. North, "Pagans, Polytheists, and the Pendulum," in *The Religious History of the Roman Empire: Pagans, Jews, and Christians* (eds. John A. North and Simon R. F. Price; Oxford: Oxford University Press, 2011), 479–504, original in *The Spread of Christianity in the the First Four Centuries: Studies in Explanation* (ed. William V. Harris; Leiden: Brill, 2005), 124–43; and a response by Michael Frede, "The Case for Pagan Monotheism in Greek and Roman Antiquity," in *One God: Pagan Monotheism in the Roman Empire* (eds., Stephen Mitchell and Peter Van Nuffelen; Cambridge: Cambridge University Press, 2010), 53–81; Maria Vittoria Cerutti, "'Pagan Monotheism'? Towards a Historical Typology," in *Monotheism between Pagans and Christians in Late Antiquity* (eds. Stephen Mitchell and Peter Van Nuffelen; Leuven: Peeters, 2010), 15–32.

[2] E.g., Mark Edwards, Review of Polymnia Athanassiadi and Michael Frede, eds. *Pagan Monotheism in Late Antiquity* (Oxford: Oxford University Press, 1999) in *JThS* 51 (2000): 339–42.

[3] E.g., "The Cult of Theos Hypsistos between Pagans, Jews, and Christians," in Athanassiadi and Frede, *Pagan Monotheism in Late Antiquity*, 81–148.

[4] "*Hypsistos*: A New Way of Exalting the Gods in Graeco-Roman Polytheism," in *The Religious History of the Roman Empire: Pagans, Jews, and Christians* (eds. John A. North and Simon R. F. Price; Oxford and New York: Oxford University Press, 2011), 139–74 (original: "*Hypsistos*: Une voie de l'exaltation des dieux dans le polythéisme gréco-romain," *AR* 7 (2005): 34–55. For a critique of Mitchell, see also Angelos Chaniotis, "Megatheism: The Search for the Almighty God and the Competition of Cults," in *One God: Pagan Monotheism*

(The Highest God) might express a monotheistic conception of the divine. She adds, however, that the religiosity of the cult belongs to the polytheism of the Imperial period, which exalted individual deities without bringing about a theological break.[5]

In Greek religion, invariably a cult or priesthood was to a particular god or goddess, as were cult statues. Similarly, one usually prayed to individual gods, or all the gods, not simply to God. In the Theos Hypsistos inscriptions, the dedications to the god or God (*theos*) is usually qualified in some way, or the god is associated with other gods. Mitchell at first described the participants as the "God-Fearers" (θεοσεβείς [*theosebeis*] or σεβόμενοι τὸν θεόν [*sebomenoi ton theon*]) such as mentioned in the *Acts of the Apostles*. His argument relied on *Acts* 16:13–18, where a slave girl calls Paul and Silas "servants of Theos Hypsistos."[6] Her words could, however, simply mean "servants of the most high God." Possibly, in some places participants in the cult, who sometimes call themselves "*theosebeis*," were the *theosebeis* known in Judaism, that is, persons interested in Judaism and participating in services, but not full-fledged converts (proselytes).[7] Interestingly, the worshippers in the Hypsistos cult, which was aniconic, seem not to have offered sacrifice.[8] If they believed in the Jewish God, would this be "pagan monotheism?"[9] They also may have been influenced by the philosophical conception of a super-supreme God.[10] However, the mystery remains.

Philo's God had several of the attributes of a Middle Platonic God, namely, that He is Being, or "the Existent One," the Good, and the One,

---

in the Roman Empire (eds. Stephen Mitchell and Peter Van Nuffelen; Cambridge: Cambridge University Press, 2010), 112–41. For Mitchell's response, see Stephen Mitchell, "Further Thoughts on the Cult of Theos Hypsistos," in *One God: Pagan Monotheism in the Roman Empire*, 167–208 (167–98).

5 Belayche, "Hypsistos," 141–42, cf. 163–64.

6 Mitchell, "The Cult of Theos Hypsistos," 94–97, 115–21. Some form of "God-Fearers" appears in Acts: 10:2, 22, 35; 13:16, 26 (where the operative word is φοβούμενος); and 13:43, 50; 16:14; 17:4, 17; and 18:7 (where the operative word is σεβόμενος). However, the classes of people to whom Acts refers often cannot be determined, and may not be in the technical sense of "*theosebeis*."

7 For Jews or Jewishness in the Theos Hypsistos inscriptions, see also Mitchell, "Further Thoughts," 185–89; for God-Fearers 189–99. He notes that seventeen Theos Hypsistos inscriptions have been designated as Jewish, twenty-three as pagan, but a remaining 178 cannot be classified simply on internal grounds as belonging to one or the other category (186–87).

8 Mitchell, "Further Thoughts," 174–75. Plutarch could have come into contact with Hypsistarians in Athens, where inscriptions have been found on the Pnyx. See Mitchell, "The Cult of Theos Hypsistos,"100–101; "Further Thoughts," 198.

9 See North, "Pagans, Polytheists, and the Pendulum," 495–96.

10 See, e.g., Henk S. Versnel, *Coping with the Gods: Wayward Readings in Greek Theology* (RGRW 173; Leiden: Brill, 2011), 262.

who had created all other gods and spiritual beings.[11] However, Philo's God, unlike the God of the philosophers, was worshipped. In contrast to other Platonists, Philo was not ashamed to assert that his God was "better than the Good, more ancient than the Monad, and more absolute than the One" (ἀγαθοῦ κρεῖττον καὶ μονάδος πρεσβύτερον καὶ ἑνὸς εἰλικρινέστερον (*Praem.* 40).[12]

As mentioned, Philo and Plutarch had somewhat different though similar starting points. Philo inherited a long tradition of a monotheistic God, the only one tolerated in official Judaism. On the other hand, the traditional religion for Plutarch was the *patrios pistis*, "the inherited faith," which involved a number of different and traditional Pan-Hellenic and local divinities.[13] But elite members of his society were acquainted with the non-traditional "Gods" of Platonism and of Stoicism. In their uniqueness, exalted character, and creativity, these "Gods" resemble the God of Judaism. Philo's task was primarily to develop a Platonic theology, while Plutarch's involved leaving the worship of Apollo somewhat intact, while giving a religious dimension to the Platonic God. Unlike Philo, he was caught between "religious Platonism," the domain of a very small elite, and the traditional polytheism of his culture.[14]

Greek philosophers, like mystagogues, had led the way for Philo and Plutarch. In the case of Philo, there is, supposedly, an intermediary, Aristobulus, an educated Jew of Alexandria of the second century B.C.E., who employed Greek philosophy and even Greek literature to illuminate the nature of God. Recently, though, Abraham and David Wasserstein have

---

[11] See David T. Runia, "The Beginnings of the End: Philo of Alexandria and Hellenistic Theology," in *Traditions of Theology: Studies in Hellenistic Theology, its Background and Aftermath* (eds. Dorothea Frede and André Laks; PhilAnt 89; Leiden: Brill, 2002), 281–316 (291); John Dillon, "Philo and Hellenistic Platonism," in *Philo of Alexandria and Post-Aristotelian Philosophy* (ed. Francesca Alesse; Studies in Philo of Alexandria 5; Leiden: Brill, 2008), 223–52 (229). On Philo's God, Runia cites Dillon, "Reclaiming the Heritage of Moses: Philo's Confrontation with Greek Philosophy," *SPhA* 7 (1995): 108–23, repr. in Dillon, *The Great Tradition* (Aldershot: Ashgate 1997, study IV); and Gretchen J. Reydams-Schils, "Stoicized Readings of Plato's *Timaeus* in Philo of Alexandria," *SPhA* 7 (1995): 85–102.

[12] On Philo's God as One, see Francesca Calabi, *God's Acting, Man's Acting: Tradition and Philosophy in Philo of Alexandria* (Studies in Philo of Alexandria 4; Leiden: Brill, 2008), 31–32, and 37–38.

[13] See Peter Van Nuffelen, "Plutarch: A Benevolent Hierarchy of Gods and Men," in his *Rethinking the Gods: Philosophical Readings of Religion in the Post-Hellenistic Period* (Cambridge: Cambridge University Press, 2011), 157–78.

[14] See Frederick E. Brenk, "Plutarch and "Pagan Monotheism," in *Plutarch in the Religious and Philosophical Discourse of Late Antiquity* (eds. Lautaro Roig Lanzillotta and Israel Muñoz Gallarate; Studies in Platonism, Neoplatonism, and the Platonic Tradition 14; Leiden: Brill, 2012), 73–84.

questioned the historical existence of Aristobulus, suspecting that he was simply a phantom figure, a late invention.[15] As far as Plutarch goes, Henk Versnel in his latest book, *Coping with the Gods*, extols the sixth century B.C.E. Presocratic philosopher Xenophanes as a brilliant monotheistic forerunner.[16] Xenophanes had enunciated the following:

Εἷς θεὸς ἔν τε θεοῖσι καὶ ἀνθρώποισι μέγιστος,
οὔτι δέμας θνητοῖσιν ὁμοίιος οὐδὲ νόημα.[17]

One God among gods and men, the greatest,
neither in form nor in thought resembling mortal beings.[18]

This might simply be a declaration of henotheism, but Jonathan Barnes notes seven other principles:

1. God is motionless.
2. God is ungenerated.
3. There is one god, greatest among gods and men.
4. God is not anthropomorphic.
5. God thinks and perceives as a whole.
6. God moves things by the power of his mind.
7. God is morally perfect.[19]

Points 1, 3, 5, and 6 are derived directly from the fragments, while the others are inferences from the difference between this God and other gods.[20] Xenophanes, however, does not mention creating a cult for this god. In his *Banquet Elegy*, lines 13–15, we learn:

Χρὴ δὲ πρῶτον μὲν θεὸν ὑμνεῖν εὔφρονας ἄνδρας
εὐφήμοις μύθοις καὶ καθαροῖσι λόγοις,
σπείσαντάς τε καὶ εὐξαμένους τὰ δίκαια δύνασθαι
πρήσσειν....

---

[15] Abraham and David Wasserstein, *The Legend of the Septuagint: From Classical Antiquity to Today* (Cambridge: Cambridge University Press, 2006), 27–35, esp. 30.

[16] Versnel, *Coping with the Gods*, 239–308. Adam Drozek, *Greek Philosophers as Theologians: The Divine Arche* (Aldershoot, Hampshire: Ashgate 2007), 15–25, esp. 24–25, sees Xenophanes as traditional, but still a monotheist.

[17] Xenophanes of Colophon, mid-sixth century B.C.E. (Hermann Diels and Walther Kranz, *Die Fragmente der Vorsokratiker* I [Zurich: Weidmann, 1964] B.23, p. 135).

[18] Versnel, *Coping with the Gods*, 244.

[19] Jonathan Barnes, *The Presocratic Philosophers I* (London: Routledge & Kegan Paul, 1979, repr., 1982), 85.

[20] Versnel, *Coping with the Gods*, 255.

First, sensible men should hymn God [the god?]
with reverent stories and pure speech,
pouring a libation and praying to accomplish what is just...
(Diels-Kranz B.1.13–15, p. 127).

Later, however, it is clear that the verses refer to Zeus. The participants are simply urged to hymn the appropriate god in a sympotic context.

Versnel's definition of monotheism is similar to that of biblical scholars like Larry Hurtado, who reconcile monotheism with a belief in the existence of other spiritual beings, even of pagan gods. Hurtado would characterize both Judaism and Christianity as monotheisms of this type.[21] In the strictest sense, one might argue that neither Judaism nor Christianity is monotheistic. Hurtado, however, found no evidence even for a cult of angels within Judaism, though aware of the omnipresence of eccentrics in religion.[22] Roberto Radice was impressed by the marginal role of angels in Philo. They can be equated with *daimones*—that is, souls without bodies, or spirits—or heroes, or even with the Platonic Ideas, (citing *Cher.* 34; *Gig.* 12; *Plant.* 14). In a few passages, Philo, by implication, even grants divinity to the stars (*Opif.* 27; cf. *Spec.* 1.209, 2.1650]).[23]

Christians, too, toyed with the belief in the gods. Versnel cites Saint Paul, 1 Cor. 8:4–6:

We know that "no idol in the world really exists," and that "there is no God but one." Indeed, even though there may be so-called gods in heaven and on earth—as in fact there are many gods and many lords—yet for us there is one God, the Father from whom are all things and for whom we exist, and one Lord, Jesus Christ, through whom are all things and through whom we exist (*NRSV*).[24]

God belongs, obviously, to a different order of being than the "so-called gods." Versnel's full definition, allowing the existence of other spiritual beings, requires worship of only one God.[25] The others must be banished from cult and reduced to the status of "powerless, wicked or demonic

[21] Larry W. Hurtado, *One God, One Lord: Early Christian Devotion and Ancient Jewish Monotheism* (London: T&T Clark, 1988; 2nd ed., 1998), 27. See also Calabi, *God's Acting*, 111–26.

[22] Hurtado, *One God* (1998), 27–35; see also 36–39.

[23] Roberto Radice, "Philo's Theology and Theory of Creation," in *The Cambridge Companion to Philo* (ed. Adam Kamesar; Cambridge: Cambridge University Press, 2009), 124–45 (129).

[24] Versnel, *Coping with the Gods*, 242, note 8.

[25] But see Cerutti, "Pagan Monotheism," on Dio Chrysostom, *Or.* 31.11 ("makes no difference, one divine power" (24 n. 40).

forces with no real significance."[26] This ironically seems to disqualify his favorite, Xenophanes, and other Greek philosophers, who offered cultic worship to the "so-called gods." And what happens to "pagan monotheism?" Later, though, Versnel seems to modify his stance to allow a cult to other gods.[27] To complicate matters, he seems to create unnecessary difficulties. For him there is a real problem in Greek philosophers simultaneously believing in one and many gods without sensing a contradiction.[28] Like most of us, they seem, rather, to have been masters at compartmentalization.[29]

Within a piece of relatively popular literature, an author could speak of supernatural causes both monotheistically and polytheistically. Greeks and Romans habitually speak of numerous gods. Yet, they also refer to God and the supernatural or divine (θεός [*theos*], τὸ δαιμόνιον [*to daimonion*] or τὸ θεῖον [*to theion*]), much as a Jew or Christian would.[30] Normally, by the time of Philo and Plutarch, an author avoids speaking of an individual god intervening in history, except in a poetic or archaistic context, such as Apollo saving his shrine at Delphi from the Galatians. Plutarch's contemporary, Pausanias, in his description of the Galatians' defeat at Delphi, avoids mention of a direct intervention of the god. Instead, the god sends "dire portents"—an earthquake, thunder, lightning, and visions of heroes—even though these contribute directly to the defeat of the Galatians (10.23.1–2). In general, when speaking historically, the reference to the supernatural would be to God, the divine, or the gods, apparently interchangeable expressions. Even terms such as providence, fate, or fortune (*tyche*) can apparently be interchanged with "God," or "the gods."

Plato's *Timaeus* figures large in this intellectual history. Most modern scholars, as apparently Plato's immediate disciples (with the exception of Aristotle) and the Old Academy, have regarded his account of creation in the *Timaeus* as allegorical or in their terminology θεωρίας ἕνεκα (for demonstration purposes [1013A]), that is, non-literally or non-temporally.[31]

---

[26] Versnel, *Coping with the Gods*, 241.

[27] Ibid, 267.

[28] Ibid, 256–60 and 267–68, citing Walter Nicolai, "Sind personale und apersonale Gottesvorstellung miteinander vereinbar oder nicht?," *Grazer Beiträge* 24 (2005): 15–29 (29), and Barnes, *Presocratic Philosophers*, 143.

[29] See, e.g., Peter Van Nuffelen, "Philo of Alexandria: Challenging Graeco-Roman Culture," in his *Rethinking the Gods*, 179–99; also Maria Vittoria Cerutti, "'Pagan Monotheism'? Towards a Historical Typology," in Mitchell and Van Nuffelen, *Monotheism between Pagans and Christians*, 15–32 (28).

[30] For works on Jewish monotheism, see Versnel, *Coping with the Gods*, 242, note 7.

[31] See, e.g., Bonazzi, "Towards Transcendence," 224. However, Jan Opsomer, "Demiurges in Early Imperial Platonism," in *Gott und die Götter bei Plutarch: Götterbilder,*

In his commentary called *On the Generation of the Soul in the* Timaeus, Plutarch claims to be challenging the dominant non-literal interpretation (1013A-F). Philo and Plutarch, however, take Plato "literally" in different ways. Both hold that God created the cosmos (Plutarch, 1014A, 1017A, 1027A).[32] Plutarch, though, insists that creation took place "in time, and not from eternity or according to infinite time" (χρόνῳ γεγονέναι and οὐκ ἐξ ἀιδίου ... οὐδὲ τὸν ἄπειρον χρόνον, 1013A, E). Thus, the cosmos (the orderly universe), as opposed to the material of the cosmos, did not exist from eternity.[33] On the other hand, Philo, against the literal reading of six days, argues that since God did not need time to create, all creation represents one moment.[34]

The clearest and most extreme views in Plutarch's corpus appear in the speech of his teacher, Ammonius, in *On the E at Delphi*, which is the final and most exalted discourse in this dialogue.[35] Though most commentators take his views, *tout court* as Plutarch's, there is actually some distance

---

Gottesbilder, Weltbilder, (ed. Rainer Hirsch-Luipold; Religionsgeschichtliche Versuche und Vorarbeiten 54; Berlin: De Gruyter, 2005), 51–100, notes that the literal interpretation by Plutarch's time was not as rare as he makes out (52–53, 65, 77, 94).

[32] David T. Runia, *Philo of Alexandria and the* Timaeus *of Plato* (Leiden: Brill, 1986), 135, claims that Philo is the first extant author to associate the goodness of Plato's Demiurge with the Judaic God in creation.

[33] His work "That According to Plato the Universe Came into Being" (Lamprias Catalogue 66) apparently treated creation in time (1013E). See Harold Cherniss, *Plutarch's Moralia* 13.1 (LCL; Cambridge: Harvard University Press; London: William Heinemann: 1976), 177, note c.

[34] See Gregory E. Sterling, "Creatio Temporalis, Aeterna, vel Continua? An Analysis of the Thought of Philo of Alexandria," *SPhA* 4 (1992): 15–41, and David T. Runia, *Philo of Alexandria. On the Creation of the Cosmos according to Moses* (PACS 1; Leiden: Brill, 2001), 124–25, for Philo and Plato vs. Plutarch and Plato, 509. See also Charles A. Anderson, *Philo of Alexandria's Views of the Physical World* (WUNT 309; Tübingen: Mohr Siebeck, 2011), 38. Philo's use of the *Timaeus* has been treated by Gregory Sterling, "'The Image of God': Becoming Like God in Philo, Paul, and Early Christianity," in *Portraits of Jesus: Studies in Christology*, (ed. Susan E. Myers; WUNT 2. Reihe, 321; Tübigen: Mohr Siebeck, 2012), 157–74 (163–64).

[35] See especially Mauro Bonazzi, "Towards Transcendence: Philo and the Renewal of Platonism in the Early Imperial Age," in *Philo of Alexandria and Post-Aristotelian Philosophy*, (ed. Francesca Alesse, Studies in Philo of Alexandria 5; Leiden: Brill, 2008), 233–52 (236–39); Jan Opsomer, "M. Annius Ammonius, a Philosophical Profile," in *The Origins of the Platonic System: Platonisms of the Early Empire and Their Philosophical Contexts* (eds. Mauro Bonazzi and Jan Opsomer; Collections des Études Classiques 23; Leuven: Peeters and Société des Études Classiques, 2009), 123–86 (147–79); John Whittaker, "Ammonius *On the E at Delphi*," *CQ* 19 (1969): 185–92. Bonazzi notes that Philo apparently did not adopt any of Eudoros's most distinctive innovations (225).

between those of "Ammonius" here and of Plutarch elsewhere.[36] Recently, for example, Jan Opsomer has recognized this disparity.[37] Ammonius claims that the being of God exists only in one moment, the now (393A-B). The words suggest Philo on creation, but would seem to be negated by Plutarch's theory of creation in time in *On the Creation of the Soul in the Timaeus*. Strictly speaking, too, time, at least as we know it, begins with the organized cosmos. Before that, time in the *Timaeus* would have had to be measured by the disorderly motions of the pre-cosmic soul and by the succession of changes during creation. Harold Cherniss has demonstrated how Plutarch, in his "literal" interpretation, did violence to the *Timaeus*, distorting, omitting, and changing his venerated master's words. This was necessary to establish his theory of a precosmic soul receiving intellect and, thus, forming the orderly cosmos.[38] The theory of intellect establishing order also appears in Plutarch's ethical writings. Rather than the cosmological theory informing the ethical, more likely the contrary was true.

In Philo's case, he had to explain the six days of creation, against the religious tradition. Plutarch faced something similar. In the *Theogony*, the standard creation account by Hesiod, a fellow Boeotian, the world comes into being from the closest thing to nothing, the void. From the void come a series of divinities and generations of gods, and somehow unexplained, the creation of man (560–614). This creation account is temporal, but mostly a case of spontaneous generation, a "theogony," with a very obscure account of the creation of human beings, rather than creation by a Demiurge. Plutarch's "literal" interpretation, then, presented an account more similar to that of Genesis and of Philo than that in Greek religion. Plato's treatise, also, is not without ethical and religious overtones. His Demiurge (Craftsman), also called God, who creates the universe, instructs the souls coming into the world on how to conduct themselves justly in this life. If virtuous, they will return to their star and enjoy a blessed life. Those, on the other hand, who live unjustly will suffer continual reincarnation "until their reason overcomes the irrational in them" (42B–D).

---

[36] E.g., Frederick E. Brenk, "Plutarch's Middle-Platonic God: About to Enter (or Remake) the Academy," in Hirsch-Luipold, *Gott und die Götter bei Plutarch*, 27–50, (repr. in Frederick E. Brenk, *With Unperfumed Voice: Studies in Plutarch, in Greek Literature, Religion and Philosophy, and in the New Testament Background* (Potsdamer Altertumswissenschaftliche Beiträge 21; Stuttgart: Steiner, 2007), 121–43); idem, "'In Learned Conversation': Plutarch's Symposiac Literature and the Elusive Authorial Voice," in *Symposion and Philanthropia in Plutarch* (eds. José Ribeiro Ferreira, Delfim Leão, Manuel Tröster, and Paula Barata Dias; Coimbra: Centro de Estudos Clássicos e Humanísticos da Universidade de Coimbra, 2009), 51–61 (28–33).

[37] Opsomer, "M. Annius Ammonius," 172–79.

[38] Cherniss, *Plutarch's Moralia* 13.1:137–49, esp. 147.

Plato employs the term "God" for the Demiurge at least thirteen times in the *Timaeus*. Later authors attributed more to Plato than what appears in his published works. According to Aëtius (ca. first century C.E.), as reported in Stobaeus (probably fifth century C.E.), Plato affirmed that God is the One, single-natured and self-natured, monadic, true Being, the Good, intellect, and Father and Maker.[39] These formulations are close to those in Philo and Plutarch. In Stoicism, God is the intellect ruling the universe, but, as David Runia observes, in Philo, God and matter do not form two complementary principles, since matter is not a cause, but an object.[40]

The Demiurge in the *Timaeus* does not ask to be worshipped. Nor does Ammonius in his speech at the end of *The E at Delphi* explicitly ask anyone to worship his God.[41] Nonetheless, worship of this Middle-Platonic God seems implied, not so much as a natural extension of the cult of Apollo as a great leap forward.[42] In the apparently earliest layers of the Hebrew Bible, the Jewish god is distinguished by his name, YHWH, and later he could be identified as "the God of Abraham, Isaac, and Jacob." Some texts, such as Exodus 15:11: "Who is like you among the gods?," or Psalm 81 (82), where the Lord stands up in the assembly of the gods and makes them all redundant, apparently reflect an original henotheistic context.[43] Philo himself had some sweating to do to explain the words of Genesis: Then God said, 'Let us make humankind to our image…'." (Gen 1:26 [NETS]).[44] He quickly linked this verse to the monotheistic following verse ("to the image of God"). He, then, paraphrased it to read: [… as Moses] "says that man was created after the image of God and in his likeness" (κατ᾽εἰκόνα θεοῦ καὶ καθ᾽ ὁμοίωσιν, *Opif*. 69, cf. 72).[45] Philo interprets the plural to refer to the "powers," something he often mentions."[46] Oddly, in an untypical passage, Plutarch also refers to the "powers." He speaks of what appears to

---

[39] Stobaeus [Wachmuth 1884] 37; see Runia, "The Beginnings of the End," 282–83.

[40] See Runia, "The Beginnings of the End," 285.

[41] Opsomer, "M. Annius Ammonius," 159, speaks of this God as an object of worship (*E Delph.*, 393B), but Ammonius's words could simply mean "reverence."

[42] See the similar explanation of the nature of Osiris in *On Isis and Osiris* 352A, 372E–F. For differences from Plato's God, see Franco Ferrari, "Der Gott Plutarchs und der Gott Platons," in Hirsch-Luipold, *Gott und die Götter bei Plutarch*, 13–26.

[43] There are many similar texts, such as Psalm 28 (29) (1) (LXX) where the psalmist addresses "the sons of God," (*Elohim* in Hebrew).

[44] See Maren R. Niehoff, *Jewish Exegesis and Homeric Scholarship in Alexandria* (Cambridge: Cambridge University Press, 2011), 181–82.

[45] For Philo's uses of the term, see Sterling, "'The Image of God.'"

[46] Besides *Opif*. 72–76, see also *Conf*. 168–183; *Fug*. 68–72; *Mut*. 30–32; *QG* 1.52. For details see Runia, *Philo of Alexandria and the* Timaeus *of Plato*, 242–49 and idem, *Philo of Alexandria* On the Creation of the Cosmos, 236–44, esp. 237–38.

be a Middle Platonic monotheistic God, while the gods and spiritual beings of all nations are described as "powers": ... there is "one *logos* directing all, and one providence which watches over all people with subordinate powers (δυναμεῖς ὑπουγοὶ) set over all things" (377F–378A).

Much of Philo's *oeuvre* constitutes an exegetical commentary on the Pentateuch, a religious document which he often explains through Platonic allegory. In reality, as in other allegorical writers, the text serves as a point of departure for theological views. Plutarch's *On the Generation of the Soul in the Timaeus* was a philosophical commentary on a small part of the *Timaeus* and not typical of most of his extant work. His essay *On Isis and Osiris*, a commentary on Egyptian religious texts and practices, however, recalls Philo's work on the Pentateuch, in that the religious text is interpreted allegorically through philosophy.[47]

Like Philo, Plutarch preferred Platonic philosophical allegory to Stoic physical allegory, euhemerism, dualism, and the like. Ammonius's speech accordingly attempts to explain the nature of the Delphic god, or better, God behind the Delphic god, through Platonic allegory. He bypasses, however, the allegorical interpretations, including ones based on number mysticism of the earlier speakers to develop the ultimate solution. This is not primarily allegorical interpretation of the nature and cult of Apollo, though it plays with etymologies of the name "Apollon," and with the Delphic rites. Rather, he substitutes a Platonic monotheistic God for the traditional god, Apollo, at Delphi. Even this is more complicated, since Ammonius does not treat Apollo simply as the traditional Delphic god. He is also the Sun (sun), already a symbol of monotheism at the time and analogous to the Idea of the Good in Plato's *Republic* 6 (507B–509C).

Both Philo and Ammonius would have been influenced by Alexandrian Platonism. Though he had an illustrious career at Athens, Ammonius is attested by a late author to have come from Alexandria. There are suggestions of this in his teaching on God in the long final speech of *On the E at Delphi* (391E–394C).[48] The starting point is Plato's *Timaeus* 27D: "... that which becomes and has no share in being and that which always is and has no part in becoming." Ammonius, however, neglects the mediating role of soul. In his speech, human beings have no part in being, since everything mortal is always coming into and passing out of existence.[49] From embryo

---

[47] See Gregory E. Sterling, "Platonizing Moses: Philo and Middle Platonism," *SPhA* 5 (1993): 96–111, who compares Philo, Chaeremon of Alexandria, Plutarch's *On Isis and Osiris*, and Numenius.

[48] Esp., 392B–393E.

[49] Opsomer, "M. Annius Ammonius," 149. See also Opsomer, 155, for Ammonius's negative depiction of the world and existence in time.

to the grave one keeps becoming a different person, continually dying. Real being can only be predicated of God, who is eternal, without beginning or end, living in instant eternity ("always in the now").[50]

Rainer Hirsch-Luipold observes that for both Philo and Plutarch the ultimate truth is to be found in religion.[51] Philo, following *Exodus*, regards God's most authentic name as being (ὁ ὤν or τὸ ὄν).[52] Unlike Philo, when speaking of God, Ammonius only employs the neuter form of the participle for "being" (τὸ ὄντως ὄν or τὸ ὄν). Strictly speaking, the expression ὁ ὤν does not figure in Ammonius's speech."[53] However, by inference, the personal, masculine form (ὁ ὤν), as in Philo, would have been appropriate. God should be addressed as "[You] are (εἶ).", or better yet, as "[You] are one (εἶ ἕν)" (393B, cf. 394C). Ammonius, however, shifts between neuter and masculine forms for "one" or the "One." For example, at 393B his words are grammatically correct (… only when Being is like this [the Being of God] is it really being (ὄντως ὄν). But if the subject is God, not His Being, as one, we find the masculine: God "being one" (εἶς ὤν) (393A). Finally, Ammonius distinguishes between Apollo and the Sun. Nor is Ammonius simply elevating Apollo to a higher rank. The traditional god Apollo, or the Sun, is simply like an image in a dream compared to what God really is. Nor does he pit God against a formidable dualistic rival.[54]

As mentioned, "Ammonius" and Plutarch do not seem to be the same person, judging by what he says elsewhere. In his dialogues, a character rarely, if ever, is simply his mouthpiece.[55] Opsomer has carefully delineated where Ammonius's statements in the speech do not coincide well with Plutarch's views elsewhere. For example, he never identifies God with "the One," which is the centerpiece of Ammonius's doctrine, or like Philo, who calls God the One or even "greater than the One." Opsomer is especially disturbed by Ammonius's extreme contrast between the being of God, and phenomenal being, including us, which being constantly in flux does not deserve the name of being. He finds Ammonius's position extreme and un-

---

[50] For difficulties with Ammonius's description of eternity, which combines new ideas with traditional ones, see Opsomer, "M. Annius Ammonius," 157.

[51] Rainer Hirsch-Luipold, "Der eine Gott bei Philon von Alexandrien und Plutarch," in Hirsch-Luipold, *Gott und die Götter bei Plutarch*, 141–68 (143), discusses the personal aspect; for the importance of religion (144).

[52] See Runia, "The Beginnings of the End," 299.

[53] Opsomer, "M. Annius Ammonius," 169.

[54] The dualism was suggested by John Dillon, "Plutarch and God: Theodicy and Cosmogony in the Thought of Plutarch," in Frede and Laks, *Traditions of Theology*, 223–38 (226), but rejected by Opsomer, "M. Annius Ammonius," 161.

[55] See, e.g., Opsomer, "Ammonius *On the E at Delphi*," 172; Brenk, "'In Learned Conversation'," 56–57.

Plutarchan, representing all visible reality in flux, without any stability. He suggests, however, that both "Ammonius" and Philo probably exaggerated in order to sharpen the contrast with divine being.[56] Opsomer even wonders who is supposedly recalling the past conversations of the dialogue, if everyone is now a different person.

In fact, in his *Platonic Questions*, Plutarch refutes this very idea of an impassable gulf between the being of God and that of human beings. The topic of *Platonic Questions* 2, "God as Father and Maker" (1001B–C), concerns God as the father of the world soul, but by extension this applies to human beings, since we, too, share in His rationality. Moreover, the stress on human beings living in constant flux and the denial of real being to them (392C–E) runs counter to *On Tranquility of Mind* 473D–E, where this idea is firmly attacked. Even more importantly, as we have seen, God is closely identified with the One in Ammonius's speech.[57] In a parallel passage in *On Isis and Osiris*, Plutarch offers an allegorical interpretation of Osiris as God. Here, however, Osiris is the First God and associated or identified with the Good and Beautiful, but never explicitly with the One (374F–375A).[58]

Eudorus, considered to be an older contemporary of Philo, is often regarded as the father of Middle Platonism.[59] His major contribution here was the existence of a supreme One, also called the supreme God (ὁ ὑπεράνω θεός), beneath which was a second One (or Monad) balanced with a Dyad. Nevertheless, unlike Eudorus, neither Ammonius nor Plutarch ever speaks of two Gods or two Ones, a higher and a lower, or balances a One against a Dyad. In some later Platonists, we find two or more Gods, one of which remains aloof, while another, possibly an exact image of the

---

[56] Opsomer, "M. Annius Ammonius," 169, citing Pierluigi Donini, "Plutarco, Ammonio e l'Academia," in *Miscellanea Plutarchea* (eds. Frederick E. Brenk and Italo Gallo; Quaderni del Giornale Filologico Ferrarese 8; Ferrara: Università di Ferrara, 1986), 97–110 (103); repr. in *Pierluigi Donini. Commentary and Tradition: Aristotelianism, Platonism, and Post-Hellenistic Philosophy* (ed. Mauro Bonazzi; Commentaria in Aristotelem Graeca et Byzantina 4; Berlin: de Gruyter, 2011), 315–26 (320).

[57] *Pace* Opsomer, "M. Annius Ammonius," 174, *On the Generation of the Soul* 1027A, does not describe God as One.

[58] For this passage, see, e.g.. Hirsch-Luipold, "Der eine Gott," 147, 150, 154. Opsomer, "M. Annius Ammonius," 159, takes "one" here not as signifiying the highest principle, as in later Platonism, but as "that which is one."

[59] On his doctrine, see Bonazzi, "Towards Transcendence," 236–238; Whittaker, "Ammonius *On the E at Delphi*," (189); (Simpl. *In Phys.* 181.7–30 = Claudio Mazzarelli, "Raccolta e interpretazione delle testimonianze e dei frammenti del medioplatonico Eudoro di Alessandria," *Rivista di Filosofia Neo-Scolastica* 77 (1985): 197–209 and 535–55, Eudoros T 3–5.

First God, and sometimes called the Demiurge, is engaged in creation and providence.[60] Neither Ammonius nor Plutarch even hint at this scheme.

Even in such a major and sublime speech at the end of a dialogue, then, Plutarch could not have endorsed all of Ammonius's views. He may, instead, have decided to suggest Ammonius's own teaching, while possibly introducing some strands of Alexandrian Platonism, including something from Eudorus. In contrast, though, with Philo and Plutarch, Eudorus's "Gods" are more principles than real or personal Gods. In any case, Eudorus, Philo, Ammonius, and Plutarch to some extent all inhaled the same philosophical and intellectual *avant-garde* air of Alexandrian Platonism. Possibly Ammonius even studied under a disciple of Eudorus. Unfortunately, Eudorus remains elusive, and elsewhere in Plutarch's works, Ammonius's views are not so extreme. The divergence suggests that, in *On the E at Delphi*, "Ammonius" is not a mirror image of Ammonius.[61]

Most striking are the parallels which John Whittaker found between Philo and "Ammonius," parallels which he attributed to Alexandrian Platonism. Opsomer, though, has taken the air out of some of Whittaker's assertions, in particular, rejecting the idea that Philo, who is never mentioned by Plutarch, influenced either him or Ammonius. Still, Opsomer notes that in Philo's *On Joseph* 126–29, we find radical flux, human existence without real being (§126), and the irrationality of fearing death, since we have already been many persons, opinions "Ammonius" would have liked.[62] Also, both Philo and "Ammonius" sharply contrast the being or becoming of this world with the being of God, flirting with the beginnings of negative theology, the unknowability of God.[63] Francesca Calabi suggests that in Philo, nonetheless, we are not devoid of all knowledge of God. Something is possible through contemplation of the world, contact with the *logos* and the powers, through revelation, practicing virtue, a noetic vision, direct

---

[60] For divergence from Eudoros, see Opsomer, "M. Annius Ammonius," 162–63, 170–72.

[61] See now Tobias Thum, *Plutarchs Dialog* De E apud Delphos. Studien und Texte zu Antike und Christentum 80 (Tübingen: Mohr Siebeck, 2013), 4–11, who attempts to minimize the importance and religiosity of Ammonius's speech; and the commentary of Hendrik Obsieger, *Plutarch: De E apud Delphos: Über das Epsilon am Apolltempel in Delphi.* Palingenesia 101 (Stuttgart: Steiner, 2013).

[62] Opsomer, "M. Annius Ammonius," 165–69, for *On Joseph* (126–28). Unlike Whittaker, however, Opsomer sees the Neopythagorean ideas in Ammonius's speech as not independent of Platonism (168).

[63] In Philo, God is incomprehensible (ἀκατάληπτος), unnameable (ἀκατανόμαστος), and unspeakable (ἄρρητος) (see e.g. Runia, "The Beginnings of the End," 304; Calabi, *God's Acting*, 39–72, esp. 39, 42–48). We can, however, deduce God's goodness from revelation (Radice, "Philo's Theology," 126).

evidence, a direct and unexpected relationship, and an initiation.[64] Similarly, Plutarch, though asking for caution in questions regarding the divine, as did the Academy in general, never speaks of the unknowability of God.

The parallels or contrasts between Philo's theology and that of the *E. Delph.* are not, however, the only issue here. The implications for religious monotheism are important. Opsomer seems to treat Ammonius's God as a glorified Apollo.[65] Rather, as argued above, "Apollo" is the name and figure behind which the real God can be found. Apollo (*A-pollon = a-polla*) is the best name for God, since allegorically it expresses his unicity or identification with Plato's One. In the dialogue, Plutarch was not writing primarily as a philosopher as in *On the Generation of the Soul in the* Timaeus. His "Ammonius" is a theologian. Moreover, as a priest of Apollo at Delphi, Plutarch had a vested interest in the cult, not just in monotheism. Even the God of "Ammonius" is not merely the Demiurge of the *Timaeus*. Rather, much like Philo, "Ammonius" attempts to explain the nature of God to educated persons acquainted with their religious traditions. His real contribution touches not so much upon his concept of Apollo, as that of one masked by Apollo. This is a much higher God, like the Jewish one, creator of the universe, exercising providence over His creation. He is also the fullness of being and, at least for "Ammonius," is unique, the only God, or the One, without parts, who deserves worship from all. The *mise-en-scène*, Delphi, contributes an aura of religion to what otherwise might seem to be mere philosophical monotheism. Worship of the traditional Apollo beside this God seemingly creates a contradiction between monotheism and polytheism, but only if our definition excludes worship of other gods, even when they are infinitely inferior to the real God. This puts Philo and Plutarch in a much closer relationship than just some sort of Alexandrian philosophical heritage. Both, on similar even if different paths, created theologies for their faiths, one essentially monotheistic, the other essentially polytheistic, theologies heavily inspired by Plato.

Arrupe House Jesuit Community
Milwaukee, USA

---

[64] Calabi, *God's Acting*, 39 and notes 2–10.
[65] Opsomer, "M. Annius Ammonius," 161.

The Studia Philonica Annual 26 (2014) 93–97

SPECIAL SECTION

PHILO'S HELLENISTIC AND HELLENISTIC JEWISH SOURCES

INTRODUCTION

GREGORY E. STERLING

Philo's knowledge of both Jewish and Hellenistic literature and thought were recognized by ancients and praised. Josephus, our earliest witness, described Philo as "a man with the highest reputation, the brother of Alexander the alabarch, and proven in philosophy" (φιλοσοφίας οὐκ ἄπειρος).[1] Others were more expansive and generous. Eusebius, the bishop of Caesarea, claimed that Philo was "a man of the highest distinction not only among us, but among pagans who pursue education." He went on to praise Philo for his control of both Jewish and Hellenistic literature. The bishop thought "the extent and the quality of his labor concerning the divine and ancestral learning is evident to all." He had the same judgment about Philo's control of Hellenistic thought: "it is not necessary to say anything about his standing in philosophical thought and the liberal arts of the pagan world, since he is reported to have surpassed all of his contemporaries, particularly in his zeal for the school of thought (ἀγωγή) of Plato and Pythagoras."[2] Eusebius was not alone in praising Philo's learning. It became a commonplace among early Christian writers who made observations about him:

---

[1] Josephus, *A.J.* 18.259. See also Eusebius, *Hist. eccl.* 2.5.4. The testimonia for Philo were collected by Leopold Cohn and conveniently printed in Leopold Cohn and Paul Wendland, *Philonis Alexandrini opera quae supersunt* (7 vols.; Berlin: Georg Reimerus, 1896–1930), 1:lxxxxv–cxiii. Hereafter abbreviated PCW. For an analysis of the titles and epithets see David T. Runia, "Philonic Nomenclature," *SPhA* 6 (1994): 1–27.

[2] Eusebius, *Hist. eccl.* 2.4.2–3.

Pseudo-Justin,[3] Pseudo-Chrysostom,[4] Jerome,[5] Augustine,[6] Cassiodorus,[7] Philo's Armenian translator,[8] and John of Damascus[9] all noted his learning or wisdom.

Eusebius's praise of Philo's control of his ancestral traditions cannot be questioned: Philo knew the Jewish Scriptures in Greek, especially the Pentateuch which functioned *de facto* as his touchstone. He cited the texts that we call Scripture 1,161 times in his writings[10] and cited or alluded to these texts a total of 8,462 times.[11] Of these citations and allusions, 97% were to the Pentateuch.[12] His ability to connect primary and secondary or tertiary lemmata in the Allegorical Commentary through catchwords or through thematic associations suggests that he knew the text incredibly well.[13] He may well have committed most of it to memory.

The biblical commentator also knew previous exegetical traditions.[14] He mentioned literal[15] and allegorical interpreters[16] numerous times in his corpus. The inconcinnities and tensions within his writings may also suggest

---

[3] Pseudo-Justin, *Cohortatio ad Gentiles* 9.2; 13.4.

[4] Pseudo-Chrysostom, *In sanctum Pascha sermo* 7.2; and the *Chronicon Paschale* (PG 92.69A).

[5] Jerome, *Jov.* 2.14; *Epist.* 29.7.1.

[6] Augustine, *Faust.* 12.39

[7] Cassiodorus, *Inst. Div. Litt.* (PL 70.1117B).

[8] Armenian translator, *Praef. in libr. Philonis De prov.* vii; and the Armenian translator of Eusebius, *Chron.* p. 213. Cf. also Eusebius, *Praep. ev.* 13.18.12.

[9] John of Damascus, *Prol. in Sac. Par.* (PG 95.1040B).

[10] Based on the index of Ioannes Leisegang, PCW 7.1:29–43.

[11] Based on the references in Jean Allenbach, et al., *Biblia patristica, Supplément: Philon d'Alexandrie* (Paris: Centre national de la recherche scientifique, 1982). I have supplied the count.

[12] For specific counts see Gregory E. Sterling, "When the Beginning Is the End: The Place of Genesis in the Commentaries of Philo," in *The Book of Genesis: Composition, Reception, and Interpretation* (ed. Craig A. Evans, Joel N. Lohr, and David L. Petersen; VTSup 152; Leiden: Brill, 2012), 427–46, esp. 437–38. See also Franz Stuhlhofer, *Der Gebrauch der Bibel von Jesus bis Euseb: Eine Statistische Untersuchung zur Kanonsgeschichte* (Monographien und Studienbücher; Wuppertal: Brockhaus, 1988), 120–123.

[13] On Philo's use of catchwords see David T. Runia, "The Structure of Philo's Allegorical Treatise *De agricultura*," SPhA 22 (2010): 87–110, esp. 94–96.

[14] On the tradition see my overview, "Philosophy as the Handmaid of Wisdom: Philosophy in the Exegetical Traditions of Alexandrian Jews," in *Philosophy in Ancient Literature* (ed. Rainer Hirsch-Luipold, Herwig Görgemanns, and Michael von Albrecht; STAC 51; Tübingen: Mohr Siebeck, 2009), 67–98.

[15] Montgomery J. Schroyer, "Alexandrian Jewish Literalists," *JBL* 55 (1936): 261–84 and David M. Hay, "References to Other Exegetes," in *Both Literal and Allegorical: Studies in Philo of Alexandria's Questions and Answers on Genesis and Exodus* (ed., David M. Hay; BJS 232; Atlanta: Scholars Press, 1991), 81–97.

[16] David M. Hay, "Philo's References to Other Allegorists," *SPh* 6 (1979–1980): 41–75, collected seventy-four references in the Philonic corpus.

the presence of earlier interpretative traditions. Unfortunately, he did not name Jewish predecessors—but neither did Josephus. In the early seventies of the previous century a group of scholars launched an effort to work through Philo's writings to unravel the exegetical traditions that he had inherited.[17] Unfortunately, the project never really materialized. Since then, but unrelated to the enterprise, one fine independent monograph[18] and another very ambitious and creative but—in my mind—problematic work have appeared.[19] The state of scholarship continues to recognize the existence of earlier and contemporary exegetical work, but lacks a consensus about how it unfolded.

Philo's knowledge of his ancestral scriptures and their interpretation was, however, only a part of his working knowledge of literature and thought. Eusebius also praised him—with hyperbolic flourish—for his knowledge of philosophy and the liberal arts.

Philo's indebtedness to Hellenistic philosophical thought is indisputable; however, the nature of his indebtedness and the use of this thought has been more difficult to assess.[20] Philo's use of Platonic thought is unambiguous. He mentioned Plato explicitly eleven times while introducing a citation,[21] cited eight different Platonic treatises a total of twenty-seven times,[22] and alluded to his writings at least 316 times.[23] This, however, hardly captures his appropriation of Platonism. He drew from Plato frequently

---

[17] Robert G. Hamerton-Kelly, "Sources and Traditions in Philo Judaeus: Prolegomena to an Analysis of His Writings," *SPh* 1 (1972): 3–26; Burton L. Mack, "Exegetical Traditions in Alexandrian Judaism: A Program for the Analysis of the Philonic Corpus," *SPh* 3 (1974–1975): 71–115; and idem, "Weisheit und Allegorie bei Philo von Alexandrien," *SPh* 5 (1978): 57–105.

[18] Thomas H. Tobin, *The Creation of Man: Philo and the History of Interpretation* (CBQMS 14; Washington, DC: Catholic Biblical Association, 1983).

[19] Richard Goulet, *La philosophie de Moïse: Essai de reconstitution d'un commentaire philosophique préphilonien de Pentateuque* (Histoire des Doctrines de l'Antiquité Classique 11; Paris: J. Vrin, 1987). For a critique see David T. Runia, review of *La philosophie de Moïse, JTS* 40 (1989): 590–602.

[20] For a survey, see Gregory E. Sterling, "'The Jewish Philosophy': Reading Moses via Hellenistic Philosophy according to Philo," in *Handbook on Philo* (ed. Torrey Seland; Grand Rapids: Eerdmans, forthcoming).

[21] Philo, *Opif.* 119, 133; *Prob.* 13; *Contempl.* 57; *Aet.* 13, 14, 16, 27, 38, 52, 141.

[22] See my list in "'The Jewish Philosophy'" for details. I drew from David T. Runia, "The Text of the Platonic Citations in Philo of Alexandria," in *Studies in Plato and the Platonic Tradition: Essays Presented to John Whittaker* (ed. Mark Joyal; Aldershot, Hampshire: Ashgate, 1997), 261–291.

[23] The count is based on the data collected by David Lincicum, "A Preliminary Index to Philo's Non-Biblical Citations and Allusions," *SPhA* 25 (2013): 139–67, esp. 156–59.

and extensively in places.[24] The same kind of data can be supplied for the Stoics, only here the evidence becomes more debatable. For example, Philo referred to a number of Stoic philosophers by name: Zeno,[25] Cleanthes,[26] Chrysippus,[27] Diogenes of Babylon,[28] Boethus of Sidon,[29] and Panaetius— all in the treatise *On the Eternity of the Cosmos*.[30] Johannes von Arnim used Philo extensively as a source in his *Stoicorum veterum fragmenta*, citing him 198 times;[31] however, Tony Long and David Sedley used him only sparingly for *The Hellenistic Philosophers*, citing him only ten times.[32] Long was critical of Philo's knowledge of Stoic philosophy and thought other sources more reliable, e.g., Cicero.[33] The point is that even when we are confident that Philo knew traditions, we need to assess how well he knew them and how he used them. There remains much research to be done in this area.

We have less of an understanding of Philo's knowledge of poetry and other fields. Although he cited Homer twenty-five times and alluded to him another forty-eight times,[34] studies on Philo's use of Homer have been limited. We have a fine treatment of the scholia[35] and two recent essays on Philo's use of Homer more broadly.[36] There is still a good deal to do. We do

---

[24] Two of the justly famous treatments are Anita Méasson, *Du char ailé de Zeus à l'Arche d'Alliance: Images et mythes platoniciens chez Philon d'Alexandrie* (Paris: Études Augustiniennes, 1986) and David T. Runia, *Philo of Alexandria and the* Timaeus *of Plato* (PhilAnt 44; Leiden: Brill, 1986).

[25] Philo, *Prob.* 53, 57, 97, 160. The last two texts use the adjectival form of the name.

[26] Philo, *Aet.* 90.

[27] Philo, *Aet.* 48, 90, 94.

[28] Philo, *Aet.* 77.

[29] Philo, *Aet.* 76, 78.

[30] Philo, *Aet.* 76.

[31] Ioannes von Arnim, *Stoicorum veterum fragmenta* (4 vols.; Leipzig: Teubner, 1905–1924).

[32] Anthony A. Long and David N. Sedley, *The Hellenistic Philosophers* (2 vols.; Cambridge: Cambridge University Press, 1987), nos. 28P, 46M, 46P, 47R, 47P, 47Q, 52A, 53P, 59H, and 67N.

[33] Anthony A. Long, "Philo on Stoic Physics," in *Philo of Alexandria and Post-Aristotelian Philosophy* (ed. Francesca Alesse; Studies in Philo of Alexandria 5; Leiden: Brill, 2008), 121–40.

[34] Both counts based on Lincicum, "A Preliminary Index to Philo's Non-Biblical Citations and Allusions," 155.

[35] Maren R. Niehoff, *Jewish Exegesis and Homeric Scholarship in Alexandria* (Cambridge: Cambridge University Press, 2011).

[36] Maren R. Niehoff, "Philo and Plutarch on Homer," in *Homer and the Bible in the Eyes of Ancient Interpreters* (ed. Maren R. Niehoff; Jerusalem Studies in Religion and Culture 16; Leiden: Brill, 2012), 127–49 and Katell Berthelot, "Philon d'Alexandrie, lecteur d'Homère: quelques elements de réflexion," in *Prolongements et renouvellements de la tradition classique* (ed. Anne Balansard, Gilles Dorival, Mireille Loubet; Textes et documents de la Méditerranée antique et mediéval; Aix-en-Provence: Université de Provence, 2011), 145–57. Prior

have a treatment of drama in Philo,[37] but again the field is hardly exhausted. There is a need for more detailed treatments of specific dramatists such as Euripides.

It was in recognition of these lacunae that the Philo of Alexandria program unit in the Society of Biblical Literature devoted two sessions of the 2013 annual meeting to Philo's Sources.[38] Eight scholars presented papers on various aspects of Philo's sources. One session concentrated on philosophical sources and the other on literary sources. The editors decided to devote a special section of the *SPhA* to essays that focused on the literary sources. As is always the case, this excluded some fine papers that hopefully will appear elsewhere. David Lincicum built on the index that he had compiled to address the issue of Philo's library.[39] What had Philo read? What did he have available to him? I provided the first full-length treatment of Philo's relationship to the most complete tragedy preserved from the Hellenistic world, Ezekiel's *Exagoge*. I argued that Philo knew and was influenced by his Jewish predecessor's play in important ways. Pura Nieto Hernández tackled the question of Philo's use of poetry in a very creative paper. She shows that Philo not only knew and valued archaic and classical poetry, but demonstrated how he adapted poetic language in his own style. Finally, it would not be right to ignore one of the greatest literary artists and thinkers of antiquity. Michael Cover explored the use of a famous Platonic myth in Philo to investigate the question of Philo's vision of God. He wrestles with the apparently divergent statements in Philo that sometimes appear to allow for a vision of the Existent and, at other times, deny a direct vision by contextualizing them. We offer these essays with the hope not that they will end discussions on these areas of research, but that they will stimulate further research and discussion.

Yale Divinity School

---

to these two studies we only had Robert Lamberton, *Homer the Theologian: Neoplatonist Allegorical Reading and the Growth of the Epic Tradition* (The Transformation of the Classical Heritage 9; Berkeley: University of California Press, 1986), 44–54, that addresses the allegorical interpretation of Homer, and W. B. McNeill, "Homer Poetry in Philo of Alexandria" (M.A. thesis, University of Miami, 1993).

[37] Erkki Koskenniemi, "Philo and Classical Drama," in *Ancient Israel, Judaism, and Christianity in Contemporary Perspective: Essays in Memory of Karl-Johan Illman* (ed. Jacob Neusner, Allan J. Avery Peck, Antii Laato, Risto Nurmela, and Karl-Gustav Sandelin; Studies in Judaism; Lanham, MD: University Press of America, 2006), 137–151.

[38] I want to express my gratitude to the chairs of the unit for their work and collaboration: Ellen Birnbaum and Ron Cox. A special word of thanks is also due to the Associate Editor and former co-chair of the program unit, Sarah Pearce who worked on this special section from the outset through the publication of this special section.

[39] Lincicum, "A Preliminary Index to Philo's Non-Biblical Citations and Allusions."

The Studia Philonica Annual 26 (2014) 99–114

PHILO'S LIBRARY

DAVID LINCICUM

Philo's explicit engagement with non-biblical authors has been a topic of enduring interest in Philonic scholarship. This has often been pursued by way of studying Philo's use of a particular author or treatise,[1] or his treatment of a philosophical *topos*. Less often does one encounter discussion of two related questions: how should we characterize the distribution and frequency of his quotations; and how might Philo have accessed those sources that he quotes? Following on from the publication of "A Preliminary Index to Philo's Non-Biblical Citations and Allusions" in a previous issue of *The Studia Philonica Annual*,[2] this article analyses the data presented there with a view to sketching an answer to those questions. In particular, the present study addresses Philonic source material in a more quantitative and formal manner than in a qualitative and material one, and asks about a means of access that will occasionally require informed historical reconstruction in lieu of direct proof. Nevertheless, considering the variety of ways in which Philo may have encountered ancient texts serves to guard against the anachronism of unreflectively viewing Philo as a modern user of books.

1. *The distribution and frequency of Philo's citations of and allusions to non-biblical literature*

First, then, we turn to examine the frequency of Philo's citations of non-biblical sources by author. Table 1 summarizes this evidence. Quotations are listed first and allusions parenthetically afterward. The case is not equally strong for an allusion in each instance, so the numbers may mask the fact that sometimes a number of proposed allusions may not alone add up to definitive proof of Philo's literary knowledge of the author in question. In the index, following the lead of Philo's learned translators,

---

[1] In many ways the standard for this important task remains the magisterial study by David T. Runia, *Philo of Alexandria and the* Timaeus *of Plato* (PhilAnt 44; Leiden: Brill, 1986).

[2] David Lincicum, "A Preliminary Index to Philo's Non-Biblical Citations and Allusions," *SPhA* 25 (2013): 139–68.

citations are considered clear verbal engagements that are marked by a citation formula, syntactical disjunction from their context, or significant verbatim repetition of a predecessor text. The difference between a quotation, an allusion, and an echo is a matter of ongoing debate in current discussion. I have operated on the basis of a generous conception of echo and allusion (without distinguishing between them) as indicating a textual recollection of lower volume than a citation, although I have mostly attempted to avoid listing references that merely supply a parallel idea, philosophical commonplace or similar lexical usage. The difficulty of considering allusions to be proof of literary knowledge can be illustrated by considering the proposed allusions to Herodotus in this list, in which it is difficult to tell whether certain turns of phrase have simply come to Philo in a process of secondary orality and may ultimately stem from the historian, whether he has read Herodotus once upon a time and recalls vestiges of his language occasionally, or whether some other relationship between the two obtained.[3] At the other end of the spectrum, however, it is equally clear that Philo treats a number of authors as "canonical" sources, important voices to whom he feels himself bound and to whom he turns again and again to express his thoughts. Here one might point to the dramatists Aeschylus, Euripides, Menander and perhaps Sophocles; the poets Pindar, Hesiod and especially Homer; Hippocrates the physician; and the philosophers Aristotle, Chrysippus, Empedocles, Heraclitus, Posidonius, Zeno and, above all, Plato.[4] As a whole, this comes as no surprise to the student of Philo, though it may be interesting to note some of the relative frequencies of his citations. Of the 133 citations represented in Table 1, just four authors make up well over half: Euripides accounts for 16 (12%), Heraclitus for 26 (20%), Homer for 24 (18%) and Plato for 18 (14%). Of the 531 allusions, Plato accounts for a staggering 315 (59%), though Aristotle (36 times), Euripides (8 times), Heraclitus (20 times), and Homer (48 times) are also strongly represented. It is also striking that, for example, he often seems to allude to positions taken by Aristotle, and mentions him by name four times (all in a single context in *Aet.* 10, 12, 16, 18) but does not seem to offer clear verbatim quotations from his writings. This gives the impression that Philo knows his positions on matters philosophical without an easy recourse to his actual words, perhaps through the commentary tradition.

[3] Herodotus, *Hist.* 1.8 in *Spec.* 4.60; 1.109 in *Flacc.* 85; 2.36 in *Spec.* 1.2; 2.65–74 in *Decal.* 77; 3.119 in *Flacc.* 85; 4.87 in *Mos.* 1.23; 5.72 in *Flacc.* 85. For Philo's knowledge of a wide variety of ancient authors, in the context of ancient *paideia*, see Monique Alexandre, "La culture profane chez Philon," in *Philon d'Alexandrie. Lyon, 11–15 Septembre 1966* (Paris: Éditions du Centre National de la Recherche Scientifique, 1967), 105–129, esp. 107–111.

[4] See "A Preliminary Index" for details.

Table 1: Frequency of quotation and allusion for non-biblical authors

Author	Quotations (Allusions)
Aeschylus	6 (9)
Aëtius	0 (7)
Anaxagoras	0 (5)
Anaxarchus	1 (0)
Anaximander	0 (1)
Antisthenes	0 (3)
Aristophanes	0 (2)
Aristotle	0 (36)
Athenaeus	0 (1)
Callimachus	0 (2)
Chrysippus	1 (3)
Cicero	0 (6)
Cleanthes	0 (1)
Critolaus	0 (2)
Democritus	0 (1)
Demosthenes	0 (6)
Diodorus Siculus	0 (3)
Empedocles	3 (3)
Epicharmus	1 (1)
(Ps.-) Epicharmus	0 (1)
Eratosthenes	1 (0)
Euripides	16 (8)
Heraclitus	26 (20)
Herodotus	1 (6)
Hesiod	5 (6)
Hippocrates	2 (2)
Homer	24 (48)
Ion?	1 (0)
Letter of Aristeas	0 (1)
Menander	3 (1)
Philolaus?	1 (0)
Pindar	3 (3)
Plato	18 (315)
Posidonius	5 (1)
Simonides	1 (0)
Solon	1 (0)
Sophocles	1 (7)
Thucydides	0 (3)
Theocritus	0 (2)
Theognis	1 (0)
Theophrastus	1 (1)
Xenophon	0 (7)
Xenophanes	0 (2)
Zeno	2 (5)

If we turn to ask about the individual works most often cited by Philo, we find the results portrayed in Table 2. This table is more useful for evidence about some authors than for others. Clearly the designation *"Fragmenta"* often encompasses multiple works, and the numbers presented in the table should be adjusted to take into consideration those cases where we can ascribe fragments to known works.[5] But our uncertainty as to the precise works from which at least some of these quotations derive injects an element of uncertainty and provisionality into this presentation. For example, Philo's intensive engagement with Heraclitus may reflect knowledge of the single work *On Nature*, while the listing of Aeschylus or Euripides' *Fragmenta* in this table obscures a broader engagement with a number of plays that today are known fragmentarily.[6] With this in mind, it is interesting to see how Philo's preferences unfold. As was generally the case in antiquity, Philo prefers the *Iliad* to the *Odyssey*, while he devotes roughly equal treatment to each of the Hesiodic works he cites. His engagements with plays and poetry are on the whole selective raids for *bon mots* ranging widely over a range of works, rather than sustained exegetical or thematic treatments of single works, and this is entirely as one would expect. Finally, it is in keeping with Philo's approach to Plato's works that the *Timaeus* is by far the most favoured Platonic work, followed by the *Phaedrus* and *Theaetetus*, and then a broad number of citations and allusions to his other works.

---

[5] The difficulties posed by fragments of literary texts can be well illustrated for Philonists by calling to mind James R. Royse's work on fragments erroneously attributed to Philo: see Royse, *The Spurious Texts of Philo of Alexandria: A Study of Textual Transmission and Corruption, with Indexes to the Major Collections of Greek Fragments* (ALGHJ 22; Leiden: Brill, 1991), esp. 1–58.

[6] Note the following attributions of fragments cited by Philo. Of Aeschylus, frg. 20* = *Argo*; frg. 139 = *Myrmidons*; frg. 159 and 162 = *Niobe*, though frg. 344, 345, 394 and 402 are all uncertain. Of Euripides, frg. 200.3–4 = *Antiope*; frg. 275.3–4 = *Auge*; fr. 420 = *Ino*; frg. 484 = *Wise Melanippe*; frg. 687–691 = *Syleus*; frg. 839 = *Chrysippus*, and frg. 893, 911, 954 and 958 are all uncertain. Of Menander, frg. 312 = *Paidion*, and frg. 786 is uncertain. Of Pindar, both frg. 33c (Snell and Maehler) and frg. 292 (Bowra) are unplaceable. Finally, of Sophocles, frg. 755, 910 and 945 are all uncertain.

Table 2: Quotations and allusions to individual works by major authors
(those quoted explicitly at least once)[7]

Aeschylus	*Eumenides*	0 (1)
Aeschylus	*Prometheus Vinctus*	0 (1)
Aeschylus	*Fragmenta*	6 (9)
Empedocles	*Fragmenta*	3 (3)
Euripides	*Hecuba*	1 (0)
Euripides	*Hippolytus*	0 (2)
Euripides	*Iphigenia Aulidensis*	0 (2)
Euripides	*Phoenissae*	1 (0)
Euripides	*Fragmenta*	15 (4)
Heraclitus	*Fragmenta*	26 (20)
Hesiod	*Works and Days*	2 (3)
Hesiod	*Theognony*	3 (3)
Homer	*Iliad*	15 (29)
Homer	*Odyssey*	10 (19)
Menander	*Fragmenta*	3 (1)
Pindar	*Nemean Odes*	0 (1)
Pindar	*Pythian Odes*	0 (1)
Pindar	*Paeans*	1 (1)
Pindar	*Fragmenta*	2 (0)
Plato	*Apology*	0 (2)
Plato	*Cratylus*	0 (11)
Plato	*Crito*	0 (1)
Plato	*Epistles*	0 (1)
Plato	*Eryxias*	0 (1)
Plato	*Gorgias*	0 (12)
Plato	*Ion*	0 (3)
Plato	*Laws*	0 (22)
Plato	*Meno*	0 (2)
Plato	*Menexenus*	1 (1)
Plato	*Phaedo*	0 (16)
Plato	*Phaedrus*	2 (61)
Plato	*Philebus*	0 (7)
Plato	*Politicus*	0 (1)
Plato	*Parmenides*	0 (1)
Plato	*Protagoras*	0 (1)
Plato	*Republic*	0 (25)
Plato	*Symposium*	1 (9)
Plato	*Sophist*	1 (3)
Plato	*Theaetetus*	3 (16)
Plato	*Timaeus*	11 (120)
Posidonius	*Fragmenta*	5 (0)
Sophocles	*Oedipus Coloneus*	0 (1)
Sophocles	*Fragmenta*	1 (6)
Zeno	*Fragmenta*	2 (5)

[7] This excludes particularly Aristotle, who has 36 allusions listed in the index, but no citations. The allusions range widely over his corpus, with concentrations in the *Nicomachean Ethics* and the *Rhetoric*.

All of this is perhaps interesting in its quantification of discrete textual engagements, but unlikely to be surprising to those familiar with Philo's works and his citation practices. These sources and authors might therefore be said to indicate some of the most important features of Philo's mental "encyclopedia," to borrow Umberto Eco's metaphor.[8]

2. *From Encyclopedia to Library: Philo and his books*

In the second part of this study, we turn now to consider whether one can move from "encyclopedia" to "library." That is, can we say anything about the ways in which Philo was likely to have accessed these works?

In his article, "'The School of Sacred Laws': The Social Setting of Philo's Treatises,"[9] Gregory E. Sterling makes a convincing case for seeing Philo as operating a kind of school in his own home or a purposed space. He makes the point that reading important figures is an activity that features in our literary reports about philosophical schools,[10] and goes on to suggest, "If our analysis is sound, then Philo must have worked with a library in which his own works became an indispensable part. This would be in keeping with the practices of philosophers who regularly had libraries," citing evidence for Aristotle, Philodemus, Plotinus and Proclus.[11] I would like to indulge in some informed speculation about what else might have belonged in that library, by drawing on our evidence for ancient private book collections and attempting a rough correlation with citation frequencies.[12] Clearly Philo's own works, the Greek Pentateuch and perhaps

---

[8] E.g., Umberto Eco, "Metaphor, Dictionary, and Encyclopedia," *New Literary History* 15.2 (1984): 255–271; cf. Paolo Desogus, "The Encyclopedia in Umberto Eco's Semiotics," *Semiotica* 192 (2012): 501–521.

[9] Gregory E. Sterling, "'The School of Sacred Laws': The Social Setting of Philo's Treatises," *VC* 53 (1999): 148–64.

[10] Ibid, 159 and n. 62.

[11] Ibid, 160 and n. 67. The suggestion that Philo's works were collected and subsequently passed to Christian Alexandrian circles has been advanced (though differing in the manner of transmission envisaged) by, e.g., D. Barthélemy, "Est-ce Hoshaya Rabba qui censura le 'Commentaire Allégorique'?" in idem, *Études d'histoire du texte de l'Ancien Testament* (OBO 21; Göttingen: Vandenhoeck & Ruprecht; Fribourg: Éditions Universitaires, 1978 [orig. 1967]), 140–73, 390–91; David T. Runia, *Philo in Early Christian Literature: A Survey* (CRINT; Assen: Van Gorcum, 1993), 22–24; Annewies van den Hoek, "The 'Catechetical' School of Early Christian Alexandria and Its Philonic Heritage," *HTR* 90.1 (1997): 59–87, esp. 84–85; and Andrew Carriker, *The Library of Eusebius of Caesarea* (VCSup 67; Leiden: Brill, 2003), 164–77.

[12] Erkki Koskenniemi, "Philo and Greek Poets," *JSJ* 41 (2010): 301–322, here 304, also suggests that "undoubtedly Philo had a private library, and it is not too bold to claim that

some other scrolls of the Greek scriptures, would have featured in the Philonic collection,[13] but I will here look beyond these works to say a bit about the Graeco-Roman possibilities in particular.

First, a few limiting factors to bear in mind. We find a near total silence in Philo's works when it comes to this question. We lack the personal letters that supply information about acquiring books and building a library that we find in Cicero's correspondence,[14] nor do we find Philo off-handedly referring to his copy (ἀντίγραφον) of a literary work,[15] much less anything approximating a catalogue of books in his possession.

We should, moreover, acknowledge a variety of potential sources for Philo's quotations and major allusions to Graeco-Roman authors, and not make the anachronistic assumption that recourse to a written continuous text was a necessary precondition for citation. One can imagine the following potential modes of encounter with a literary text:

1) *Lines committed to memory during the course of education*

Philo explicitly mentions the role that reading and "inquiry into the writings of the poets" (τὴν ἱστορίαν τῶν παρὰ ποιηταῖς) played in his education in Grammar (*Congr.* 74–76), and it is likely that his education would have supplied him with an enduring familiarity with some classics of Graeco-Roman culture. In fact, if we follow Raffaella Cribiore and Teresa Morgan in looking at the significant authors that feature in literary school exercises in the papyri, we find a recurrent presence of authors like Aeschylus (3x), Euripides (20x), Hesiod (2x), Homer and Homerica (*Iliad* 33x; *Odyssey* 6x; and Homerica 33x); Isocrates (8x); Menander (26x); Sophocles (1x) and Theognis (2x).[16] Especially Homer has a consistent presence over a long period of time in school exercises, as do Euripides and

---

he enjoyed its treasures with his friends, that is, learned fellow Jews and Gentiles leaning to Judaism."

[13] On the question of private ownership of books, see below.

[14] On which, see esp. T. Keith Dix, "'Beware of promising your library to anyone': Assembling a Private Library at Rome," in *Ancient Libraries* (eds. Jason König, Katarina Oikonomopolou, and Greg Woolf; Cambridge: Cambridge University Press, 2013), 209–234.

[15] He only uses the term once, in *Legat.* 315, to refer to a copy of a letter.

[16] Raffaella Cribiore, "Literary School Exercises," *ZPE* 116 (1997): 53–60 (with corrigenda in *ZPE* 117 [1997]: 162); cf. eadem, *Writing, Teachers, and Students in Graeco-Roman Egypt* (Atlanta: Scholars Press, 1996); eadem, *Gymnastics of the Mind: Greek Education in Hellenistic and Roman Egypt* (Princeton: Princeton University Press, 2001). See also the appendices in Teresa Morgan, *Literate Education in the Hellenistic and Roman Worlds* (Cambridge: Cambridge University Press, 1998).

Menander (the latter beginning in the second century B.C.E.).[17] This clearly corresponds to a significant element in Philo's literary indebtedness.

But it may also be worth noting that a striking majority of the Homeric school papyri concern the first two books of the *Iliad* and the *Odyssey*, with much less coverage of the later books.[18] This suggests, of course, that the reading of Homer was often begun in educational contexts, but that training did not always equally cover the rest of the long epic poems. Philo's indebtedness to the Homeric works, by contrast, as shown in Table 3, ranges widely across both works. This may suggest, though no more, that Philo had a more significant and ongoing exposure to Homer than merely what he might have derived from his initial education.

[17] See the previous footnote. Also see Raffaella Cribiore, "Education in the Papyri," in *The Oxford Handbook of Papyrology* (ed. Roger S. Bagnall; Oxford: Oxford University Press, 2009), 320–37: "Homer was the author that students came to know in detail, and the thousand or so extant Homeric papyri confirm his popularity among the cultivated public. Both students and the general public vastly preferred the *Iliad* to the *Odyssey*. The grammarians read the first six books of the *Iliad* in detail, and their more advanced students went through the whole work" (329).

[18] But see Traianos Gagos, Nikos Litinas, and Nancy E. Priest, "Homerica Varia Michiganensia," *BASP* 41 (2004): 39–84, esp. 44–50, for two papyri that may preserve school exercises with Homer, *Iliad* 24.507–513 (P.Mich. inv. 1217b) and *Iliad* 24.681–685, 723–728 (P.Mich. inv. 4162b).

Table 3: Attestation of Homeric works by book

Iliad   *Odyssey*

Book		Book	
1	1 (5)	1	0 (1)
2	2 (4)	2	0 (0)
3	1 (1)	3	0 (0)
4	1 (0)	4	2 (2)
5	0 (3)	5	0 (0)
6	3 (1)	6	1 (0)
7	0 (0)	7	1 (0)
8	0 (0)	8	0 (0)
9	1 (1)	9	0 (2)
10	0 (0)	10	0 (0)
11	0 (0)	11	1 (4)
12	0 (1)	12	2 (4)
13	1 (2)	13	0 (0)
14	0 (1)	14	1 (0)
15	2 (1)	15	0 (1)
16	0 (0)	16	0 (0)
17	0 (1)	17	1 (1)
18	0 (4)	18	0 (0)
19	0 (0)	19	0 (0)
20	2 (1)	20	0 (3)
21	0 (0)	21	0 (1)
22	0 (2)	22	0 (0)
23	0 (0)	23	0 (0)
24	1 (1)	24	0 (0)

2) *Encounter with texts via the medium of performance.*

Philo indicates that he had attended the theatre and says, "Recently, when some players were putting on a tragedy and reciting those lines from Euripides..." (*Prob.* 141). We should not forget that there was a lively ongoing performance of dramas—especially those deemed classical by the scholars of the Mouseion—that would have provided another context for Philo's knowledge of the dramatic works in particular, one major subset of the authors he quotes with some regularity.[19] Given the robust inter-penetration of oral and textual means of encountering and assimilating compositions in Greco-Roman antiquity, together with the significant role played by memory in storage and recall of aurally received texts, we should not discount the way such performances may have mediated literary works to Philo.

3) *Use of doxographical handbooks.*

As David T. Runia has elegantly shown, Philo made use of the full range of scholarly literature available to him in his day, including the collections of opinion we now refer to as doxographies.[20] So we must caution against assuming that simply because Philo knows the position of a philosopher or a thinker, he must therefore have read and analyzed such works directly. There are intermediate channels through which such opinions may well have been mediated to Philo.

4) *Disputation and study in a house of prayer and school.*

In the same way that Philo may have encountered a number of these texts in his initial education, he may have continued to debate and teach them in the context of the Jewish house of prayer or house of study. Philo tends to assimilate the house of prayer to the model of the philosophical school in his presentation of it (so *Spec.* 2.62; cf. *Prob.* 81–82; *Somn.* 2.127; *Mos.* 2.211–212, 215–216), and while it is clear that he envisages primarily the study of the Torah, it is not unlikely that other discussions involving culturally significant literature took place there as well. It is equally possible that the school formed the social location in which Philo might have encountered classic literary texts from his Jewish predecessors, who may have grappled as he did with reconciling philosophical thought with biblical faith. Unless we are prepared to conceive of Philo as a radical innovator in introducing

---

[19] Cf. also *Ebr.* 177; *Agr.* 35; *Abr.* 134; *Legat.* 359 for some statements that reflect Philo's complex stance toward the theatre, on which see, e.g., Erkki Koskenniemi, "Philo and Classical Drama," in *Ancient Israel, Judaism, and Christianity in Contemporary Perspective: Essays in Memory of Karl-Johan Illman* (ed. Jacob Neusner, et al.; Lanham: University Press of America, 2006), 137–51.

[20] See David T. Runia, "Philo and Hellenistic Doxography," in *Philo of Alexandria and Post-Aristotelian Philosophy* (ed. Francesca Alesse; Studies in Philo of Alexandria 5; Leiden: Brill, 2008), 13–54. Doxographical material may be found in, e.g., *Opif.* 7–8; 170–171; 54; *Abr.* 162–163; *Ebr.* 170–202; *Mut.* 10, 67; *Somn.* 1.14–16, 21–24, 25, 30–34, 52–56, 145, 184; *Her.* 246; *Aet.* 7–19; *Prov.* 2.89, *Contempl.* 14–16, etc. Other sorts of handbooks, for example of historiographical works, may also have been available to Philo.

non-Jewish philosophical and literary texts into discussion of the Greek scriptures, we must countenance a social space in which Philo himself may have been inducted into these discussions and continued to debate with other exegetes and teachers.[21]

5) *Re-use of his own notes and excerpta.*

The tradition of making notes from one's reading is well-known in antiquity,[22] and it is entirely plausible to imagine Philo engaging in the contemporary practice of keeping wax tablets or another form of writing material by his side while reading scrolls, and then jotting down important or felicitous excerpts for later re-use in the composition of his treatises. This need not deny to Philo direct literary encounter with the authors whom he cites, but does introduce some level of distance between Philo and the works he cites. Certain citations recur in Philo (e.g., Aeschylus, frg. 162 Radt, or certain lines of Euripides or Plato), but one is also struck by the general spread of his citations over a broad range of authors and their works, and this breadth could suggest a more sustained encounter with at least some texts than might be envisaged in the somewhat more episodic models mentioned above.

---

[21] I am grateful to interlocutors (including Joan Taylor) at the SBL Philo Session in Baltimore (November 2013) for raising this suggestion when the paper was originally presented. My gratitude is owed as well to Sarah Pearce and Ellen Birnbaum for the kind invitation to present, to other members of the Philo of Alexandria Group for helpful discussion, and to Sarah Pearce and Gregory Sterling for helpful editorial improvements and bibliographical suggestions.

[22] See Henry Chadwick, "Florilegium" *RAC* 7:1131–1160; Christopher D. Stanley, *Paul and the Language of Scripture: Citation Technique in the Pauline Epistles and Contemporary Literature* (SNTSMS 74; Cambridge: Cambridge University Press, 1992), 73–78; idem, "The Importance of 4QTanḥumim (4Q176)," *RevQ* 15 (1992) 569–582; Martin C. Albl, *"And Scripture Cannot Be Broken": The Form and Function of the Early Christian Testimonia Collections* (NovTSup 96; Leiden: Brill, 1999), 70–81; Lutz Doering, "Excerpted Texts in Second Temple Judaism. A Survey of the Evidence," in *Selecta colligere, II: Beiträge zur Technik des Sammelns und Kompilierens griechischer Texte von der Antike bis zum Humanismus* (eds. Rosa Maria Piccione and Matthias Perkams; Alessandria: Edizioni dell-Orso, 2005), 1–38. Stanley points especially to Xenophon, *Mem.* 1.6.14; Aristotle, *Top.* 1.14; Athenaeus, *Deipn.* 8.336d; Plutarch, *Mor.* 464F; Cicero, *Inv.* 2.4; Pliny the Younger, *Ep.* 3.5; 6.20.5; Aulus Gellius, *Noct. att.*, 17.21.1; cf. also 4Q175. For the continuation of the practice in the patristic period, note esp. Robert Devreesse, "Chaines Exégétiques Grecques," *DBSup* 1:1084–1233.

6) *Reading and returning directly to the continuous written texts.*

Finally, then, we might name the model that is most often tacitly assumed, that of Philo reading continuous texts (or having them read aloud to him by a servant) and remembering key arguments, turns of phrase or quotations, to which he may then later have returned for re-use.

This variety of possible modes of encounter, each plausible in certain circumstances, suggests that we must beware of retrojecting an anachronistically bookish mentality, as though Philo mirrored his modern critics and were some ancient academic in a study surrounded by books. Some of these models require direct recourse to written texts (5 and 6), while others place a greater emphasis on memory and orality (1, 2 and 4) or intermediary texts (3). Nevertheless, it is not unreasonable to envisage Philo as an ancient user of a library, and even an owner of a personal collection of books himself. Philo, of course, fits the general profile of others who owned books in antiquity: wealthy, learned, self-sufficient, and philosophically inclined, and it is worth pausing briefly to call attention to the collecting activity of wealthy *literati* in antiquity. In some particularly learned studies, George W. Houston has analyzed the composition of a number of private libraries, on the basis of both lists of books that have been preserved in papyri, and concentrations of papyri that have been found together in particular sites.[23] The interpretation of these data is not without difficulty, but a plausible picture emerges of a concern among some members of the learned elite to gather together a collection of important books, often with a uniting theme, to serve as a resource, we assume, for education and reflection. Perhaps the most spectacular of these finds are those from the so-called Villa of the Papyri in Herculaneum.[24] These consist of a large number of carbonized papyrus rolls, ranging from 700 to 1,100 scrolls, with probably just over half by Philodemus. The suggestion has plausibly been advanced that at one point this was Philodemus's own collection, though it outlived the poet-philosopher and came into other hands. It also contains a number of Epicurean writers, as well as works by the Stoic Chrysippus and

[23] George W. Houston, "Papyrological Evidence for Book Collections and Libraries in the Roman Empire," in *Ancient Literacies: The Culture of Reading in Greece and Rome* (ed. William A. Johnson; Oxford: Oxford University Press, 2009), 233–67; idem, "The Non-Philodemus Book Collection in the Villa of the Papyri," in *Ancient Libraries* (eds. Jason König, Katarina Oikonomopolou, and Greg Woolf; Cambridge: Cambridge University Press, 2013), 183–208.

[24] For a recent overview, see David Sider, "The Books of the Villa of the Papyri," in *The Villa of the Papyri at Herculaneum* (ed. Mantha Zarmakoupi; Sozomena: Studies in the Recovery of Ancient Texts 1; Berlin: Walter de Gruyter, 2010), 115–27; idem, "The Special Case of Herculaneum," in *The Oxford Handbook of Papyrology*, 303–19, with bibliography.

Epicurus himself.[25] This seems to be a carefully acquired and focused library that developed over a relatively sustained period of time, but there are also other examples of book collections that appear less focused and much smaller.[26]

We also see glimpses of intellectuals going about the business of book-collecting. Cicero left a trail of letters indicating a concern for his book holdings over a number of years, and it seems that his library was particularly in use when he was writing.[27] One might also point to the lively correspondence indicating a search for books among literary friends in P. Oxy. XVIII 2192, a papyrus letter with up to four hands, with requests such as "Make and send me copies of Books 6 and 7 of Hypsicrates' *Characters in Comedy*," or, "of Seleucus's work on the *Tenses* make copies and send me as many (books) as you find, apart from those I possess."[28] The concern to search out and acquire significant books indicates a lively social enterprise of reading, as well as an effort to collect what seem to be relatively obscure titles.

But even if Philo is clearly interested in books, and so might be characterized as the library-going type, can we say whether he might have preferred an institutional or his own private library? Did Philo, for example, go to the Mouseion or the Serapeion, taking advantage of the famous Alexandrian Library?[29]

Philo does mention the Muses a couple of times in passing (*Prob.* 62; *Aet.* 55) but nowhere mentions explicitly either the Mouseion, with its

[25] See the descriptive catalogue in Houston, "Non-Philodemus Book Collection," 197–208.

[26] For these, see esp. Houston, "Papyrological Evidence." Note also Roger S. Bagnall, "An Owner of Literary Papyri," *CP* 87 (1992): 137–40, who supplies by interesting detective work an example of a set of four literary papyri probably owned by a land-owning woman, Aurelia Ptolemais. There are some slight indications for private ownership of books in roughly contemporary Jewish and Christian sources (cf. 1 Macc. 1:56–57; 2 Macc. 2:13–15; 2 Tim 4:13). More broadly, see Harry Y. Gamble, *Books and Readers in the Early Church* (New Haven: Yale University Press, 1995), esp. 174–76, 186–89 and notes; and H. Gregory Snyder, *Teachers and Texts in the Ancient World* (London: Routledge, 2000).

[27] See Dix, "'Beware of Promising Your Library to Anyone.'" As Sarah Pearce has pointed out to me in private communication: "Cicero also lambasts Cleopatra VII for not having provided him with some promised books, presumably from Alexandria"; cf. Cicero, *Att.* 15.15.

[28] See the re-edition of this papyrus by Rasalia Hatzilambrou in Dirk Obbink, "Readers and Intellectuals," in *Oxyrhynchus: A City and Its Texts* (ed. Alan K. Bowman; Graeco-Roman Memoirs 93; London: Egypt Exploration Society, 2007), 271–86, esp. 282–86. For discussion, note William A. Johnson, *Readers and Reading Culture in the High Roman Empire: A Study of Elite Communities* (Oxford: Oxford University Press, 2010), 179–92.

[29] J. Harold Ellens, "Philo Judaeus and the Ancient Library of Alexandria," *SBLSP* 26 (1987): 439–42, remains entirely in the realm of conjecture.

famous library, or the Serapeion, which housed a smaller lending library later.[30] Philo does refer to the "libraries" (βιβλιοθήκαις) that adorn the Sebasteum, or temple to Caesar, built in Alexandria to commemorate its surrender to Augustus in 30 B.C.E. (*Legat.* 151).[31] Notably, perhaps, Philo expressly mentions the complex as a temple to someone other than the one God of Judaism, and though he speaks with admiration it may also indicate some distance. Philo seems to show knowledge of authors who were treated as canonical by the scholars of the Mouseion—e.g., Aeschylus, Sophocles, Euripides, Pindar and so forth[32]—but this may arguably be because he lived in a society in which the cultural ideals had been shaped by this centuries-old tradition of collection and emphasis.[33] Our knowledge of the Alexandrian Library, its policies and practices is distinctly thin for the first century, though some have seen a restriction of horizon to the finer points of grammar and syntax among the Alexandrian scholars in this period.[34] Although it is an argument from silence, it is worth noting that, whereas the *Letter of Aristeas* calls explicit attention to the Library, and makes the rationale for the translation of the Hebrew Bible its absence in

---

[30] The precise relationship of the two libraries is murky, but it does seem as though there are two distinct libraries (apart from the libraries of the Sebasteum, which Philo mentions). Epiphanius says that the translation of the Septuagint was placed "in the first library" (ἐν τῇ πρώτῃ βιβλιοθήκῃ), but goes on to mention a "daughter" library in the Serapeion (Ἐγένετο δὲ αὐτῇ τῇ βιβλιοθήκῃ ἑτέρα, ἡ θυγάτηρ αὐτῆς ὀνομασθεῖσα ἄνω ἐν τῷ Σεραπείῳ); see Epiphanius, *de mens. et pond.* lines 325–327 (Moutsoulas). The Byzantine monk Johannes Tzetzes, drawing on older sources in his preface to Aristophanes, mentions two libraries, one within the palace precincts (presumably in the Mouseion) and one outside it; cf. Georg Kaibel, *Comicorum graecorum fragmenta* (Berlin: Weidmann, 1899), 1:19. For discussion, see Rudolf Pfeiffer, *History of Classical Scholarship: From the Beginnings to the End of the Hellenistic Age* (Oxford: Clarendon, 1968), 99–102; Peter Marshall Fraser, *Ptolemaic Alexandria* (Oxford: Clarendon, 1972), 1:320–335; Gamble, *Books and Readers*, 177–81; cf. "Library," *Brill's New Pauly*.

[31] On which, see Fraser, *Ptolemaic Alexandria*, 1:24–25.

[32] Cf. Herwig Maehler, "Alexandria, the Mouseion, and Cultural Identity," in *Alexandria, Real and Imagined* (eds. Anthony Hirst and Michael Silk; Aldershot: Ashgate, 2004), 1–14.

[33] "A museum in the Greek world was organized as a confraternity devoted to the worship of the Muses; the museum head was the officiating priest of the cult" (Obbink, "Readers and Intellectuals," 281; cf. Maehler, "Alexandria, the Mouseion, and Cultural Identity."

[34] See the useful presentation in Myrto Hatzimichali, "Ashes to Ashes? The Library of Alexandria after 48 BC," in *Ancient Libraries* (eds. Jason König, Katarina Oikonomopolou, and Greg Woolf; Cambridge: Cambridge University Press, 2013), 167–82. For the limitations of our knowledge about the Library, see Roger S. Bagnall, "Alexandria: Library of Dreams," *APSP* 146 (2002): 348–62 (who also notes that the precise relationship between the Library and the Mouseion is also unclear in ancient sources).

that achievement (9–11, 29–31, 39), Philo's adaptation of the Aristeas legend in *Mos* 2.25–44 passes over the Library in silence.

We may find one small hint, whose importance should not be over-stated, in Philo's portrait of the ideal person in his treatise on Abraham, that may push us toward preferring to see Philo as making use of his own library:

> The man of worth on the other hand, having acquired a desire for a quiet life, withdraws from the public and loves solitude, and his choice is to be unnoticed by the many, not because he is misanthropical, for he is eminently a philan-thropist, but because he has rejected vice which is welcomed by the multitude who rejoice at what calls for mourning and grieve where it is well to be glad. And therefore he mostly secludes himself at home (οἴκοι) and scarcely ever crosses his threshold, or else because of the frequency of visitors he leaves the town and spends his days in some lonely farm, finding pleasanter society in those noblest of the whole human race whose bodies time has turned into dust but the flame of their virtues is kept alive by the written records which have survived them in poetry or in prose and serve to promote the growth of goodness in the soul. (*Abr.* 22–23 PLCL)[35]

Interesting in the present connection is that the withdrawal from society does not leave the worthy person "bookless," but there is access to "written records" (γραφαί) by past notables who have written poetry and prose. When one compares this with Philo's famous complaint in *Spec.* 3.1–6, in which he laments the fact that he was ripped from his philosophy and contemplation to the "vast sea of civil cares," we may be justified in seeing his remarks as at least partially autobiographical. In this sense, then, Philo may have longed for retirement to a country refuge where he would indulge in the reading of his books—precisely the type of activity in which we see Cicero engaging, and arguably the purpose of the Villa of Papyri in Herculaneum as well.

So, then, with the *comparanda* in view, even in the lack of explicit evidence, we may rightly assume that Philo will have possessed a cache of private books. It may be possible to draw some cautious lines between the frequency and breadth of his cited authors and his ownership of those books. Working especially from the data in Table 2, and bearing in mind the caveats previously enumerated, it is reasonable to suppose that, in addition to his own works, Philo will have owned a modest philosophical library that included many works of Plato, but also perhaps works by Empedocles, Heraclitus, Posidonius, and Zeno, as well as others whom he did not find occasion to cite as often. Less certain is whether Philo might

---

[35] This recalls the similar picture drawn in *Contempl.* 19–20.

have also owned copies of the literary works whose words pepper his prose, but his broad familiarity with the works of Homer and Hesiod suggest it is not improbable. With this in view, therefore, we may be justified in offering this sketch of the rough contours of a *bibliotheca philonica*.

                                          Mansfield College, Oxford

The Studia Philonica Annual 26 (2014) 115–133

FROM THE THICK MARSHES OF THE NILE
TO THE THRONE OF GOD:
Moses in Ezekiel the Tragedian and Philo of Alexandria

GREGORY E. STERLING

On two different occasions, Philo mentioned reactions of audiences to plays in a theater when he was present. While noting the different ways that humans respond to stimuli, he wrote: "When I have been in the theatre, I have often noticed that some are so moved by a melody sung by the actors on the stage or performed by the musicians that they are aroused and spontaneously join in an outburst of approval." He noted that "others are so unaffected that one might suppose that in this way they are no different than the lifeless benches on which they are sitting." Still others, "are so repulsed that they leave the performance and as they depart, cover their ears with each of their hands..."[1] On another occasion he commented on the reaction of an audience to a couplet from Euripides's *Auge* that praised freedom: "I saw the entire audience stand up in enthusiasm to their full height and raise their voices together powerfully with continuous shouts of approval both for the sentiment and for the poet."[2]

While the descriptions in these statements are dramatic, I understand them to refer to actual experiences that Philo had in the theater. Philo knew classical drama. He mentioned all three of the major tragedians by name: Aeschylus,[3] Sophocles,[4] and Euripides.[5] He cited Aeschylus six times[6] and

---

[1] Philo, *Ebr.* 177.

[2] Philo, *Prob.* 141; cf. also *Anim.* 23.

[3] Philo, *Prob.* 143.

[4] Philo, *Prob.* 19.

[5] Philo, *Prob.* 99, 116, 141.

[6] Philo, *Prob.* 143 cited *TrGF* 3:20 (=Bruno Snell *et al.* eds., *Tragicorum graecorum fragmenta* (5 vols.; Göttingen: Vandenhoeck & Ruprecht, 1981–2004); Philo, *Aet.* 49 cited *TrGF* 3:139; Philo, *Anim.* 47 cited *TrGF* 3:162; Philo, *Prov.* 2.8 cited *TrGF* 3:344; and Philo, *Prov.* 2.90 cited *TrGF* 3:345. I owe these references and those below to the index of David Lincicum, "A Preliminary Index to Philo's Non-Biblical Citations and Allusions," *SPhA* 25 (2013): 139–67. On the reference in *Anim.* 47 see David Lincicum, "Aeschylus in Philo, *Anim.* 47 and *QE* 2.6," *SPhA* 25 (2013): 65–68.

alluded to lines from his tragedies nine more times.[7] He only cited Sophocles once,[8] although he alluded to lines from him seven times.[9] His favorite classical tragedian was Euripides: he cited him seventeen times[10] and alluded to lines from his plays another eight times.[11] The Alexandrian Jew appears to have known other tragedians as well, such as Ion[12] and two anonymous tragedians.[13]

Philo's tastes were not restricted to the serious: he also knew comedies. He alluded to Aristophanes, the most famous representative of Old Comedy twice,[14] and cited Menander, the celebrated playwright of the New Comedy three times[15] and alluded to him once.[16] He did not cite any of the known figures of the Middle Comedy; however, he did know comedies beyond Athens and cited Epicharmus, the Sicilian writer of comedies, once[17] and alluded to him once.[18] On another occasion he alluded to an unidentified comic poet.[19] Philo's enjoyment of Greek tragedy and comedy is not surprising: one of the Jewish translators in Pseudo-Aristeas indicated

[7] Philo, *Ebr.* 126 alluded to *Eum.* 107; Philo, *Opif.* 132 alluded to *Prom.* 90; Philo, *Opif.* 144; *Mos.* 1.279; *Spec.* 4.14; 4.236; *Virt.* 80 alluded to *TrGF* 3:162 (although this may be through Plato, *Resp.* 3.391E); Philo, *Sacr.* 93 alluded to *TrGF* 3:394; and Philo, *Aet.* 139 alluded to *TrGF* 3:402.

[8] Philo, *Prob.* 19 cited *TrGF* 4:755.

[9] Philo, *Ios.* 48 alluded to *Hipp.* (?); Philo, *Prob.* 42 alluded to *Oed. col.* 1293; Philo, *Gig.* 56; *Ebr.* 8; *QG* 4.159 alluded to *TrGF* 4:910; and Philo, *Spec.* 1.74; 3.50 alluded to *TrGF* 4:945.

[10] Philo, *Prob.* 116 cited *Hec.* 548–551; Philo, *Ios.* 78 cited *Phoen.* 521; Philo, *Spec.* 4.47 cited *TrGF* 5:200.3–4; Philo, *Prob.* 141 cited *TrGF* 5:275.3–4; Philo, *Somn.* 1.154; *Mos.* 1.31 cited *TrGF* 5:420; Philo, *Leg.* 3.202; *Ios.* 78; *Prob.* 25 cited *TrGF* 5:687; Philo, *Prob.* 98–104 cited *TrGF* 5:839.8–14; Philo, *Leg.* 1.5; *Aet.* 5, 144 cited *TrGF* 5:839.12–14; Philo *Prob.* 145 cited *TrGF* 5:839.1; Philo, *QG* 4.203 alluded to *TrGF* 5:954; Philo, *Prob.* 22 cited *TrGF* 5:958.

[11] Philo, *Ios.* 48 alluded to *Hipp.* (?); Philo, *QG* 4.211 alluded to *Hipp.* 331; Philo, *Mos.* 1.135; *Spec.* 2.133 alluded to *Iph. aul.* 122; Philo, *Somn.* 1.172 alluded to *TrGF* 5:484; Philo, *Mut.* 152 alluded to *TrGF* 5:484.1; Philo, *Aet.* 57 alluded to *TrGF* 5:839.12–14; Philo, *Cher.* 26 alluded to *TrGF* 5:911.

[12] Philo, *Prob.* 134 cited *TrGF* 1:53.

[13] Philo, *Prob.* 145 alluded to *TrGF* 2:318 and Philo, *Aet.* 27 alluded to *TrGF* 2:327a.

[14] Philo, *Opif.* 312 alluded to *Av.* 971 and to *Ran.* 382.

[15] Philo, *Her.* 5 cited frg. 312 (Alfred Körte and Andreas Thierfelder, *Menandri quae supersunt* [2 vols.; Bibliotheca scriptorium Graecorum et Romanorum Teubneriana; Leipzig: Teubner, 1957–1959], hereafter KT); Philo, *QG* 4.120 cited frg. 581 (Theodor Kock, ed., *Comicorum Atticorum fragmenta* [3 vols.; Leipzig: Teubner, 1880–1888], hereafter *CAF*); and Philo *Abr.* 134 cited frg. 786 KT.

[16] Philo, *Mos.* 2.13 alluded to frg. 786 KT.

[17] Philo, *QG* 4.203 cited frg. 260 (R. Kassel and C. Austin, eds., *Poetae comici graeci* [8 vols.; Berlin: de Gruyter, 1983–2001], hereafter *PCG*).

[18] Philo *Post.* 214 alluded to frg. 214 *PCG*. Cf. also Philo, *Sacr.* 35 alluding to Ps-Epicharmus frg. 271 *PCG*.

[19] Philo, *Contempl.* 43 alluded to *PCG* 8:475.

to the king that his idea of relaxation was "to observe whatever is performed with decorum."[20] Philo apparently followed the advice.[21]

Did Philo know any Jewish playwrights or plays? Through a twist of fate, the best preserved tragedy that we have from the Hellenistic world is the *Exagoge* of Ezekiel.[22] While the date and provenance of Ezekiel are debatable, I place him in Egypt in the second century B.C.E.[23] Philo never mentioned Ezekiel by name or openly cited any of his plays, but this is hardly a surprise: he did not mention Jewish predecessors by name. The closest that Philo came to naming Jewish predecessors was in his preface to the *Life of Moses* where he wrote: "I will relate the story of Moses as I have learned it both from the sacred books which he left behind as marvelous monuments of his wisdom and from certain elders of the nation."[24] Who were the elders? Was Ezekiel's *Exagoge* in Philo's library or did he see a version of the play performed?[25]

I propose to examine the relationship between Ezekiel's *Exagoge*[26] and Philo of Alexandria's *Life of Moses*[27] in three areas: verbal parallels, exegetical traditions, and thematic similarities. While it would be possible to consider the relationship between Ezekiel and the entire Philonic corpus, I will concentrate on the *Life of Moses* since it has the most numerous parallels

[20] Let. Aris. 284.

[21] For a treatment of Philo's relationship to classical drama see Erkki Koskenniemi, "Philo and Classical Drama," in *Ancient Israel, Judaism, and Christianity in Contemporary Perspective: Essays in Memory of Karl-Johan Illman* (eds. Jacob Neusner et al.; Studies in Judaism; Lanham, MD: University Press of America, 2006), 137–51. See also the fine treatment of David Lincicum, "Philo's Library," elsewhere in this issue of *SPhA*.

[22] There are seventeen fragments preserving 269 lines in iambic trimeter that Alexander Polyhistor cited which were in turn cited by Eusebius, *Praep. ev.* 9.28–29. Clement, *Strom.* 1.23.155.1–5 and 6–7 has parallels to frgs 1 and 2 and Eustathius, *Commentary on the Hexameron* has a parallel to frg. 17. There is another fragment preserved in Epiphanius, *PAN.* 64.29.6–30.1 (=frg. 18), but I do not consider this to belong to the *Exagoge*, although it is possibly from another work of Ezekiel.

[23] The *termini* are the translation of Exodus into Greek (third century BCE) and Alexander Polyhistor (ca. 110–post 40 BCE). See Felix Jacoby, ed,, *Die Fragmente der grichischen Historiker* (3 vols. in 16 parts; Leiden: Brill, 1923–1969), no. 273, hereafter *FGrH*.

[24] Philo, *Mos.* 1.4.

[25] There has not been a study dedicated to this issue. Carl R. Holladay, *Fragments from Hellenistic Jewish Authors. Volume 2: Poets* (SBLTT 30/SBLSPS 12; Atlanta: Scholars Press, 1989), 301–529, esp. 317, and Howard Jacobson, *The Exagoge of Ezekiel* (Cambridge: Cambridge University Press, 1983), esp. 38–39, both thought that Philo probably knew Ezekiel. David T. Runia, "God and Man in Philo of Alexandria," *JTS* 39 (1988): 48–75, esp. 53, was less sanguine about the possibility.

[26] I have used the edition of Holladay, *Poets*, 301–529 and consulted Jacobson, *The Exagoge of Ezekiel.*

[27] I have used the text of Leopold Cohn, ed., *Philonis Alexandrini opera quae supersunt. Volume 4* (Berlin: Georg Reimerus, 1902; reprinted Berlin: de Gruyter, 1962).

and offers us the opportunity to ask whether Philo was influenced by Ezekiel's play in a more sustained way rather than exploring a series of isolated occurrences.[28] I assume that both Ezekiel and Philo used a form of the Greek text of Exodus as their base.[29] I have compared both to the Göttingen *Septuaginta*.[30] I am only concerned with occurrences where Ezekiel and Philo agree in departing from the biblical text. A common departure from the Greek Bible does not demonstrate dependence; there are a number of other possibilities such as variant readings, similar embellishments of a narrative by authors who think in Hellenic terms, and common exegetical traditions that both may attest. I will try to take these factors into account as I work through the similarities. I am distinguishing verbal parallels from exegetical traditions by using the latter for the texts where there are common interpretations but no verbal parallels. I have reserved the category of thematic parallels for similar concepts that are not directly grounded in a common exegetical tradition. We want to ask whether the evidence suggests that Philo knew Ezekiel directly—either through having observed a performance or having a copy of the play in front of him.

Verbal Parallels

The first parallels that we will explore are the places where Ezekiel and Philo retold the biblical story by using an identical word or phrase that does not appear in the Greek Bible. These could be called echoes in some circles, but I have elected to call them parallels since we are concerned primarily with the issue of whether Philo knew Ezekiel rather than the influence of Ezekiel on Philo's retelling of Moses.[31] I have found fifteen places where this occurs. In each case I have also looked to see if another Jewish author writing in Greek used the same term or expression in

[28] Unfortunately, *QE* is not extant until Exod 12:2 or it would have been a natural section of the Philonic corpus to use as a point of comparison.

[29] On Philo's use of Exodus see Gregory E. Sterling "The People of the Covenant or the People of God: Exodus in Philo of Alexandria," in *The Book of Exodus: Composition, Reception, and Interpretation* (eds. Thomas B. Dozeman, Craig A. Evans, and Joel N. Lohr; Formation and Interpretation of Old Testament Literature; Leiden: Brill, forthcoming).

[30] John William Wevers, ed., *Septuaginta Vetus Testamentum Graecum. Volume 2.1: Exodus* (Göttingen: Vandenhoeck & Ruprecht, 1991).

[31] For the larger issue of intertextuality see especially Richard B. Hays, *Echoes of Scripture in the Letters of Paul* (New Haven: Yale University Press, 1989) and Richard B. Hays, Stefan Alkier, and Leroy A. Huizenga, eds., *Reading the Bible Intertextually* (Waco, TX: Baylor University Press, 2009).

retelling the Exodus story. The most obvious place to look is Josephus who probably knew both Ezekiel's *Exagoge*[32] and Philo's *Life of Moses*.[33] This means that if Josephus is the only parallel to Ezekiel and Philo, it may reflect the historian's dependence on one of his predecessors rather than an independent tradition.

1. The first verbal echo occurs in the rehearsal of Exod 1 when Ezekiel and Philo retold Pharaoh's decision to oppress the Hebrew people. The Greek has, "Come let us outwit them (κατασοφισώμεθα αὐτούς)."[34] Ezekiel and Philo preferred the verb "contrive" (μηχανάομαι) rather than "outwit" (κατασοφίζομαι).[35] It is worth noting that Philo used the verb "outwit" three times elsewhere but never in connection with Exod 1.[36] Josephus used a completely different expression when he retold Exod 1:10,[37] but did use the verb "contrive" (μηχανάομαι) later in a generalizing expression that referred to Pharaoh's machinations.[38]

2. The largest number of verbal echoes cluster around the retelling of Exod 2, especially the story of Moses's birth and adoption. There are three verbal echoes in the retelling of the exposure of Moses (nos. 2–4). The Greek Bible explained the rationale of Moses's parents' decision to put him in an ark: "since they were not able to keep him hidden" (οὐκ ἠδύνατο ... κρύπτειν).[39] Ezekiel and Philo preferred a participial form of "escape notice" (λανθάνω), although Ezekiel used it as a strict analogy to the negative expression in Exodus while Philo used it to describe their success in keeping Moses out of sight for three months.[40] Josephus used the same expression.[41] While this could reflect dependence, it could also be a common stylistic improvement of the LXX.

3. According to Exodus, Moses's parents' inability to keep him concealed led his mother to construct an ark and place him in it (καὶ ἐνέβαλεν

---

[32] So Jacobson, *The Exagoge of Ezekiel*, 37–39. Cf. also pp. 5–6. He was followed by Louis Feldman, *Josephus's Interpretation of the Bible* (Hellenistic Culture and Society 27; Berkeley: University of California Press, 1998), 52, 175.

[33] See Gregory E. Sterling, "'A Man of the Highest Repute': Did Josephus Knew the Writings of Philo?" *SPhA* 25 (2013): 101–113.

[34] Exod 1:10.

[35] Ezekiel 7–9, esp. 8; Philo, *Mos.* 1.8.

[36] Philo, *Leg.* 3.82; *Spec.* 3.186; *Flacc.* 42.

[37] Josephus, *A.J.* 2.203, "they (the Egyptians) thought up all sorts of ill treatments for them" (καὶ ταλαιπωρίας αὐτοῖς ποικίλας ἐπενόουν).

[38] Josephus, *A.J.* 2.209, "no one can overpower the will of God no matter how many devices he contrived for this purpose" (οὐδὲ μυρίας τέχνας ἐπὶ τούτῳ μηχανησάμενος).

[39] Exod 2:3.

[40] Ezekiel 15; Philo, *Mos.* 1.9.

[41] Josephus, *A.J.* 2.209, 215, 218 (*bis*), 219.

τὸ παιδίον εἰς αὐτήν).⁴² Ezekiel and Philo omitted the ark and suggested that Moses was exposed on the bank of the river. Ezekiel followed the biblical text and had the mother expose her child (ὑπεξέθηκεν); Philo had both parents expose him (ἐκτιθέασι).⁴³ It is important to note that while Ezekiel used a fuller form of the verb, both forms were used for infant exposure.⁴⁴ By contrast, Josephus goes into detail about the ark, suggesting that Moses's parents went to some lengths to make sure that it was river worthy.⁴⁵ Interestingly, the author of Acts in the New Testament knew the tradition of Moses's exposure and used the same verb as Philo.⁴⁶

4. In the biblical text Moses's mother set the ark "in the marsh at the river" (εἰς τὸ ἕλος παρὰ τὸν ποταμόν).⁴⁷ Ezekiel and Philo qualified the marsh almost identically: Ezekiel had Moses's mother set him "in a thickly grown marsh" (λάσιον εἰς ἕλος δασύ) while Philo suggested that Pharaoh's daughter found the child "in the thickest part of the marsh" (ἐν τῷ δασυτάτῳ τῶν ἑλῶν).⁴⁸ The common use of "thick" (δασύς) to describe the marsh is striking: it is the type of word that once heard or read might well remain in the memory.

5. The striking similarities continue in the description of the discovery of Moses (nos. 5–7). Ezekiel and Philo replaced the aorist infinitive of the biblical text "to wash" (λούσασθαι)⁴⁹ with the noun "bathing" (λουτροῖς) when they related Pharaoh's daughter's decision to go to the river.⁵⁰ This could easily be an accidental agreement due to reworking the biblical text.

6. According to the biblical text, when the royal princess saw Moses in the ark, "she said: 'He is from the children of the Hebrews.'"⁵¹ Ezekiel and

⁴² Exod 2:3.

⁴³ Ezekiel 16; Philo, *Mos.* 1.10. See also §11.

⁴⁴ See the examples in Holladay, *Poets*, 413. Philo, *Mos.* 1.14, uses ἐκκεῖμαι, also meaning "expose." See Herodotus 1.110. On the issue of infanticide in Philo, see Adele Reinhartz, "Philo on Infanticide," *SPhA* 4 (1992): 42–58, esp. 51; Maren R. Niehoff, *Philo on Jewish Identity and Culture* (TSAJ 86; Tübingen: Mohr Siebeck, 2001), 163–74; Daniel R. Schwartz, "Did the Jews Practice Infant Exposure and Infanticide in Antiquity?" *SPhA* 16 (2004): 61–95; and Maren R. Niehoff, "Response to Daniel R. Schwartz," *SPhA* 17 (2005): 99–101.

⁴⁵ Josephus, *A.J.* 2.220–221. Compare the elaborations of later Jewish traditions cited by Louis Ginzberg, *Legends of the Jews* (7 vols.; trans. Henrietta Szold and Paul Radin; Philadelphia: The Jewish Publication Society of America, 1909–1938; repr. with foreword by James L. Kugel; Baltimore: The Johns Hopkins University Press, 1998), 2:265.

⁴⁶ Acts 7:21, "when he had been exposed" (ἐκτεθέντος δὲ αὐτοῦ).

⁴⁷ Exod 2:3. See also 2:5.

⁴⁸ Ezekiel 17; Philo, *Mos.* 1.14.

⁴⁹ Exod 2:5.

⁵⁰ Ezekiel 20; Philo, *Mos.* 1.14.

⁵¹ Exod 2:6.

Philo dropped the *oratio recta* and had Pharaoh's daughter recognize (γινώσκω) that he was from the Hebrews. They altered the syntax from the literal translation of the biblical text[52] to a similar and more idiomatic Greek construction.[53]

7. The biblical text did not mention the approach of Moses's sister;[54] however, Ezekiel and Philo did by using the same participle: Miriam ran to Pharaoh's daughter (προσδραμοῦσα).[55] The description of Miriam's approach could be due to a common attempt to fill in the narrative; however, the agreement in the participle is noteworthy.

8. The verbal echoes continue in later parts of Ezekiel, but not with the same degree of frequency. Ezekiel and Philo embellished the biblical text by adding that he received a royal upbringing (τροφὴ βασιλική)[56] and education. They agree in wording on the former and in concept on the latter. Philo, in particular, expatiated on Moses's education.[57] Other ancient authors commented on Moses's education, although I am not aware of any other writer who used the same expression "royal upbringing."[58]

9. There are two verbal parallels in the retelling of the burning bush (nos. 9–10). In contrast to the biblical text that describes it as "this great sight" (τὸ ὅραμα τὸ μέγα τοῦτο),[59] Ezekiel and Philo called it a "portent" (τεράστιον).[60] Josephus used a similar, although not identical expression.[61]

10. Moses objected that he was not qualified to lead the Hebrews out of Egypt because "I am weak-voiced and halting" (ἰσχνόφωνος καὶ βραδύγλωσσος ἐγώ εἰμι).[62] Ezekiel and Philo expanded this by adding that Moses

---

[52] Exod 2:6, זה מילדי העברים ותאמר is rendered καὶ ἔφη Ἀπὸ τῶν παιδίων τῶν Ἐβραίων τοῦτο in the LXX.

[53] Ezekiel 22, ἔγνω δ' Ἐβραῖον ὄντα. Philo, *Mos.* 1.15, γνοῦσαν δ' ὅτι τῶν Ἐβραίων ἐστί.

[54] Exod 2:7.

[55] Ezekiel 23; Philo, *Mos.* 1.16, who used it in the accusative rather than the nominative case.

[56] Exod 2:11 has nothing along these lines. See Ezekiel 36–37 for both the upbringing and the education. Ezekiel used the plural for "royal upbringing." Philo, *Mos.* 1.20 and 1.8, used the singular for Moses's "royal upbringing."

[57] Philo, *Mos.* 1.20–24.

[58] See, for example, Josephus, *A.J.* 2.236–237, "he was educated with great care" (ἐτρέφετο οὖν πολλῆς ἐπιμελείας τυγχάνων) and Acts 7:22, "and Moses was educated in all the wisdom of the Egyptians" (καὶ ἐπαιδεύθη Μωυσῆς ἐν πάσῃ σοφίᾳ Αἰγυπτίων).

[59] Exod 3:3.

[60] Ezekiel 91; Philo, *Mos.* 1.71.

[61] Josephus, *A.J.* 2.265, called it "an amazing portent" (τέρας ... θαυμάσιον).

[62] Exod 4:10.

claimed that he was "not eloquent" (οὐκ εὔλογος).[63] There are several variants in the manuscript tradition for the LXX that include "not eloquent" (οὐκ εὔλογος),[64] "not fluent" (οὐκ εὔγλωσσος),[65] and "not smooth speaking" (οὐκ εὔλαλος).[66] The manuscripts for Philo have the same variations.[67] This may be a case of an alternate text, although this is not certain since we also have to allow for scribal adaptation to the text of the LXX familiar to them.

11. There are three verbal echoes relating to the plagues (nos. 11–13). The first appears to be a common expansion of the biblical text. The first plague turned not only the rivers into blood, but all of the bodies of water.[68] Ezekiel and Philo both included "springs" (πηγαί) in their descriptions.[69] Josephus also mentioned "springs" among the sources of water affected.[70]

12. The sixth plague in Exodus is introduced with the command: "Take your hands full of furnace soot" (αἰθάλη).[71] Ezekiel and Philo changed this to "furnace ashes" (τέφρα).[72] I am not aware of another author who used the same expression for this plague.

13. Both Ezekiel and Philo mentioned the destruction of the fruit (καρποί) when the hail struck,[73] a specification omitted in Exodus although it does mention trees.[74] Josephus also mentioned "fruit" in his version of the plagues.[75]

14. In the exodus proper there are two echoes (nos. 14–15). The first is the common description of the despoiling of the Egyptians as repayment for the way that the Egyptians treated them. Both make an explicit point of saying that this is a "payment" (μισθός) for past treatment,[76] a detail not mentioned in the biblical narrative. While the despoiling of the Egyptians

---

[63] Ezekiel 113–115, esp. 113; Philo, *Mos.* 1.83. It is worth noting that Exod 6:12 reads ἐγὼ δὲ ἄλογός εἰμι. Jacobson, *The Exagoge of Ezekiel*, 204 n. 32 suggested that this lay behind this reading.

[64] F F$^{b\ c}$ M *ol*–29*–135–707^{txt} *et al.*

[65] 29^c 628 18.

[66] 72–426 131^c–313^c–414^c–551 19–108^{txtc} *et al.*

[67] εὔγλωττος GH^2 and εὔλαλος V^{2}OK^2

[68] Exod 7:19.

[69] Ezekiel 133–134; Philo, *Mos.* 1.99. Some mss of Philo omit πηγαί (BEMA), a move that brought Philo's text closer to the biblical text.

[70] Josephus, *A.J.* 2.294.

[71] Exod 9:8.

[72] Ezekiel 136, ἔπειτα τέφραν οἷς καμιναίαν πάσω. Philo, *Mos.* 1.127, τέφραν ἀπὸ καμίνου λαμβάνοθσι ταῖς χερσίν.

[73] Ezekiel, 143; Philo, *Mos.* 1.119.

[74] Exod 9:25. See also Ps 104:33 that mentions the vineyards and figs trees specifically.

[75] Josephus, *A.J.* 2.305.

[76] Ezekiel 162–166, esp. 166; Philo, *Mos.* 1.141.

was common in later retellings, Ezekiel and Philo are unique in their version (see no. 10 under Exegetical Traditions below).

15. The two also replaced the biblical description of the passage of the children of Israel through the sea, "into the midst of the sea on dry ground" (εἰς μέσον τῆς θαλάσσης κατὰ τὸ ξηράν),[77] with "through the salty path" (ἀλυρᾶς δι᾽ ἀτραποῦ)[78] or "through the dry path" (διὰ ξηρᾶς ἀτραποῦ).[79] The use of "path" (ἀτραπός) is a striking formulation in the retelling of the exodus; it does occur again in the *Third Sibylline Oracle*.[80]

What can we say about the verbal parallels? They are not of equal weight. Some could easily be common improvements or variations of the biblical text (nos. 2, 5, 6, 9, 11, and 13); however, others—in fact the majority—appear to be striking parallels that are not easily dismissed (nos. 1, 3, 4, 7, 8, 10, 12, 14, 15). It is further worth noting that the verbal parallels are distributed through the fragments (eight from fragment 1 [nos. 1–8)], one from fragment 2 [no. 9], one from fragment 10 [no. 10], four from fragment 13 [nos. 11–14], and one from fragment 15 [no. 15]), although the greatest number of parallels are concentrated in the retelling of Moses's birth (nos. 2–7) and the plagues (nos. 11–13). The quantity of the verbal parallels and their broad distribution across the fragments of Ezekiel suggest that Philo knew Ezekiel's *Exagoge*.

There is one other verbal similarity that we should note, although it takes us beyond the scope of *The Life of Moses*. In *On the Migration of Abraham*, Philo wrote: "The hierophant (Moses) quite appropriately entitled one entire sacred book of the legislation Exodus (Ἐξαγωγή), having found a name appropriate to the oracles it contains."[81] Philo's name for the second scroll is striking: it reminds us of the title of Ezekiel's play. Philo used ἔξοδος to describe the journey out of Egypt, but not as the title for the

---

[77] Exod 14:22.

[78] Ezekiel 229.

[79] Philo, *Mos.* 1.179; 2.254, ἐπὶ ξηρᾶς ἀτραποῦ. Cf. Artapanus, frg. 3 (Eusebius, *Praep. ev.* 9.27.36), διὰ ξηρᾶς ὁδοῦ.

[80] *Sib. Or.* 3.248–249, "when the people of twelve tribes left Egypt and journeyed down the path (ἀταρπὸν ὁδεύσει) with God-sent leaders ... "

[81] Philo, *Migr.* 14. See also *Her.* 14, 251; and *Somn.* 1.117, where Philo used the title to introduce a citation from Exodus: *Her.* 14 (Exod 14:14), 251 (Exod 19:18); and *Somn.* 1.117 (Exod 10:23). Philo used ἐξαγωγή in the title for the *Quaestiones in Exodum*. See Eusebius, *Hist. eccl.* 2.18.1. On this title see James R. Royse, "Philo of Alexandria, *Quaestiones in Exodum* 2.62–68: Critical Edition," *SPhA* 24 (2012): 4–5. On Philo's knowledge of the names of biblical books see Helmut Burkhardt, *Die Inspiration heiliger Schriften bei Philo von Alexandrien* (2d ed.; Basel: Brunnen, 1992), 73–74; Naomi G. Cohen, "The Names of the Separate Books of the Pentateuch in Philo's Writings," *SPhA* 9 (1997): 54–78, esp. 58–61; eadem, *Philo's Scriptures: Citations from the Prophets and Writings. Evidence for a Haftarah Cycle in Second Temple Judaism* (JSJSup 123; Leiden: Brill, 2007), 25–53, esp. 29–33.

book.[82] Why did he use Ἐξαγωγή rather than ἔξοδος? Naomi Cohen suggested that Philo was influenced by the title of Ezekiel's play.[83] Her suggestion is worth serious consideration since Philo is the only author whom we know called the scroll by Ἐξαγωγή: all other ancient witnesses to the name use Ἔξοδος in various forms.[84] It may well be that Philo elected to give the name of the book the cognate that reflects the dramatic or literary title that he knew.

The Exegetical Traditions

The second category that we will use is exegetical tradition. Here we are looking for traditions that in one way or another go beyond the biblical text. In this case there are no verbal parallels, only similar exegetical moves to make sense of the text. I have found thirteen examples of common exegetical traditions. We will also consider the extent to which the same exegetical tradition is attested in other Jewish works, with the same stipulations noted for verbal parallels.

1. Ezekiel and Philo both omitted the story of the midwives in their versions of Pharaoh's machinations, probably to remove any hint of complicity.[85] Josephus appears to have been sensitive to this implication, but reacted differently by making the midwives Egyptians thus distancing the Hebrews themselves.[86]

2. Another major omission shared by Ezekiel and Philo is the absence of the ark. This meant that Moses could not be set on the river but on the bank of the river. In Ezekiel, Moses's mother set her infant "at the edge of the river" (παρ᾽ ἄκρα ποταμοῦ) and Pharaoh's daughter drew him "from the moist bank of the river" (ὑγρᾶς ἀνεῖλε ποταμίας ἀπ᾽ ἠόνος).[87] Philo had both parents set him "on the banks of the river" (παρὰ τὰς ὄχθας τοῦ ποταμοῦ).[88] The two thus knew a common exegetical tradition, but used different

---

[82] Philo used ἔξοδος 20x, 10x for the journey from Egypt: *Migr.* 15, 151; *Her.* 273; *Mos.* 1.105, 122, 268; 2.248; *Hypoth.* 8.6.1, 2, 5.

[83] Cohen, "The Names of the Separate Books of the Pentateuch in Philo's Writings," 58–61 and eadem, *Philo's Scriptures*, 29–33. The title of Ezekiel's work was mentioned by Polyhistor (Eusebius, *Praep. ev.* 9.28.12 = frg. 13) and Clement, *Strom.* 1.23.55.1 (= frg. 1A).

[84] See Wevers, *Exodus*, 65, lists twenty-one variations of the *inscriptio*: all use ἔξοδος. It is worth noting that Aristobulus does use ἐξαγωγή to describe the exodus, but not as a title for the book (frg. 2.11).

[85] Ezekiel 8–13; Philo, *Mos.* 1.8.

[86] Josephus, *A.J.* 2.206–207.

[87] Ezekiel 31.

[88] Ezekiel 17; Philo, *Mos.* 1.10.

words to describe the river's bank: Ezekiel used ἠϊών while Philo opted for the more prosaic ὄχθη. The author of Acts also omitted the ark and—like Ezekiel and Philo[89]—said that Moses was exposed, although it is not clear from the abbreviated retelling of Exod 2 in Acts 7 whether this was the result of a telescoping of the text or a reference to the same exegetical tradition.[90]

3. According to the biblical text, Moses's sister watched what would happen to her infant brother "from a distance" (μακρόθεν).[91] Ezekiel and Philo suggested that she stood nearby, although they do not agree in wording: the former used "near by" (πέλας)[92] and the latter "a little way off" (μικρὸν ἄποθεν).[93] Josephus has a similar but different version: he said that Miriam walked along beside the ark.[94]

4. Ezekiel and Philo also agree in the timing of the naming of Moses. In the biblical tradition he was named after his mother brought the weaned Moses to the house of Pharaoh,[95] while in Ezekiel and Philo he was named when Pharaoh's daughter found him on the bank of the Nile,[96] a tradition that Josephus also knew.[97]

5. When he was grown, the biblical text suggests that Moses became aware of the distress of his own people and went out to see them.[98] Ezekiel and Philo state that he broke with Pharaoh when he came to understand Pharaoh's evil machinations.[99] This could be a common independent move to explain Moses's break with his past, although the similarity of the agreement is worth noting.

6. Ezekiel and Philo retell the story of the burning bush in two similar ways that depart from the biblical text. Both elaborate on the condition of the bush that was not consumed by the flame.[100] Ezekiel wrote: "its growth remains entirely green."[101] Philo said, "it remained as it was before it began

---

[89] Ezekiel 16–17; Philo, *Mos.* 1.10, 14. See Exod 2:3.

[90] Acts 7:21 "when he had been exposed, Pharaoh's daughter rescued him and raised him as her own son."

[91] Exod 2:4.

[92] Ezekiel 18.

[93] Philo, *Mos.* 1.12.

[94] Josephus, *A.J.* 2.221.

[95] Exod 2:10.

[96] Ezekiel 30–31; Philo, *Mos.* 1.17.

[97] Josephus, *A.J.* 2.228.

[98] Exod 2:11, κατανοήσας δὲ τὸν πόνον αὐτῶν.

[99] Ezekiel 40–41, πρὸς ἔργα γὰρ / θυμός μ' ἄνωγε καὶ τέχνασμα βασιλέως; Philo, *Mos.* 1.33, εἰ μὴ κατεῖδεν ἐν τῇ χώρᾳ μέγα καινουργηθὲν ὑπὸ τοῦ βασιλέως ἀσέβημα. Philo then related the events of Exod 1 (§§34–39).

[100] Exod 3:3, τί ὅτι οὐ κατακαίεται ὁ βάτος.

[101] Ezekiel 90–95, esp. 92.

to burn; it lost nothing but, on the contrary, gained in brightness."[102] These could easily be independent expansions of authors who wanted to enhance the dramatic quality of the biblical narrative. Josephus has a similar expansion. He wrote: "the fire ... left the green throughout the bush and its bloom was left unharmed, nor was one of its fruit bearing branches consumed."[103] Later Jewish interpretations concentrated on the celestial fire, although they did note and elaborate on the significance of the bush as a thornbush.[104]

7. The next agreement is more complex. In the biblical text, "the angel of the LORD appeared to Moses in a flame of fire from the bush" (ὤφθη δὲ αὐτῷ ἄγγελος κυρίου ἐν πυρὶ φλόγος ἐκ τοῦ βάτου).[105] Ezekiel had God say: "From the bush the divine word shines out to you" (ὁ δ᾽ ἐκ βάτου σοι θεῖος ἐκλάμπει λόγος).[106] The expression "divine word" has been understood from "divine speech" to the "divine Logos."[107] If the latter were the case, Ezekiel would be among the first Jews to attest a belief in the Logos. For the present we do not need to adjudicate this debate but to ask whether Philo was aware of the interpretation. The commentator described the flame that Moses saw and then said: "someone might suppose that this was the Image of the Existent, but let it be called an angel because it announced the things that were about to occur with a silence clearer than a voice by means of a vision that accomplished great things."[108] For Philo, the Logos was the Image of God.[109] He appears to know the interpretation in Ezekiel, but rejected it in favor of preserving the language of the biblical text.

8. The next exegetical tradition is also involved. Ezekiel wrote that when God spoke to Moses from the bush, he said: "I am the God of your ancestors, about whom you speak/Abraham, Isaac, and Jacob the third./ I have remembered them and my gifts (to them)."[110] This is based on Exod 3:6, "I am the God of your ancestor, the God of Abraham, the God of Isaac, and the God of Jacob." This is clear, but what are the "gifts"? This appears to draw from Exod 2:24: "God remembered his covenant with Abraham, Isaac, and Jacob." Ezekiel may have conflated the two texts and called the

---

[102] Philo, *Mos.* 1.68. See also 1.65.

[103] Josephus, *A.J.* 2.267.

[104] Ginzberg, *Legends of the Jews*, 2:303; 5:415–416.

[105] Exod 3:2.

[106] Ezekiel 99.

[107] For options see Howard Jacobson, "Mysticism and Apocalyptic in Ezekiel's *Exagoge*," *Illinois Classical Studies* 6 (1981): 272–93 and the summary discussion in Holladay, *Poets*, 455.

[108] Philo, *Mos.* 1.66.

[109] Philo, *Opif.* 25; *Leg.* 3.96; *Her.* 231; *Spec.* 1.81; 3.83, 207; *QG* 2.62.

[110] Ezekiel 104–106.

covenant God's gifts. The substitution of "gifts" for "covenant" may have been a way for Ezekiel to minimize national claims of the Hebrews of his day. Philo omitted all of these references in his *Life of Moses*. He did know the tradition that the covenant was linked with gifts. The treatise *On the Migration of Abraham* interprets God's covenant with Abraham in Genesis 17 as five "gifts" (δωρεαί).[111] Thus both Ezekiel and Philo omitted the reference to the covenant in the text of Exod 2. While this is an argument from silence, it is worth noting that both Ezekiel and Philo not only agree in their omission, but understand the covenant as a gift.[112]

9. The first sign that God gave Moses to assure him that the divine presence would be with him was turning his rod into a snake.[113] Both Ezekiel and Philo expand the description of the snake and Moses's fear.[114] These are likely common expansions that we should expect in later retellings.

10. The next four common interpretations deal with the exodus proper (nos. 10–13). Ezekiel and Philo agreed in stating that the Israelites were unarmed when they left the land. The Hebrew text does not make this point. The MT of Exod 13:18 reads, "the children of Israel went up from Egypt in battle array" (עלו בני ישראל מארץ מצרים וחמשים) which the Greek renders "the children of Israel went up out of Egypt in the fifth generation," (πέμπτη δὲ γενεᾷ ἀνέβησαν οἱ υἱοὶ Ἰσραὴλ ἐκ γῆς Αἰγύπτου), reading a number (חמש="five") in the place of a participle (חמשים = "arrayed for battle"). Ezekiel and Philo made the unarmed nature of the Hebrews explicit;[115] however, this was a common tradition as early as Demetrius.[116]

11. The next tradition is similar: the biblical text suggests that Moses stretched his hand out over the sea and a south wind blew all night causing the sea to be dried up.[117] Ezekiel and Philo have the sea split immediately when Moses struck it with his rod. There are two differences: in the biblical

[111] Philo, *Migr.* 1–127. Cf. also *Mut.* 52.

[112] This has been addressed in detail by William Horbury, "Ezekiel Tragicus 106: δωρήματα," *VT* 36 (1986): 37–51, esp. 42–45, although he makes the connections by pointing out the use of the "gifts of God" in l. 35. See also Anna Maria Schwemer, "Zum Verhältnis von Diatheke und Nomos in den Schriften der jüdischen Diaspora Ägyptens in hellenistisch-römischer Zeit," in *Bund und Thora: Zur theologischer Begriffsgeschichte in alttestamentlicher frühjüdischer und urchristlicher Tradition* (eds. Friedrich Avemarie and Hermann Lichtenberger; WUNT 92; Tübingen: Mohr [Siebeck], 1996), 67–109, esp. 92–101.

[113] Exod 4:3.

[114] Ezekiel 122–126; Philo, *Mos.* 1.77.

[115] Ezekiel 210; Philo, *Mos.* 1.170.

[116] Demetrius, frg. 5 (Eusebius, *Praep. ev.* 9.29.16); Wis 10:20; Josephus, *A.J.* 2.321. Contrast, Pseudo-Philo, *L.A.B.* 10.3, who thought that they were armed.

[117] Exod 14:16, 21.

text, Moses stretched his hand out over the sea; in Ezekiel and Philo, he struck it with his rod.[118] In the biblical text, the wind dried the sea over the course of the night; in Ezekiel and Philo the sea split as soon as Moses struck it with his rod.[119] Artapanus, Pseudo-Philo, and Josephus also knew the tradition of Moses striking the sea and splitting it.[120]

12. Both Ezekiel and Philo expanded the role of the pillar of fire that guided the Israelites.[121] Ezekiel and Philo both suggested that God caused fire to appear behind the Hebrews, although they have slightly different understandings of it. In Ezekiel a great flame appeared to the Egyptians;[122] in Philo, the vision of God flashed rays of fire.[123] Artapanus and Josephus also thought that fire was involved in the destruction of the Egyptians,[124] a tradition shared with later Jewish interpreters.[125]

13. There is one other tradition that we should mention. The biblical text says that the entire Egyptian army was destroyed: "not even one of them was left."[126] This created a problem for Ezekiel who needed to narrate the story without having the action appear on the stage. He chose to do what other tragedians had done: he had a messenger report the destruction, in this case, an Egyptian survivor, a point that is made clear from the first person narration and Eusebius's introductory frame.[127] Philo followed the biblical text and emphasized the complete destruction of the Egyptian army "so that not even a torch-bearer was left to announce to the Egyptians the sudden disaster."[128] Howard Jacobson thought that this point—shared by Josephus[129]—was a direct polemic against Ezekiel in defense of a more literal reading of the biblical text.[130] However, the expression used by Philo

---

[118] Ezekiel 227–228; Philo, *Mos.* 1.177.

[119] Ezekiel 227–228; Philo, *Mos.* 1.177, although Philo also recorded the tradition about the wind (§176). See Exod 14:21.

[120] Artapanus, frg. 3 (Eusebius, *Praep. ev.* 9.27.36); Pseudo-Philo, *L.A.B.* 10.5; Josephus, *A.J.* 2.338. Later Jewish interpreters have an elaborate scheme for the interactions between God and Moses at the Sea. They emphasize the role of God in parting the waters. See Ginzberg, *Legends of the Jews*, 4:18–20.

[121] Exod 14:24.

[122] Ezekiel 234.

[123] Philo, *Mos.* 2.254.

[124] Artapanus frg. 3 (Eusebius, *Praep. ev.* 9.27.37) and Josephus, *A.J.* 2.343.

[125] Ginzberg, *Legends of the Jews*, 4:27; 6:9.

[126] Exod 14:29.

[127] Ezekiel 202, 204, 211, 214, 215, 218, 223, 230, 213, 235, 238, 239, 240. See also the introductory frame to frg. 15 (Eusebius, *Praep. ev.* 9.29.14).

[128] Philo, *Mos.* 1.179.

[129] Josephus, *A.J.* 2.344, although Josephus did not mention the destruction of even torch-bearers.

[130] Jacobson, *The Exagoge of Ezekiel*, 152.

and Josephus is a trope that emphasized the complete destruction of an army.[131] I see no need to understand this as a polemic; it reflects the fact that Philo did not have the same constraint that Ezekiel faced and followed the biblical text more closely.

Most of the exegetical traditions have parallels in other texts—hardly a surprise, especially in Josephus who knew the texts. The number of exegetical agreements is impressive. This is not the case of an isolated agreement but of sustained agreements across the entire story. The exegetical parallels are distributed widely across the fragments: four from fragment 1 (nos. 1–4), one from fragment 2 (no. 5), one from fragment 8 (no. 6), two from fragment nine (nos. 7–8), one from fragment 12 (no. 9), and four from fragment 15 (nos. 10–13). As was the case with the verbal parallels, the quantity of the exegetical parallels and the distribution of the parallels across the entire work of Ezekiel suggests that Philo knew the full play.

Thematic Parallel

The final point of comparison is the most famous. In fragments six and seven, Ezekiel narrated a dream that Moses had and his father-in-law's—Raguel's—interpretation of the dream.[132] Moses said: "There appeared to be on the summit of Mount Sinai a certain great throne that reached up to a vale of heaven.[133] On it sat a certain noble person who had a diadem and a great scepter in his left hand. With his right hand, he motioned to me and I stood before the throne." The vision of the divine throne on Sinai is not surprising, but the next statements are: "he handed me the scepter and told me to sit on the throne. He gave me the royal diadem and vacated the throne. I saw the entire circle of the earth, beneath the earth and above heaven." Then in a statement that reminds us of Joseph's dream,[134] Moses said: "a large group of stars fell on their knees before me; I numbered them all and they passed by me like a company of soldiers." Raguel interpreted the dream to signify that Moses will sit as humanity's judge on the throne with the power to perceive the past, present, and future.

---

[131] See Obad 18 (LXX). F. H. Colson pointed this out in PLCL 6:368–369 n. a.

[132] Ezekiel 68–89.

[133] There is a problem with the text. The major issue for our purposes is whether to read "Sinai" (Σιναίου) or not. The text is corrupt. The best reading is Sinai in my judgment. Even if we read "lofty" (αἰπεινοῦ)–as Jacobson suggests–we would naturally identify the mountain with Sinai. For details on the mss and emendations see Holladay, *Poets*, 439–440 n. 72.

[134] Gen 37:9.

The dream and its interpretation are a clear expansion of the biblical text and have been the subject of extensive discussion.[135] I am inclined to think that Ezekiel has drawn on two statements from Exodus for the inspiration of this dream. The first is based on the five theophanies that occur on Mount Sinai in Exodus. [136] More specifically, the background is either the third or—more likely—the fifth theophany. In the third ascent, Moses took Aaron, Nadab, Abihu, and seventy of the elders up with him and had a vision of God.[137] He then proceeded further up the mountain with Joshua where he remained forty days and forty nights.[138] In the fifth ascent, Moses saw God's glory.[139]

These statements could suffice to explain the vision, but not the invitation for Moses to sit on God's throne. The most likely background for this move is the statement in Exod 7:1, "behold, I have set you as god to Pharaoh," at least this would explain why God vacated the divine throne and installed Moses upon it. While the play will go on to remind Moses that he is mortal,[140] the dream suggests that he is—in some way—divine. If Ezekiel drew any inspiration for this from the biblical text, the obvious place to turn is Exod 7:1. The absence of any direct allusion has led interpreters to look for parallels of figures on divine thrones in Hellenistic or Jewish sources; the parallels selected determine the interpretation.[141] While the background may be complex, it is hard to exclude Exod 7:1.

[135] Lucien Cerfaux, "Influence des Mystères sur la Judaïsme Alexandrin avant Philon," *Le Muséon* 37 (1924): 29–88, esp. 54–58; Erwin R. Goodenough, *By Light, Light: The Mystic Gospel of Hellenistic Judaism* (New Haven: Yale University Press, 1935; repr. by Amsterdam: Philo Press, 1969), 290; idem, *Jewish Symbols in the Greco-Roman Period* (13 vols.; Bollingen Series 37; New York: Pantheon Books, 1953–1968), 9:101, who understood the dream as an example of Orphic mysticism; Wayne Meeks, "Moses as God and King," in *Religions in Antiquity: Essays in Memory of E. R. Goodenough* (ed. Jacob Neusner; SHR 14; Leiden: E. J. Brill, 1968), 354–371; Esther Starobinski-Safran, "Un poète judéo-hellénistique: Ezéchiel le tragique," *MH* 31 (1974): 216–224; Carl R. Holladay, "Portrait of Moses in Ezekiel the Tragedian," *SBLSP* (1976): 447–52; Howard Jacobson, "Mysticism and Apocalyptic in Ezekiel's *Exagoge*," *Illinois Classical Studies* 6 (1981): 272–293; and Pieter van der Horst, "Moses' Throne Vision in Ezekiel the Dramatist," *JJS* 34 (1983): 21–29.

[136] Exod 19:3–14; 19:20–25; 24:1–11 and 24:12–32:15; 32:30–34; 34:1–18.

[137] Exod 24:1–11.

[138] Exod 24:12–32:15.

[139] Exod 34:1–28 which includes the anticipated vision of 33:17–23.

[140] Ezekiel 102.

[141] The sharpest debate has been between van der Horst and Jacobson. Van der Horst, "Moses' Throne Vision in Ezekiel the Dramatist," 21–29, argued for a background in mysticism and the Enochic literature in particular; Jacobson, *The Exagoge of Ezekiel*, 89–97 and idem, "Mysticism and Apocalyptic in Ezekiel's *Exagoge*," 272–93, argued that the dream was a polemic against the mystical view; and van der Horst, "Some Notes on the *Exagoge* of Ezekiel," *Mnemosyne* 37 (1984): 354–75, offered a rejoinder.

Is there any evidence that Philo knew this dream or its interpretation? He did not repeat the dream or the interpretation; however, on two occasions, he hinted at divine status for Moses in his *Life of Moses*. The first occurs in an excursus in which Philo reflected on Moses's authority.[142] The key passage comes immediately after Philo argued that the elements of the cosmos obeyed Moses because he was God's friend and as God's friend had a share in God's possession.[143] This led him to narrate Moses's ascent on Mount Sinai. He wrote: "For he was named god and king of the entire nation and entered into the darkness where God was, that is, into the unseen, invisible, incorporeal, and archetypal reality of what exists."[144] The reference to Moses as god is to Exod 7:1. The reference to Moses as king is part of the larger portrait of Moses in book 1 of the *Life of Moses*.[145] The entrance into the darkness is a reference to Moses's ascent on Sinai.

The question that we need to pose is did Philo draw any inspiration for the combination of cosmic, royal, and divine qualities from Ezekiel's *Exagoge*? Many have answered affirmatively based on the obvious concurrence of the key elements,[146] but by no means all.[147] The issue is not whether Philo thought that Moses shared in the essence of God; he was clear in his writings that the gap between the truly Existent and humans was real. The issue is whether he thought that Moses had participated in the divine in ways that other mortals had not.[148]

---

[142] Philo, *Mos.* 1.148–162.

[143] Ibid., 1.156–157.

[144] Ibid., *Mos.* 1.158.

[145] Ibid., *Mos.* 1.334; 2.1–7.

[146] See Wayne A. Meeks, *The Prophet King: Moses Traditions and the Johannine Christo-logy* (NovTSup 14; Leiden: Brill, 1965), 147–49, 153, 156–57; idem, "Moses as God and King," 354–71; van der Horst, "Moses' Throne Vision in Ezekiel the Dramatist," 21–29, esp. 25–26; Maarten J. J. Menken, "The Provenance and Meaning of the Old Testament Quotations in John 6:31," *NovT* 30 (1988): 39–56, esp. 49–51; Martha Himmelfarb, *Ascent to Heaven in Jewish and Christian Apocalypses* (New York: Oxford University Press, 1993), 48–49, 70–71; and Peder Borgen, *Philo of Alexandria, An Exegete for His Time* (NovTSup 86; Leiden: Brill, 1997), 201–205.

[147] The most important challenges have come from Carl R. Holladay, *Theios Aner in Hellenistic Judaism: A Critique of the Use of This Category in New Testament Christology* (SBLDS40; Missoula, MT: Scholars Press, 1977), 108–129; Runia, "God and Man in Philo of Alexandria," 53–63; and Louis H. Feldman, *Philo's Portrayal of Moses in the Context of Ancient Judaism* (CJAS 15; South Bend: University of Notre Dame Press, 2007), 339–348.

[148] On this issue see Naomi Janowitz, "'You Are Gods': Multiple Divine Beings in Late Antique Jewish Theology," in *With Letters of Light: Studies in the Dead Sea Scrolls, Early Jewish Apocalypticism, Magic, and Mysticism in Honor of Rachel Elior* (eds. Daphna V. Arbel and Andrei A. Orlov; Berlin: de Gruyter, 2010), 349–64, esp. 352–57. See especially the article of David Litwa, "The Deification of Moses in Philo of Alexandria," elsewhere in this volume.

A text that has not received the attention that it deserves in the debate is Philo's treatment of Exod 24:2 in the *Questions and Answers on Exodus*. The biblical text specified that only Moses should ascend Mount Sinai. Philo explained why: "For when the prophetic mind becomes divinely inspired and filled with God, it becomes like the monad, not being at all mixed with any of those things associated with duality." The prophetic mind reminds us of Raguel's interpretation more than it reminds us of Moses's dream; however, the reference to the monad is the element that Philo elected to expand. He continued: "But he who is revolved into the nature of unity is said to come near God in a kind of family relation, for having given up and left behind all mortal kinds, he is changed into the divine so that such men become kin to God and truly divine."[149] The point that I wish to make is that Philo had no hesitation in calling Moses divine in association with his experience on Sinai. While he did not allude to Exod 7:1—he rarely cited secondary lemmata in the *Questions and Answers*[150]—it was likely in the background of his exposition.

This may also explain—in part—why Philo presented the death of Moses as he did at the end of the *Life of Moses*. Philo wrote: "Later, at the time when he was about to set off on his migration from here to heaven, having left mortal life to become immortal, he was summoned by the Father who converted his dual nature—body and soul—into the nature of the indivisible monad and transformed him through and through into mind pure as the sunlight."[151] While there is no reference to Moses as god here, it is clear that a type of apotheosis has occurred, an apotheosis that is similar to the earlier experience at Sinai.

Conclusion

Had Philo either watched a performance of Ezekiel's *Exagoge* or read a copy of the play? I am not asking whether Ezekiel was a major source for Philo's *Life of Moses*: the scope and the scale of the two works are so different that this is not a realistic way to pose the question. I am asking whether Ezekiel's portrait of Moses served as one of the influences on Philo's portrayal in the *Life of Moses*.

---

[149] Philo, *QE* 2.29.

[150] See David T. Runia, "Secondary Texts in Philo's *Quaestiones*," in *Both Literal and Allegorical: Studies in Philo of Alexandria's* Questions and Answers on Genesis and Exodus (ed. David M. Hay; BJS 232; Atlanta: Scholars Press, 1991), 47–79.

[151] Philo, *Mos.* 2.288. This is the first part of a longer Greek sentence that goes on to mention the fact that Moses prophesied to each tribe and even his own death.

I am inclined to think that it was. The number of verbal parallels and exegetical traditions that the two shared is impressive. Philo did not use Ezekiel's *Exagoge* as a basis for his portrait of Moses—the biblical text served this role; however, Philo apparently liked a number of Ezekiel's turns of phrases and interpretive moves well enough that they became part of his own reading of the story of Exodus. Ezekiel had no authoritative status for Philo; the commentator could depart from him as well as accept him depending on his own judgments. Philo apparently found the retelling of Moses's birth, the story of the burning bush, and—I think—the dream of Moses intriguing.

If I am right, it means that we should not think of Philo as someone who lived in isolation working in his study or offering lectures to students. Rather, he was someone who appreciated the theater and either watched or read the script of one Jewish play enough times that selections from it became a part of his own reading of the biblical text.

Yale Divinity School

The Studia Philonica Annual 26 (2014) 135–149

PHILO AND GREEK POETRY

PURA NIETO HERNÁNDEZ

This paper falls into two parts. In the first, I show that, contrary to what some scholars have maintained, Philo held archaic and classical Greek poetry in high esteem, and believed that it was an important source of moral education. In the second, I offer some examples of Philo's creative adaptation of poetic language and motifs, which confirm his deep engagement with the classical tradition.

I. *Introduction*

Philo, who, as is well known, follows Plato's philosophical positions more often than not, has, like Plato himself, an ambivalent relationship to poetry. Beyond the fact that he cites directly and frequently the best Greek poets (from Homer to the tragedians),[1] his own writing is often highly poetical. He uses terms, phrases and constructions that are unique to poetry (often, clearly Homeric), in a way similar to Plato's own. Philo, nevertheless, does not limit himself to the direct quotation or the clear allusion to previous poetry. He rather uses poetic language in highly creative ways: some of his phrases have a poetic, almost traditional, ring to them, but when examined carefully they turn out to be Philo's own inventions. Thus, he appears to have no superficial acquaintance with the poetic tradition, but rather a deep knowledge of it. And yet, at the same time, in some passages he denounces the false fictions of the poets and of the arts in general, as if he were endorsing Plato's famous indictments against poetry.[2] This has produced among scholars a perception that Philo's view of Greek culture is not

---

[1] On the knowledge of the tradition that Philo exhibits in his work see now David Lincicum, "A Preliminary Index to Philo's non-Biblical Citations and Allusions." *SPhA* 25 (2013): 139–67.

[2] Stephen Halliwell in his book *Between Ecstasy and Truth. Interpretations of Greek Poetics from Homer to Longinus* (Oxford: Oxford University Press 2011), 155–207, has recently highlighted Plato's own ambivalent attitude towards poetry and poets.

entirely positive, or at least that it is nuanced if not outright contradictory. Thus Robert Lamberton could write in 1986 that "most of his [Philo's] citations of Homer are purely rhetorical and decorative, and give little indication of what Philo may have thought the lines meant—if anything— beyond the literal."[3] And yet, three pages later, commenting on *Prov.* 2.40– 41, Lamberton writes: "Philo was well acquainted with the standard Stoic allegories of Homeric myth, and of Greek myth in general. He clearly respected Homer not only as a poet, but as a theologian as well."[4] Recently, however, scholars such as Maren Niehoff and Katell Berthelot have made good cases in defense of Philo's serious engagement with the Greek tradition and with Homeric poetry in particular.[5] This is also my view. In what follows I provide some further evidence of the depth of Philo's assimilation of Homeric poetry.

II. *Philo on Greek Poetry*

Philo cites (or alludes to) Homer's text over sixty times and mentions Homer by name four times.[6] Two of these passages describe Homer as "the greatest and most famous poet,"[7] and the poet "par excellence."[8] Philo

---

[3] Robert Lamberton, *Homer the Theologian. Neoplatonist Allegorical Reading and the Growth of the Epic Tradition* (Berkeley: University of California Press, 1986), 49.

[4] Ibid, 51.

[5] See Maren R. Niehoff, *Jewish Exegesis and Homeric Scholarship in Alexandria* (Cambridge: Cambridge University Press, 2011); eadem, "Philo and Plutarch on Homer," in *Homer and the Bible in the Eyes of Ancient Interpreters*, (ed., Maren R. Niehoff; Jerusalem Studies in Religion and Culture 16; Leiden: Brill, 2012), 127–49; and Katell Berthelot, "Philon d'Alexandrie, lecteur d' Homère: quelques éléments de réflexion," in *Prolongements et renouvellements de la tradition classique*, (eds., Anne Balansard, Gilles Dorival, Mireille Loubet; Textes et documents de la Méditerranée antique et médiévale; Aix-en-Provence: Université de Provence, 2011), 145–57. Berthelot describes four different ways in which Philo relates to Homer: 1. Direct citation; 2. Evocation of Homer as the greatest of the poets; 3. Stylistic allusions or reminiscences; and 4. A more indirect connection, i.e., the way in which Philo takes the interpretations of Homer that were current in his time as a model for his own interpretation of biblical texts. After enumerating these possibilities, Berthelot concentrates on Philo as reader and advocate of Homer, his use of the Homeric texts for his exegesis of Scripture and for his apologetic writings, and concludes with Philo's view of the Bible's superiority to Homer.

[6] The lists provided in volume 10 of PLCL are helpful but neither exact nor exhaustive.

[7] *Conf.* 4, ὁ μέγιστος καὶ δοκιμώτατος τῶν ποιητῶν Ὅμηρος. The passage offers a direct quotation of *Od.* 11.315, 318, on the piling up of Mounts Ossa, Pelion and Olympus on top of each other. All translations of Philo's text are from the PLCL.

also—as is usual in the rest of the Greek tradition—often refers to him simply as ὁ ποιητής, an apellation that Philo, we should note, employs regularly for God. Despite the fact that he never quite calls Homer "divine"[9] or "sacred,"[10] Philo constantly has recourse to Homer's verses as authoritative on a variety of matters, to illustrate, reinforce, or even justify his own argumentation.[11] This is understandable, given that in no small number of passages Philo speaks of the fundamental role of poets in the moral education of both Greeks and barbarians and, more significantly, in his own education. Thus in *Agr.* 18.4 Philo explains that he will extirpate from souls all passions and licentious tendencies and instead implant "the diligent search of what wise poets have written," which in his view comes second only to learning to read and write easily. In *Spec.* 1.343, he again speaks of the moral value of poetry, since "song charms away the passions and controls the irregular element in us with its rhythm, the discordant with its melodies, the immoderate with its measures." He continues, "And each of these three assumes every variety of form, as the musicians and poets testify, belief in whom necessarily becomes habitual in those who have received a good education."

Two other passages highlight the importance of poets as teachers of wisdom and morality for public, social life:

Prob. 143: "And if we are justified in listening to the poets,—and why should we not, since they are our educators through all our days, and as parents in private life teach wisdom to their children, so do they in public life to their cities—"

And

---

[8] *Abr.* 10.1: ποιητὴς Ὅμηρος, μυρίων ποιητῶν ὄντων, κατ᾽ ἐξοχὴν λέγεται. The two other passages with Homer's name are *Prob.* 31: Ὅμηρος μὲν οὖν „ποιμένας λαῶν" εἴωθε καλεῖν τοὺς βασιλέας, "Homer often calls kings 'shepherds of the people'"; and *Leg.* 80–82: Πρωτέως, ὃν εἰσήγαγεν Ὅμηρος μεταβολὰς παντοίας ἐνδεχόμενον, "Proteus whom Homer represented as admitting every kind of transfiguration."

[9] Berthelot, "Philon d'Alexandrie, lecteur d' Homère," 147.

[10] Niehoff, "Philo and Plutarch on Homer," 130 n. 21.

[11] Berthelot, "Philon d'Alexandrie, lecteur d' Homère," 156, indicates that Philo does not use Homer usually as a historian, something we do find in Josephus; on the other hand, Josephus never uses him to explain or clarify the biblical text, which is in fact Philo's main purpose in his use of Homer's poetry. But, as we will see (infra p. 6), Philo occasionally cites Homer as authority on historical matters, for instance at *Contempl.* 17. On the importance of the Homeric poems as canonical texts throughout Greek-speaking antiquity, see Margalit Finkelberg, "Decanonising Homer: Reception of the Homeric Poems in Antiquity and Modernity," in *Homer and the Bible in the Eyes of Ancient Interpreters,* (ed. Maren R. Niehoff; Leiden: Brill, 2012), 15–28, esp. 16–17, with bibliography.

Sacr. 78: "No doubt it is profitable, if not for the acquisition of perfect virtue, at any rate for the life of civic virtue, to feed the mind on ancient and time-honoured thoughts, to trace the venerable tradition of noble deeds, which historians and all the family of poets have handed down to the memory of their own and future generations."

Poetry can also be a moral remedy for a bad upbringing, even among barbarians:

Prob. 98: "The freedom of the virtuous is also vouched for by the poets and prose writers, in whose thoughts Greeks and barbarians alike are reared almost from the cradle, and so gain improvement of character and restamp into sterling coin every bit of metal in their souls which has been debased by a faulty upbringing and mode of life."

Only philosophy seems to occupy a higher place in intellectual endeavors; but still the study of the poets is a prerequisite, as Philo says speaking of his own education: "when first I was incited by the goads of philosophy to desire her I consorted in early youth with one of her handmaids, Grammar, and all that I begat by her, writing, reading and study of the writings of the poets, I dedicated to her mistress."[12]

Despite all this praise for poetry, Philo is also keenly aware of its limitations. Thus, for example, in the passage of *Sacr.* 78 just cited, he goes on to measure poetry against the wisdom that is God-inspired,[13] where direct contemplation replaces hearing. In *Opif.* 4.2 he affirms the inability of human poets to sing the beauty of the creative act of God, and in several other passages he condemns the poets' mythical fictions, especially in regard to their representation of many gods or of false characters, and also warns about the attractiveness of their language, which charms people into believing these falsehoods.[14] Philo also criticizes poets in contrast to either his own truthfulness as a writer, or to the truthfulness of the Lawgiver.[15] It

---

[12] Philo, *Congr.* 75. This passage, together with the story of Abraham, Sarah, and her slave girl (*Cher.* 5), with whom Abraham is able to conceive a child, has suggested to some interpreters (Colson, *PLCL* I, xvi n. f) a connection with the allegorical interpretation of Penelope's maids in the *Odyssey*: the suitors, unable to have Penelope (=Wisdom), content themselves with her servants. For this analogy and the many other images that Philo applies to the encyclical training, see Karl Olav Sandnes, *Challenge of Homer: School, Pagan Poets and Early Christianity* (Library of New Testament Studies 400; London: Continuum International Publishing, 2009), 71–72.

[13] Sandnes, *Challenge of Homer*, 75: "Philo was concerned that encyclical studies could distract one from the most important thing, namely to 'see God'; i.e. to know the God of Israel. This, according to Philo, was the summit of philosophy."

[14] See *Spec.* 2.164; *Opif.* 157 (poets and sophists, critized); *Contempl.* 1.6; *Spec.* 1.28–30.

[15] Lamberton, *Homer the Theologian*, 48: "It is puzzling to find that in spite of his frequent indications of his concern with, and knowledge of, pagan myth and his application

is well known that in several passages he notes the condemnation of all arts by the Lawgiver on account of the corrupting effect they have on the soul, since they falsify reality (see *Gig.* 58 with explicit reference to the expulsion of all arts from Moses' Republic, and, with the same idea, *Spec.* 1. 28–30).

Philo does affirm that the value of poetry is that, by providing examples of the heroes of the past who suffered, we learn to control the vain fantasies of our imagination,[16] although some scholars have taken this remark in a negative sense. For example, one writes: "It is, however, worth noticing that Philo is here mentioning examples that should not be imitated but rather avoided. In the light of what he writes elsewhere, it seems likely that this implicitly conveys a critical attitude towards Greek literature."[17] I would see this in a different light, and stress rather Philo's respect and admiration for the Greek tradition as an excellent accomplishment of humankind to the point that, more than once, even when he cannot accept the literal truth of a Homeric or poetic passage, he still finds something fruitful and good about it. For example, when he cites the passage at *Od.* 17.485 in which gods are described as travelling among men, Philo says: "The current story may not be a true one, but it is at all events good and profitable for us that it should be current" (*Somn.* 1.233).[18]

III. *Philo and Greek Poetry*

There is no question, then, that Philo is proud of his own cultural education and that he approves it for others too.[19] He exhibits his excellent knowledge

---

to scripture of techniques unquestionably derivative from pagan exegesis, he nevertheless repeatedly denies that there is a mythic element in scripture."

[16] Philo, *Congr.* 15: "For grammar teaches us to study literature in the poets and historians, and will thus produce intelligence and wealth of knowledge. It will teach us also to despise the vain delusions of our empty imagination by showing us the calamities which heroes and demi-gods who are celebrated in such literature are said to have undergone."

[17] Sandnes, *Challenge of Homer*, 75. In his footnote 20 he continues "The examples to be pursued, Philo takes from the heroes of Jewish tradition," with reference to Alan Mendelson, *Secular Education in Philo of Alexandria* (HUCM 7; Cincinnati, OH: Hebrew Union College Press, 1982), 6.

[18] Cf. Lamberton, *Homer the Theologian*, 49, commenting on this same passage: "Even when the truth of Homeric poetry is treated as dubious or unacceptable, that poetry is seen to have redeeming value."

[19] I subscribe to Sterling's hypothesis that Philo had his own school with his own disciples; see Gregory E. Sterling, "'The School of Sacred Laws': The Social Setting of Philo's Treatises" *VC* 53 (1999): 148–164 and idem, "The place of Philo of Alexandria in the study of Christian origins," in *Philo und das Neue Testament: wechselseitige Wahrnehmungen;*

of the tradition constantly and in at least two fundamental ways: 1) by frequent direct citations of one or several lines of poetry; 2) by imitating poetic expression in his own language in a creative way. I offer examples of each.

1) *Direct citations of poetry:*

Often when Philo cites a sizable portion of Homer's text (at least a full half line) the text of the citation coincides with the text of Homer that we have received from the direct tradition. One passage is of particular interest, inasmuch as Philo mentions its precise location in the *Iliad*: "in the beginning of the thirteenth rhapsody." As far as I can tell, Philo is the first (or one of the first) to refer to a specific book of Homer in this way. I have not found any text previous to the first century c.e. that uses the term *rhapsodia* ("book") in this modern fashion. The grammarian Aristonicus (known to have been active in the Augustan period and so, probably, a younger contemporary of Philo) does in fact use *rhapsodia* in this way, applied to specific books that correspond to our numeration, and also gives numbers for them.[20] I suggest that Philo's manner of citing is an important testimony to his familiarity with contemporary philological and critical scholarship.[21]

The pasage in question is *Contempl.* 16–17:

αἱ γὰρ χρημάτων καὶ κτημάτων ἐπιμέλειαι τοὺς χρόνους ἀναλίσκουσι· χρόνου δὲ φείδεσθαι καλόν, ἐπειδὴ κατὰ τὸν ἰατρὸν Ἱπποκράτην „ὁ μὲν βίος βραχύς, ἡ δὲ τέχνη μακρή." τοῦτό μοι δοκεῖ καὶ Ὅμηρος αἰνίξασθαι ἐν Ἰλιάδι κατὰ τὴν ἀρχὴν τῆς τρισκαιδεκάτης ῥαψῳδίας διὰ τούτων τῶν ἐπῶν·

„Μυσῶν τ᾿ ἀγχεμάχων καὶ ἀγαυῶν Ἱππημολγῶν,
γλακτοφάγων ἀβίων τε, δικαιοτάτων ἀνθρώπων,"

ὡς τῆς μὲν περὶ βίον σπουδῆς καὶ χρηματισμὸν ἀδικίαν γεννώσης διὰ τὸ ἄνισον, δικαιοσύνην δὲ τῆς ἐναντίας προαιρέσεως ἕνεκα ἰσότητος, καθ᾿ ἣν ὁ τῆς φύσεως πλοῦτος ὥρισται καὶ παρευημερεῖ τὸν ἐν ταῖς κεναῖς δόξαις.

Colson renders this:

---

1. *Internationales Symposium zum Corpus Judaeo-Hellenisticum*, 1–4. Mai 2003, Eisenach-Jena (eds. Roland Deines and Karl-Wilhelm Niebuhr; Tübingen: Mohr Siebeck, 2004), 29–40. As Sterling acknowledges, even if likely to be true and attractive, this remains indemonstrable.

[20] In his work *De signis Iliadis / Odysseae*, which we have only in fragments transmitted in the scholia to the Homeric poems.

[21] Cf. Niehoff, *Jewish Exegesis and Homeric Scholarship*, 139. In her excellent work, Niehoff gives much more evidence that demonstrates Philo's acquaintance with current problems of Homeric scholarship.

For taking care of wealth and possessions consumes time and to economize time is an excellent thing since according to the physician Hippocrates 'life is short but art is long.' The same idea is suggested I think by Homer in the *Iliad* at the beginning of the thirteenth book in the lines
The Mysians fighting hand to hand, and noble Mare's-milk-drinkers—
Nought else but milk sustains their life, these men of perfect justice.
The idea conveyed is that injustice is bred by anxious thought for the means of life and for money-making, justice by holding and following the opposite creed. The first entails inequality, the second equality, the principle by which nature's wealth is regulated and so stands superior to the wealth of vain opinion.

Colson notes (PLCL 9:123 n. d) that the passage cites lines 5–6 of *Iliad* 13, and that ἀβίων is taken by some as a proper name but is interpreted by others as equivalent to "having no fixed means of subsistence," that is, nomadic, and he adds: "Philo evidently takes it as an adjective meaning without βίος in the sense of means of life."[22]

This reading of the Homeric lines was not new at the time of Philo. Already Aeschylus in his *Prometheus Unbound* (F 196 Nauck) mentions a Scythian tribe who are the most just and most hospitable of mortals, who do not know agriculture, and for whom the land renders its fruits spontaneously.[23] Strabo, in a long pasage on the Scythians (7.3.9), gathers

---

[22] In fact, as the Homeric scholia and the lexicographical tradition attest, the word was interpreted as either derived from alpha privative and βίη and meaning "without violence," (this seems to be the Homeric interpretation) or βίος, "life, means of life," and so meaning "without means of existence;" or else as derived from βιός, "bow" with either a privative or copulative alpha and so giving the opposites "bowless" or "archers." The lines, as Lawrence Kim, *Homer between History and Fiction in Imperial Greek Literature* (Cambridge: Cambridge University Press, 2010), 193 writes, "had inspired intense debate among ancient scholars of Homer and geography: Ephorus, Aristarchus, and the historian Nicolaus of Damascus (late first century BCE) had all weighed in on various problems presented by the verses." On this Homeric passage see also Richard Janko, *The Iliad, a Commentary, Volume 4: Books 13–16* (6 vols.; ed. Geoffrey S. Kirk; Cambridge: Cambridge University Press, 1985–1993), commentary ad loc., Steve Reece "The Ἄβιοι and the Γάβιοι: An Aeschylean Solution to a Homeric Problem" *AJPh* 122 (2001): 564–470 and A. Ivancic, "Die hellenistischen Kommentare zu Homer Il. 13, 3–6. Zur Idealisierung des Barbarenbildes," in *Hellenismus. Beiträge zur Erforschung von Akkulturation und politischer Ordnung in den Staaten des hellenistischen Zeitalters: Akten des Internationalen Hellenismus-Kolloquiums, 9.-14. März 1994 in Berlin* (ed. Bernd Funck; Tübingen: J.C.B. Mohr (Paul Siebeck), 1996), 671–692. Although Ivancic presents quite a full dossier of attestations, he does not mention the Philonic passage and the point of his paper is rather to explain the idealization of the Scythians in later sources.

[23] Janko, *The Iliad, a Commentary*, commentary ad 13.4–7, explains that these Hippemolgoi are "no doubt a nomadic Scythian tribe across the Danube, like the milk-drinking Massagetai (Hdt. 1.216)." Note, though, that Homer does not indicate that the Hippemolgoi were Scythians. On Aeschylus' passage, see Pierre Vidal–Naquet, *The Black Hunter: Forms of Thought and Forms of Society in the Greek World* (Baltimore: Johns Hopkins University Press, 1986), 22, who compares them to other utopian societies in Homer. To

what Ephorus, the fourth-century B.C.E. historian, had written about this people. Ephorus, says Strabo, was reacting against his predecessors who had presented the Scythians only as cruel enough to eat human flesh and had failed to tell about other Scythians who were their opposite: "for there are some of the Scythian Nomads who feed only on mare's milk, and excel all men in justice." Strabo continues: "Then Ephorus reasons out the cause as follows: since they are frugal in their ways of living and not money-getters, they not only are orderly towards one another, because they have all things in common, their wives, children, the whole of their kin and everything," but, he goes on, "also remain invincible and unconquered by outsiders, because they have nothing to be enslaved for."[24] As we can see, Strabo, following Ephorus, offers an interpretation similar to Philo's, although Philo concentrates on this people's frugality and lack of interest in possessions. Strabo also indicates that these Scythians were already known to the poets, with specific reference to the Homeric passage (*Il.* 13) and to Hesiod. The phrase δικαιοτάτων ἀνθρώπων must have been a gloss (that is, an explanation of the word ἄβιοι), already in Homer, who has a fondness for etymological word-play with proper names.[25] Thus, the Homeric text itself invited this type of reading. The Homeric lines, then, had already been taken to mean that the Abioi were the most just because of their particularly sparse way of life. Philo may have also had before his eyes here the interpretation provided by his contemporary Nicolaus of Damascus

---

this may be added two fragments of the Hesiodic *Catalogue of Women*: 150 and 151 (Merkel-bach-West). Frg. 150, from a papyrus, mentions several poorly known and idealized peoples, among them some "Scythian Hyppemolgoi" (Σκύ[θ]ας ἱππημο[λγού]ς, 115); frg. 151, very short, comes from Ephorus via Strabo and mentions some "milk-eaters" (Γλακτοφάγων). On this last fragment see next page and Ivancic, "Die hellenistischen Kommentare," 676.

[24] Translation of Horace Leonard Jones, *The Geography of Strabo* (8 vols.; LCL; Cambridge: Harvard University Press, 1917–1949). For Ephorus' fragment see Felix Jacoby, *Die Fragmente der griechischen Historiker*, (3 vols. in 16 parts; Leiden: Brill, 1923–1969), no. 70, frg. 42, and the article on Ephorus by Victor Parker in *Brill's New Jacoby*.

[25] Cf. Janko, *The Iliad, a Commentary*, commentary ad loc. and Reece, "The Ἄβιοι and the Γάβιοι," 466: "The fact that there is a schema etymologicum in the collocation of Ἱππημολγῶν and γλακτοφάγων should incline us toward the view that δικαιοτάτων ἀνθρώπων, too, is a gloss. And the overall contrast that Homer is drawing between the unceasing toil and violence of the Trojans and Achaeans fighting by the ships and the comparative utopia of the noble Hippemolgoi and just Abioi of the north and east lends further support to the view that Homer is engaging in etymological wordplay here—that he intends Ἄβιοι to be understood as 'those who are without violence.' Zeus' eyes are seeking a respite from the violence of battle as they gaze further and further afield." See also *ibid*, 468, for "Homer's penchant for finding etymological significance in proper names."

(who is well-known as an important source of Josephus),[26] who relates the same story, but mentioning only Homer as his source:

V, 73: Γαλακτοφάγοι, Σκυθικὸν ἔθνος, ἄοικοί εἰσιν, ὥσπερ καὶ οἱ πλεῖστοι Σκυθῶν, τροφὴν δ' ἔχουσι γάλα μόνον ἵππειον, ἐξ οὗ τυροποιοῦντες ἐσθίουσι καὶ πίνουσι, καί εἰσι διὰ τοῦτο δυσμαχώτατοι, σὺν αὐτοῖς πάντη τὴν τροφὴν ἔχοντες. (2) Οὗτοι καὶ Δαρεῖον ἐτρέψαντο. (3) Εἰσὶ δὲ καὶ δικαιότατοι, κοινὰ ἔχοντες τά τε κτήματα καὶ τὰς γυναῖκας, ὥστε τοὺς μὲν πρεσβυτέρους αὐτῶν πατέρας ὀνομάζειν, τοὺς δὲ νεωτέρους παῖδας, τοὺς δ' ἥλικας ἀδελφούς. (...) (5) Τούτων καὶ Ὅμηρος μέμνηται ἐν οἷς φησιν·
Μυσῶν τ' ἀγχεμάχων καὶ ἀγαυῶν Ἱππημολγῶν,
Γλακτοφάγων ἀβίων τε, δικαιοτάτων ἀνθρώπων.
Ἀβίους δ' αὐτοὺς λέγει ἢ διὰ τὸ γῆν μὴ γεωργεῖν ἢ διὰ (15) τὸ ἀοίκους εἶναι ἢ διὰ τὸ χρῆσθαι τούτους μόνους τόξοις· βιὸν γὰρ λέγει τὸ τόξον. (6) Παρὰ τούτοις οὐδὲ εἷς οὔτε φθόνων, ὥς φασιν, οὔτε μισῶν οὔτε φοβούμενος ἱστορήθη διὰ τὴν τοῦ βίου κοινότητα καὶ δικαιοσύνην. (7) μάχιμοι δ' αὐτῶν οὐχ ἧττον αἱ γυναῖκες ἢ οἱ ἄνδρες, καὶ συμπολεμοῦσιν αὐτοῖς ὅταν δέῃ.

The Milk-eaters, a Scythian tribe, were nomads, as the majority of Scythians are too and their nutrition is only mare-milk which is the source of their food (in the form of cheese) and of their drink. For this reason they are inconquerable, because they always have with them their food—they routed even Darius. They are also extremely just, and they have everything in common, their goods and their wives, so that all adults they call fathers, and young people children and those of the same age, brothers .... Also Homer mentions them in those lines where he says ... (citation of *Il.* 13.5–6). He calls them *abious*, because they did not labor the land, or because they do not have an ancestral land, or because they were the only ones to use bows (since the bow is called *bios*). No one of them has been reported as being envious, as they say, or full of hatred, or fearful, thanks to the communality and justice of their lives.[27]

But what is interesting in *Contempl.* 17, apart from the fact that Philo shows a knowledge of the book-division of the *Iliad* and his interpretation of the way of life of these Hyppemolgoi, is that he also says τοῦτό μοι δοκεῖ καὶ Ὅμηρος αἰνίξασθαι: "it seems to me that Homer hints at this too." The use of the verb αἰνίττομαι is a clear indication that Philo is launching one of his allegorical interpretations and here, as often, he uses an etymological analysis as his starting point.[28] Although, as we have seen, the Homeric text invites this kind of analysis, Philo superimposes on the Homeric gloss his

---

[26] On the brilliant career and influence of Nicolaus of Damascus and his work see Mark Toher, "On the Use of Nicolaus' Historical Fragments," *Classical Antiquity* 8 (1989): 159–72, especially 161–62.

[27] Translation is mine. See K. Müller, *Fragmenta historicorum Graecorum* (Paris: Didot, 1841–1870; reprint, Frankfurt-Main: Minerva, 1975), 3 (hereafter FHG). See now *Brill's New Jacoby*, Nicolaus FGrH 90 F 104 from Joann. Stob. *Anth.* III 1 [Π. ἀρετῆς], 200.

[28] Cf. Lambert, *Homer the Theologian*, 48.

own interpretation: *abioi* is, at the same time, "lacking in violence" (ἀ-βίη) and "lacking in means of life" or frugal (ἀ-βίος), an ideal community that lives perfect lives free of material ambitions. He seems, then, to have in mind a community much closer to the one described in the text of Nicolaus of Damascus and which, in its basic outline, goes back at least to Ephorus. Philo, nevertheless, does not mention Ephorus (whom it is quite clear he must have known) or any other contemporary historian.[29] Instead, he prefers the authority of Homer, as historian and moral teacher, and feels free to interpret him liberally, since Homer himself does not provide any explanation for the outstanding justice of the Hyppemolgoi.

2) *Poetical expressions:*

Often, when he refers to an expression as poetical, Philo speaks of the poets (οἱ ποιηταί), the "family of poets" (τὸ ποιητικὸν γένος), "among poets" (παρὰ ποιηταῖς), "according to the poetic expression" (κατὰ τὸ ποιητικόν), "that poetic saying" (τὸ ποιητικὸν ἐκεῖνο), etc. In a majority of these cases the word or expression used comes from Homer (Philo tends to be more specific in his attribution when citing other poets). But there are many cases in which Philo cites one or two words from Homer but changes the rest of the phrase, so that it is possible to recognize the Homeric allusion, but to see, at the same time, that Philo is handling it in what seems to be an original and creative fashion. Most scholars have taken these poetic expressions in Philo to be mere adornment and see in them no other purpose than stylistic embellishment. That Philo's language is exceptionally rich is no novelty, but it may be interesting to reflect more closely on how highly poetic his language sometimes is, and on his motives for such implicit allusions. Here are two examples:

1. *Somn.* 2.249 (poetic expression: ἀμβρόσιον ... φάρμακον: "ambrosian drug"):

καὶ ψυχῇ δ' εὐδαίμονι τὸ ἱερώτατον ἔκπωμα προτεινούσῃ τὸν ἑαυτῆς λογισμὸν τίς ἐπιχεῖ τοὺς ἱεροὺς κυάθους τῆς πρὸς ἀλήθειαν εὐφροσύνης, ὅτι μὴ <ὁ> οἰνοχόος

---

[29] Ephorus's *Universal History*, as is well known, was extremely popular up until the time of Philo. In addition, he was one of the main sources of historians contemporary with Philo, such as Nicolaus of Damascus, Diodorus Siculus, Timagenes, and Strabo (see Klaus Meister, "Ephorus" in *Brill's New Pauly*. Antiquity volumes edited by: Hubert Cancik and Helmuth Schneider. Brill Online, 2014. Reference. Brown University. 22 February 2014 <http://referenceworks.brillonline.com/entries/brill-s-new-pauly/ephorus-e331660> First appeared online: 2006. First Print Edition: 9789004122598, 20110510). The likelihood that Philo knew him either directly or indirectly is high.

τοῦ θεοῦ καὶ συμποσίαρχος λόγος, οὐ διαφέρων τοῦ πόματος, ἀλλ' αὐτὸς ἄκρατος ὤν, τὸ γάνωμα, τὸ ἥδυσμα, ἡ ἀνάχυσις, ἡ εὐθυμία, τὸ χαρᾶς, τὸ εὐφροσύνης (5) ἀμβρόσιον, ἵνα καὶ αὐτοὶ ποιητικοῖς ὀνόμασι χρησώμεθα, φάρμακον;

And, when the happy soul holds out the sacred goblet of its own reason, who is it that pours into it the holy cupfolds of true gladness, but the Word, the Cup-Bearer of God and Master of the feast, who is also none other than the draught which he pours—his own self free from all dilution, the delight, the sweetening, the exhilaration, the merriment, the ambrosian drug (to take for our own use the poet's terms) whose medicine gives joy and gladness? (Trans. Colson and Whitaker)

As far as I can see the phrase "ambrosian drug" is a hapax. I expect that the expression τὸ χαρᾶς, τὸ εὐφροσύνης ἀμβρόσιον ... φάρμακον was created by Philo himself and is unique. *Pharmakon* is of course common, but *ambrosios* is an adjective used only by poets. Hence, the parenthesis in Colson's translation should be placed immediately after "ambrosial," as it is in the Greek. The compound phrase is not to be found in any other author: not even Plato, in his most poetical moments, uses it (he doesn't ever use the adjective ἀμβρόσιος, although he employs φάρμακον often); in Philo's own works this is the only instance of the adjective. Philo's combination may have been inspired by something like the *Homeric Hymn to Demeter* 49: οὐδέ ποτ' ἀμβροσίης καὶ νέκταρος ἡδυπότοιο πάσσατ' ἀκηχεμένη, "in her affliction she did not ever eat ambrosia nor the sweet drink nectar;" or the Homeric passage where the Cyclops, after drinking Maron's wine, describes it as ἀμβροσίης καὶ νέκταρός ἐστιν ἀπορρώξ, ("it is an efflux of ambrosia and nectar," *Od.* 9.359),[30] in combination with *Od.* 1.261: φάρμακον ἀνδροφόνον "man-killing poison." But Philo has transformed the modest Homeric "man-killing poison" into its opposite, "drug of immortality," and what may superficially seem a normal poetic expression ἀμβρόσιον ... φάρμακον, that could have been used by Homer and other poets, is, in fact, judging from the evidence we possess, an ingenious creation of Philo's.

The passage in which the expression is found is highly emotional, as it describes what I would call a mystical experience. Philo creates a crescendo with a run of nouns in apposition (5 in total) that culminates in the phrase noted here. He is talking about the divine Logos, the Cup-Bearer who is identical with the draught he pours. To describe such an experience he forces his language to a maximum of expresssion, and prosaic wording seems insufficient for such enthusiasm. It is, then, not mere embellishment but a way of intensifying the significance and emotional quality of the passage. Finally, he may also have found inspiration in another favorite

---

[30] Before that Odysseus himself has described it as a θεῖον ποτόν, *Od.* 9.205.

author, Menander, one of whose *sententiae* (1.587 Jäkel) reads: Ψυχῆς νοσούσης ἐστὶ φάρμακον λόγος.[31]

My second example involves a quite different kind of effect:

2. *Spec.* 1.74:

τρίτον δ' ὅτι τὰ μὲν τῆς ἀγρίας ὕλης πρὸς οὐδὲν ὄφελος, „ἄχθος" δ' ὡς οἱ ποιηταί φασι „γῆς" (…).

Thirdly, because the plants of the wild kind of vegetation are of no use, but only, as the poets say, 'a burden to the soil.'

Colson's note cites *Il.* 18.104 and *Od.* 20.379 (on the suitors talking to Telemachus about the beggar-Odysseus: αὕτως ἄχθος ἀρούρης). Colson adds in the note that both passages have ἄχθος ἀρούρης, although Plato has the form γῆς ἄχθη in *Theaet.* 176d. In all these cases, Colson continues, the phrase is applied to human beings, and so also by Philo at *Mos.* 1.30 (some men) and *Congr.* 171 (Adam and Eve on Eden); but he applies it to herds in *Spec.* 3.50.

Colson's note, informative as it is, fails to recognize the Homeric passage that Philo surely has in mind here, namely *Il.* 18.104, where Achilles, in despair over the recent death of Patroclus, expresses his guilt at not having been able to protect his companion: ἀλλ' ἧμαι παρὰ νηυσὶν ἐτώσιον ἄχθος ἀρούρης "but I'm sitting here by the ships, a useless burden upon the earth." Philo has written πρὸς οὐδὲν ὄφελος "of no benefit" instead of the ἐτώσιον "useless" of the *Iliad*, replacing the poetical (and by his time obsolete) ἐτώσιον, and adapting the line, as if via Plato's citation, by altering ἀρούρης to γῆς.

The passage of *Theaet.* 176d indeed already alters the Homeric ἐτώσιον to the more prosaic ἄλλως, "vainly":

ἀγάλλονται γὰρ τῷ ὀνείδει καὶ οἴονται ἀκούειν ὅτι οὐ λῆροί εἰσι, γῆς ἄλλως ἄχθη, ἀλλ' ἄνδρες οἵους δεῖ ἐν πόλει τοὺς σωθησομένους.

[such men] are ready enough to glory in the reproach, and think that it means not that they are mere rubbish, cumbering the ground to no purpose, but that

---

[31] On this pasage of Philo and the Logos as God's Cup-Bearer, Dillon had already pointed out the possibility of a reference to an allegorical identification of Ganymede with the divine Logos; see John Dillon, "Ganymede as the Logos: Traces of a Forgotten Allegorization in Philo?" *CQ* 31 (1981): 183–85. Menander's sentence may, in turn, be based in other poetical phrases such as Aesch. *Prometheus* 379, ψυχῆς νοσούσης εἰσὶν ἰατροὶ λόγοι. *Cf.* Pseudo-Plutarch, *Consolation to Apollonius* 6: κράτιστον δὴ πρὸς ἀλυππίαν φάρμακον ὁ λόγος …

they have the kind of qualities that are necessary for survival in the community.[32]

But to fully understand Philo's use of the expression, this *Theaetetus* passage is insufficient. For one thing, Plato here uses the plural ἄχθη whereas Philo's passage has the singular ἄχθος, like Homer.[33] We do better to look to *Apol.* 28d.4, where Plato paraphrases more closely Achilles' words:

'Αὐτίκα,' φησί, 'τεθναίην, δίκην ἐπιθεὶς τῷ ἀδικοῦντι, ἵνα μὴ ἐνθάδε μένω καταγέλαστος παρὰ νηυσὶ κορωνίσιν ἄχθος ἀρούρης.' μὴ αὐτὸν οἴει φροντίσαι θανάτου καὶ κινδύνου;"[34]

'Let me die at once,' he said, 'when once I have given the wrongdoer his deserts, rather than remain here, a laughingstock by the curved ships, a burden upon the earth.'

Note how here Plato has changed the Homeric passage in several ways: μένω "remain" replaces ἧμαι "I'm sitting," and καταγέλαστος "laughable" replaces ἐτώσιον "useless." He also adds an epithet for the ships, "curved," that, although traditional, is nevertheless absent in the Homeric passage.

It is also important to note that while in Plato the word ἄχθος is not at all common (in addition to *Theaetetus* and *Apology* cited above, it is found only in *Crat.* 121a and *Phaedr.* 252c), Philo, on the other hand, uses it more often than any prose author up to his day. I have counted forty-two uses, of which only ten are in the plural.[35] All others are in the singular, as in the passage under discussion.[36] Despite this, the phrase ἄχθος γῆς only recurs in one other Philonic passage:

τὰ δὲ μηδαμῇ χρήσιμα τῷ βίῳ ζῆν εἰ καὶ λυσιτελὲς ἀλλ' οὖν περιττὸν „ἄχθος γῆς", (5) ὡς εἶπέ τις (*Spec.* 3.50).

(Philo is here writing about animals contaminated by intercourse with humans and made by that fact unclean and so useless) "And, when things serve no

---

[32] Translation by M. J. Levett, rev. Myles F. Burnyeat in John M. Cooper and D.S. Hutchinson, eds., *Plato. Complete Works* (Indianapolis: Hackett, 1997), 157–234.

[33] And, in fact, the whole ancient epos that we know; see Homer, *Il.* 12.452; 18.104; 20.247; *Od.* 3.312; 9.233; 20.379; Hesiod *Op.* 692; *Scut.* 400; *frg.* 239 West-Merkelbach. I have not found any uses of the word at all in the *Homeric Hymns*.

[34] Translation by G.M.A. Grubbe in Cooper, *Plato. Complete Works*, 17–36.

[35] In four of these plural uses, we find the word together with γῆς, which would be closer to *Theaet.* 176d: Philo, *Agr.* 21; *Contempl.* 171; *Mos.* 1.30. Philo does not include in any of these passages a phrase like "as someone said," or "to use the poets' words," etc., which are his usual markers of citations or allusions.

[36] See also Peder Borgen, Kåre Fuglseth and Roald Skarsten, *The Philo Index. A Complete Greek Word Index to the Writings of Philo of Alexandria. Lemmatised and Computergenerated.* (UniTrel Studieserie 25; Tronheim: NTNU, 1997), s.v. ἄχθος.

purpose in life, their survival, even if it can be turned to some account, is just a superfluity, 'cumbering the earth,' as the poet puts it."

As we see, Colson's translation supplies what is only implicit in the Greek, for Philo does not mention poet or poets. Rather, he uses another of his formulas to indicate a quotation, ὡς εἶπέ τις, "as someone said," relying on the knowledgeable reader to recognize the source. My point, however, is to highlight what Philo's use of this poetic phrase reveals about his creative style of appropriation: in *Spec.* 3.50, as in *Spec.* 1.74, he applies to plants and animals a poetic expression used in his sources metaphorically of people, and does so in contexts that are rather lowly in comparison both to Homer and Plato's *Apology*. This is the reverse of the way ἀμβρόσιον φάρμακον served as an instance of elevated expression, for here the passages are not highly emotive but rather humble. They reflect a kind of joke, by which a phrase with such a high poetic pedigree and used metaphorically in sober contexts is applied in a more strictly literal way to useless plants and animals that do indeed weigh upon the earth.

But there is still more to the phrase ἄχθος γῆς. We find it also used by the comic writer Eupolis and, possibly, Menander. Eupolis's text (Austin 96.68 and 69) comes from papyri and the attribution is clear.[37] Regarding the possible fragment by Menander, although it is included in Alfred Körte and Andreas Thierfelder's edition,[38] it should be noted that the Philo passage is, in fact, the source for it and the attribution of the fragment to Menander's *Dis expaton* is conjectural. Richard Reitzenstein[39] recognized the trimeter and, comparing it to Plautus, *Bacch.* 820 *terrai odium ambulant*, assigned it to Menander's play. In both cases (if we accept the words as Menander's) we have only fragments deprived of context, and it is therefore impossible to know whether the expression is applied to people or to plants and animals; nevertheless, we have some indication that, long before Philo, the expression ἄχθος γῆς was used in comedy and may well have already become a comic cliché. This would reinforce the sense that a kind of joke or comic bathos is implicit in Philo's use of the expression.

---

[37]   ϲτάτου ϲπ[
       κουϲιμοικο[
       τῆϲ γῆϲ μ(ὲν) ἄχθο[ϲ ἄ-
       χθοϲ μ(ὲν) ἐπεὶ καμ[
       κουφότηϲ δ(ὲ) ἐπεὶ .[(70)

[38] Alfred Körte and Andreas Thierfelder, eds., *Menandri quae supersunt* (2 vols.; 2nd ed.;. Leipzig: Teubner, 1959). The fragment (K- T 113) reads: περιττὸν ἄχθος ὄντα γῆς, ὡς εἶπέ τις.

[39] Richard Reitzenstein, "Philologische Kleinigkeiten." *Hermes* 65 (1930): 77–91, esp. 77–81.

At this stage, I am in the process of examining several other cases in which Philo adapts an expression from Homer or other poets to his own context, in the process both inviting the reader to recognize how he has altered the phrasing or the tone of the original and how intimately conversant he was with the antiquarian scholarship of his own time. As the above examples show, Philo was a canny and subtle reader, and teasing out the implications of his adaptations is no easy task—nor, I think, was it meant to be; Philo expected much of his cleverest readers. But there is also a preliminary job to be done, and that is to collect a more or less complete register of Philo's allusions to poetry. The two exercises are not unrelated, since it is precisely Philo's tendency to alter his citations in nuanced ways that makes them sometimes difficult to detect. I hope in the future to fill in the gaps in this important area of Philonic scholarship.

Brown University

The Studia Philonica Annual 26 (2014) 151–167

THE SUN AND THE CHARIOT:

The *Republic* and the *Phaedrus* as Sources for Rival Platonic Paradigms of Psychic Vision in Philo's Biblical Commentaries

MICHAEL COVER*

Introduction

Philonic Questions and Platonic Sources

One of the more intractable questions for students of Philo's mystical thought regards the content of contemplative vision. Does the sage see God himself, the Logos, God's powers, or some combination of these?[1] Some, like David Winston, argue that for Philo, God in himself remains completely transcendent and unknowable. The content of the sage's vision and the source of his knowledge is limited to the Logos.[2] In this, Philo anticipates the mystical thought of Plotinus and Gregory of Nyssa.[3]

While agreeing with this general picture, others, like Bernard McGinn, Ellen Birnbaum, and Rowan Williams, judge that attributing such philosophical consistency to Philo does not accurately reflect the wide variety of statements that the Alexandrian makes on the subject. So, for example, McGinn notes that "some [Philonic] texts, at least, seem to hold out the

---

* This is a revised version of a paper presented to the Philo of Alexandria section at the annual meeting of the Society of Biblical Literature in Baltimore, Maryland, November 24, 2013. I am grateful to the participants in the section for their helpful suggestions, with special thanks to David Runia, Gregory Sterling, and Sarah Pearce.

[1] The question has been framed this way most recently by Scott Mackie, "Seeing God in Philo of Alexandria: The Logos, the Powers, or the Existent One?" *SPhA* 21 (2009): 25–47.

[2] David Winston, *Logos and Mystical Theology in Philo of Alexandria* (Cincinnati: Hebrew Union College Press, 1985), 15, 44.

[3] Gregory of Nyssa, *De Vita Moysis*, 2.162–163. For a recent overview of this apophatic tradition, including Philo, see Ilaria Ramelli, "The Divine as Inaccessible Object of Knowledge in Ancient Platonism: A Common Philosophical Pattern across Religious Traditions," *JHI* 75 (2014): 167–88. For the import of this contemplative question in the Trinitarian debates of the fourth century and Augustine's eschatological view of the vision of God, see Michel Barnes, "The Visible Christ and the Invisible Trinity: Mt. 5:8 in Augustine's Trinitarian Theology of 400," *Modern Theology* 19 (2003): 329–55.

possibility for vision of the Existent in himself, not, of course, a comprehension or understanding of his nature, but some form of contact with that which is."[4]

While this second position better accounts for the diversity of views present in Philo's corpus, it does not really answer the Philonic question, but simply poses it afresh: what is one to make of Philo's seemingly contradictory statements about the content of contemplative vision, if they cannot be philosophically harmonized? One solution, suggested by Ellen Birnbaum, is that reading Philo's statements on contemplative vision in light of their respective commentary series provides a key to understanding their diversity. The Exposition of the Law, Philo's most popularly oriented commentary series, offers a simplified view of contemplation in which God himself is the object of psychic vision. The Allegorical Commentary, on the other hand, Philo's most philosophically and exegetically sophisticated work, highlights the role of the Logos and other intermediaries as the actual content of the sage's contemplation.[5]

Despite the strengths of Birnbaum's hypothesis, it cannot, as Scott Mackie has observed,[6] account for all the evidence. For example, in *Praem.* 40–46, a famous passage at the end of the Exposition of the Law, Philo expressly denies that a direct vision of God is possible; while in *Leg.* 3.100–101, a critical passage at the beginning of the Allegorical Commentary, Philo suggests that an unmediated vision of God himself is the ultimate end of Moses's mystical ascent.

Clearly then, there are other factors influencing Philo's thought. In investigating these further factors, I will focus particularly in this article on the role various Platonic sources (which Philo knew firsthand) play in shaping the diversity of Philo's views of psychic vision. It is my contention

---

[4] Bernard McGinn, *The Presence of God: A History of Western Mysticism. Volume One: The Foundations of Mysticism* (New York: Crossroad, 1991), 40. See also Michael B. Cover, "Lifting the Veil: 2 Corinthians 3:7–18 in Light of Jewish Homiletic and Commentary Traditions" (Ph.D. diss., The University of Notre Dame, 2013), 257–67; Mackie, "Seeing God in Philo," 34–36; and Rowan Williams, *Arius: Heresy and Tradition* (Grand Rapids: Eerdmans, 2001 [1987], 120: "Whether Philo had a doctrine of 'mystical union' in any strict sense remains debatable; but (despite the logical difficulties involved in such a position) he *does* seem to have believed that there could be a relation to God other than in his world-related aspect as Logos." See also Ellen Birnbaum, *The Place of Judaism in Philo's Thought: Israel, Jews, and Proselytes* (BJS 290; SPhM 2; Atlanta: Scholars Press, 1996), 80: "although Philo occasionally seems to speak without qualification about the possibility of seeing God, at other times he claims that God can be seen only through apprehension of His various intermediaries." See also eadem, "What Does Philo Mean by 'Seeing God'? Some Methodological Considerations," *SBLSP* 34 (1995): 535–52.

[5] Birnbaum, *Place of Judaism*, 89–90.

[6] Mackie, "Seeing God," 45–47.

that this diversity can be explained in part by Philo's deference to the myths and images of his various Platonic intertexts.

The Agōn of Platonic Images in Philo's Works

Interpreters of Plato, like interpreters of Philo, face the challenge of a corpus that both invites and defies systematization. Literary critics have long pointed out that Plato's use of the dialogue genre allows him to veil his own philosophical views behind a dramatic mask. His statement in the (probably) spurious seventh letter that "no writing of mine exists" cautions us against presuming that the fictional Socrates simply speaks *in persona Platonis*.[7] No less complicating is the fact that even Socrates's longer speeches are not comprised solely of argument or dialectical exchange, but are interwoven with mythical digressions and hymnic reveries. Despite his notorious banishment of the poets from the republic, Socrates remained "greedy for images" (*Resp.* 488a) to supplement his more analytic thought.[8]

It is precisely the unsystematic nature of Plato's myths, coupled with their imaginative appeal, that suggests them as a source for diversity in Philo's thought.[9] In fact, both of the aberrant passages mentioned above (*Praem.* 40–46 and *Leg.* 3.100–101) owe a debt to the images of Socrates. In the case of *Praem.* 46, the dominant image is that of the sun from *Republic* 6; in *Leg.* 3.100, by contrast, Philo depends on the Phaedran image of the chariot soul and its mythic ascent. It might fairly be argued that—alongside the *Timaeus*, whose influence on Philo's thought seems to be all-pervasive[10]—the *Republic's* sun has exercised the greatest influence on Philo's understanding of psychic vision. This, after all is the *locus classicus* appealed to by Winston and Erwin R. Goodenough, which suggests (with the

---

[7] Plato, *Ep. 7*, 341c. For a stimulating analysis of several Platonic dialogues, including the *Republic* and the *Phaedrus*, in light of their dramatic form, see Richard Rutherford, *The Art of Plato: Ten Essays in Platonic Interpretation* (London: Duckworth, 1995).

[8] Grubbe's translation. In the text of *Resp.* 488a, ἄκουε δ᾽ οὖν τῆς εἰκονος, ἵν᾽ ἔτι μᾶλλον ἴδης ὡς γλίσχρως εἰκάζω, Socrates more literally boasts of "how greedily I employ images."

[9] Earlier studies of the influence of Platonic myth on Philo's thought include Thomas H. Billings, *The Platonism of Philo Judaeus* (Chicago: University of Chicago Press, 1919), esp. chapter 4; and Pierre Boyancé, "Sur l'exégèse hellénistique du 'Phèdre' (Phèdre 246e)," in *Miscellanea di studi alessandrini in memoria di Augusto Rostagni* (Torino: Bottega d'Erasmo, 1963), 45–53; and idem, "Études philoniennes," *REG* 76 (1963): 210–29. More recently, see Anita Méasson, *Du char ailé de Zeus à l'Arche d'Alliance: Images et mythes platoniciens chez Philon d'Alexandrie* (Paris: Études Augustiniennes, 1986).

[10] For Philo's use of the *Timaeus*, see David T. Runia, *Philo of Alexandria and the Timaeus of Plato* (PhilAnt 44; Leiden: Brill, 1986).

majority opinion) that for Philo, as for Plotinus, one always and only sees God by means of his Logos, "God by god, light by light."[11]

As many readers have noticed, however, images from the *Phaedrus* also heavily color Philo's mystical thought, in ways that rival the *Republic*.[12] It is thus worth asking not only how Philo harmonizes various Platonic images, but in what ways the independent voices of these dialogues compete with one another as authoritative sources. It is my argument that while the *Republic*'s image of the sun and its rays does suggest to Philo a theory of complete divine transcendence and contemplative intermediacy through the Logos—and surely this represents Philo's more common position—the myth of the Phaedran chariot raises the possibility of the soul's unmediated vision of God in himself, even if such vision still entailed qualified knowledge, was usually not attained, and, at times, is declared to be impossible in Philo's works.[13] To be clear, I am not arguing that Philo ever suggests that Moses might know God's nature fully. What is in question is whether the knowledge or vision of God that a human being can achieve is uniformly mediated by the Logos in Philo's thought or whether it might be conveyed by way of some more immediate "relation" (Williams) or "form of contact" (McGinn) in certain cases.

Since the influence of the *Phaedrus* on Philo's thought provokes the more philosophically problematic thesis—that one might have unmediated vision of God—and has been less frequently discussed in Anglophone scholarship, I will focus my remarks on the use of Phaedran intertexts in *Leg.* 3.100–101. My argument will proceed in three stages. First, I will present evidence that suggests that Philo, in *Leg.* 3.100–101, offers the possibility of a vision of God that does not directly depend on seeing the Logos; second, I will examine Phaedran intertexts in this passage, which

---

[11] Philo, *Praem.* 46; Plotinus, *Enn.* 5.1.7: "But we say the Intellect is an image of that [Good]; for we must speak more plainly; first of all we must say that what has come into being must be in a way that [Good] and retain much of it and be a likeness of it, as light is of the sun. But Intellect is not that [Good]." See also *Enn.* 5.1.6.28 and 5.3.17: "And this is the soul's true end: to touch that light [of the One] and see it by itself, not by another light, but by the light which is also its means of seeing (δι'οὗ καὶ ὁρᾷ). It must see that light by which it is enlightened: for we do not see the sun by another light than his own. How then can this happen? Take away everything!" Further, Winston, *Logos and Mystical Theology*, 44, nn. 8–9; and Erwin R. Goodenough, *By Light, Light: The Mystic Gospel of Hellenistic Judaism* (New Haven: Yale University Press, 1935).

[12] So Boyancé, "Études philoniennes," 81 (as quoted by Méasson): "Il semble en particulier que deux traités ont, en raison de leur sujet, été ainsi particulièrement rapprochés, le *Phèdre* (ou plus exactement le mythe du *Phèdre*) et le *Timée*."

[13] For some counterexamples, where Philo alludes to the *Phaedrus* but does not permit the soul any degree of vision of τὸ ὄν, see *Opif.* 69–70 and *Mut.* 16.

suggest that Plato's chariot myth has shaped Philo's vision; third, I will corroborate my conclusions by turning to the reception history of the *Phaedrus* myth among the Neoplatonists. Particularly, one finds an allegorical reading of the *Phaedrus* myth in the thought of Iamblichus of Chalcis which, if known by Philo, would offer exegetical support for his position. In the conclusion, I raise a critical counterexample to *Leg.* 3.100–101, found in *Mut.* 7–17, in which Philo's appeal to the *Phaedrus* myth does not lead to his portrayal of an unmediated vision of God, but in fact, a mediated one. This counterexample exposes the explanatory limits of the strong version of the current hypothesis (that the *Phaedrus* myth always suggests to Philo an unmediated vision of God; the *Republic*, a mediated one) and also points to further factors which may help explain the diversity in Philo's mystical thought in the Allegorical Commentary.

Following Zeus: The Heavenly Charioteer and the Celestial Demiurge

The Possibility of Unmediated Vision of God in Philo (Leg. 3.100–101)

The starting point of this argument is Philo's remarkable description of the vision of God in *Leg.* 3.101. Here, Philo depicts the vision of the soul that resembles Moses himself:

οὗτός ἐστι Μωϋσῆς ὁ λέγων «Ἐμφάνισον μοι σαυτόν, γνωστῶς ἴδω σε» (Exod 33:13). Μὴ γὰρ ἐμφανισθείης μοι δι' οὐρανοῦ ἢ γῆς ἢ ὕδατος ἢ ἀέρος ἤ τινος ἁπλῶς τῶν ἐν γενέσει, μηδὲ κατοπτρισαίμην ἐν ἄλλῳ τινὶ τὴν σὴν ἰδέαν ἢ ἐν σοὶ τῷ θεῷ·

This [purer mind] is Moses, who is saying "Make yourself clear to me, let me see you and know you" (Exod 33:13); do not be revealed to me through heaven or earth or water or air or through any of other things in your creation, neither let me see your form reflected in anything other than you yourself, O God![14]

Is Philo's Moses in *Leg.* 3.101 asking for a mirror-vision through God's eternal Logos-image, or by the phrase ἐν σοὶ τῷ θεῷ is he is asking for something more? While both sides can and have been argued, I think the least problematic reading of *this* text is that Philo's Moses is in fact asking for (and capable of receiving) a more direct vision.[15]

---

[14] Philo, *Leg.* 3.101.

[15] Sarah Pearce helpfully points out to me that Moses's negative request here echoes and affirms the second commandment. Moses's inclusion of the elements suggests his desire not to approach God by way of graven images (see LXX Exod 20:4, wherein three of Philo's four elements are mentioned!). And yet, Moses does not stop with the elements, but

Admittedly, however, the passage is ambiguous. One objection to it might be that the passage's central verb, κατοπτρίζεσθαι, most naturally connotes indirect vision.[16] One might thereby argue that the verb κατοπτρισαίμην implies an indirect vision of God's form. A second, related objection is that in requesting a vision of God's ἰδέα, Moses is speaking not of a direct vision of God, but of his εἰκών, that is, his Logos.[17] Let us consider these objections in turn.

First, suppose one concedes, for the sake of argument, that κατοπτρισαίμην most naturally implies indirect vision; this seems plausible given the verb's prepositional prefix and Philo's uses of the cognate noun elsewhere. It does not thereby follow, however, that the first objection holds, for Philo uses the verb here *in the negative* following a disjunction. In other words, κατοπτρισαίμην signifies the kind of indirect vision Moses wishes to avoid (see *Leg.* 3.97–99). Thus Rudolph Bultmann argues:

> Certainly, the meaning here is not "nothing created shall reflect you toward me, O God, but you yourself shall be the mirror in which I see you," so that God would be regarded as the mirror of himself (thus Lietzmann, 113). Rather, for the ἤ-clause an ἰδοίμην is to be inferred from the κατοπτρισαίμην.[18]

The same reply might be made to the ἰδέα objection as well. It too stands on the negative side of the disjunction, and represents the Logos-vision Moses seeks to transcend. Even if one does understand ἰδέαν as the object of Bultmann's ἰδοίμην, this need not point exclusively to a vision of the Logos. As I will subsequently argue, Philo may instead be echoing Plato's vocabulary from the *Phaedrus* and mean ἰδέα in that mythic register and not as a philosophical substitute for εἰκών or λόγος.

This understanding of *Leg.* 3.101 garners further support from two important linguistic considerations. First, when Moses does speak positively of his vision, he uses the arthrous form of God (ὁ θεός), which usually refers to God himself and not the anarthrous form (θεός), which more

---

goes on to reject τινος ἁπλῶς τῶν ἐν γενέσει, "frankly, anything at all that has come to be." The force of the indefinite pronoun may thus suggest the revelatory inadequacy of both material and immaterial mediation, of both physical and ideal creation.

[16] For this meaning, see Volker Rabens, "Transformation through Contemplation: New Light from Philo on 2 Corinthians 3:18" (paper presented at the annual meeting of the SBL, Chicago, Il., 17 November 2012), 2; M. David Litwa, "Transformation through a Mirror: Moses in 2 Cor 3.18," *JSNT* 34 (2012): 285–97, esp. 292.

[17] Philo does, in at least one place, identify the Logos with God's image and idea (*Somn.* 2.45–46: <ὁ θεὸς> τὸν ὅλον ἐσφράγισε κόσμον εἰκόνι καὶ ἰδέᾳ, τῷ ἑαυτοῦ λόγῳ).

[18] Rudolph Bultmann, *The Second Letter to the Corinthians* (trans. Roy A. Harrisville; Minneapolis: Augsburg, 1985 [1976]), 94.

commonly refers to the Logos.[19] Similarly, the phrase τινος ἁπλῶς τῶν ἐν γενέσει could be understood to include the Logos, since Philo speaks of the Logos in several places as having "come into existence," most critically for this argument, in *Leg.* 3.175.[20]

As a confirmation of this reading, I turn to the immediately foregoing paragraph, *Leg.* 3.100, which provides some critical contextualization. There, Philo writes:

ἔστι δέ τις τελεώτερος καὶ μᾶλλον κεκαθαρμένος νοῦς τὰ μεγάλα μυστήρια μυηθείς, ὅστις οὐκ ἀπὸ τῶν γεγονότων τὸ αἴτιον γνωρίζει, ὡς ἂν ἀπὸ σκιᾶς τὸ μένον, ἀλλ᾽ ὑπερκύψας τὸ γενητὸν ἔμφασιν ἐναργῆ τοῦ ἀγενήτου λαμβάνει, (Α) ὡς ἀπ᾽ αὐτου (i) αὐτὸν καταλαμβάνειν καὶ (ii) τὴν σκιὰν αὐτοῦ, (Β) ὅπερ ἦν τόν τε λόγον καὶ τόνδε τὸν κόσμον.

There is a more perfect and more purified mind that has been initiated into the great mysteries, which does not know the Cause from what has come to be, as one may learn what is actually there from its shadow. Rather, having transcended those things which are generated, it receives a clear impression of the ungenerated One, (A) so that it (i) comprehends him from himself and (ii) [it comprehends] his shadow—(B) which was [to comprehend] both the Logos and this world.[21]

The critical phrase on which my interpretation depends is the last one. What does Philo mean to clarify by clause (B), "both the Logos and this world?" Do "(i') the Logos and (ii') this world," refer one for one to (i) God and (ii) his shadow?[22] Or should the entirety of clause (B) be taken to explicate only (ii), God's shadow?

Admittedly, Philo's language here does come quite close to that of Plotinus in *Enn.* 5.3.17. One might argue that Moses's comprehension "of God from Himself" is identical to Plotinus's soul seeing [the One] "by itself," by that same light "through which it sees" (δι᾽οὗ καὶ ὁρᾷ).[23] It would

---

[19] Thus, e.g., Williams, *Arius*, 120: "*Ho theos* [for Philo] means God in his own mysterious being, *theos* God as purposive and active in respect of creation." See also, e.g., John 1:1.

[20] For the implication that the Logos belongs to the created order, despite also being "above" creation, see *Leg.* 3.175: καὶ ὁ λόγος δὲ τοῦ θεοῦ ὑπεράνω παντός ἐστι τοῦ κόσμου καὶ πρεσβύτατος καὶ γενικώτατος τῶν ὅσα γέγονε. Elsewhere in the Allegorical Commentary, however, Philo presents a slightly more nuanced view, claiming that the Logos is a kind of distinguishing borderland (μεθόριος) between the creature (τὸ γενόμενον) and Creator (ὁ πεποιηκώς), who is neither uncreated as God nor created as human beings (οὔτε ἀγένητος ὡς ὁ θεός, οὔτε γενητὸς ὡς ὑμεῖς) (*Her.* 205).

[21] Philo, *Leg.* 3.100.

[22] So Litwa, "Transformation through a Mirror," 292–93.

[23] Philo himself argues this position in the famous passage from the Exposition of the Law mentioned above (*Praem.* 46).

be odd, one might further contend, to introduce the Logos but then presuppose a vision of God without him.

Reasonable as these objections are, the second option seems the more probable reading of this particular text: (ii) "God's shadow" signifies both (B) "the Logos and this world." This reading finds support a few chapters earlier in the same treatise, where Philo explicitly calls the Logos God's shadow (σκιὰ θεοῦ ὁ λόγος αὐτοῦ ἐστιν, ᾧ καθάπερ ὀργάνῳ προσχρήσαμενος ἐκοσμοποίει; *Leg.* 3.96). Philo thus uses the term "shadow" to refer both to God's material world and to the creative power by which that world came to be. To behold neither of these, however—neither the material creation nor the immaterial Logos—will satisfy the fully-initiated Mosaic mind.

A second argument for this reading stems from Moses's stated desire to receive an impression of the ἀγένητος. Mackie has argued that, with one exception, Philo describes the Logos as "originated" or γενητός.[24] If the Logos is thus both σκία and γενητός, then it cannot be the object or mediator of the vision requested by Moses in *Leg.* 3.100–101.

One final argument in support of this view arises from what has elsewhere been called prepositional metaphysics.[25] Moses's use of the prepositional phrase ἀπ᾿ αὐτοῦ in his request to understand God "from himself" (*Leg.* 3.100) does not indicate the same instrumental causality usually attributed to the Logos with the dative or the preposition διά.[26] Contrast Plotinus, *Enn.* 5.3.17, and Philo, *Praem.* 45, where both the instrumental dative and the prepositional phrase δι᾿ οὗ present Intellect or Logos as the instrumental cause of the soul's vision.[27] Direct vision from God in himself is requested. Just what such a vision *epistemologically* entails for Moses and for those whose souls resemble him—a mystical experience, an allegorical encounter with Scripture, or both—Philo does not say.[28]

[24] Mackie, "Seeing God in Philo," 35, argues that only in *Cher.* 86 does Philo explicitly call the Logos ἀγένητος.

[25] Gregory E. Sterling, "Prepositional Metaphysics in Jewish Wisdom Speculation and Early Christological Liturgical Texts," *SPhA* 9 (1997): 219–38.

[26] See *Cher.* 126–127, where God (ὁ θεός) is similarly identified as the ὑφ᾿ οὗ, the δημιουργός, and the αἴτιον; while the Word of God (λόγος θεοῦ) is identified as the δι᾿ οὗ, the ἐργαλεῖον, and the ὄργανον. See also 1 Cor 8:6.

[27] To support this stance, note that whereas the Word is called the ὄργανον in *Leg.* 3.96, it is God the αἴτιον which is sought in *Leg.* 3.100; *Cf. Cher.* 126–127.

[28] Ramelli, "Divine as Inaccessible Object," 171, cites *Leg.* 3.100 as evidence for Philo's belief that some knowledge of God seems to be possible, even as his essence remains unknowable. Intriguingly, Ramelli reads this passage as pointing not to further apophatic experience on Moses's part, but to the kataphatic corrective of scriptural revelation: "Human intellects cannot grasp the divine essence, but some help to this end can come from the revelation of God in Scripture … It is a gnoseological factor in that it allows human beings to know something of the divinity, which would otherwise be precluded."

Phaedran Echoes in the Legum allegoriae

Having set out my reading of *Leg.* 3.100–101 in the foregoing section, I turn now to the identification of Phaedran echoes in this passage. Few images in Plato's dialogues rival that of the Phaedran chariot myth (*Phaedr.* 246a–257b) in poetic grandeur and imaginative potential.[29] At first blush, however, it is not clear that *Leg.* 3.100–101 makes reference to this myth at all.[30] Allusions to the *Phaedrus's* iconic *nous* charioteer and his white and black horses are absent. Philo does not invoke the Phaedran myth in this passage as unambiguously as he does elsewhere.[31] Nonetheless, there are several indications that Philo has Plato's *Phaedrus* in mind.

To hear these echoes, it will be necessary briefly to rehearse a few more details from Plato's myth. In the *Phaedrus*, the chariot soul, spurred on by *eros*, ascends into the supra-heavenly realm in order to see the forms. Many chariot souls attempt this journey, but with varying degrees of success, depending on the obedience of horses and rider. Those charioteer minds that have both good and bad horses tightly under control may manage to continue riding in the noetic realm and enjoy an uninterrupted vision of the forms, albeit with some difficulty;[32] the majority of charioteers, however, cannot so dexterously control their steeds and are pulled back under the heavens and lose this more perfect vision.[33] In a further elaboration of this image, Socrates divides the various kinds of charioteers, now in truly mythic terms, according to the kind of god they follow. Some follow Hera, some follow Apollo, but the highest and steadiest kind of soul follows Zeus, who as a master charioteer and "great leader in heaven" guides his

---

Whether or not Philo has scripture in view here, Ramelli is certainly correct in noting that this passage seems to indicate some "gnoseological" supplement to Philo's core apophatic minimalism.

[29] So Michael J. B. Allen, *Marsilio Ficino: Commentaries on Plato. Volume One: Phaedrus and Ion* (ITRL 34; Cambridge, Mass.: Harvard University Press, 2008), ix, speaks of the chariot myth as "one of Plato's most dazzling and memorable" scenes and "the most self-consciously poetic in terms of its diction, gorgeous rhythms and figures, dramatic juxtapositions, elaborate allegory, and symphonic structure."

[30] Méasson does not discuss the Phaedran echoes in *Leg.* 3.100–101 and treats *Leg.* 3.97–100 only once in a passing discussion of astrology (Méasson, "Du char ailé," 393, n. 430). This is hardly surprising, however, given the density with which Phaedran language permeates Philo's thought. I will, moreover, use some of Méasson's own criteria to identify the Phaedran references in this passage (see below).

[31] Philo alludes more clearly to both the sun and the chariot together in *Praem.* 36–46.

[32] Plato, *Phaedr.* 248a: μόγις καθορῶσα τὰ ὄντα.

[33] Plato, *Phaedr.* 248ab.

train of perfected souls in perpetual contemplative orbit.[34] Each chariot soul is said to imitate the "form and practice" of the God it follows.[35]

This outline of Plato's myth supplies the context necessary to understand *Leg.* 3.100–101 as a reading of the *Phaedrus*. First, Philo interprets the vision that Moses requests in Exod 33:13 in terms that echo the vision attributed to the gods in Plato's *Phaedrus*. Just as Moses asks to see God apart from anything that is generated or originate (*Leg.* 3.101: τινος ἁπλῶς τῶν ἐν γενέσει), so Socrates speaks of how the divine minds beholds "justice itself, moderation itself, and knowledge—not [knowledge] which is linked to origination (οὐχ ᾗ γένεσις πρόσεστιν) … but knowledge which exists in respect to that which really is."[36]

A second, more probative clue that the *Phaedrus* stands behind this contemplative passage comes in Philo's description of the Mosaic mind in *Leg.* 3.100. There Philo speaks of how the purified νοῦς … "having looked over those things which are generated (ὑπερκύψας τὸ γενητόν) … receives a clear impression of the ungenerated One."[37] This myth of noetic ascent, particularly the verb ὑπερκύψας, strongly echoes several constitutive elements of the Phaedran journey, not only in its location in the ὑπερουράνιος τόπος,[38] but also the soul's journey above the created order. Thus, Socrates speaks of the best human souls lifting up the heads of their charioteers (ὑπερῆρεν) to the place beyond heaven,[39] and likewise of our

> memory of those things which once our soul saw, as it went along in the company of God and <u>looked above</u> those things which now we say exist and <u>lifted up our heads</u> to that which really is.
>
> ἀνάμνησις ἐκείνων ἅ ποτ᾽ εἶδεν ἡμῶν ἡ ψυχὴ συμπορευθεῖσα θεῷ καὶ <u>ὑπεριδοῦσα</u> ἃ νῦν εἶναί φαμεν, καὶ <u>ἀνακύψασα</u> εἰς τὸ ὂν ὄντως.[40]

Ascent and surpassing sight of the Existent (τὸ ὂν ὄντως),[41] the two key elements of Mosaic vision in *Leg.* 3.100–101, can both be derived from

---

34   Plato, *Phaedr.* 246d–247e, 253ab.

35   Plato, *Phaedr.* 253ab.

36   Plato, *Phaedr.* 247d.

37   Méasson, "Du char ailé," 381, identifies Philo's use of ὑπερκύψας in *Opif.* 70 as an allusion to *Phaedr.* 249c: "Le participe ὑπερκύψας est sans doute encore une allusion au *Phèdre.*" For further support, see Roger M. Jones, "Posidonius and the Flight of the Mind through the Universe," *CP* 21 (1926): 97–113 (102).

38   Plato, *Phaedr.* 247c.

39   Plato, *Phaedr.* 248a.

40   Plato, *Phaedr.* 249c.

41   While Plato (and later Platonists) may have intended/taken τὸ ὂν ὄντως to refer to the ideal realm more generally, Philo often refers to the transcendent God with the neuter

Socrates's description of the chariot soul's vision of the existent in the *Phaedrus*.

Finally, Moses requests in *Leg.* 3.101 to see God's "very form" (τὴν σὴν ἰδέαν). If in fact "form" is to be taken positively as content of the vision Moses requests (see discussion above), this echoes not only Num 12:18 (that God spoke with Moses ἐν εἴδει),[42] but also the Phaedran notion that each chariot soul first "looks toward the nature of their own god and acquires their practices" and then attempts to lead their lovers to follow "the practice and form" (εἰς τὸ ἐκείνου ἐπιτήδευμα καὶ ἰδέαν) of the god they imitate.[43] In philosophical terms, "form" might point to the Logos. Elsewhere Philo, like some later Neoplatonists, would identify this form—and in fact the Phaedran god himself—with the Logos, distinguishing between god (θεῷ) and the Existent (τὸ ὂν ὄντως) in *Phaedr.* 249c.[44] In *Leg.* 3.100–101, however, since Moses rules out seeing by means of the Logos, Philo has little choice other than to identify both the charioteer god *and* the Existent from the myth with God in himself, the Jewish Demiurge of the cosmos.[45]

Neoplatonic Interpretations of the Phaedran Zeus

This final exegetical point, that Philo in *Leg.* 3.100–101 implicitly identifies the Existent himself/Demiurge (rather than the Logos/*organon*) with Zeus, finds support in later Neoplatonic interpretation of the *Phaedrus* myth. It bears noting first, however, that Plotinus would certainly have objected to Philo's reading of the *Phaedrus* in *Leg.* 3.100–101 as I have construed it. For Plotinus, there can be no question of seeing the One. The Phaedran Zeus, moreover, represents not the One or even Intellect, but the World Soul, which Winston has argued is the Neoplatonic analogue to Philo's Logos.[46]

τὸ ὄν (see, e.g., *Mut.* 7: τὸ ὄν, ὅ ἐστι πρὸς ἀλήθειαν ὄν). It is thus plausible that he could have read this passage as speaking about the *visio Dei*.

[42] Cited by Philo in *Leg.* 3.103.

[43] Plato, *Phaedr.* 253ab.

[44] As mentioned above, Philo identifies the Logos with God's image and idea in *Somn.* 2.45–46 (<ὁ θεὸς> τὸν ὅλον ἐσφράγισε κόσμον εἰκόνι καὶ ἰδέα, τῷ ἑαυτοῦ λόγῳ); however, the context there points to the Word's role as paradigm in and for creation, as ἰδέα ἰδεῶν (*Migr.* 103; *Opif.* 69), rather than as a manifestation of God's self *per se*. Moreover, the ἰδέα of *Phaedr.* 253ab clearly has a literal, mythic significance, and does not refer to God's immaterial form. It would be strange indeed to think of the Logos as in some sense the transcendent form of the particular Demiurge.

[45] For the Demiurge/Logos distinction, see *Cher.* 126–127.

[46] Plotinus, *Enn.* 5.8.9, 10, 12, 13. See the discussion of this subject in Allen, *Marsilio Ficino*, xiii–xiv. For Philo's Logos as the functional equivalent of the World Soul, see Winston, *Logos and Mystical Theology*, 15.

Clearly, then, Winston's suggestion that the Logos is the content of Moses' vision in *Leg.* 3.100–101 jibes well with the Plotinian reading of the *Phaedrus*. The later Renaissance Christian Neoplatonist Marcello Ficino, in his commentary on the *Phaedrus* (ca. 1460s), would further identify Zeus the charioteer not with God the Father but with Christ the Logos. True to the Plotinian position, Ficino transformed Zeus into the "Jupiter-Christ," "the first, last, and sovereign charioteer at the head of the hosts of the saved returning to God."[47]

It seems unwarranted, however, to rule out the reading of *Leg.* 3.100–101 that I have proposed on the grounds that it does not agree with Plotinus's position. Philo, after all, is at most a *Middle* Platonist and does not need to follow Plotinus on every point.[48] There is, moreover, at least one Neoplatonist reader of the *Phaedrus* who lends *exegetical* support to the thesis that a first century Platonist might identify the Phaedran Zeus with God himself rather than the Logos. The support in this case comes from Iamblichus of Chalcis.

Iamblichus was a student of Porphyry who elaborated his master's already complex systematization of Plato's thought. Like Plotinus, Iamblichus posited the ontological ineffability and incomprehensibility of the One.[49] However, as an exegete of Plato's images, particularly the images of the *Phaedrus*, Iamblichus differs from Plotinus in an important respect. Unlike Plotinus, who identifies the Phaedran Zeus with the World Soul, Iamblichus identifies Zeus with the Demiurge. The relevant fragment comes from Hermias's commentary on *Phaedr.* 246e:

Ὁ μέντοι θεῖος Ἰάμβλιχος τοῦ τοῦ Διὸς ὀνόματος δραξάμενος ἐπὶ τὸν ἕνα δημιουργὸν τοῦ κόσμου, περὶ οὗ καὶ ἐν Τιμαίῳ εἴρηται, μεταφέρει τὸν λόγον.[50]

The divine Iamblichus, however, drawing on the name 'Zeus', refers the subject of the present passage to the single Demiurge of the cosmos, who is described also in the *Timaeus*.

By interpreting Zeus as the Demiurge rather than the World Soul, Iamblichus provides an ancient exegetical precedent for interpreting the Phaedran Zeus as the "one Craftsman of the cosmos." If such a tradition existed in the first century, Philo could have drawn on it to construct a

---

[47] Allen, *Marsilio Ficino*, xi.

[48] For the question of whether Philo was a Middle Platonist, properly speaking, see the special section "Philo and Middle Platonism," in *SPhA* 5 (1993): 95–155.

[49] In Iamblichus's reworking of Neoplatonic metaphysics, the most transcendent figure is παντελῶς ἄρρητον. See John M. Dillon, *Iamblichi Chalcidensis: In Platonis Dialogos Commentariorum Fragmenta* (PhilAnt 23; Leiden: Brill, 1973), 32.

[50] Iamblichus, *In Phaedrum*, Fr. 3a, in Dillon, *Iamblichi*, 95.

narrative of Mosaic ascent to see the Demiurge, even if the philosophical implications of this narrative remained underdetermined. This would not have prevented Philo from identifying Zeus with the Logos in other passages, as indeed I will demonstrate in a subsequent section that he does (see discussion of *Mut.* 7–17 below).

The Sun and the Chariot (Praem. 36–46)

Thus far, I have argued that in *Leg.* 3.100–101, the image of the Phaedran charioteer leads Philo to endorse a portrait of Moses's unmediated vision of God. Where the chariot ascends high enough, even God's Logos-light becomes shadow. The *Phaedrus*, however, was not always interpreted in this way. Neither did it always win its struggle with the *Republic* to structure Philo's account of mystical experience. Thus, in *Praem.* 36–46, as Philo deftly fuses images from the *Phaedrus* and the *Republic*, the strength of Plato's sun eclipses the "form" of the divine charioteer and obscures the sage's vision of the Existent:

> That charioteer [of the noetic realm], ringed as he was with beams of undiluted light, was beyond [the visionary's] sight or conjecture, for the eye was darkened by the dazzling beams .... The Father and Savior perceiving the sincerity of his yearning in pity gave power to the penetration of his eyesight .... Yet the vision only showed that He is, not what He is.[51]

In this passage, the motif of limited vision from the *Republic* reins in the visionary optimism of the *Phaedrus*. *Praem.* 36–46 thus further illustrates the central claim of this article that Philo's contemplative vision is controlled by *both* (a) the commentary series and (b) his Platonic intertexts. And yet, neither of these controls ultimately determines Philo's thought. In fact, careful attention to the contexts of *Leg.* 3.100–101 and *Praem.* 36–46 suggests yet a third factor that helped shape Philo's mystical vision: (c) the biblical persona upon which each contemplative pattern is based.

Could it be that Philo found the image of the sun particularly fitting to the narrative of the Jacob/Israel soul (as represented in *Praem.* 40–46), detecting an analogy between the gradual ascent out of Plato's cave and Jacob's progressive ascent up a heavenly ladder?[52] Did Moses, to the contrary, the ascender of Sinai and tabernacle visionary, who sees God face to face in Exod 33:11, outstrip the visionary patterns of Philo's second

---

[51] Philo, *Praem.* 38–39. See also *Opif.* 69–70.
[52] See Philo, *Praem.* 43, who mentions τις οὐράνιος κλῖμαξ.

ethical trinity (Abraham, Isaac, and Jacob) and call to mind the unmediated vision of the charioteer soul in the *Phaedrus*?

Such a concept would have a peculiarly Phaedran ring. Just as Plato claims that chariot souls follow their gods with different degrees of success, so Philo asserts that Abraham, Jacob, and Moses did not all rise to the same heights and stability of vision. For many, like Abraham, though they follow in the train of the divine Demiurge, see only God with his powers, a "second-best voyage" in Philo's estimation.[53] It is for Moses and souls like him that Philo reserves the highest Phaedran vision.

Addressing a Counterexample: Limited Mosaic Vision in Mut. 7–17

In explaining the differences between *Leg.* 3.100–101 and *Praem.* 36–46, I appealed to three criteria: (a) commentary series, (b) Platonic images, and (c) biblical exemplar. What, however, is one to do with a passage from the Allegorical Commentary like *Mut.* 7–17, in which Philo clearly rules out any vision of the existent?

> μὴ μέντοι νομίσῃς τὸ ὄν, ὅ ἐστι πρὸς ἀλήθειαν ὄν, ὑπ᾽ ἀνθρώπου τινὸς καταλαμβάνεσθαι.[54]

> Do not think that the Existent, which truly exists, is comprehensible by any human being.

This limitation, it would seem, applies even to Moses in this case. To make this point, after quoting Exod 33:13 (*Mut.* 8)—the lemma cited also in *Leg.* 3.101—Philo then adds God's response to Moses's request, Exod 33:23 (*Mut.* 9): "you shall see my back, but my face you shall not see." Philo interprets this divine reply to mean that Moses's vision is restricted to "the back" which is μετὰ τὸ ὄν (*Mut.* 9, 10), that which is "after" or "below" the Existent; seeing the Existent himself ("my face") is clearly precluded.

To complicate matters further, a couple of sections later, Philo again echoes the *Phaedrus*. In line with his stance in this treatise, however, he claims that the mind's vision is limited to the Logos, who appears to be the divine charioteer leading of the heavenly train, rather than the Demiurge:

> νοῦς ... ἔγνω ἡνιοχούμενον καὶ κυβερνώμενον [τὸν κόσμον] ὑπὸ ἡγεμόνος, οὗ τῆς ἀρχῆς φαντασίαν ἔλαβε. διὸ λέγεται «ὤφθη» οὐ τὸ ὄν, ἀλλὰ κύριος.[55]

---

[53] Philo, *Abr.* 123.
[54] Philo, *Mut.* 7.
[55] Philo, *Mut.* 16–17.

Mind recognized that [the world] was being driven and piloted by a ruler, whose governance he perceived. Therefore it is said that "the Lord" (not the Existent) was seen [by it/Abraham].

Mut. 7–17 thus problematizes the thesis of this article on three scores: (a) as is perhaps typical of the allegorical commentary, Philo presents here the more typical Platonic view of mediated vision; (b) the Phaedran myth (*Mut.* 16–17), however, admits the intermediary role of the Logos, who is implicitly identified as the charioteer; and (c) even Moses's vision falls short of the God who is (*Mut.* 7–9).

The best resolution to this tension between *Leg.* 3.100–101 and *Mut.* 7–17 may simply be a theory of Philonic sources. As Thomas Tobin and others have convincingly argued, to a certain degree, Philo's thought defies systematization because of the conservative and anthological character of his commentaries.[56] It seems clear, in this case, that two very different Moseses appear in *Leg.* 3.101 and *Mut.* 8–9.[57] Before conceding Philonic incoherence, however, I want to offer a possible *exegetical* explanation of the counterexample of *Mut.* 7–17, one that might help mitigate the failure of (b) the Phaedran allusion and (c) the Mosaic persona to produce a theory of unmediated vision. To do this, one needs to consider two additional determinative factors in Philo's exegesis: (d) the length of the biblical lemma Philo interprets; and (e) the context of Mosaic citations within the exegetical structure of the Allegorical Commentary.

As is common in his commentaries, Philo often draws different messages from "the same" biblical text by (d) altering the length of his scriptural pericope. Whereas in *Mut.* 8–9 Philo takes as his lemma Exod 33:13–23, considering both Moses's question and God's response, in *Leg.* 3.101 Philo interprets only Exod 33:13. By focusing in an atomistic fashion on Moses's question (Exod 33:13) in *Leg.* 3.101, Philo functionally bypasses the scriptural response of God and opens the possibility that the Moses soul might attain what he seeks.

Philo's dependence upon the length of his biblical lemma helps to explain this exegetical discrepancy to a degree. It does not, however, solve

[56] See Thomas H. Tobin, S.J., *The Creation of Man: Philo and the History of Interpretation* (CBQMS 14; Washington, DC: Catholic Biblical Association of America, 1983).

[57] Similar significant inconsistencies can be witnessed in Philo's treatment of other biblical figures, such as Philo's various depictions of Adam, who is viewed as both a voluntary and an involuntary sinner, depending on the treatise/context. I am grateful to Michael Francis for alerting me to this in his paper "The Origins of Voluntary Sin: Cain as a Voluntary Sinner according to Philo of Alexandria," presented in the Apocrypha and Cognate Literature section of the Midwest Regional SBL Meeting, Bourbonnais, Il., Feb 7–9, 2014.

the hermeneutical problem, but merely pushes it back a stage. *If* Philo chooses to interpret a longer portion of Exodus 33:13–23 in *Mut.* 8–9, why has he done so? The (b) Phaedran allusion has not led to a theory of unmediated vision; and Moses' limited vision in *Mut.* 8–9 still seems to undermine the thesis that (c) variant views on contemplation can be attributed to variant biblical paradigmatic *personae*.

To further account for the tension between these two passages, one needs to consider one final factor influencing Philo's depictions of Moses in the Allegorical Commentary: in each allegorical treatise, the texts of Exodus which give rise to descriptions of Moses's vision (e) are *secondary* lemmata, that is, they supplement the primary biblical text (from Genesis) that Philo is commenting on in his treatise. In the case of *Leg.* 3.101, the primary subject of the allegory is Adam, the first human being in paradise; in the case of *Mut.* 8–9, the primary subject is Abraham, an ethical exemplar outside of Eden.

This is important, I would suggest, because it may be that Philo adapts his portrait of Moses in these commentaries to mirror the primary spiritual model of each treatise. In discussing Abraham as a contemplative model in *Mut.* 7–17, Gen 17:1 serves as Philo's primary text. Philo understands the Septuagintal phrase καὶ ὤφθη κύριος τῷ Ἀβραάμ to imply that Abraham "saw" God's regal power (κύριος), but not the Existent himself.[58] The limited version of Moses's visionary potential in *Mut.* 7–8, including the length of the secondary lemma interpreted by Philo, may thus depend on the scope of vision possible for Abraham, who is the primary paradigmatic subject grounding the discussion.

Focusing on the centrality of Abraham rather than Moses in *De mutatione nominum* also helps resolve (b) the failure of the *Phaedrus* in this pericope to produce a theory of unmediated vision of God. In *Mut.* 16, it is the mind like Abraham, and *not* the mind like Moses, which is the subject of the *limited* Phaedran vision. Thus, in *Mut.* 16, as in *Praem.* 40–46, it is the Abraham or the Jacob soul (respectively), but not the Moses soul, which fails to follow the Demiurge, but turns after the train of the Logos. In *Leg.* 3.100–101, to the contrary, as Philo considers the original Adamic human being in paradise, Moses emerges with higher visionary potential.

---

[58] Philo, *Mut.* 15.

Conclusion

Addressing the counterexample of *Mut.* 7–17 has helped refine our growing list of features that govern Philonic exegesis. Philo's statements on Moses's contemplative vision gain an exegetical coherence (if not a philosophical consistency) when one considers: (a) the commentary series, (b) his Platonic intertexts, (c) the biblical figure that serves as contemplative paradigm, (d) the length of his biblical citation, and (e) the primary biblical lemma from Genesis to which the Moses exemplum is subordinated.

As regards (b) Philo's Platonic sources, which have been the primary subjects of this article, one can say in conclusion that the images and narrative contours of the *Phaedrus* myth, while sometimes at odds with the images from the *Republic*, ultimately provide the basis for ranking multiple levels of visionary attainment in Philo. The *Phaedrus* raises the possibility that one might see the really Existent (τὸ ὂν ὄντως).[59] While this idea sits uneasily with the apophatic emphasis of much of Philo's mystical thought, and while the *Phaedrus* myth itself might admit other interpretations, Philo did not completely eliminate this Platonic trope from his writings. Faithful to his sources, Philo reserves a place for unmediated vision of the Existent as he interprets the figure of Moses.

Marquette University

---

[59] Plato, *Phaedr.* 249c.

The Studia Philonica Annual 26 (2014) 169–216

BIBLIOGRAPHY SECTION

PHILO OF ALEXANDRIA
AN ANNOTATED BIBLIOGRAPHY 2011

D. T. Runia, K. Berthelot, E. Birnbaum, A. C. Geljon, H. M. Keizer,
J. Leonhardt-Balzer, J. P. Martín, M. R. Niehoff, S. J. K. Pearce,
T. Seland, S. Weisser

2011[1]

F. Alesse, '*Prohairesis* in Philo of Alexandria,' in S. Inowlocki and B. Decharneux (edd.), *Philon d'Alexandrie. Un penseur à l'intersection des cultures gréco-romaine, orientale, juive et chrétienne*, Monothéismes et philosophie (Turnhout 2011) 185–204.

The article studies the usage and connotations of the term προαίρεσις in Philo and aims to identify possible philosophical positions in Philo's application of the term. The author through a selection of passages (e.g. *Sacr.* 11–14) collects the meanings of προαίρεσις found in Philo—general rule or conduct of life, and particular intention or purpose of action, all of which can be morally neutral, or positive, or negative—and tries to link them to a possible philosophical tradition. She then discusses in more detail the philosophical traditions that had made use of the term (esp. Aristotelian, but also Cynic, Platonic and Sceptical). She concludes that προαίρεσις in Philo always presupposes an antithesis between truth and falsity, be it in cognitive, metaphysical, ethical or religious matters, and that Philo summons and rearranges all the philosophical traditions he finds useful to support as coherent as possible an interpretation of Scripture. The article also contains a rich bibliography of studies on this term in ancient philosophy. (HMK)

[1] This bibliography has been prepared by the members of the International Philo Bibliography Project under the leadership of D. T. Runia (Melbourne). The principles on which the annotated bibliography is based have been outlined in *SPhA* 2 (1990) 141–142, and are largely based on those used to compile the 'mother works,' R-R, RRS and RRS2 (on the inclusion of works in languages outside the scholarly mainstream see esp. RRS2 xii). The division of the work this year is as follows: material in English (and Dutch) by D. T. Runia (DTR), E. Birnbaum (EB), A. C. Geljon (ACG) and S. J. K. Pearce (SJKP); in French by K. Berthelot (KB) and Sharon Weisser (SW) with assistance from other team members; in Italian by H. M. Keizer (HMK); in German by Jutta Leonhardt-Balzer (JLB); in Spanish and Portuguese by J. P. Martín (JPM); in Scandinavian languages (and by Scandinavian scholars) by T. Seland (TS), and in Hebrew and by Israeli scholars by M. R. Niehoff (MRN). Once again this year much benefit has been derived from the related bibliographical labours of L. Perrone (Bologna) and his team in the journal *Adamantius* (studies on the

F. Alesse, 'La 'radice alla mente' in Phil. Alex. *Quod deter*. 84–85. Breve analisi di una metafora astrologica,' *MHNH* 11 (2011) 218–228.

The article argues that Philo of Alexandria employs the Platonic simile of man as a 'celestial plant' (*Tim*. 90a2–b1) in a way that reveals an astrological presupposition. Philo specifies (unlike Plato) that this celestial plant has its roots in the sphere of fixed stars, i.e. in the part of the physical world that is characterised by regular and uniform motion. Philo's adaptation of the Platonic simile is to be read in the light of astrological theories about influences of the planets (with their irregular, not uniform motions), against which the human mind must be protected. To support this thesis, the article reviews the use of the 'root' metaphor in (a possibly astrological) relation to the soul and the passions in Philo (esp. *Post*. 163 and *Congr*. 56) and Plato, and in the first and second century c.e. (esp. Plutarch). (HMK, based on the author's summary)

M. Alesso, 'Qué son las potencias del alma en los textos de Filón,' *Circe de clásicos y modernos* 15 (2011) 15–26.

The article gives the results of an investigation on the role of powers (δυνάμεις) in Philo's allegorical treatises. The analysis proceeds on three levels: (1) the powers that form the allegory of the Ark and its accessories: when the five powers join to the Logos, they correspond to the number six, as the six cities of refuge which were given to the Levites in Num 35:15; (2) the powers that collaborate with God when in Gen 1:26 we read the plural '*let us* make the man in *our* image, according to *our* likeness'; (3) the powers of the human soul and especially those of the ascetic–Jacob—represented by his two wives, Rachel and Leah. (JPM)

M. Alexandre Jr. (ed.), *Fílon de Alexandria nas origens da cultura ocidental*, Centro de Estudos Clássicos (Lisbon 2011).

This volume contains lectures and communications held on Philo and related subjects at a conference in the Faculty of Letters in Lisbon on 15 March 2011 as well as other studies carried out in the framework of the *Centro de Estudos Clássicos, Projecto Fílon de Alexandrian nas Origens da Cultura Ocidental*. The papers are separately summarized in this bibliography. (JPM)

Alexandrian tradition). Other scholars who have given assistance this year are Marta Alesso, Giovanni Benedetto, Carlos Lévy, John J. Pilch, Sofía Torallas Tovar and Sami Yli-Karjanmaa. This year once again I owe much to my former Leiden colleague M. R. J. Hofstede, who laid a secure foundation for the bibliography through his extremely thorough electronic searches. However, the bibliography remains inevitably incomplete, because much work on Philo is tucked away in monographs and articles, the titles of which do not mention his name. Scholars are encouraged to get in touch with members of the team if they spot omissions (addresses below in 'Notes on Contributors'). In order to preserve continuity with previous years, the bibliography retains its own customary stylistic conventions and has not changed to those of the Society of Biblical Literature used in the remainder of the Annual. Investigations continue in relation to the possibility of making an online version of the Bibliography which will cover the entire history of Philonic scholarship, including the material included in G-G.

M. ALEXANDRE JR., 'Fílon de Alexandria na Interpretação das Escrituras,' in IDEM (ed.), *Fílon de Alexandria nas origens da cultura ocidental*, Centro de Estudos Clássicos (Lisbon 2011) 9–22.

The article connects Philo's hermeneutics with his theory of the origin of language. Adam is the first who gives beings their name, but there are two states of Adam, heavenly and earthly, and two periods in his life, before and after his fall and expulsion from paradise. Human language follows this descending path and then rises again towards the primary language. The final stage of this rise occurs via the allegorical reading of Moses' text, which is prior to Greek philosophy, and allows human beings to acquire the knowledge of first truths. (JPM)

M. ALEXANDRE JR., 'Fílon entre os sofistas de Alexandria. A Sofística Alexandrina sob o olhar crítico de Fílon de Alexandria,' in IDEM (ed.), *Fílon de Alexandria nas origens da cultura ocidental*, Centro de Estudos Clássicos (Lisbon 2011) 121–136.

The author undertakes to examine the place of Philo in the Alexandrian tradition of sophistic rhetoric, especially on education and culture. Philo shows two uses of the term 'sophist': on the one hand, he highlights the value of Alexandrian sophistic in the philosopher's education, specifically on in the areas of composition and argumentation; on the other hand, he also represents another tendency in speaking of the Sophists in a pejorative sense as manipulators of language. (JPM)

MONIQUE ALEXANDRE, 'Monarchie divine et dieux des nations chez Philon d'Alexandrie,' in S. INOWLOCKI and B. DECHARNEUX (edd.), *Philon d'Alexandrie. Un penseur à l'intersection des cultures gréco-romaine, orientale, juive et chrétienne*, Monothéismes et philosophie (Turnhout 2011) 117–147.

It is the scriptural framework, and more precisely the two first commands of the Decalogue, which stands at the basis of Philo's elaboration of the opposition between divine monarchy and pagan polytheism. Despite this biblical anchor, Philo's criticism of pagan polytheism has to be seen in the context of its diverse contemporaneous Hellenistic and Alexandrian manifestations, and also as nourished by the philosophical critique of traditional religion. Philo's condemnation of polytheism is sustained by a conceptualization of the terminology of polytheism and divine monarchy. Through semantic innovations regarding the terms πολύθεος and μοναρχία, Philo provides a political model which dwells as much on the biblical motif of divine monarchy as on the philosophical tradition concerning the sovereignty of Zeus. On several occasions Philo provides a hierarchical model of the different erroneous beliefs in a plurality of gods, beginning with the divinization of the cosmos and its elements and extending down to Egyptian zoolatry. Finally, the mention of the pagan gods, the presence of certain formulations (such as 'God of gods,' 'sensible gods' or 'God of the intelligible gods'), the utilization of Homeric formula referring to the gods, and the adoption of the pagan tradition of allegorical readings of the gods by Philo raise the question of the radical nature of the opposition between divine monarchy and polyarchy in his thought. (SW)

C. A. Anderson, *Philo of Alexandria's Views of the Physical World*, Wissenschaftliche Untersuchungen zum Neuen Testament 2.309 (Tübingen 2011).

The monograph is a revised version of a dissertation prepared at the University of Cambridge under the direction of Markus Bockmuehl. Its aim is to examine the ambivalent, seemingly contradictory claims about the 'ethical status' of the physical and sense-perceptible world in Philo's thought. Its method is primarily lexical. The author has selected six key terms for Philo's description of the world and its creation and gives a thorough analysis of their contextual use throughout the entire Philonic corpus, taking account of their background in the LXX, Jewish literature and Greek philosophy. The first four terms οὐσία, ὕλη, γένεσις and γενητός are examined together. It is concluded on the basis of their usage that they depict an overall negative ethical status for the sensible realm. The following three chapters discuss positive terminology, the first examining the use of the term κόσμος, the second the term φύσις in the senses of creative power, essential nature and universal nature, the third φύσις in the meaning of cosmic order. The use of both these terms is consistently highly positive. The remainder of the study proceeds to offer an explanation for this apparent ambivalence in Philo's views. The first step is to examine higher and lower approaches to God. The author distinguishes between indirect and direct ways of seeing God and higher and lower categories of people engaged in that search. Philo's pronouncements depend on the perspective that he takes on a question, as revealed in the different kinds of commentaries on scripture that he wrote. This can be called 'Philo's multi-perspectivalism' (p. 167) and it furnishes the key to the many apparent contradictions in his statements. In the final chapter the author reaches his conclusions. Philo's ambivalence about the ethical status of the sense-perceptible world runs very deep. At a more superficial level the world is praised and it can lead to recognition of the creator. At a deeper level, however, to know and have communion with God is to reject the world completely. Although the passages indicating this view are much fewer in number than the positive ones, they represent his deepest and truest thought. In reaching this view Philo takes a more negative stance than scripture (both the LXX and Paul) and Greek philosophy, particularly Plato and the Stoa. He is closer to the pessimistic Middle Platonist thinkers such as Plutarch or Numenius, or even the Gnostics (though his recognition of God the good creator makes him at most a pre-Gnostic). The source of his pessimism is a strong mystical-ascetic impulse, which operates at an underlying level in his psyche and leads to strong condemnation of all that has to do with the body and its impulses. There is a correspondence between this negative perspective and Philo's use of allegory. When set free from the constraints of the literal meaning, Philo's interpretations tend to move to a negative view of the material world. Further research is needed to show whether this attitude is continued in Patristic authors on whom Philo has exerted influence. See further the review by D. T. Runia in *SPhA* vol. 24, pp. 252–255. (DTR)

S. Badilita, 'Caïn, figure du mal chez Philon d'Alexandrie,' in Y.-M. Blanchard, B. Pouderon and M. Scopello (edd.), *Les forces du bien et du mal aux premiers siècles de l'Église: Actes du Colloque de Tours, septembre 2008*, Théologie historique 118 (Paris 2011) 239–252.

An important principle in Philo's thought is that God cannot be the source of evil. Evil arises in human beings themselves. For Philo the most important representative of vice and evil is Cain. He devotes four allegorical treatises to the discussion of Cain: *Cher.*, *Sacr.*, *Det.* and *Post.* Philo explains the name of Cain as meaning 'possession,' and Cain is an example of the mind who thinks that all things are his own possession, which means that he is a lover of himself. He suffers from self-conceit (□□□□□□). He is placed opposite to Abel, who represents the lover of God. Cain is also presented as a sophist, i.e. he thinks that the human mind is the measure of all things. After the killing of Abel, Cain rejects repentance. In Philo's exegesis he says to God: 'The charge against me is too great to be liberated from.' Because in the Bible the death of Cain is never mentioned Philo argues that an evil person will live for ever. (ACG)

K. Berthelot, 'Grecs, Barbares et Juifs dans l'œuvre de Philon,' in S. Inowlocki and B. Decharneux (edd.), *Philon d'Alexandrie. Un penseur à l'intersection des cultures gréco-romaine, orientale, juive et chrétienne,* Monothéismes et philosophie (Turnhout 2011) 47–61.

In order to speak about humankind as a whole, Philo often uses the expression 'Greeks and barbarians,' which reflects a Greek perception of the world; he never uses the traditional Jewish distinction between Israel and the nations (*goyim*). Even if Hebrew as a language can be considered 'barbarian,' in Philo's writings Israel is never counted among the barbarian peoples. Jews are not Greeks either, a statement that corresponds to the social situation of Jews in Egypt during the Roman period. Although they were still culturally Greek to a great extent, they were not considered Greeks by the Roman administration, and therefore were treated like Egyptians (that is, barbarians). Philo's construction of Israel as neither Greek nor barbarian differs from the way Roman or pro-Roman authors viewed the place of Rome among Greeks and barbarians, because these authors understood Rome as a continuation of the Greek world. For Philo, on the contrary, the Law of Moses inspired the Greek world. In the end, Philo contrasts both Greeks and barbarians with the people of Israel, which stands on its own and is not included among the nations. The key to understand Philo's position lies in Balaam's prophecy in Num 23:9 ('a people dwelling alone, and not reckoning itself among the nations'), which Philo paraphrases in *Mos.* 1.278. For Philo, Israel is both separated from the rest of humankind and closely connected with it through its spiritual call to be the priest of the nations. (KB)

K. Berthelot, 'Philo's Perception of the Roman Empire,' *Journal for the Study of Judaism* 42 (2011) 166–187.

Philo's perception of Rome is less positive than has generally been argued. Although he appreciated the *Pax romana* and the religious freedom generally enjoyed by Jews in the Roman Empire, he was nevertheless critical of Rome. In particular, he rejected the idea that the Roman empire was the outcome of divine providence (πρόνοια) and would last forever. Before tackling Philo's position on this matter the article analyzes this idea in Roman or pro-Roman literature and examines Josephus' way of coping with the claim that the empire would last forever. Although Philo nowhere explicitly states that the Roman empire will come to an end, an analysis of his use of chance or fortune (τύχη) in the *Legat.* in connection with Gaius and of his general vision of the instability of worldly empires leads to the conclusion that he expected Roman rule to fade away in the end, and Israel to blossom as no other nation ever had in the past. Philo thus implicitly opposed the spiritual kingship of Israel to the worldly and transitory dominion of Rome. (KB)

K. Berthelot, 'The Canaanites who 'Trusted in God': an Original Interpretation of the Fate of the Canaanites in Rabbinic Literature,' *Journal for the Jewish Studies* 62 (2011) 233–261.

The article discusses the issue of the fate of the Canaanites at the time of the conquest according to some rabbinic sources that contain an unusual tradition, according to which some of the Canaanites obeyed God's will and left the Land that was to be given to the children of Israel. Acknowledging their merit, God gave them another land in Africa and allowed that the Land of Israel be called 'Canaan'. It is argued that this tradition does not merely represent an attempt to defend the right of Israel to the Land, but reflects a genuine theological and ethical questioning about the fate of the Canaanites and, more generally, about the ability of Gentiles to know and obey God's commandments. The exceptional character of this rabbinic tradition is emphasized through a comparison with a similar yet different tradition in Philo's *Hypoth*. Philo argues that it is sounder to suppose that the children of Israel settled in the Land in a peaceful way rather than to imagine that they conquered the Land by force. Philo, however, does not present the autochtonous populations as having done something commendable and does not praise them for their faith or their goodwill towards their invaders. His purpose is to show that Moses was no charlatan, as some people argued. Rather, Moses won the respect of the people whose country the children of Israel came to seize and thus the Canaanites willingly gave pieces of land to Israel. Philo's reasoning and hermeneutical approach thus differ significantly from that of the Sages. (KB)

K. BERTHELOT, 'Philon d'Alexandrie, lecteur d'Homère: quelques éléments de réflexion,' in A. BALANSARD, G. DORIVAL and M. LOUBET (edd.), *Prolongements et renouvellements de la tradition classique: en hommage à Didier Pralon*, Textes et documents de la Méditerranée antique et médiévale (Aix-en-Provence 2011) 145–157.

Philo was very familiar with Homer. He quotes the *Iliad* and the *Odyssey* roughly sixty times, and there are also numerous allusions or reminiscences in addition to the explicit quotations. Moreover, he also knows exegetical traditions concerning Homer's work. In the debate about the morality or immorality of the Homeric corpus, Philo stands on the side of Homer, fully concurring with those who develop an allegorical reading of the Greek poet. Homer's wisdom is so great in Philo's eyes that he sometimes quotes an Homeric verse in order to support his interpretation of a biblical passage (*Od.* 7.36 in *Mut.* 179-180 for instance). Quoting Homer may even provide the Jewish exegete with a weapon in order to defend the meaning of a biblical passage in response to those (probably within the Jewish community) who were critical of the literal meaning of the text. Philo therefore saw much that was harmonious between the Bible and Homer's work, even if the former was much holier. The superiority of the Bible was beyond doubt for Philo, who makes it explicit in some cases (as in *QG* 4.20). However, Philo's work is the greatest homage to the work of Homer ever paid by a Jew in Antiquity. (KB)

K. BERTHELOT, M. R. NIEHOFF, and M. SIMONETTI, 'Discussione su The Cambridge Companion to Philo a cura di A. Kamesar,' *Annali di Storia dell'Esegesi* 28 (2011) 367–390.

This threefold discussion of *The Cambridge Companion to Philo* published in 2009 (see *SPhA* vol. 24 p. 198) opens with Katell Berthelot's contribution (in English, 9 pp.) in which a summary of the various chapters is followed by critical and constructive observations, notably on chapters 1 (on Philo's family and times, by D. Schwartz), 7 (on Philo and the New Testament, by Folkert Siegert) and 9 (on Philo and Rabbinic literature, by David Winston). Berthelot characterizes the Companion as an extremely valuable synthesis of modern research on Philo. The second contribution to the discussion, by Maren Niehoff (in English, 4 pp.), highlights first what she considers strengths of the book (particular points in various chapters, and in general the tenor to appreciate Philo in his own right), while the weaker aspects of the volume for Niehoff are represented by chapters 1 and 7. She qualifies the Companion nonetheless as an excellent introduction and important research tool. The third part of the discussion, by Manlio Simonetti (in Italian, 11 pp.), again reviews the successive chapters of the book (which he judges very favourably) by means of supportive as well as critical observations and comments. This contribution concludes with a reflection on the fact (emphasised by Runia in *Philo in Early Christian Literature*, 1993) that knowledge of Philo's *oeuvre* is attested only from Clement of Alexandria onwards, and only in Alexandria. What may have been the distribution of the cultural movement represented by Philo? Since all authors or texts that can be connected with it are Alexandrian (Pseudo-Aristeas, Aristobulus, *Wisdom*), Simonetti proposes the hypothesis that Hellenistic Judaism of the Philonic type was a religious, philosophical and cultural movement which was restricted to Alexandria, and which became influential only in Christian context thanks to Clement, Origen and Eusebius. (HMK)

E. Birnbaum, 'Who Celebrated on Pharos with the Jews? Conflicting Philonic Currents and Their Implications,' in S. Inowlocki and B. Dechar-neux (edd.), *Philon d'Alexandrie. Un penseur à l'intersection des cultures gréco-romaine, orientale, juive et chrétienne*, Monothéismes et philosophie (Turnhout 2011) 63–82.

Philo's account in *Mos.* 2.41–44 of an annual celebration on the island of Pharos to commemorate the translation of the Hebrew Bible into Greek is somewhat contradictory. Although he depicts the coming together of Jews and non-Jews to celebrate, Philo's observation that the Jewish nation has not prospered for many years and that this situation has cast a shadow on things related to the nation hints at its possible social isolation. Philo's description of the festival thus suggests, on one hand, cultural intermingling, harmony of values, and positive social interaction, and, on the other hand, cultural difference, disharmony of values, and social hostility. The author examines these conflicting currents, which are expressed in different ways throughout Philo's works. Turning to the question posed in the title, she then considers various possibilities for who constituted the 'multitudes of others' (*Mos.* 2.41) who joined the Jews on Pharos. While it is unlikely that Philo invented the details of his account, evidence from his works and outside sources—both of which testify to much hostility against the Jews—do not allow any positive identification of the Jews' co-celebrants. Nonetheless the study calls attention to this intriguing festival and the social situation of the Jews in Alexandria. In the notes there is discussion of such aspects of the gathering as the nature of the thanksgiving prayers and the condition of Pharos in Philo's time and also include a rare 16th-century reference to the festival. (EB)

R. Bloch, *Moses und der Mythos: die Auseinandersetzung mit der griechi-schen Mythologie bei jüdisch-hellenistischen Autoren*, Journal for the Study of Judaism Supplements 145 (Leiden 2011).

The book studies the attitude towards myth, and particularly its criticism in Hellenistic-Jewish authors. The main focus is on Josephus, but also, as background, on other texts such as the Septuagint, Ps.-Orphic fragments, Ps.-Eupolemus, Artapanus, Ezechiel Tragicus, Aristobulus, Ps.Aristeas, the Sibylline Oracles, Ps.Phocylides, the epic authors Theodotos and Philo, and also including Philo of Alexandria. Like Josephus, Philo claims that Moses did not create myths, but presented truths (*Opif.* 2). Philo criticizes the invented Greek myths (*Det.* 125; *Cher.* 91). The biblical account is not a myth (*Gig.* 7). The second commandment forbids the creation of myths (*Decal.* 156); proponents of myths are represented by Cain and Esau (*Post.* 52). Myths are to be shunned because they are unreliable (*Sacr.* 13), opposed to truth, inciting polytheism and not the veneration of the one God (*Aet.* 56; *Deus* 155). Philo argues with Jewish opponents who describe the story of the tower of Babel as myth, comparable to Homeric myths (*Conf.* 2–5). He reads the biblical narratives allegorically (*Conf.* 15ff; other biblical stories: *Opif.* 157; *Agr.* 97). Greek myths are also read allegorically and used as symbols of a certain behavior and its consequences (*Spec.* 3.43–45; *Cher.* 78; *Decal.* 149). Philo even defends them against his nephew's accusations of immorality (*Prov.* 2.40–41), but he also corrects them to suit his own interpretation (*Congr.* 57). In all this he acts like many of his pagan philosophical counterparts. (JLB)

G. Bolognesi, 'Marginal Notes on the Armenian Translation of the *Quaestiones et Solutiones in Genesim* by Philo,' in S. Mancini Lombardi and P. Pontani (edd.), *Studies on the Ancient Armenian Version of Philo's Works*, Studies in Philo of Alexandria 6 (Leiden 2011) 45–50.

English version of the article originally written in Italian by the late Italian scholar who played a key role in the study of the Armenian Philo in his country. See the summary at R-R 7010. (DTR)

A. Botica, *The Concept of Intention in the Bible, Philo of Alexandria, and the early Rabbinic Literature: a Study in Human Intentionality in the Area of Criminal, Cultic and Religious and Ethical Law*, Perspectives on Hebrew Scriptures and its Contexts 9 (Piscataway N.J. 2011).

Based on a dissertation completed in 2007 at Hebrew Union College in Cincinnati, this study addresses the question, 'what role did intention—or the state of mind of a person—play in the worldview of ... Biblical, Hellenistic and Early rabbinic Judaism?' (p. 1). As the representative of Hellenistic Judaism, Philo is allotted nearly 150 pages. The section is divided into two main parts, on criminal law and then the areas of cult, piety, and ethics/ philosophy. In the area of criminal law, Philo is more influenced by Greek and Alexandrian ideas and vocabulary than Roman ones, but the Pentateuch, esp. Exod 21:12–14, remains an important source. Philo mentions different nuances of intention and appears to contribute his own distinct interpretation of biblical law regarding specific cases of liability before the divine court, limited or secondary culpability simply for intending an act, and liability for the attempt to murder and for murderous intent (pp. 239–240). With regard to cultic, spiritual and ethical cases, Philo places even more emphasis on inwardness, as reflected in his spiritualization of cultic elements and acts and his focus on intention, concern with divine examination of thought, and discussion of 'intentions, words, and actions.' Influenced by external sources such as Platonic and Hellenistic philosophy, Philo's understanding of intent shows more sophistication and varied vocabulary than the Bible. (EB)

M. Broze, 'L'Égypte de Philon d'Alexandrie: approches d'un discours ambigu,' in S. Inowlocki and B. Decharneux (edd.), *Philon d'Alexandrie. Un penseur à l'intersection des cultures gréco-romaine, orientale, juive et chrétienne,* Monothéismes et philosophie (Turnhout 2011) 105–113.

Despite Philo's harsh and relentless criticism of Egypt, one passage discloses a more positive stance. In *Mos.* 1:23–24, the learned Egyptians are described as teaching to Moses the allegorical method. In other words, it is the Egyptians who introduce the young Moses to symbolic philosophy. The author argues that Moses' role as the one who makes the divine word accessible is similar to that of the Egyptian God Toth, the inventor of the hieroglyph—a function that will later be assigned to Hermes Trismegistus in the Hermetic literature. (SW)

F. Calabi, 'Le repos de Dieu chez Philon d'Alexandrie,' in S. Inowlocki and B. Decharneux (edd.), *Philon d'Alexandrie. Un penseur à l'intersection des cultures gréco-romaine, orientale, juive et chrétienne,* Monothéismes et philosophie (Turnhout 2011) 185–204.

In six days God created the world, and on the seventh day he rested. The questions prompted by this biblical statement are: (1) in what sense can God's activity have a temporal duration? (2) in what sense did God complete his work, when he is unchangeable and his work is continuous? and (3) what does 'rest' mean for a God who certainly does not become tired? The biblical text (Gen 2:2) moreover presents a variant reading: whereas the Hebrew text says that God completed his work on the seventh day, the LXX and other witnesses (and also Philo) read that it occurred on the sixth. The article, which is rich in bibliographical references, analyses Philo's interpretation, esp. in *Opif.* and *Leg.* 1, of God's creative activity and God's resting from it on the Sabbath. Philo's views can be related to those of Aristobulus (fr. 5 God's rest on the Sabbath does not mean inactivity but fixation of the created order) and Aristotle (the *energeia* of the unmoved mover). For Philo, the rest on the Sabbath is identified with the activity of reflection or contemplation. (HMK)

F. Calabi, 'Metafore del *logos* in Filone di Alessandria,' in R. Radice and M. Sordi (edd.), *Dal Logos dei Greci e dei Romani al Logos di Dio* (Milano 2011) 65–84.

When speaking of the *Logos* Philo uses throughout his work a rich variety of metaphors, which he derives from the Bible or from Greek tradition. God in his being or essence is unknowable and inexpressible: the same according to Philo holds true for his *Logos* and his (other) 'powers'. It is therefore only their role and their actions that can be discussed, and this with the help of images or metaphors (*via analogiae*). The *Logos* has the role of intermediary between God and the created world, a role both in the latter's formation and in its maintenance. Calabi's study focuses on the image of light (Plato's sun, and the light of Gen 1) and its corollaries (shadow, eye) used by Philo to describe this role, and on the image of nourishment or bread (for the soul) as represented in particular by the manna of Exod 16. The λόγος in this context is repeatedly put on a par with ῥῆμα, notably because of Deut 8:3. With these and other images Philo brings out the variety of functions of the *Logos* as present both in the cosmos and in the individual human being. (HMK)

M. Ceglarek, *Die Rede von der Gegenwart Gottes, Christi und des Geistes: eine Untersuchung zu den Briefen des Apostels Paulus*, Europäische Hochschul-schriften: Reihe 23, Theologie Band 911 (Frankfurt am Main 2011), esp. 103–152.

The author discusses Philo's concepts of God as both transcendent and immanent. The distinction between the transcendent God and his immanent powers enables him to maintain both positions. Another aspect of the presence of the transcendent God is the Logos, the guide of the rational soul. Places of the divine presence are reason and the soul of the virtuous, but also the Temple in Jerusalem and the cosmos as a whole as house of God. The spirit is another way in which God is present, and Philo's view in this matter is twofold. On the one hand he holds that every person has been equipped with a spirit: it is not an eschatological gift but the divine breath, which gives reason to humankind and enables human beings to be capable of virtue. It can also be lost, if the material nature of a person takes precedence over reason and the spirit is driven out of the human soul. On the other hand, the advent of the divine spirit can expel the human mind temporarily in an ecstatic state, because mortal things cannot cohabit with immortal ones. Usually the presence of the divine spirit is linked to particular virtue, e.g. in the case of Abraham. Yet not only ecstatic phenomena are related to the arrival of the divine spirit. Prophecy is also connected to its presence. In sum, God's presence inside the world and especially inside the human soul, generally depends on virtue. (JLB)

N. G. Cohen, 'Philo's Place in the Chain of Jewish Tradition,' *Tradition* 44 (2011) 9–17.

In this article, written for a broad readership within Jewish Studies, the author argues that Philo's works show the continual development of a profound commitment as a Jew and loyalty to the Jewish tradition. Building on her earlier studies, Cohen argues that Philo expressed himself in 'the idiosyncratic religious vocabulary' of the Jewish tradition (p. 10), and that such vocabulary deals with aspects of the *Torah she–be'al peh* (the Oral Torah). Correct understanding of Philo as a Jew must, she argues, pay attention to the 'idio-syncratic' Jewish connotation of his use of otherwise standard Greek terms (δόγμα, λόγος, νόμος etc.). (SJKP)

M.-H. Congourdeau, 'De l'exil à la migration. À propos de *La migration d'Abraham* de Philon,' *Christus* 230 (2011) 169–175.

The article provides a general overview of the theme of migration in *Migr.* Abraham leaves his country, i.e. he departs from the sensible to the intelligible world. Examples of other migrants are Joseph and Jacob, who returns to his homeland. Philo emphasizes the help of God during the journey. Abraham's migration is also a journey into one's inner self. At the same time the migration is a voyage into the interior meaning of scripture. (ACG)

J. T. Conroy Jr., 'Philo's "Death of the Soul": Is This Only a Metaphor?,' *The Studia Philonica Annual* 23 (2011) 23–40.

Acknowledging that Philo's references to 'death of the soul' are widely recognized as metaphorical, Conroy sets out to show that the question posed in his subtitle should nonetheless be answered in the negative. He begins by establishing that true life, or immortality, refers ontologically—i.e., not metaphorically—to the soul's continued existence after its separation from the body. He then considers passages understood by D. Zeller and E. Wasserman to be metaphorical but argues that these may also be understood non-metaphorically to indicate 'an ontological shift,' spiritual death, actual immortality of the soul, or unhappiness as a real consequence of spiritual death in contrast to true life made possible by the practice of wisdom. After adducing additional examples, he explains that Philo was influenced by the Hellenistic concept of a hierarchical chain of being which placed 'Being' at the top and inanimate beings at the bottom and rational creatures above irrational ones. Humans can move up and down in the hierarchy so that a human whose rationality has departed or who has chosen to live a life of vice can be transformed into the nature of a beast even while retaining human form. Similarly the death of the rational part of the soul may not signify the death of the entire soul but instead may indicate the non-metaphorical transformation of the rational human soul into the soul of a beast. (EB)

L. S. Cook, *On the Question of the "Cessation of Prophecy" in Ancient Judaism*, Texts and Studies in Ancient Judaism 145 (Tübingen 2011).

In this well-researched monograph the author deals with his subject in three extensive parts, comprising fourteen chapters. Philo is dealt with in Chapter Eight (pp. 88-103). Part One deals with the ancients texts, a review of modern literature, and a summary and assessment. Part Two (chapters four to twelve) deals with the question 'did Second Temple Jews believe Prophecy had ceased?' In the final Part he briefly reassess modern debates and draws his conclusions. In his treatment of Philo the author deals with his view of both the ancient prophets and his own ecstatic experiences. Setting aside his own inspired experiences, Philo does not seem to assert that true prophecy was to be found among the Jews of his own day. All those he names as true prophets come from Israel's distant past. Hence the conclusion of Cook is that Philo does support the conclusion that prophecy had ceased. This is also the general conclusion of this work, namely that Second Temple Jews did, on the whole, tend to believe that prophecy had ceased in the Persian period (p. 191). (TS)

R. R. Cox, 'Travelling the Royal Road: the Soteriology of Philo of Alexandria,' in D. M. Gurtner (ed.), *This World and the World to Come: Soteriology in Early Judaism* (London 2011) 167–180.

For Philo, salvation is the death of the soul to the material body and the return of the soul to its heavenly origins. Developing Platonic ideas, he regards the goal of human life as assimilation to God (cf. *Opif.* 144); in order to attain the virtue of well-being, the soul must adopt the ways of God. Attainment of this virtue, for Philo, is profoundly linked to the activity of allegorical exegesis of Scripture, which reveals the route to virtue through the examples of the Patriarchs and their embodiment of the natural law, by which they followed God. The path to virtue is hard, as symbolized by the tortuous migrations of Abraham and Jacob; the achievement of virtue without effort, represented by Isaac, is reserved for very few. The different descriptions of the deaths of the patriarchs and of Moses reveal, in Philo's thinking, 'a gradation of rewards,' matching the highest degree of virtue attained in life to the closest proximity to God (cf. *Sacr.* 5-10; *Fug.* 168; *Somn.* 2.232). For Philo, salvation is not just a human work, but rather the result of God's providence; the Logos is 'the primary catalyst for salvation,' by which the Deity draws the perfect human being to itself. The Logos is 'best suited for this assistance' because of its kinship with the rational soul of human beings. (SJKP)

B. Decharneux, 'Le Logos philonien comme fondation paradoxale de l'Évangile de Jean,' in S. Inowlocki and B. Decharneux (edd.), *Philon d'Alexandrie. Un penseur à l'intersection des cultures gréco-romaine, orientale, juive et chrétienne,* Monothéismes et philosophie (Turnhout 2011) 317–333.

In proposing the hypothesis that the Prologue of John represents a first synthesis of views present in the first Christian communities around John, the article first reviews five hypotheses on the nature of the Prologue formulated in earlier research, one of which is that the Prologue shows direct or indirect influence from the Philonic corpus. The author supports the view that no direct or indirect influence from Philo on John's Prologue can be demonstrated, but only a common background for the two. He concludes that the Prologue is not a speculative or hymnal prelude, but represents a theological necessity, which is to unite the different components of John's Gospel by means of a logos-centred Christology. (HMK)

B. Dolna, 'The Hidden and the Revealed Torah in Philo,' in A. Lange and K. De Troyer (edd.), *The Qumran Legal Texts between the Hebrew Bible and its Interpretation* (Leuven 2011).

In this article the author asks whether a concept of hidden Torah existed alongside a revealed one in Philo's works, similar to concepts of Torah *nigleh* and *nistar* in Qumran writings. For Philo, the revealed Torah is an imitation of the 'true' laws, the unwritten divine Logos, embodied in the lives of the patriarchs and of Moses. It is a 'hidden Torah,' revealed by Moses himself. Despite his full commitment to the revealed Torah, it is evident that Philo works with a model of Law 'which surpasses the Mosaic Law itself' (p. 97). Understanding of this 'hidden Torah' can only be achieved through allegorical interpretation of the revealed Torah. There are formal similarities between the Qumran concepts of Torah *nigleh* and *nistar* and Philo's understanding of Torah. But there are also key differences, notably, the mystic-philosophical aspect of Philo's concept of the hidden Torah which leads to a universalistic understanding of Judaism. (SJKP)

M. Duarte, 'Λόγος ἐνδιάθετος e προφορικός na Formação da Cristologia Patrística,' in M. Alexandre Jr. (ed.), *Fílon de Alexandria nas origens da cultura ocidental,* Centro de Estudos Clássicos (Lisbon 2011) 47–79.

After considering the relevant background in Greek philosophy, the author discusses the reception of the Philonic distinction between ἐνδιάθετος λόγος and προφορικός λόγος and its echoes in the first centuries of Christian literature. The distinction was developed by Theophilus of Antioch, Tatian, Justin, Hippolytus and others. But during the fourth century, in the context of the dispute with Arianism, the issue was forgotten or covered in silence. It was explicitly rejected by orthodox authors such as Cyril of Jerusalem, Athanasius of Alexandria, Gregory of Nyssa and John Chrysostom. The assignment of the terms ἐνδιάθετος and προφορικός to Jesus the Logos was also condemned by the Arians in the Council of Sirmium in 358. (JPM)

T. Faia, 'Embaixada de Calígula, Agustina Bessa-Luís e uma Memória de Fílon de Alexandria,' in M. Alexandre Jr. (ed.), *Fílon de Alexandria nas origens da cultura ocidental*, Centro de Estudos Clássicos (Lisbon 2011) 37–467.

The paper reviews a book by A. Bessa-Luís which treats Philo's embassy to the Emperor Caligula and evokes the contrast between Philo, who loved his people and ancestral traditions, and Caligula, who believed he was able to subjugate anyone. Bessa-Luís argues that this contrast remains topical in contemporary Europe. (JPM)

M. Fernandes, 'O Profetismo no Tratado *De Iosepho* de Fílon de Alexandria,' in M. Alexandre Jr. (ed.), *Fílon de Alexandria nas origens da cultura ocidental*, Centro de Estudos Clássicos (Lisbon 2011) 81–90.

Analyses *Ios.* and argues that the figure of Joseph represents a kind of prophet. Prophetic functions can be seen in the prediction of misfortunes, the interventions to save his land and his people, the speech in the name of God, the revelation of secrets (*Ios.* 90–95), divine inspiration (*Ios.* 107), the interpretation of dreams (*Ios.* 121) and mediation regarding divine will (*Ios.* 241–245). (JPM)

M. Fernandes, 'Φύσις no Tratado de Fílon de Alexandria *De Iosepho*,' in M. Alexandre Jr. (ed.), *Fílon de Alexandria nas origens da cultura ocidental*, Centro de Estudos Clássicos (Lisbon 2011) 111–120.

The paper analyses the entry □□□□□ in the best-known dictionaries of Greek language, including the Liddell-Scott and Bailly, and notes that Philo is absent in all of them. Dictionaries assign some meanings of the term to the Christian period, but when the author studies the occurrences of the term in the treatise *Ios.* he reaches the conclusion that Philo testifies to meanings such as 'substance,' 'essence' and 'acting universal principle' before Christianity. (JPM)

A. C. Geljon, 'Philo's Influence on Didymus the Blind,' in S. Inowlocki and B. Decharneux (edd.), *Philon d'Alexandrie. Un penseur à l'intersection des cultures gréco-romaine, orientale, juive et chrétienne*, Monothéismes et philosophie (Turnhout 2011) 357–372.

This article examines some interesting examples of Didymus' use of Philo. The Alexandrian exegete borrows his allegorical interpretation of Cain as vice and Abel as virtue from Philo, to whom he also refers by name (*Gen. Comm.* 119.1–10). An anonymous reference to Philo is found in *Zach. Comm.* 3.273, where Didymus explains the difference between horseman and rider. Philonic elements are also encountered in Didymus' interpretation of Ps. 22 LXX as indicating the soul's moral progress towards virtue. Finally, Didymus shows a great interest in Philo's explanation of numbers, and he derives some arithmological material from him (*Gen. Comm.* 183.22–184.21). (ACG)

D. A. GIULEA, 'The Noetic Turn in Jewish Thought,' *Journal for the Study of Judaism* 42 (2011) 23–58.

By 'noetic turn,' the author means the reconceptualization of biblical and apocalyptic ontological and epistemological categories (e.g. God, angels, heavens), generally thought of according to the norms of everyday knowledge, into noetic categories. The heavenly mysteries are understood not by direct vision, hearing, dreams, but by noetic perception. This development introduces new ideas about the nature of the realities of the heavenly world, about revelation, and about human capacity for noetic perception. It begins with Philo, who introduces Plato's distinction between the noetic/intellectual and the sense-perceptible into Jewish thought. Thus, while Philo still holds to the notion of heaven as the place of divine indwelling, access to that realm is to be attained through noetic perception. In place of the biblical/apocalyptic categories of transportation to heaven, direct vision, dreams or other methods of access, Philo has the intellect make the upward journey to the heavenly realm. Philo is also the 'real initiator' of negative language for describing the intellectually inaccessible aspect of God. The remainder of the article explores the 'noetic turn' in early Christian and medieval Jewish thought. (SJKP)

M. GOODMAN, 'Philo as a Philosopher in Rome,' in S. INOWLOCKI and B. DECHARNEUX (edd.), *Philon d'Alexandrie. Un penseur à l'intersection des cultures gréco-romaine, orientale, juive et chrétienne*, Monothéismes et philosophie (Turnhout 2011) 37–45.

The article investigates Josephus' account in *Ant.* 18.259–260 of Philo's participation in the embassy to the emperor Gaius, and particularly the emphasis that he places on Philo's role as philosopher. It was unusual for a philosopher to represent his community at this time (there are no other examples in the early Imperial period). Philo certainly saw himself as a philosopher, but Gaius may not have recognized him as such. Most of his writings would not have been seen as philosophical. Platonist philosophers were very scarce in Rome at this time and in general philosophers were accepted but fairly marginalised. Josephus may also have had his own reasons for emphasizing Philo's reputation in philosophy. It is probably safest to conclude that Gaius, if he did see Philo as a philosopher, would have categorized him not so much as a Platonist but 'as an outstandingly articulate representative of the barbarian philosophy of Judaism' (p. 45). (DTR)

E. S. GRUEN, 'Jews and Greeks as Philosophers: a Challenge to Otherness,' in D. C. HARLOW, K. MARTIN HOGAN, M. GOFF and J. KAMINSKY (edd.), *The "Other" in Second Temple Judaism: Essays in Honor of John J. Collins* (Grand Rapids Mich. 2011) 402–422.

In contrast to hostile views of the Other in the biblical narrative and later Jewish history, during the Hellenistic period the relationship between Jews and Gentiles, especially Greeks, was 'far more complex and ambivalent' (p. 403). To illustrate this relationship, Gruen focuses on Greek views of Jews as philosophers and Jewish views of Greek philosophers as dependent on Jewish lore. In the former category, he considers evidence from Theophrastus, Clearchus of Soli, and Megasthenes. In the latter category, he discusses the *Letter of Aristeas*, Aristobulus, Philo, and Josephus. Following in the steps of Aristobulus, Philo claims that teachings from Heraclitus, Hesiod and Plato were already propounded by Moses and—perhaps with some sense of humor—finds biblical sources that anticipate ideas expressed by Zeno, the Stoics, Socrates, and other Greek philosophers. Philo also portrays Moses as having been educated by both learned Egyptians and Greeks. Among the wise, just, and virtuous, Philo recognizes the seven sages of Greece, Persian *magi*, Indian gymnosophists and Jewish Essenes, and thereby further reflects high regard for others as philosophers. (EB)

E. S. GRUEN, *Rethinking the Other in Antiquity.* Martin Classical Lectures (Princeton 2011).

Aiming to show that Greeks, Romans, and Jews 'had far more mixed, nuanced, and complex opinions about other peoples' than is often thought (p. 3), Gruen examines a range of sources in two sections: 'Impressions of the 'Other,' which considers attitudes toward and evaluations of others, and 'Connections with the 'Other,' which focuses on tales and traditions that emphasize linkages rather than differences. Philo is mentioned in passing primarily in the second section as an example of someone who called for high regard to be shown to foreigners who have abandoned their homelands and way of life (p. 306, cf. pp. 291–292); who viewed Moses as an earlier proponent or even the source of the teachings of several Greek philosophers but also as the recipient of Egyptian and Greek training in his youth (pp. 319–320); and who recognized among the wise, just, and virtuous, such figures as the seven sages of Greece, the Persian *magi*, Indian gymnosophists, and Jewish Essenes. (EB)

N. GUPTA, 'The Question of Coherence in Philo's Cultic Imagery: a Socio-literary Approach,' *Journal for the Study of the Pseudepigrapha* 20 (2011) 277–297.

Although Philo's works are often regarded as lacking in coherence, Gupta focuses on Philo's cultic imagery to show that he is in fact a coherent writer. With each cultic element, Gupta first discusses Philo's attitude toward the role of the cultic aspect itself and then turns to his symbolic interpretation of these elements on a macrocosmic and microcosmic level. Thus for Philo the physical temple—God's dwelling place—offers an important, tangible way to serve God and unite the community of His worshippers. As a macrocosm, the temple represents the entire universe, the heavens, the world of ideas, and/or divine wisdom. On a microcosmic level, the temple is the soul, mind, and/or reason. After similarly considering Philo's discussions of priests, sacrifices, and worshippers (the latter two being closely linked), Gupta acknowledges that Philo is not *consistent* because he does not present a 'single image' of cultic elements (p. 291). Nonetheless he is *coherent* in relating cultic elements (the 'source domain') on a macrocosmic level 'to the 'world' or the cosmic *logos*' (the 'target domain') and on a microcosmic level to the soul, mind, and virtues (pp. 291–292). Philo also demonstrates coherence in the purpose of his images, which is 'to promote Judaism as the pinnacle of religious aspiration' (p. 293) and to provide diasporic Jewish communities with a meaningful way to understand Jewish cultic worship and their own Jewish identity. (EB)

M. HARL, 'L'association du Cosmos au culte sacerdotal selon Philon d'Alexandrie,' in A. BALANSARD, G. DORIVAL and M. LOUBET (edd.), *Prolongements et renouvellements de la tradition classique: en hommage à Didier Pralon*, Textes et documents de la Méditerranée antique et médiévale (Aix-en-Provence 2011) 173–186.

The author analyses the motive of the association of the cosmos with the priestly cult through the examination of three main texts: *Leg.* 1.82–96, *Mos.* 2.133–135, *Somn.* 1.203–215. The association of the universe with the priestly liturgy is conducted through three main ideas: (1) the sacerdotal vestment constitutes an imitation of the cosmos; (2) the cosmos is the model of perfect virtue and (3) it functions as an intercessor. For Philo, the vestment of the priest, being a figuration and a reproduction of the cosmos, functions as a model which can give access to the knowledge of God. Moreover, Philo's associates the priest's breast-plate (λογεῖον) with the Logos, in its acceptation as the cohesive principle conferring unity upon beings. The depiction of the cosmos as the son of the father, pervaded by the divine logos and attesting to the perfect accord and harmony in nature explains its exemplarity as the model of perfect virtue and accounts for the idea that priesthood should be understood as obedience to the laws. Finally, in a similar way to human consciousness, the cosmos functions as an accuser, a witness and an intercessor (παράκλητος). Then, under Philo's pen, the cosmos becomes the first sanctuary devoted to the cult of God. (SW)

J. G. HARRISSON, 'Jewish Memory and Identity in the First Century AD: Philo and Josephus on Dreams,' in M. BOMMAS (ed.), *Cultural Memory and Identity in Ancient Societies* (London 2011) 61–78.

The article focuses on the significance of cultural and autobiographical memory as major factors in the construction of cultural identity. Specifically, it explores the 'conflict and interplay of identities within Philo and Josephus … whose Jewish cultural memory and sense of identity had to be reconciled with a Greco-Roman literary output' (p. 61). The study focuses on their writings on dreams as a way to explore the interconnections of identities in both authors. Based on an examination of *Somn.*, Philo's approach to dreams is seen as combining both Greek and Jewish 'intellectual identities' (the use of dream inter-preters; skill in dream interpretation connected to the moral status of the interpreter; the influence of Greek philosophy as a framework for exploring the significance of dreams). Unlike Josephus, Philo almost completely ignores the culture of Rome; his chief concerns are with Jewish culture, Egyptian culture and the intellectually dominant Greek culture. (SJKP)

M. HATZIMICHALI, *Potamo of Alexandria and the Emergence of Eclecticism in Late Hellenistic Philosophy* (Cambridge 2011).

It is likely that the self-style 'eclectic' philosopher Potamo was a leading figure on the philosophical scene in Alexandria when Philo received his training. The monograph discusses in detail both the context of his work and what we can determine about his thought on the basis of very limited evidence (some information on epistemology, physics and ethics, and also two comments on Aristotle's *De caelo*). Philo's thought is not included in the volume on chronological grounds 'as his main period of activity falls about a genera-tion after Potamo's' (p. 4) and also because the latter should be seen as a late product of Hellenistic philosophy rather than a witness to the beginnings of Imperial philosophy. But various references are made to Philo (to the list in the index on p. 194 can be added pp. 53, 59) and obviously anything we know about Potamo's thought will contribute an under-standing of the background to Philo's philosophical knowledge. See further the review by D. T. Runia in *SPhA* vol. 25, pp. 236–237. (DTR)

C. T. R. Hayward, 'Saint Jerome, Jewish Learning, and the Symbolism of the Number Eight,' in A. Andreopoulos, A. Casiday and C. Harrison (edd.), *Meditations of the Heart: the Psalms in Early Christian Thought and Practice: Essays in Honour of Andrew Louth* (Turnhout 2011) 141–159.

The article studies Jerome's interpretation of the number eight in the heading of Ps 6. Philo is used twice in this context. Firstly, he is thought to be the cause of Ambrose's appreciation of the number eight in *Ep.* 44.13–14, where the seven physical and irrational parts of the human being are complemented and completed by the soul as the eighth (*QG* 1.75; *Det.* 168). Secondly, Philo provides a model for Jerome's selection of passages from the Pentateuch which attest to the importance of the number eight. Important texts are *Spec.* 2.211–213 and *QG* 3.49. (JLB).

S. Inowlocki and B. Decharneux, *Philon d'Alexandrie. Un penseur à l'intersection des cultures gréco-romaine, orientale, juive et chrétienne*, Monothéismes et philosophie (Turnhout 2011).

This volume contains the papers of the conference on Philo organised at the Free University of Brussels and held from 26 to 28 June 2007. As the editors state in their introduction, the theme of the conference was chosen in order to proceed beyond the customary antithesis between Judaism and Hellenism which has long dominated Philonic studies. The aim was to explore a complex reality which is expressed through the simple fact that Philo was an Alexandrian. In addition it is important to give a voice to many different methodologies, whether those of philology, philosophy, theology, history, literature or sociology. The conference theme flows from the conviction that only a pluralistic approach to Philo' *œuvre* will allow us to gain an adequate understanding of his thought. After the keynote address of David Runia the remaining papers are divided into three sections: Philo between Jerusalem and Rome, exploring him and his work in a Jewish, Roman and Alexandrian context (five papers); Between Athens and Alexandria, exploring the Philonic corpus from the viewpoint of philology and philosophy (eight papers); and 'Le temps des relectures' (The time of rereading), exploring the relations between Philo and the New Testament and also his subsequent *Nachleben* (seven papers). All twenty-one papers are summarized separately in this bibliography. (DTR)

S. Inowlocki, 'Relectures apologétiques de Philon par Eusèbe de Césarée: le cas d'Enoch et des Thérapeutes,' in Eadem and B. Decharneux (edd.), *Philon d'Alexandrie. Un penseur à l'intersection des cultures gréco-romaine, orientale, juive et chrétienne*, Monothéismes et philosophie (Turnhout 2011) 373–391.

This study aims to demonstrate how in the *Praeparatio Evangelica* and the *Demonstratio Evangelica* the person and work of Philo contribute to Eusebius' apologetic purpose. Philo is cited as 'the Hebrew,' i.e. one who belongs to the ancient tradition of believers in the true God represented by the Hebrews, embodied in particular by the pre-Mosaic patriarchs and continued by the followers of Christ. Philo's influence is not limited to those places where his work is expressly quoted. The article focuses on Eusebius' discussion and interpretation of the patriarch Enoch, identifying similarities with Philo's treatment, and also on Eusebius' description in *DE* 1.8 of the ecclesiastical order, which evokes Philo's description of the Therapeutae in *Contempl.* 12–13. It is concluded that Philo's influence on

Eusebius is unmistakeable, but that the Bishop profoundly modifies Philo's thought and adapts it to his own apologetic aims. (HMK)

O. Kaiser, 'Aretê and Pathos bei Philo von Alexandrien,' *Deutero-canonical and Cognate Literature Yearbook* (2011) 379–429.

Kaiser introduces Philo as Middle Platonist and exegete of the Torah, in whose thought virtue and passion play a major role. This can already seen from the number of occurrences of ἀρετή and πάθος in his works, which is exceeded only by the term θεός. Philo's idea of virtue follows the Aristotelian concept of the right middle between the extremes, while passion is the unbridled urge against one's created nature, and therefore always objectionable. Humankind is nevertheless subject to this urge, because God only created the mind and virtuous part of the soul, the other was left to God's co-workers whom he appears to address in Gen 1:26. The material life in itself, e.g. wealth and procreation, is not seen as negative; it only becomes so when desire takes over and the passions are no longer subject to reason. Human beings carry the responsibility for their lives in spite of God's foreknowledge and plan. Humankind has been given reason, and *paideia* (education) further guides towards virtue. There are three kinds of goods, the spiritual (virtue), the bodily (health) and the external ones (wealth). Material goods (wealth and health) are neither good nor bad. If used towards the common good they are beneficial, as goals in themselves they are unsuitable. They may, however, be allowed to play a greater role in youth than in later life. Virtue carries as reward the eternal life of the soul, while vice leads to eternal death. There is no concept of divine judgment except in this consequence of one's life decisions, but there is a brief hint that the soul of those who cling to the material world might be reborn repeatedly until they finally separate from it and ascend. (JLB)

S. Kottek, 'Les Esseniens et la medicine,' *Histoire des sciences medicales* 45 (2011) 315–320.

Besides Josephus and Pliny the Elder, Philo is used as a source of information about the Essenes and the Therapeutae with whom he had personal contact. The focus is on the hygienic and medical aspects of their way of life. The members of the communities take their meals in common, bathe in cold water and are clothed modestly. They observe the Sabbath strictly. The Essenes show a great interest in books about medicine and study the virtues of medicinal plants. (ACG)

R. S. Kraemer, *Unreliable Witnesses: Religion, Gender, and History in the Greco-Roman Mediterranean* (Oxford 2011).

In this book Kraemer explores the ways in which ancient ideas about gender have shaped the written record of women's religious practice in the Greco-Roman Mediterranean. It is offered as a critical retrospective of the author's own work in this field, and includes a substantial chapter (pp. 57–116) in which she reconsiders her earlier studies on Philo's Therapeutrides described in the *Contempl*. She notes Philo's repeated emphasis on the equal participation of women in the community's practices, even though women members are discussed by him only in the context of the weekly meetings or the Feast of Fifty of the Therapeutae. It is uncertain how much of the rest of Philo's account of the community includes the female members. In her previous studies on the subject, Kraemer took Philo's account to be 'rooted in social reality.' Since then, she explains, she has changed her mind on two key issues: (1) Philo has either invented or so shaped the account of the Therapeutae 'as to make them virtually inaccessible to us'; and (2) his portrayal of the Therapeutae is 'generated out of a combination of Philo's exegetical interests,' especially Genesis 1–3 and Exodus 15. In line with her earlier work, Kraemer continues to hold that Philo purposely shows the Therapeutrides as 'masculinized,' but now sees this conception in a broader context as 'part of a larger pattern of de-emphasizing many aspects of ancient gender norms' for women and men. (SJKP)

F. LEDEGANG, *Philo van Alexandrië Over de tien woorden, De Decalogo* (Budel, Netherlands 2011).

Dutch translation of *Decal.* with copious explanatory footnotes. In the introduction attention is paid to Philo's life, his writings, his thought, his relation with the rabbis and the contents of the treatise. See the review by D. T. Runia elsewhere in this volume. (ACG)

C. LÉVY, 'La notion de signe chez Philon d'Alexandrie,' in S. INOWLOCKI and B. DECHARNEUX (edd.), *Philon d'Alexandrie. Un penseur à l'intersection des cultures gréco-romaine, orientale, juive et chrétienne,* Monothéismes et philosophie (Turnhout 2011) 149–161.

The notion of sign (σημεῖον) was a hotly debated issue between the Sceptics and the Stoics. Although Philo seems aware of the complexity of the issue and of the polemic that it triggered, he intentionally dismisses the logical and linguistic Hellenistic concerns over the notion of sign in order to align himself with the Platonic usage of the term (*Phdr.* 244c). It is the theological and cosmological outlook which articulates Philo's use of the term, for the sign constitutes in his eyes the expression of transcendence, the fulcrum of the divine manifestation to human beings. In the last part of the paper, the author claims that 'symbol' (σύμβολον) and 'sign' (σημεῖον) are not exact synonyms in Philo's thought. The exegete's task is to transform the exclusively divine sign into a symbol standing on the borders between the human and divine realms. (SW)

C. LÉVY, 'L'aristotélisme, parent pauvre de la pensée philonienne?,' in T. BÉNATOUÏL, E. MAFFI and F. TRABATTONI (edd.), *Plato, Aristotle, or Both? Dialogues between Platonism and Aristotelianism in Antiquity,* Europaea memoria. Reihe 1 Studien, Band 85. Diatribai 4 (Hildesheim 2011) 17–33.

The aim of the article is to establish the status of Aristotelianism within Philo's thought, particularly in relation to the role played by Platonism and Stoicism. Lévy first reviews a number of recent studies, particularly those of Bos (RRS2 9824) and Niehoff (RRS2 20666). These studies all focus on the question of the relation between God and the cosmos. Less attention has been paid to Philo's view of Aristotle's ethics. As can be seen in his interpretation of the figure of Joseph, Philo's takes a vigorous anti-Aristotelian position, though in some contexts it can be relativised. The final part of the article focuses on the key text of *Aet.* Its authenticity is defended with the observation of a key parallel between the work's exordium and the reference to oracles, signs and prodigies in *Mos.* 1.76. It is true that Aristotle is praised in §10 and §16, but the reference to the ὁρατὸς θεός must be ambivalent because it disqualifies him as a philosopher of absolute transcendance. In addition the three definitions of the cosmos found in *Aet.* 4 also must be read negatively from the viewpoint of a transcendant philosophy. For Philo Aristotle will always come in the second place in comparison with Plato, but it is to his credit that he showed that there is no absolute incompatibility between the Bible and Aristotelianism and so can be regarded as a pioneer of developments that took place in the medieval period. (DTR)

Y. Li, 'A Comparative Study of Philo's Allegory and Origen's Allegory [Chinese],' *China Graduate School of Theology Journal* 50 (2011) 47–74.

In order to establish a universal Judaism, Philo adopted an allegorical approach to the Bible. Origen adopted a similar approach as Philo in order to establish a universal Christianity. Both of them produced a synthesis of Hebrew and Greek cultures. Philo's hermeneutics included four theoretical principles and two methodological guidelines. In addressing a particular theological theme, he usually employed four methodological steps. Building on Philo, Origen developed a more comprehensive approach to allegorical interpretation. Origen believed that there are three kinds of wisdom, and he accordingly divided the meaning of Scripture into three levels. His allegorical interpretation was guided by two theological principles. The process of interpretation involved five basic steps, and Origen employed these steps flexibly. In Philo's interpretation, the biblical 'God of Abraham' became 'Plato's God.' However, Origen brought out a 'Triune' God through his allegorical interpretation. Judging from the development of Christianity after Origen, his allegorical method was a success. (DTR; based on author's abstract)

D. Lincicum, 'Philo on Phinehas and the Levites: Observing an Exegetical Connection,' *Bulletin for Biblical Research* 21 (2011) 43–49.

Philo makes an exegetical connection between the narrative of the golden calf (Exod 32) and Phinehas's response to the apostasy in Moab (Num 25). The article seeks to show that there are a number of ways in which Philo makes connections between these two texts, reading each text in the light of the other and making 'subtle exegetical modifications' in order to effect the relationship between the narratives: connections between idolatry and punishment; priority of right worship over family ties; substitution of the number of those killed in Numbers (24,000) for the number of those worshippers of the golden calf killed by the Levites in Exodus (3,000); Phinehas's reward of the priesthood as a clarification of the Levites' blessing, thus interpreting the latter as receiving the priesthood on account of their sacred violence. This connection has not been sufficiently noted in debates over Philo's views on sacred violence, though it does not settle the question. This conclusion strengthens the possibility, noted by others, that Paul makes a similar interpretative link between these texts in 1 Cor 10. (SJKP)

W. Loader, *Philo, Josephus, and the Testaments on Sexuality: Attitudes towards Sexuality in the Writings of Philo and Josephus and in the Testaments of the Twelve Patriarchs* (Grand Rapids 2011), esp. 1–258.

The study under review is the fourth volume of a larger project entitled 'Attitudes towards Sexuality in Judaism and Christianity in the Hellenistic Greco-Roman Era.' This project follows on from the earlier study on the Septuagint, sexuality and the New Testament, in which the impact of the LXX on Philo and the New Testament was examined (see the summary in *SPhA* vol. 19, pp. 166–167). When completed, the entire project of seven volumes in all will offer a panoramic view of issues of sexuality (taken in a broad sense) as recorded in preserved Jewish and early Christian texts during the Second Temple period. In the present volume Philo's thought on all aspects of sexuality is thoroughly researched and the results presented in a treatment of monographic length. In a brief introductory section Loader first outlines his subject, reviews the existing literature and makes some methodological remarks, noting the difference between gender and sexuality. The first part of his investigation focuses on the beginnings of human relations in Gen 1–3. The chief method used is a careful reading of the texts and the judgement of their author in the context of his own time. A key question is the relation between sex and procreation. For Philo the purpose of sexual intercourse is procreation and this is coupled with an insistence on controlling the passions, but it need not preclude a positive attitude towards the practice of sexual relations between husband and wife. An extensive section is devoted to the consequences of the events in paradise and life beyond its borders, followed by a treatment of sexuality in the remainder of Philo's exegesis (both literal and allegorical) of the events described in Genesis and Exodus. The final part relating to Philo deals with sexual issues in the Exposition of the Law. Here Loader has the opportunity to examine a wide range of aspects of sexuality, such as adultery, incest, intermarriage, prostitution and so on. Other aspects relate to the Ten Commandments and these are treated separately. The study concludes that there can be no question of an absolute dualism in Philo which declares the body or its parts as evil. 'Human sexuality is not a flaw, let alone an evil (p. 253).' According to Philo it is God and the divine order which he creates that has made woman inferior to man. Although standing on the biblical text as it were, Philo also has an eye for political and community issues, including the Augustan reforms relating to sex and marriage. See further the review by G. E. Sterling in *SPhA* vol. 24, pp. 262–266. (DTR)

E. Z. LYONS, *Hellenic Philosophers as Ambassadors to the Roman Empire: Performance, Parrhesia, and Power* (diss. University of Michigan 2011).

The dissertation examines the relationship of philosophers to those in power in terms of their activities as advocates and ambassadors for their communities. It focuses on four Hellenic philosophers who took on embassies to the Roman state: Carneades, whose spectacular rhetorical displays during his embassy 155 B.C.E. were long remembered by the Romans; Philo of Alexandria, who was forced by dire circumstances to take on an embassy to Gaius Caligula on behalf of the Jews in his native city; Plutarch, who spent his life as a member of the Roman elite and a Greek philosopher negotiating between his people and Roman officials; and Themistius, a philosopher of the late imperial period who served ostensibly as an ambassador for the Constantinopolitan senate, but in reality was a representative of the Emperor to the citizenry. A pattern emerges of forceful and energetic philosophical advocacy degenerating into impotent panegyric, even as Greek philosophy and philosophers become progressively more powerful and influential in the Imperial government. (DTR; based on author's abstract at DAI-A 72/08)

S. MANCINI LOMBARDI and P. PONTANI (edd.), *Studies on the Ancient Armenian Version of Philo's Works*, Studies in Philo of Alexandria 6 (Leiden 2011).

This valuable study is the first volume of collected studies on Armenian tradition of Philo's writings. Most of the contributors are members of the Italian School of Armenian studies which was established by the late Giancarlo Bolognesi, Professor at the Catholic University in Milan. As G. Uluhogian writes in her introduction, the volume can be considered as a companion to another collective volume, *Italian Studies on Philo of Alexandria* (see RRS2 20326), which focuses on the Greek versions of Philo's writings. The volume serves as an introduction to the Armenian Philo, including its *Nachleben* in the Armenian Christian tradition. It contains eight studies, which are separately summarized in this bibliography. Summaries of the articles are also given by G. Uluhogian in the above-mentioned Introduction (pp. 1–6). See further the review by A. Terian in *SPhA* vol. 24, pp. 266–269. (DTR)

E. Matusova, '1 Enoch in the Context of Philo's Writings,' in A. Lange, E. Tov, M. Weigold and B. H. Reynolds III (edd.), *The Dead Sea Scrolls in Context: Integrating the Dead Sea Scrolls in the Study of Ancient Texts, Languages, and Cultures,* Vetus Testamentum Supplements 140 (Leiden 2011) 1.385–397.

The article explores the following questions: how widely known and how significant was *1 Enoch* in the Second Temple period?; and is there substantial evidence for readers of *1 Enoch* among Hellenistic Jewish groups apart from those connected with the fragments from Qumran Caves 1 and 4? It aims to show that the works of Philo provide a 'reliable source of such evidence' (p. 386), based on the identification of evidence for Philo's knowledge and use of specifically Enochic subjects incorporated into his commentary on Scripture. The discussion focuses on the Greek fragments of *1 Enoch*, and, by way of example, on sections from two Philonic commentaries (*Gig.* and *Deus*). The author concludes that Philo's commentaries contain many allusions to *1 Enoch*; that such allusions lie deep within the Philonic text; and 'that the extant parts of the Greek translation [of *1 Enoch*] are semantically reflected in Philo's text' (p. 397). The connection between *1 Enoch* and Qumran is thus by no means exclusive. Philo's evidence shows that the Greek translation of *1 Enoch* was known not only at Qumran but also in first-century Alexandria. (SJKP)

A. M. Mazzanti, 'Il λόγος nell'antropologia di Filone d'Alessandria: considerazione sulla creazione dell'uomo in *De opificio mundi* e in *Legum Allegoriae*,' in R. Radice and M. Sordi (edd.), *Dal Logos dei Greci e dei Romani al Logos di Dio* (Milano 2011) 85–101.

The article discusses Philo's view of the human *logos* through a study of Philo's comments on the creation of man as found in *Opif.* (esp. 69, 73, 119, 139, 165) and in *Leg.* (esp. 2.27–28, 3.116–118, 3.153-156). The points of departure are of course the two anthropological texts Gen 1:26–27 (man created in the image and likeness of God) and Gen 2:7 (God breathing into his nostrils the breath of life), leading to the idea of a 'double creation' which has been much discussed among scholars of Philo. The author analyses the specific role and significance of the human *logos* as related to and distinct from the metaphysical *Logos*, the human νοῦς (Philo repeatedly speaks about ▯▯▯▯ ▯▯▯ ▯▯▯▯▯ in one breath), the πνεῦμα θεῖον, the λογισμός, and the ὀρθὸς λόγος. Essential for the human *logos* is a normative aspect (indicated by the added qualification ὀρθός) which it derives from its relationship with the divine and metaphysical *Logos*. (HMK)

D. S. Meca, J. A. López Férez, A. Díaz Hernandez and A. Martínez Lorca, *Pensadores judíos: de Fílon de Alejandría a Walter Benjamin*, Coleccío Judaica (Palma de Mallorca 2011).

This volume presents the papers from conferences organised by the Instituto de Relaciones Culturales Baleares-Israel, in collaboration with UNED (Distance University, Spain) in Palma de Mallorca. In these conferences, Jewish thinkers from all times were presented from different perspectives. The three most interesting papers from the viewpoint of Philonic studes are: A. Piñero Sáenz, 'La versión al griego de la biblia hebrea (LXX, setenta, septuaginta). Su impacto cultural y religioso' (pp. 123–142); J. María Nieto Ibáñez, 'Flavio Josefo, un clásico del judaísmo' (pp. 177–202) and J. A. López Férez, 'Filón de Alejandría: obra y pensamiento' (pp. 203–270). (DTR; based on information supplied by S. Torallas Tovar)

J. Mélèze Modrzejewski, 'Philon d'Alexandrie notable juif et philosophe politique. La bible d'Alexandrie: quand le judaisme rencontre le monde grec,' *Le Monde de la Bible* (2011) 50–55.

Brief and straightforward introduction to Philo. Some remarks are made on the Roman citizenship of his brother. Philo's writings have survived because of the interest that the Church fathers had in them. Central in Philo's thought are the Law and the lawgiver Moses. The Greek philosophers are disciples of Moses, and they have only partial knowledge of truth. Philo believes he is able to unveil to whole truth through his exegesis. (ACG)

K. Mielcarek, 'Swięte Miasto w pismach Filona z Aleksandrii i Józefa Flawiusza [Polish: The Holy City in the Writings of Philo of Alexandria and Josephus Flavius],' in B. Strzałkowska (ed.), *Więcej szczęścia w dawaniu aniżeli braniu: Księga Pamiątkowa dla Księdza Profesora Waldemara Chrostowskiego w 60. Rocznicę urodziń [Polish: The Greater Blessing Is in Giving than in Receiving: Commemorative Volume for Rev. Prof. Waldemar Chrostowski on his 60th birthday]* (Warsaw 2011) 1091–1103.

Ninety-six percent of the references to the Holy City in the Septuagint use the word Ἰερουσαλήμ (reflecting the Semitic *Yerûsalaim*), while only thirty-six references speak of the Greek name Ἰεροσόλυμα. Both Philo and Josephus devote much attention to the Holy City, but, for the most part, diligently avoid the name with its Semitic coloring. Yet when they do refer to the Semitic term—in very important passages—each interprets it differently. Philo sought the archetype of 'Jerusalem' in the interior of each believer, for whom God's idea of peace is precious. Josephus' use of the semiticizing form illustrates the difficulty that the Hellenistic world has vis-à-vis its etymological sense. As for the above, more Hellenistic term, Philo develops the neologism ἱερόπολις to indicate the close connection between the city and the sanctuary. Recognizing the popularity of the form Hierosolyma in his day, Josephus tends to change biblical references to τὸ ἱερόν and ὁ ναός so as to distinguish the Jerusalem Temple from pagan temples. (DTR; based on an abstract by John J. Pilch)

W. Moon, *Your Love is Better than Wine: a Reading of Love in the Gospel according to John* (diss. The Claremont Graduate University 2011).

The Fourth Gospel presents the doctrine of love by repeating the terms for love, such as ἀγαπή and φιλός and their cognate verbs. It further enriches the doctrine by adopting metaphors and symbols that signify love, lovers, and/or love deities in the first-century Mediterranean world. This study explores the nature and functions of love in John and its environment in order to examine what traditions and ideas resonate with the Johannine concept of love, why the Gospel so stresses love, and what the target of love is. Two primary methodologies of this study include the history of ideas coined by Arthur O. Lovejoy in a form slightly modified with intertextual theories, and Dennis R. MacDonald's mimesis criticism. The purpose of this study is not to determine the exact sources or literary models for Johannine love. Nevertheless, it gives substantial consideration to Philo of Alexandria and his primary ante-texts, because Wayne A. Meeks effectively argued that the Johannine definition of Jesus as the only seer of God radically contradicts Philo's concept of Israel, the one who sees God. This dissertation demonstrates that the verbal and thematic similarities between Philo and John are dense, and that both authors use part of the Jewish Scriptures, Plato, Hesiod, and Euripides. Nevertheless, their objectives differ from each other. Philo consults his literary elders to elaborate Moses and his law, while the evangelist brings out the theme of love from the same elders. The dissertation further proposes that the fourth evangelist uses the royal typology of Solomon, rather than any other coming anointed one expected by the Jewish Scripture, in order to defend the Johannine community against the religio-legal system of Moses supported by Philonic Judaism. By taking the loving and wise image of Solomon as the primary type of messiah, the Gospel effectively combines other authorities of love, such as Eros and Dionysus, into the character of Jesus. Furthermore, Solomon has a solid connection with the Jewish sapiential traditions most competitive to Moses and his Pentateuchal traditions. (DTR; based on author's summary in DAI-A 72/06)

J. Moreau, 'Entre Écriture sainte et *paideia*: le langage exégétique de Philon d'Alexandrie. Étude sur la *pistis* d'Abraham dans le *Quis rerum divinarum heres sit* 90–95,' in S. Inowlocki and B. Decharneux (edd.), *Philon d'Alexandrie. Un penseur à l'intersection des cultures gréco-romaine, orientale, juive et chrétienne*, Monothéismes et philosophie (Turnhout 2011) 241–263.

The author offers a literary, philological and philosophical analysis of the exegetical method displayed by Philo in Her. 90–95, in which Philo, commenting upon Gen 15:6, elaborates on the concept of Abraham's faith (πίστις). Philo's borrowing of Greek philosophical language and of biblical imagery creates a new and unique discourse. Abraham's act of faith is understood as a purification from the sensible world, which aims at lifting the sensible realm, without dismissing it, to the intelligible one—a task similar to that of the exegete. By disclosing the intelligible and universal meaning of the letter of the text, the exegete weaves a connection between the human and divine realm. This corresponds to what the author labels Philo's 'noological' perspective, which puts the stress on the communication between God and the world through the intermediary of the intellect. (SW)

A. Muhling, *Blickt auf Abraham, euren Vater: Abraham als Identifikationsfigur des Judentums in der Zeit des Exils und des Zweiten Tempels*, Forschungen zur Religion und Literatur des Alten und Neuen Testaments 236 (Göttingen 2011).

This volume, a revised version of the author's 2008 dissertation (Ruprecht-Karls University, Heidelberg), investigates the use of the Abraham character as an 'Identification figure' in the biblical traditions and in the writings of the Hellenistic-Roman time, both from within and outside the Septuagint, and including the New Testament. By 'Identification figure,' the author means a social character that through real or ascribed characteristics becomes an ideal for one or more other characters, and thus comes to represent a source of one's own identity. The section on Philo is rather brief, and deals with the Abraham character as described in *Abr.* It is suggested that in Philo's descriptions of Abraham a strong apologetic interest is expressed for a non-Jewish audience: the figure of Abraham shows that the Jewish traditions are not in contradiction to Greek philosophy, that Abraham is depicted as a Stoic wise man, as an archetypal figure in following the law of nature, and also as an exemplary proselyte. Philo's work on Abraham thus represent both an apologetic and recruiting attitude vis-à-vis the Gentiles. (TS)

O. Munnich, 'La fugacité de la vie humane (*De Josepho* § 125–147): la place des motifs traditionnels dans l'élaboration de la pensée philonienne,' in S. Inowlocki and B. Decharneux (edd.), *Philon d'Alexandrie. Un penseur à l'intersection des cultures gréco-romaine, orientale, juive et chrétienne,* Monothéismes et philosophie (Turnhout 2011) 163–183.

Biblical and Greek parallels to Philo's treatise *Ios.* are analysed in order to show the singular way in which Philo reworks traditional material and themes. Philo's reorientation of philosophical, literary and biblical topoi brings forth a pessimistic picture of the human world, which stresses the fragility of human existence and the impossibility to comprehend the world. It is in the sphere of this precarious and instable world that Joseph, the stateman (πολιτικός), emerges as the one in charge of bringing discernment (κριτικός). (SW)

O. Munnich, 'Travail sur la langue et sur le texte dans l'exégèse de Philon d'Alexandrie,' in A. Balansard, G. Dorival and M. Loubet (edd.), *Prolongements et renouvellements de la tradition classique: en hommage à Didier Pralon,* Textes et documents de la Méditerranée antique et médiévale (Aix-en-Provence 2011) 203–216.

Selected examples of Philonic texts (*Ios.* 126, *Fug.* 132–136, *Her.* 94–95) are presented and analysed in order to cast light on the function of the Greek language and of the scriptural text in Philo's exegesis. The author points to the dynamic and mutual cross-fertilization of the philosophical language by the semantic network offered by the language of the Bible. In the second part of the paper the author focuses on Philo's quotations from the Bible and shows that changes in the order of the words, deliberate shortenings or reformulations of the LXX lemmata serve the purposes of his argumentation. (SW)

G. Muradyan, 'The Armenian Version of Philo Alexandrinus. Translation Technique, Biblical Citations,' in S. Mancini Lombardi and P. Pontani (edd.), *Studies on the Ancient Armenian Version of Philo's Works,* Studies in Philo of Alexandria 6 (Leiden 2011) 51–85.

The article gives an overview of the translation techniques used by the translators of the Armenian corpus. The translations are very literal, but there is certainly not always a one-to-one correspondence, as can be seen in the analysis of doublets in the Armenian. This and other factors mean that a retranslation from the Armenian to Greek, as attempted by Siegert, 'cannot be considered as something absolute' (p. 52). The author lists numerous examples of doublets, where one Greek word is translated by two Armenian words, and concludes that, compared with other Hellenizing texts, these are very common in the Philonic corpus. The article then moves on to an examination of 'Grecisms' in the Armenian versions of Philo's texts, again making general comments followed by a long list of examples in terminology, morphology and syntax. Finally the article analyses the translation of biblical passages found in *Leg.* 1 and *QG* 1 as compared with the translation of the same passages in the Armenian Bible. It emerges that the method of the translator of Philo and the lexical equivalents that he uses are independent of his precedessor, so that his version of the texts is quite different from those in the Armenian Bible, but that nevertheless he is familiar with the latter and sometimes undergoes its influence. Once again a long list of examples is presented in order to illustrate this conclusion. (DTR)

M. R. NIEHOFF, *Jewish Exegesis and Homeric Scholarship in Alexandria* (Cambridge 2011).

This book explores for the first time systematically the relations between the interpreters of the two classical canons of Western civilization: the Jewish Bible and the Homeric epics, both of which were submitted to meticulous study in Hellenistic Alexandria. It is argued that the Jewish interpreters engaged so deeply with the approaches of their Greek colleagues that their work cannot be understood without taking into account this historical background. Jewish interpreters adopted diverse positions, some approaching the Scriptures from a radically literary and critical perspective, others stressing the uniqueness of the Bible and the limited applicability of critical methods. The book covers all known stages of biblical interpretation in Alexandria, ranging from the earliest fragments of Demetrius and Aristobulus and the *Letter of Aristeas* to Philo's anonymous colleagues as portrayed in his polemics as well as Philo's own writings. Each of these epochs is treated in a separate section of the book. Philo's works are examined in the last two sections, once for evidence of his colleagues and once for his own sake. Three chapters offer detailed analyses of different biblical interpretations by Philo's colleagues, one showing how they compared the story of Tower of Babel to a similar Homeric story, another investigating their historical contextualization of the Binding of Isaac and yet another gathering pieces of evidence for their text-critical approach. Three additional chapters focus on Philo's different series of works, which are investigated each in its own right. Philo emerges as conservative in comparison to his colleagues, defending the sanctity and uniqueness of the biblical text, while at the same offering the first synthesis of allegory and literary criticism, a combination which became popular among subsequent Platonists. See also the review by F. Siegert in *SPhA* vol. 23, pp. 243–252. (MRN)

M. R. NIEHOFF, 'Recherche homérique et exégèse biblique à Alexandrie: un fragment sur la Tour de Babel préservé par Philon,' in S. INOWLOCKI and B. DECHARNEUX (edd.), *Philon d'Alexandrie. Un penseur à l'intersection des cultures gréco-romaine, orientale, juive et chrétienne*, Monothéismes et philosophie (Turnhout 2011) 83–103.

This article is the French version of chapter four in the author's book *Jewish Exegesis and Homeric Scholarship in Alexandria* (Cambridge 2011), on which see above. It focuses on a group of Philo's colleagues, whose interpretation of the story of the Tower of Babel he strongly criticizes. These anonymous interpreters identified in the Biblical story a myth similar to the Homeric myth of Aloaedes' sons piling up mountains in order to reach heaven. Not only is the biblical text submitted to critical literary analysis, but even its historical sources are identified. Philo's colleagues thus anticipated modern Bible scholarship by almost two thousand years. (MRN)

M. R. Niehoff, 'Jüdische Bibelexegese im Spiegel alexandrinischer Homerforschung,' *Biblische Notizen* NF 148 (2011) 19–33.

This article is a German summary of the author's *Jewish Exegesis and Homeric Scholarship in Alexandria* (Cambridge 2011), on which see above. (MRN)

M. R. Niehoff, 'Philo's Exposition in a Roman Context,' *The Studia Philonica Annual* 23 (2011) 1–21.

This article argues that Philo's series of treatises called 'The Exposition' must be appreciated as one of his later works, written in the context of the Embassy to Gaius. In particular, Philo's radical change in his style of writing, namely from systematic Bible commentary to biographies of the forefathers, is best understood in light of Philo's new interests and new audiences in Rome. The article shows how the biographies of Moses and Joseph engage Roman discourses and rely on notions of Roman Stoicism. (MRN)

F. Nobilio, 'Le chemin de l'Esprit dans l'œuvre de Philon d'Alexandrie en dans l'Évangile de Jean,' in S. Inowlocki and B. Decharneux (edd.), *Philon d'Alexandrie. Un penseur à l'intersection des cultures gréco-romaine, orientale, juive et chrétienne,* Monothéismes et philosophie (Turnhout 2011) 283–315.

A study of πνεῦμα in Philo and the Gospel according to John, which leads to the conclusion that Philo and John, when speaking of the Spirit, deal with the same themes but give them a different temporal location. The article identifies and discusses the following four themes, which in both authors are developed in a similar way, but with different temporal reference: (1) Spirit and wind (humanity's high vocation: for Philo belonging to the human constitution, for John requiring to be born again in Christ); (2) Spirit and breath (the human soul 'sealed' by the life-giving Spirit: for Philo from the 'beginning,' for John at the 'end'); (3) Spirit and worship (the way of the Spirit: for Philo leading towards the truth, for John leading into the truth); and (4) Spirit and scripture (inspiration: for Philo inspired exegesis, for John inspired writing). There is no ground for supposing any direct textual influence of Philo on John, but it appears probable that John was acquainted with Philo's pneumatology. (HMK)

S. Nordgaard Svendsen, 'Paul's Appropriation of Philo's Theory of 'Two Men' in 1 Corinthians 15:45–49,' *New Testament Studies* 57 (2011) 348–365.

This essay focuses on Paul's interactions with Philo's theory of two men in 1 Cor 15:45–49. It argues that instead of rejecting that theory, Paul transforms and reinterprets it in such way as to substantiate his own doctrine of the resurrection as developed in 1 Cor 15:35–58, that is, his doctrine of eschatological bodily change. The essay provides an analysis of Philo's theory of two men as well as an exegesis of the biblical passage. An important premise in Nordgaard's argumentation is that he assumes that both Paul and the Corinthian sceptics knew certain ideas of Philo's, and possibly, that they knew them through familiarity with some of Philo's writings. Furthermore, the author argues that Paul's reasoning in this passage is close to incomprehensible if we do not presume that Philo's views was rather well-known and accepted by Paul's critics. Hence the reason why Paul chose to deal with this theory of Philo was to demonstrate that the theory on the basis of which his critics had rejected his doctrine of the resurrection in fact supports it when properly understood. (TS)

P. VAN NUFFELEN, *Rethinking the Gods: Philosophical Readings of Religion in the Post-Hellenistic Period* (Cambridge 2011).

Post-Hellenistic philosophy (1st cent. BCE–2nd cent. CE) exhibits a unity of assumptions and approaches, which include a return to classical thinkers and an openness to new sources of authority, including religion. This study focuses on how various post-Hellenistic writers adopted and transformed the notions of religion as a source of philosophical knowledge propounded by wise ancient figures and of a hierarchical view of the universe that encompasses human and divine realms. Writing between the time of Varro and Cicero and later Plutarch, Philo is an important witness to the continuation of post-Hellenistic tendencies during this period. Drawing upon Greco-Roman culture while dismissing some of its key aspects, Philo stands apart in his primary allegiance to Jewish tradition and denial of polytheism. Thus while using mystery language as a metaphor for philosophy, he rejects real mystery cults. Similarly, while accepting the notion of a divine hierarchy, he insists that 'only the apex of it is truly God and thus deserves worship and honour' (p. 212). Despite his commitment to the idea of a divine monarchy, Philo also recognizes the abilities of a 'natural ruler,' like the biblical Joseph, to bring order into earthly rulerships. These examples show how Philo can adopt Greco-Roman concepts and vocabulary but still promote his ideas about monotheism and the truth of Jewish tradition. (EB)

M. OLIVIERI, 'Philo's *De Providentia*: a Work Between Two Traditions,' in S. MANCINI LOMBARDI and P. PONTANI (edd.), *Studies on the Ancient Armenian Version of Philo's Works,* Studies in Philo of Alexandria 6 (Leiden 2011) 87–124.

The textual tradition of *Prov.* I and II is entirely indirect. For the two books an Armenian translation survives, while of the second there are a number of extensive fragments transmitted by Eusebius in his *Praeparatio Evangelica*. This is a happy circumstance because it allows the variants in the Greek text to be compared with the Armenian tradition and vice versa. The article moves in four stages. Firstly, the author raises general questions associated with the work as a whole. Eusebius in his list of Philo's works only mentions a single book of *Prov.*, but nevertheless examination of the contents of *Prov.* I makes it probable that it is authentic. However, there is a difference in quality and quantity between the two books, which suggests that *Prov.* I may in fact be an abridged version of the original and that the Armenian translator combined two works in different states of transmission. The author also points out that the division of the text into paragraphs is unsatisfactory for the entire tradition and proposes to adopt a division which is a combination of those of Aucher–Richter for the Armenian and Mras for the Greek. Secondly, the Armenian translation is used to determine a stemma for the transmission of the Greek text in Eusebius. Comparison of the two traditions reveal errors that are more ancient than the oldest manuscripts, some of which go back to earlier than the 3rd century. Thirdly, Olivieri examines the relation between the extent Armenian codices. Comparison with the Greek fragments permits the editor to evaluate many Armenian variants with certainty. Through examination of the 12 main manuscripts a stemma for the tradition can be established. This is not an easy task, since we are dealing with an open *recensio*, with contamination between the various branches of the tradition, as can seen in marginal notes and interlinear corrections in the witnesses. The resultant stemma is thus very complex. An excerpt that gives a good example of the relation between all the witnesses and the transfer of glosses from one branch of the tradition to another is *Prov.* 2.99.2 preserved in Eusebius. Finally on the last page of the article the author brings together all the results of his research in a single table, which presents the combined stemma of both the Greek and the Armenian tradition of Philo's treatise. (DTR)

J. Otto, 'Conflicting Christian Reactions to Philo's Ark Door Exegesis,' *Theoforum* 43 (2011) 89–98.

The article compares and contrasts two Patristic adaptations of Philo's allegorical exegesis of Noah's ark in terms of the human body, and in particular the identification of the ark's door with the orifice by which excrement leaves it. After first recounting early Christian attitudes as seen in the legend of Philo Christianus, the author quotes the Greek text and gives an English translation of *QG* 2.6 (though not indicating where this Greek text is found). She then cites and discusses Ambrose's use of the Philonic theme in *De Noe* 8.24. Ambrose not only accepts the exegesis, but links it to Paul's use of the image of the body in 1 Cor 12:22–23, enabling him to extend the allegory into the context of Christian revelation and promote a Christological reading of Gen 6. Philo's explanation of the human body thus comes to symbolize the body of the church. Elsewhere, however, Ambrose criticizes Philo for the limitations of his Jewish 'carnal exegesis,' which meant that he confined his interpretation of Gen 2:15 to the moral aspect and did not understand its spiritual import. The article then turns to Augustine's treatment of the same Philonic exegesis of the ark in *Contra Faustum* 12.39. He accepts Philo's allegorical method and his interpretation of the ark in terms of the human body, but in the particular case of the door he is repelled by its crudeness. Philo illustrates the futility of Jewish exegesis which searches for truth in the Old Testament without looking through the lens of Christ. Augustine's attitude thus differs from that of his mentor, for whom Philo's exegesis was at least half-way correct. (DTR)

J. Otto, 'An Education in Virtue: Philosophical Speculation and Religious Observance in the Thought of Philo of Alexandria,' *Dionysius* 29 (2011) 135–146.

Philo regards both philosophy and contemplation as well as practical observance of the Torah as paths to piety (εὐσέβεια). This does not distinguish him from his predecessors, e.g. Aristobulus, but in Philo the identification of philosophy and piety is particularly prominent. Some scholars (e.g. J. E. Taylor) propose that in the Diaspora the observance of the Jewish customs could appear as participation in a philosophical school, others (e.g. A. Mendelson, N. G. Cohen) regard Philo rather as member of a special group with an interest in making Jewish traditions compatible with philosophy by means of allegory. Otto agrees with D. T. Runia, who warns against the description of the Jews as a philosophical school or a number of schools, because the term αἵρεσις occurs only once (*Contempl.* 29). Philo emphasizes that, like the Greek philosophical schools, the Torah teaches philosophical truths as well as practical virtue, but unlike them the Torah is not exclusive. It is accessible to all Jews, turning them into a philosopher race. The encyclical subjects prepare for philosophy, which is a path to virtue. The observance of the Torah also leads to virtue, and the Jews are trained in its theory and practice. The best path combines philosophy and the practical observance of the Torah. (JLB)

E. PARKER, 'A Portrait of Many Colours: Philo's Account of Roman Political Administration of Alexandria,' *Dionysius* 29 (2011) 147–156.

The article explores how Philo's portrait of the patriarch Joseph as statesman might shed light on Philo's own views of relations between Rome and Judea, and, secondly, how Philo's criticism of contemporary politics expresses 'the dangerous consequences implicit in *De Iosepho*' (p. 148). Following discussion of the goal and genre of *Ios.*, *Flacc.*, and *Legat.*, the author examines the development of Philo's views on the statesman in *Ios.*, and the critical terms and concepts of his interpretation of the latter that function in the historical-apologetic treatises. In conclusion it is argued that politicians of Philo's time have 'actualized the potential dangers he ascribed to the statesman' (p. 148). (SJKP)

D. PASTORELLI, 'La lecture de Lv 5, 20–26 par Philon, *Lois spéciales* 1, 237: la conscience accusatrice, un paraclet pour le péché volontaire,' in A. BALANSARD, G. DORIVAL AND M. LOUBET (edd.), *Prolongements et renouvellements de la tradition classique: en hommage à Didier Pralon,* Textes et documents de la Méditerranée antique et médiévale (Aix-en-Provence 2011) 217–228.

In *Spec.* 1.237 Philo links together the notion of moral consciousness (expressed by the terms συνειδός and ἔλεγχος) and that of the intercessor (παράκλητος). The insertion of Philo's own metaphor of the tribunal of consciousness into the more traditional Jewish notion of intercession constitutes a unique association of the moral and cultic spheres. It is also the only case in Philo's *œuvre* in which consciousness is depicted as leaving the borders of human interiority. (SW)

P. A. PATTERSON, *Visions of Christ: The Anthropomorphite Controversy of 399 CE* (diss. Saint Louis University 2011).

The dissertation was published in 2012 by Mohr Siebeck in the series Studien und Texte zu Antike und Christentum. It will be summarized in next year's bibliography. (DTR)

L. PERRONE, 'Origenes pro domo sua: Self-quotations and (Re)construction of a Literary Œuvre,' in S. KACZMARKEK and H. PIETRAS (edd.), *Origeniana Decima: Origen as Writer* (Leuven 2011) 3–38, esp. 12–15.

As part of a section on Origen's quotations of other writers, brief remarks are made on his references to Philo. Most are anonymous. It was not indispensable to quote Philo by name because he was regarded as belonging to the same tradition as Origen himself. (DTR)

P. PONTANI, 'Saying (Almost) the Same Thing. On Some Relevant Differences Between Greek-Language Originals and their Armenian Translations,' in S. MANCINI LOMBARDI and P. PONTANI (edd.), *Studies on the Ancient Armenian Version of Philo's Works,* Studies in Philo of Alexandria 6 (Leiden 2011) 125–146.

The title of the article is based on Umberto Eco's classic work on translation, but it also accurately defines the relationship between the Armenian translations of Philo's writings and their Greek originals. This relationship has usually been described either positively in terms of 'perfect adherence' or negatively as 'slavish subservience,' and so these works have not been studied as independent works in their own right. For this reason most of the research on them has been done by classical philologists and not by scholars of Armenian literature. For example, much effort has been expended on producing exact lexical equivalents and only texts that are philologically relevant have been studied. The author argues for a new approach, which takes seriously the independence of the Armenian translator. She notes that the Armenian translations are part of a living tradition that goes right through to the 18th century. The case of Aucher's translations is of relevance here, because they are frequently judged in terms of their accuracy in relation to the original meaning, yet are in fact Latin translations of an Armenian text. Various examples are given of how he had to make interpretations in his translation because of the ambiguity of his original and how his version sometimes diverges from the Armenian text. The final part of the article turns to the Armenian translation itself. Here it is very possible that the translator has intervened and deviated from his Greek model. An example is found in *QG* 2.59, where the distinction between ψυχή and πνεῦμα is annulled. □n her final words the author recommends that the Armenian text should be opened up to all the interpretations which it is capable of offering. They should no longer be deprived of 'their own voice' (p. 146). (DTR)

R. RADICE, 'Logos tra stoicismo e platonismo. Il problema di Filone,' in R. RADICE and M. SORDI (edd.), *Dal Logos dei Greci e dei Romani al Logos di Dio* (Milano 2011) 131–145.

Philo in *Opif.* (esp. 24–25) combines two creation theories, one Stoic (key concepts the *logos* and the *dynameis*) and the other Platonic (key concept the noetic cosmos). His predecessors in this approach are Posidonius (adopting Platonic concepts in Stoicism) and Antiochus of Ascalon (adopting Stoic concepts in Platonism). Philo's fusion of theories, however, is more than just eclectic: it leads to a new 'Mosaic' philosophy. His predecessor in Alexandrian Judaism is in this respect Aristobulus, who inserted the Stoic *dynameis* in an Aristotelian system. All four thinkers in different ways are concerned with reconciling divine freedom from exertion (or divine transcendence) with divine engagement in creation. Radice's thesis is that Jewish-Alexandrian theology has chosen the Stoic *logos* concept as its philosophic basis, in conjunction with the (Stoic) allegorical method. It was the tradition of the allegorical method of interpretation, rather than the tradition of a specific philosophy, that encouraged Jewish exegetes to apply originally immanentist (Stoic) concepts such as λόγος, πνεῦμα, δυνάμεις and πρόνοια in the transcendentalist (and therefore more Platonic) context of biblical exegesis. (HMK)

I. L. E. Ramelli, 'The Birth of the Rome–Alexandria Connection: the Early Sources on Mark and Philo, and the Petrine Tradition,' *The Studia Philonica Annual* 23 (2011) 69–95.

Tradition (reported by Eusebius *HE* 2.15-16) records that Mark the Evangelist went from Rome to Alexandria, while Philo, as we well know from his own work, went from Alexandria to Rome and back. The article analyzes, with many excursuses, the sources in which this 'Rome-Alexandria connection' is first found. It focuses on Clement of Alexandria as source for the above tradition (his *Hypotyposeis* are Eusebius' source in *HE* 2.15), and hypothesizes that the tradition is probably Alexandrian. The tradition also reports that Mark's Gospel is a written account of the teaching of Peter, hence Petrine tradition. The article also focuses on Eusebius' information on Philo, including the latter's encounter with Peter, and finds many similarities between Eusebius' portraits of Philo and Origen, two great Alexandrian scholars of philosophy and the Bible each with an impressive *œuvre*. The Rome-Alexandria connection as exemplified by Philo is found also in Jerome, who depends on Eusebius. The final part of the article discusses a letter of Clement on a Secret (or Mystical) Gospel of Mark, which can be taken as another source supporting the Rome-Alexandria connection. However, the letter is of doubtful authenticity (found in an 18th century manuscript discovered by Morton Smith in 1958). (HMK)

E. Regev, 'From Qumran to Alexandria and Rome: Qumranic Halakhah in Josephus and Philo,' in A. I. Baumgarten, H. Eshel, R. Katzoff and S. Tzoref (edd.), *Halakhah in the Light of Epigraphy*, Journal of Ancient Judaism Supplements 3 (Göttingen 2011) 43–63.

The article seeks to show that both Philo and Josephus adopted several laws otherwise known in the Temple Scroll, MMT and the *Book of Jubilees*. This conclusion would serve to extend our knowledge of the impact of Qumranic halakhah well beyond the circles of the Qumran sectarians, but it also raises questions of method with regard to scholars' definitions of such halakhic positions as 'sectarian.' Building on an earlier study of 2002 which focused on Josephus, co-authored with D. Nakman, the author identifies in the works of Josephus (*Ant.* 3–4; *Ap.*) and Philo (*Spec.* and *Virt.*) several laws corresponding to laws that in other texts appear to be distinctive of the Pharisees, Sadducees or Qumran community. In the case of Philo, Pharisaic halakhah is identified in five cases (*Spec.* 2.162; 1.76–78; 3.137–143; 3.80; 1.152); Sadducean halakhah in at least two cases (*Spec.* 3.181–183, 195; 1.72); and Qumranic halakhah in at least five examples (*Virt.* 159; *Virt.* 95; *Spec.* 3.206; *Spec.* 2.179–180; *Spec.* 1.110–111). The evidence in the case of both Philo and Josephus shows their 'halakhic eclecticism' with regard to the teaching of the Pharisees, Sadducees, and Qumran community. In their presentation of the law, both authors chose not to follow 'one single halakhic school' (p. 52). Others no doubt did the same in holding 'a mixture of halakhic opinions' in the first century C.E. (p. 53). Why did Philo and Josephus follow Qumranic halakhah? The author concludes that they must have been drawn to it for personal reasons as well as because of their knowledge of the Essenes. In the case of Philo, his preferences for Qumranic halakhah, with its emphasis on Temple cult, may be explained by his preeminent interest in the Jerusalem Temple and its sacrificial system, and the importance of its priesthood, and by his conception of the priesthood of the entire Jewish people. (SJKP)

C. M. Rios, 'Exílio, Diáspora e Saudades de Jerusalém: Estudo em Jeremias 29:1-14 em Fílon de Alexandria,' in M. Alexandre Jr. (ed.), *Fílon de Alexandria nas origens da cultura ocidental,* Centro de Estudos Clássicos (Lisbon 2011) 91–109.

The author presents a careful reading of the letter of Jer 29:1-14, and compares it with some passages by Philo, especially *Flacc.* 46. Both, though showing some differences, focus on the same subject, namely the relationship with Jerusalem that Jews have who are separated from the homeland, either by exile or through diaspora. In both texts the following common features appear: positive regard for the land where they are installed; recommendation to live in peace with the nations; disavowal of or silence in relation to the apocalyptic announcements; and hope of returning to Jerusalem when it is God's will. (JPM)

P. Robertson, 'Toward an Understanding of Philo's and Cicero's Treatment of Sacrifice,' *The Studia Philonica Annual* 23 (2011) 41–67.

Philo's works abound in information about the meaning of sacrifice and its correct performance. In this article the author focuses on the question of why Philo wrote so much about the details of physical aspects of Jewish sacrifice, seeking to explain this question by situating Philo's ideas in the wider cultural context of Roman thought, and drawing on theoretical models from the work of Bourdieu, Foucault and Rappaport. Based on an examination of texts drawn from *Spec.* 1–2, the author emphasizes Philo's insistence on a fundamental connection between spiritual and physical aspects of sacrifice. Cicero's writings on sacrifice reveal many similarities to Philonic thinking on the subject. Both Philo and Cicero understand the sacrificial system as 'a tool for hierarchical organization' (p. 65); both try to 'universalize' the significance of sacrifice; both promote a sense of an institutional—rather than individual—relationship with the divine. A significant factor in differences of emphasis and purpose is explained according to the author by the fact that Philo was not a priest ('Philo is outside the innermost circle and thus carves out an authority based on meaning that is exterior to institutional claims of religious form but dependent on them'), while Cicero was part of the augural college ('fully within the innermost circle and … content to reaffirm the institutional claims of form while attacking those explicating meaning' (p. 67)). (SJKP)

D. Roure, 'Forgiveness in Ben Sira and in Philo of Alexandria,' *Studia Monastica* 53 (2011) 7–19.

The article would appear to be an English translation of the earlier contribution published in Catalan (RRS2 20279). It compares the positions of Ben Sira and Philo of Alexandria on the topic of obtaining pardon in Hellenistic Judaism. The study attempts to determine whether Philo was able to find proposals related to his own concerns in the positions of Ben Sira. There are cases in which it is possible to observe the same tradition in the two authors. Furthermore, the study of their terminology clearly reveals a network of relations. Having carried out an analysis of vocabulary, the study then comparatively examines the conceptions developed by each of the authors in the following sections: (1) the relation between sacrifice for sin and ethical attitude; (2) the path to conversion and the example of Enoch; (3) from the example of the Fathers to the intercession of the Patriarchs; (4) the God of grace and pardon. The conclusion sets out the results of the study, emphasizing the extent to which Ben Sira is one of Philo's sources in this question, and also the extent to which Philo, in accordance with his cultural and philosophical positions, develops some of Ben Sira's own traditions. (DTR; based on author's abstract)

D. T. Runia, 'Why Philo of Alexandria is an Important Writer and Thinker,' in S. Inowlocki and B. Decharneux (edd.), *Philon d'Alexandrie. Un penseur à l'intersection des cultures gréco-romaine, orientale, juive et chrétienne,* Monothéismes et philosophie (Turnhout 2011) 13–33.

The paper is the text of the keynote lecture at the conference on Philo held in Brussels in June 2007. It aims to show why Philo is an important writer and thinker. In the first part it demonstrates that knowledge of Philo contributes to no less than seven areas of scholarly study: Judaism, Classics, Ancient Philosophy, Ancient History, New Testament and *Umwelt*, Patristics and Gnosticism (illustrated by a seven-pointed star on p. 16). The second part then gives an example of Philo's importance by examining his attitude towards the religion of the cosmos as it developed in the Greco-Roman world and in particular his views on the divinization of the heavenly bodies. In the final part of the lecture the author shows how this theme illustrates the seven areas of study outlined in the first part. It concludes by emphasizing that Philo is worth reading not only as a source, but also for his own particular voice. There are two aspects of his thought that make him distinct and special. The first is his positive attitude as a Jew towards the Greek heritage. The second is the spiritual depth and creativity of his allegories, which indicate that for him the biblical text and the philosophical doctrines located in it are not just objects of study but are relevant to the life of the soul. (DTR)

D. T. Runia, 'Ancient Philosophy and the New Testament: "Exemplar" as Example,' in A. B. McGowan and K. Richards (edd.), *Method and Meaning: Essays on New Testament Interpretation in Honor of Harold W. Attridge,* Society of Biblical Literature Resources for Biblical Study 67 (Atlanta 2011) 347–361.

Contributors to the Festschrift in honour of the distinguished Yale scholar of New Testament and related fields were asked to write on a designated area of ancient studies. The first part of the contribution would focus on how this area related to New Testament studies, the second would give an example of this relation in practice. The author was assigned the field of ancient philosophy. He first outlines the very limited number of direct references to ancient philosophy in the New Testament, but observes that many New Testament scholars are well-versed in the study of ancient philosophy. Many parallels have been noted between the two corpora, but these are of limited value on their own. If an analysis is made of how New Testament scholars utilize material from ancient philosophy to aid the study of the New Testament, a four-fold typology of approaches emerges: (1) sociological and literary; (2) the study of terminology and conceptuality; (3) contextualizing New Testament themes in relation to ancient philosophical doctrines; (4) using such doctrines as an essential key to the understanding of specific texts. In the second part of the article this typology is illustrated with an example drawn from Hebrews, a book on which the honorand has written an authoritative commentary. It focuses on Hebr 8:4–5, where the phrase ὑπόδειγμα καὶ σκιά is used, translated by Attridge as 'a shadowy copy.' It is part of the language of model and copy that occurs in the Letter and which many interpreters have seen as at least partly inspired by Platonic philosophy. It is to be agreed with Hurst (RRS 9033) that ὑπόδειγμα cannot in fact bear the meaning 'copy.' Nevertheless evidence from Philo shows that the term is best translated 'exemplar' and can refer to both model and copy. In addition Philonic parallels make it quite clear that to deny any influence of Platonic dualism in Hebr 8:1–5 and 9:23–24 flies in the face of the evidence. In the final part of the article this example is related to the typology outlined earlier. The example illustrates the fourth category, i.e. we cannot understand the biblical text without reference to the doctrines of ancient philosophy. (DTR)

D. T. Runia, A. C. Geljon, K. Berthelot, E. Birnbaum,. H. M. Keizer, J. Leonhardt Balzer, J. P. Martín, M. R. Niehoff and T. Seland, 'Philo of Alexandria: an Annotated Bibliography 2008,' *The Studia Philonica Annual* 23 (2011) 97–159.

The yearly annotated bibliography of Philonic studies prepared by the members of the International Philo Bibliography Project covers the year 2008 (132 items), with addenda for the years 1995–2007 (17 items), and provisional lists for the years 2009–11. (DTR)

D. T. Runia, and G. E. Sterling (edd.), *The Studia Philonica Annual*, Vol. 23 (Atlanta 2011).

The twenty-third volume of the Journal dedicated to Philonic studies contains four articles, the usual bibliography section (see summary below), and twelve book reviews. These are followed by the customary News and Notes section, Notes on contributors and Instructions for contributors. The articles are summarized elsewhere in this bibliography. (DTR)

D. Satran, 'Philo of Alexandria,' in A.-J. Levine and M. Z. Brettler (edd.), *The Jewish Annotated New Testament* (New York 2011) 572–575.

Annotated by Jewish scholars, this volume has as one of its aims to highlight 'aspects of first- and second-century Judaism that enrich the understanding of the New Testament' (p. xi). In the section on Literature, the essay on Philo discusses his life, works, thought, and influence. Although Philo was a contemporary of Jesus, he evinces no knowledge of Jesus or his followers. Likewise, despite similar ideas between Philo and such NT books as the Gospel of John (esp. with reference to the *Logos*), the Epistle to the Hebrews, and some Pauline letters, it is unlikely that NT writers knew Philo's works directly. Later Church Fathers, however, used and cited Philo's writings, were especially influenced by his way of reading Scripture, and even envisioned him as a Christian. Philo's commitment to both Scripture and Greek philosophy foreshadows the medieval endeavor among Jews, Christians, and Muslims to harmonize these two sources. The author concludes that 'Philo's Hellenistic Judaism' provided later Christians with 'the exegetical and theological tools to forge their new identity' (p. 575). (EB)

L. Saudelli, 'Les fragments d'Héraclite et leur signification dans le *corpus philonicum*: le cas du fr. 60 DK,' in S. Inowlocki and B. Decharneux (edd.), *Philon d'Alexandrie. Un penseur à l'intersection des cultures gréco-romaine, orientale, juive et chrétienne*, Monothéismes et philosophie (Turnhout 2011) 265–280.

This article discusses the passages in which Philo refers to the saying by Heraclitus: 'the way up and down is one and the same' (fr. 60 DK). In *Aet.* 109 Philo interprets the expression as indicating the transformation of the elements, i.e. the replacement of the one by the other. Philo also quotes the Heraclitean *dictum* in *Somn.* 1.156, associating it with Jacob's ladder. He takes it to refer to the fluidity of human affairs. In the same way Philo alludes to the saying in *Mos.* 1.21, remarking that Fortune moves human affairs up and down (parallel in *Ios.* 135–136). Philo's passages have parallels in Plutarch (*E Delph.* 392B–D) and Seneca (*Ep.* 58.22). The author concludes that for Philo Heraclitus' saying expresses the continuous transformation of every aspect of reality into its opposite. Philo applies it in cosmology, psychology and anthropology. (ACG)

G. Sᴇʟʟɪɴ, *Allegorie – Metapher – Mythos – Schrift. Beiträge zur religiösen Sprache im Neuen Testament und in seiner Umwelt*, edited by D. Sᴀ̈ɴɢᴇʀ, Novum Testamentum et orbis antiquus 90 (Göttingen 2011).

This collection of studies by the distinguished German New Testament scholar contains two articles pertaining to Philonic studies which have been summarized in earlier bibliographies and are now reprinted in an unaltered form except corrections of mistakes, updated orthography and unified quotations: 'Gotteserkenntnis und Gotteserfahrung bei Philon von Alexandrien,' first published in 1992 (pp. 57–77 = RRS 9279); 'Die Allegorese und die Anfänge der Schriftauslegung,' first published in 1997 (pp. 9–56, esp. 29–49 = RRS 9772). (JLB)

R. Sɢᴀʀʙɪ, 'Philo's Stylemes vs Armenian Translation Stylemes,' in S. Mᴀɴᴄɪɴɪ Lᴏᴍʙᴀʀᴅɪ and P. Pᴏɴᴛᴀɴɪ (edd.), *Studies on the Ancient Armenian Version of Philo's Works*, Studies in Philo of Alexandria 6 (Leiden 2011) 147–154.

According to the author Philo's style is complex and even tending to the tortuous, because he is seeking to express the correspondences between the physical and the metaphysical worlds. The article explores how this complexity is rendered in the Armenian versions of his work, taking as his examples the rendering of stylemes and lexemes (esp. 'double translations') in *Contempl.* 1, 6, 20 and *Spec.* 1.288. He concludes that in evaluating the contribution of the Armenian translators it is necessary to set aside preconceptions in the application of inter-textual methodology. (DTR)

M. E. Sʜɪʀɪɴɪᴀɴ, 'Philo and the *Book of Causes* by Grigor Abasean,' in S. Mᴀɴᴄɪɴɪ Lᴏᴍʙᴀʀᴅɪ and P. Pᴏɴᴛᴀɴɪ (edd.), *Studies on the Ancient Armenian Version of Philo's Works*, Studies in Philo of Alexandria 6 (Leiden 2011) 155–189.

The main focus of this important article is the *Book of Causes* by the 12th cent. Armenian theologian Grigor Abasean, which has so far remained unpublished. But it also contains much valuable information on the Armenian tradition of Philo's writings. It first asks why Philo's writings were of more interest to the Armenians than to other Christian groups. Various answers can be given, including the attraction of the allegorical method and the need for philosophy in order to defend theological and dogmatic positions. The *Book of Causes* can be called the first extant Armenian encyclopaedia of commentaries. It offers an introduction to the study of two major components of the Armenian school curriculum, the books of the Bible, which are called 'wide,' and selected works by Greek philosophers and Christian theologians, which are called 'subtle.' The work contains no less than ten passages relating to Philo's life, education and writings. The author lists the titles of these passages and presents the text and translation of the most important of them. The longest and most important is the first 'Cause' which gives a lengthy account of Philo in his Jewish context. Another text discusses why Philo wrote *Prov.* and gives information on the interlocutors in his dialogues, Alexander and Lysimachus. We also read in one of the 'Causes' that Philo was appointed governor of the city of Alexandria. Various 'causes' give lists and accounts of Philo's writings, including an explanation of the order of the seven groups of writings in the Armenian corpus. The final section of the article discusses information on Philo's education and his intellectual capacities, and in particular investigates the interpretation of the term 'encyclical studies' in the Armenian tradition, which may preserve some older traditions from earlier times. The author concludes with pertinent observations on how the traditionalism of Armenian culture allows us to find interesting material in medieval texts, including information on Philo. (DTR)

F. Siegert, 'Philon et la philologie alexandrine. Aux origines du fonda-mentalisme chrétien,' in S. Inowlocki and B. Decharneux (edd.), *Philon d'Alexandrie. Un penseur à l'intersection des cultures gréco-romaine, orientale, juive et chrétienne*, Monothéismes et philosophie (Turnhout 2011) 393–402.

Philo totally ignores the method of approaching an ancient text that was applied by the Alexandrian philologists. He avoids difficulties that arise in reading the Bible, which is a collection of ancient and sometimes difficult texts. The Alexandrians had to face the problem of myth. According to Eratosthenes it was forbidden to look for historical information in mythical passages of Homer. Philo solves the problem by utilising the method of allegorical interpretation. Philo's rejection of Alexandrian philology is shown through a comparison between him and Strabo. In contrast to Strabo Philo does not read the text critically, and, for instance, does not make conjectures. Similarly he ignores the historical aspects of the text. Philo influenced the Fathers of the church and it was due to his authority that a critical-historical approach of the Bible was not developed. (ACG)

A. Sirinian, "Armenian Philo': a Survey of the Literature,' in S. Mancini Lombardi and P. Pontani (edd.), *Studies on the Ancient Armenian Version of Philo's Works*, Studies in Philo of Alexandria 6 (Leiden 2011) 7–44.

The Armenian corpus of Philonic works is of great importance for Philonic studies but also for the history of Armenian literature. At the beginning of her valuable survey of the 'Armenian Philo' the author notes that these works were initially studied from a Western Hellenocentric approach because they yielded new texts which had not survived in the original. But gradually there has been a movement to study them in their own right as a product of the Armenian tradition, the result of a fruitful exchange between Greek and Armenian scholars. In the first section the author describes how the Armenian Philo was discovered in the late 18th century by Giovanni Zohrab and Giovanni Battista Aucher and first publicised by Angelo Mai. Next there is an account of Aucher's two still unsurpassed editions of 1822 and 1826, and also of the third volume of Philonic works published by Garegin Zarbhanalean in 1892. The significant contribution of the English scholar Frederick Conybeare is also described at some length. The third section gives a comprehensive list of the thirteen works in the Armenian Philonic corpus. The fourth section is entitled 'The twentieth century: the age of translations.' It notes that almost no work has been done on the text of the corpus after Aucher and Zarbhanalean. An account is then given of translations into English, French and German, followed by a brief description of research on the language and reception of the works. The fifth and final section examines the current state of research and gives six suggested areas for future areas of study. The article ends with three appendices giving bibliographical references for (1) studies in linguistics and translation technique, (2) studies in textual history, and (3) works published after the year 2000. (DTR)

J. SMITH, *Christ the Ideal King*, Wissenschaftliche Untersuchungen zum Neuen Testament 2.313 (Tübingen 2011).

The book as a whole studies Ephesians and the depiction of Christ as the ideal king. As background there is a long survey of the ideal king in ancient times, starting with Greco-Roman thought. Philo is discussed in the chapter on the ideal king in Jewish literature (Bible, Psalms of Solomon, Qumran, Sibylline Oracles, Aristeas, Philo, Josephus, Testaments of the Twelve Patriarchs). The account of Philo is based on *Legat.*, *Ios.* and *Mos.* In *Legat.* Gaius is criticised as a bad ruler, while Augustus is praised as a good example of a king. *Ios.* describes Joseph as the ideal Hellenistic king and statesman full of virtue, wisdom and charisma. *Mos.* presents Moses as the ideal philosopher king, legislator, priest and prophet, thus combining the ideals of Greek and Jewish expectations in virtue, wisdom and behaviour, and even imitating the divine. He brings peace, benefactions, justice (legislation) and communes with the deity (priest and prophet), thus being 'God's vice-regent on earth.' (JLB)

G. J. STEYN, '"On Earth as it is in Heaven ..." The Heavenly Sanctuary Motif in Hebrews 8:5 and its Textual Connection with the "Shadowy Copy" [ὑποδείγματι σκίᾳ] of LXX Exodus 25:40,' *HTS Teologiese Studies/Theological Studies* 67 (2011) 6 pages (electronic publication DOI:10.4102/hts.v67i1.885).

The paper investigates the Greek, Jewish and early Christian backgrounds of the quotation of Exod 25:40 in Hebr 8:5, where the writer draws on the motif of the earthly sanctuary modelled on the heavenly sanctuary. Among the authors who use this theme is Philo, who cites Exod 25:40 at *Leg.* 3.102 and alludes to it in *QE* 2.52. The quoted text in Hebrews is in exact agreement with neither the LXX or Philo. The common differences that Hebrews and Philo have against the LXX can be explained through common knowledge of a cultic, and perhaps even a liturgical tradition. (DTR)

İ. TASPINAR, 'Yahudi Geleneğinde İlahî Kelâm Tasavvuru: İskenderiyeli Philo ve Logos Doktrini [Turkish: The Divine Word Conception in Judaic Tradition: Philo of Alexandria and the Doctrine of Logos],' *Milel ve Nihal* 8 (2011) 143–164.

'Logos,' which was an important term used in relation to the world and human beings, both in a transcendental and immanent sense, in ancient Greek philosophy, also had an impact on Jewish philosophy and theology, which was under the influence of Greek culture. Philo was the first Jewish philosopher who utilized the term 'Logos' with a philosophical approach while retaining major precepts of Jewish belief. The doctrine of Logos exists at the very heart of Philo's thought system in order to explain the creation and the relations between God and the universe and God and humanity. The paper deals with the place of the Logos, which would later influence concepts such as 'Son,' 'Messiah,' 'Holy Spirit' and 'Trinity' in Christian theology, in Philo's thought system by examining key texts in his treatises. (DTR; based on the author's abstract)

C. Tassin, *Les juifs d'Alexandrie et leur écrits*, Les Suppléments aux Cahiers Évangile 156 (Paris 2011), esp. 59–69.

Some themes in Philo's thought are briefly treated and illustrated with the translation of a key text: Abraham (*Virt.* 218–221, *Abr.* 70), the flood (*QG* 2.3), the invisible God (*Mut.* 7–9), God's manifestation on Mount Sinai (*Decal.* 33, 46), the exegesis of the furnishings of the tabernacle (*Mos.* 2.88) and the limits of allegorical interpretation (*Migr.* 89–93). In his comments the author also points out parallels in the Targum. (ACG)

T. H. Tobin SJ, 'Hellenistic Judaism and the New Testament,' in A. B. McGowan and K. Richards (edd.), *Method and Meaning: Essays on New Testament Interpretation in Honor of Harold W. Attridge,* Society of Biblical Literature Resources for Biblical Study 67 (Atlanta 2011) 363–380.

The article follows on from the one on ancient philosophy and the New Testament by D. T. Runia (see above). Both are part of a Festschrift in honour of the distinguished Yale scholar of New Testament and related fields. The designated area of ancient studies assigned to Tobin was Hellenistic Judaism. He commences with the two obvious yet crucial observations that the New Testament was written in Greek, the language also used by Hellenistic Jews, and that the scriptures cited in it are Jewish scriptures written in Greek. The article examines the kinship between Hellenistic Judaism and the early Christian movement at three levels, that of organization, beliefs and ethical practice. Extensive reference is made to Philo in the discussion of the second and third of these levels. In the area of beliefs a first example of kinship is the language of 'conversion,' used both by Philo and by Paul (and by the author of Luke-Acts when speaking about Paul). A more complex example is the figure of the Logos. Tobin gives a brief description of Philo's doctrine and its links with philosophical themes in Stoicism and Middle Platonism. He then compares it briefly with related concepts and language used in John, Colossians and Hebrews. In his discussion of the influence of Hellenistic Judaism on early Christian ethics, Tobin shows how Philo and other writers redescribed the commandments of the Law in terms of the doctrine of virtue as developed in Greek ethics. This background helps us to understand Paul's redirection and transformation of Hellenistic-Jewish ideas in his Letter to the Galatians. Tobin concludes that there was 'little sense of distance' between Hellenistic Jews and early Christians, but that the ways in which Christians appropriated the traditions of Hellenistic Judaism would ultimately become unacceptable to the vast majority of Jews. (DTR)

P. J. Tomson, 'Le temple céleste: pensée platonisante et orientation apocalyptique dans l'Épître aux Hébreux,' in S. Inowlocki and B. Decharneux (edd.), *Philon d'Alexandrie. Un penseur à l'intersection des cultures gréco-romaine, orientale, juive et chrétienne,* Monothéismes et philosophie (Turnhout 2011) 337–356.

After a discussion on the date and authorship of the Epistle to the Hebrews, the author turns to the question of its 'Platonic' or 'Philonic' elements. Despite some similarities with

Philo (i.e. the idea of a celestial prototype associated to that of the sanctuary) and the use of Platonic terminology, the Epistle is less philosophical and more apocalyptically oriented than Philo—an orientation that has to be seen in line with the Judeo-Christian apocalyptic tradition. At the end of the paper, the author raises the question of oriental or even Babylonian influences on Plato and 'the books of Moses,' which could explain the coexistence of anomalous elements not only in the Epistle but also in the Septuagint and Philo. (SW)

S. Torallas Tovar, 'Orphic Hymn 86 "To Dream": On Orphic Sleep and Philo,' in M. Herrero de Jáuregui, A. I. Jiménez San Cristóbal, E. R. Luján Martínez, R. M. Hernández, M. A. Santamaría Álvarez and S. Torallas Tovar (edd.), *Tracing Orpheus: Studies of Orphic Fragments*, Sozomena 86 (Berlin 2011) 405–411.

In this brief article, published in a Festschrift in honour of the distinguished Spanish scholar of ancient religion, Alberto Bernabé, the author focuses on *Orphic hymn* 86 dedicated to Oneiros, characterized as a messanger of revelations about the future who awakens the mind during sleep. First parallels in Plutarch involving the transition of the initiate from darkness into light are cited. The author then notes that a similar transition is found in the writings of Philo, for example when describing Abraham's awakening from his Chaldean slumber in *Abr.* 70. Although Philo's dream theories appear to be largely inspired by Platonism, many motifs found in the Orphic fragments can also be identified, namely 'the state of sleep as a state of revelation, the presence of 'light' in the initiation, and the condition of purity or spiritual perfection required for the soul to reach revelation' (p. 411). (DTR)

S. Torallas Tovar, 'La lengua de Filón de Alejandría en el panorama lingüistico del Egipto Romano,' in M. Alexandre Jr. (ed.), *Fílon de Alexandria nas origens da cultura ocidental*, Centro de Estudos Clássicos (Lisbon 2011) 23–36.

In her paper the author observes that the studies on the language of Philo generally consider the background of the LXX and Greek philosophy, but should also take into consideration the socio-linguistic Alexandrian context of his time. Our knowledge of this linguistic context is constantly growing due to studies on papyri from that period. The vocabulary of Philo contains elements from popular usage, with roots in Aristophanic comedy and Demosthenic rhetoric. Other terms exhibiting sarcasm or invective that appear for the first time in Philo, such as 'calamus killer' (καλαμοσφάκτης) or 'disturbing of public order' (ταραξίπολις), may derive from the popular language of his time or could be the result of the Philo's lexical originality. (JPM)

O. S. Vardazaryan, 'The 'Armenian Philo': a Remnant of an Unknown Tradition,' in S. Mancini Lombardi and P. Pontani (edd.), *Studies on the Ancient Armenian Version of Philo's Works*, Studies in Philo of Alexandria 6 (Leiden 2011) 191–216.

This important article, which draws on the author's research as distilled in her Russian monograph summarized in RRS2 20694, takes the Armenian medieval tradition of study of Philo's writings as its starting-point and asks why this took place and where it derived its knowledge of Philo from. It thus covers some of the same ground as the article by M. E. Shirinian summarized above. The extensive use of Philo's writings in school practice is without parallel in other Christian traditions and has resulted in a unique scholiography. The author first discusses the information on the legend of Philo Christianus. She then moves on to Philo's role as a 'spiritual' exegete. The Armenian corpus is not regarded as a set of casual texts, but rather as a complex of seven 'writings' illustrating spiritual progress and climaxing in the contemplation described in *Contempl.* Armenian scholiasts fully accepted Philo's allegorical method. He is described as 'most subtle in the interpretation and understanding of the Divine Scripture,' with the term 'subtle' corresponding to the phrase θεωρία λεπτή in Greek ecclesiastical literature, e.g. in Basil of Caesarea and Cyril of Alexandria. The remainder of the article focuses on why the Armenians attached so much significance to the Philonic heritage at a time when in Patristic literature there was a loss of interest in his writings (5th–6th cent. c.e.). The author puts forward the hypothesis that there is a connection with the practice of catechesis, which the Armenians took over from the Jerusalem church. An important intermediary may have been the *Catecheses* of Cyril of Jerusalem. Later this tradition was modified through the development of the monastic tradition in Armenian, which was the context for the teaching of theology. (DTR)

J. B. Wallace, *Snatched into Paradise (2 Cor 12:1–10). Paul's Heavenly Journey in the Context of Early Christian Experience*, Beihefte zur Zeitschrift für die neutestamentliche Wissenschaft 179 (Berlin 2011).

As background to the study of his chosen passage, 2 Cor 12:1-10, the author devotes two chapters to the examination of the motif of heavenly ascents in the Greco-Roman and Jewish worlds. In the second of these, the chapter on Ascent to heaven in ancient Judaism and Christianity (pp. 95–168), Philo is disappointingly dealt with in just a few pages (pp. 107–108 and 144–146). The first of these sections deals with Philo's Moses, especially as represented by *Mos.* 1.158. The second deals with heavenly ascent as religious practice, dealing primarily with *Opif.* 70-71, emphasizing that the flight Philo describes is a flight of the mind (p. 146). In the rest of this volume, Philo is only referred to twice. (TS)

J. Weinberg, 'La quête de Philon dans l'historiographie juive du XVIᵉ s.,' in S. Inowlocki and B. Decharneux (edd.), *Philon d'Alexandrie. Un penseur à l'intersection des cultures gréco-romaine, orientale, juive et chrétienne*, Monothéismes et philosophie (Turnhout 2011) 403–432.

The contribution is a translation of an article published in English (RRS 8870) more than twenty years earlier and has not been updated. Some additional bibliographical references, including the author's landmark study on Azariah de' Rossi (RRS 20188) are given in the first footnote. (DTR)

S. Weisser, 'La figure du progressant ou la proximité de la sagesse,' in S. Inowlocki and B. Decharneux (edd.), *Philon d'Alexandrie. Un penseur à l'intersection des cultures gréco-romaine, orientale, juive et chrétienne*, Monothéismes et philosophie (Turnhout 2011) 221–239.

The author analyzes the category of the 'one in progress' (□ προκόπτων) in the Philonic corpus—a notion that should be distinguished from the general notion of progress. This category, which is symbolized by the biblical characters of Aaron, Lot and Hagar, is determined by three main features: (1) the intermediate degree of the appropriate actions (καθήκοντα); (2) moderation of the passions (μετριοπάθεια); and (3) an incomplete representation of divinity. Philo's elaboration on the 'one in progress' is rooted in the contemporaneous debates between the Stoics and the Platonists on this issue. Philo's main innovation lies in attributing to the 'one in progress' a particular relation to God and in the crystallization of this intermediary level. This consolidation can be considered as a first step towards the constitution of the different stages of spiritual progress which will play a significant role in early Christian spirituality. (SW)

S. Weisser, 'Philo's Therapeutae and Essenes: a Precedent for the Exceptional Condemnation of Slavery in Gregory of Nyssa?,' in K. Berthelot and M. Morgenstern (edd.), *The Quest for a Common Humanity: Human Dignity and Otherness in the Religious Traditions of the Mediterranean*, Numen Book Series 134 (Leiden 2011) 289–310.

The paper presents an analysis of the argumentative structure of the first unequivocal condemnation of slavery formulated by the Cappadocian father, Gregory of Nyssa, in his *Homily on Ecclesiastes*. Three central interconnected claims inform the condemnation, spanning the anthropological, physical and theological domains: (1) all people are equal and free; (2) slavery is a transgression of the order of nature; and (3) slavery is a transgression of the divine order. The arguments used by Philo in order to explain the refusal of slavery by the Therapeutae and Essenes bear a close similarity to those of Gregory, although they do not constitute a condemnation of slavery per se. Both Gregory and Philo's views should not be considered as aiming at the establishment of social justice, but rather address the vanity and arrogance of slave ownership. (SW)

M. Wiener, 'Εὐσέβεια et 'crainte de Dieu' dans la Septante,' in J. Joosten and E. Bons (edd.), *Septuagint Vocabulary: Pre-History, Usage, Reception*, SBL Septuagint and Cognate Studies 58 (Atlanta 2011) 101–156.

The term εὐσέβεια occurs in the LXX about 60 times. It is absent in the Pentateuch, and most occurrences are in the texts that are written in Greek directly. The Hebrew equivalent is mostly translated with φόβος θεοῦ. The author first examines the meaning of φόβος, σέβας and εὐσέβεια in Greek literature. φόβος means fear or anxiety, whereas σέβας refers to awe in a religious sense. The word σέβας passed into disuse and was replaced by εὐσέβεια. In classical times εὐσέβεια was used in a religious context: awe or respect for the gods. Secondly, he discusses the philosophical criticism of fear for the gods. He then treats the use of εὐσέβεια and φόβος θεοῦ in Jewish-Hellenistic literature. For Philo εὐσέβεια is an important virtue: it is the queen of virtues and the source of other virtues. It consists in knowledge of God and is the source of a virtuous life. Philo regards φόβος as something negative; in itself it is a passion. At the same time fear of God is the lowest step on the spiritual path to God. (ACG)

W. T. Wilson, *Philo of Alexandria On Virtues. Introduction, Translation, and Commentary*, Philo of Alexandria Commentary Series 3 (Leiden 2011).

The third volume in the Philo of Alexandria Commentary Series, like the first on *Opif.* (RRS2 3108), is devoted to a treatise in the Exposition of the Law, the *Virt.* The Commentary follows by and large the formula established by the first two volumes in the series. It commences with a General Introduction by the series editor, Gregory E. Sterling. There follows an introduction to the treatise in six sub-sections. The first two discuss the place of the treatise in the Philonic corpus and in Philo's life. The next examines the difficult questions of the title and the integrity of the work, noting that the transmission in the manuscripts is varied and complex, with only a single (though excellent) manuscript containing the four parts of the work as presented in the *editio maior* of C–W. There is also much variation in the titles of the work and its parts in the manuscripts. In the end Wilson, despite caveats, follows the conventional title and contents as found in C-W and also in the LCL. Next an analysis is given of the treatise's contents. Wilson notes that the final two shorter sections on repentance and nobility should be seen as adjuncts to the treatment of humanity (φιλανθρωπία), rather than as independent virtues. The next section on the treatise's character and aim focuses primarily on the subject of humanity and ancillary topics, which occupy three-fourths of the work. Philo's presentation of Mosaic humanity incorporates a large number of referents and social situations, and has a clear apologetic purpose. A useful comparison can be made with Dionysius of Halicarnassus' description of the origins of the Roman *ethnos* in his *Antiquitates romanae*. As for the treatise's intended audience, the author agrees with Birnbaum that it is probably operating at a number of different levels and has both Jews and non-Jews in mind. The final sub-section of the Introduction treats the work's *Nachleben*, which is confined to the extensive use of it made by Clement of Alexandria (although Josephus may have known the work, his usage is not clear enough to be included under this label). The English translation that follows is divided into the four conventional sections of the work: on courage, humanity, repentance and nobility. The commentary is based on the sub-divisions of the translation. The first part on courage is divided into two chapters, the second on humanity into sixteen, while the last two are not further sub-divided. The commentary on each chapter is then divided into Analysis/General comments, Detailed comments, Parallel exegesis and *Nachleben*. Extensive indices round off the work. The commentary focuses on the contents of the treatise, with relatively little attention to textual and stylistic matters. It collects and presents a vast amount of valuable parallel material from Greek and Jewish traditions, as well as giving much interpretative insight into Philo's aims and methods. See further the review by D. Konstan in *SPhA* vol. 23, pp. 169–172. (DTR)

J. D. Worthington, *Creation in Paul and Philo*, Wissenschaftliche Untersuchungen zum Neuen Testament 2.317 (Tübingen 2011).

The monograph is a revised version of the author's Durham dissertation prepared under the supervision of Francis Watson. Its focus is on Pauline protology as expressed in the letters to the Romans and the Corinthians and seen against the background of the writings of Philo, particular his treatise on the Mosaic creation account *Opif*. The proposal of the study is formulated at its outset as follows (p. 3): 'Paul's interpretation of creation, like Philo's in his commentary, contains three interwoven aspects: the beginning of the world, the beginning of humanity, and God's intentions before the beginning.' The book is organised on the basis of this proposal. It commences with the theme of God's thoughts prior to creation. Philo's thought here is strongly based on the Platonic *Timaeus*, whereas for Paul it focuses on the cross of Christ. For Philo God's pre-deliberations have an 'ontic-structural focus' as compared to Paul, for whom they have a 'historical-redemptive focus' (p. 76). The second part moves to the 'beginning of the world.' The main topics here are the creation of light on day one (Gen 1:2–5) and the creation of everything else on the second to sixth days (Gen 1:6–31). For Philo the creation of light is paradigmatic for the embodiment of less pure light in the heavenly bodies. For Paul it is connected to the personal illumination of believers (2 Cor 4:6) and is not dimmed by alliance with a body.

The third and final part has as its subject the beginnings of humanity. As for the creations of the remaining days, for Philo they indicate God's sovereign activity and the propriety of the ontic order, enabling the world to be prepared for humanity according to the divine purpose. Paul's main concern with the beginning of the world is found in the passage on the resurrection of bodies in 1 Cor 15:35–41, where the understanding of the beginning informs the answers he gives to questions raised by 'resurrection-ontology' (p. 134). The third and final part of the study treats the beginning of humanity, with a focus on exegesis of Gen 1:27, 2:7 and 5:3, which are treated separately. Worthington cannot avoid delving into the complexities of Philo's readings of these texts. His emphasis on the role played by the 'before' of creation yields valuable insights. Both Philo and Paul use contrasts (whether negative or positive) between the first two texts to deepen their understanding of humanity's creation and relation to God. The study as a whole is an excellent example of how Philonic material can be used to illuminate Paul, despite the marked differences in their thought-worlds. See further the review by B. A. Pearson in *SPhA* vol. 24, pp. 255–259. (DTR)

B. Wyss, 'Philon und die Philologen,' *Biblische Notizen* 148 (2011) 67–83.

The article attempts to reconstruct the intellectual milieu of Philo's Alexandria. Searching for first century scholars with the epithet 'the Alexandrian,' Wyss finds an increased number of experts in philology and grammar, due to the influence of the great library. Philo's work (esp. *Agr.*) is the main surviving evidence of their methods. They study literature and prepare commentaries. They also study language and dialectics. Philo displays knowledge of grammatical details as well as the appreciation of the subject in general, an awareness of which, he insists, is required to participate in academic discourse, even if the perfect do not need its rules any longer. The subject itself continues to exist, even if its individual practitioners die. Yet grammar itself only has the role of servant in relation to philosophy (*Congr.* 148). In Philo's writings there is evidence of a range of grammatical methods and discourse of his time. He does not hesitate to use them for his exegesis, and in *Sacr.* there is even a structural parallel to the *Onomasticon* of Julius Pollux. (JLB)

D. Zeller, *Studien zu Philo und Paulus*, Bonner Biblische Beiträge 165 (Göttingen 2011).

The volume contains a second selection of articles by the German scholar of New Testament and Ancient Religions who passed away earlier this year (see the notice in News and Notes on p. 264). An earlier volume focusing on the New Testament and its Hellenistic Umwelt was published in 2006 in the same series (it contained no articles on Philo). The present volume collects articles on Philo and Paul, whom the author had compared on the subject of grace in his important monograph published in 1990 (RRS 9076). The first six articles reprint studies on or related to Philo: 'Gott bei Philo von Alexandrien' (2003, summary in RRS2 203136); 'Schöpfungsglaube und fremde Religion bei Philo von Alexandrien' (2008, summary in *SPhA* vol. 23, p. 140); 'Leben und Tod der Seele in der allegorischen Exegese Philo's. Gebrauch und Ursprung einer Metapher' (1995, RRS 9596; see also next item); 'Philo's spiritualisierende Eschatologie und ihre Nachwirkung bei den Kirchenvätern' (1997, RRS2 9792); 'Philonische Logos-Theologie im Hintergrund des Konflikts von 1Kor 1–4?' (2004, RRS2 204145); 'Die angebliche enthusiastische oder spiritualistische Front in 1Kor 15' (2001, RRS2 20193). Regrettably the volume is not indexed. (DTR)

D. ZELLER, 'Leben und Tod der Seele in der allegorischen Exegese Philo's. Gebrauch und Ursprung einer Metapher,' in IDEM (ed.), *Studien zu Philo und Paulus* (Göttingen 2011) 55–99.

Updated German translation of the author's important article on the metaphor of the death of the soul as utilized by Philo in his allegorical interpretation of the Bible. It was first published in *SPhA* 7 (1995) 19–55 (summary at RRS 9596). See the previous entry. (DTR)

Extra items from before 2011

K. Hult, *Theodore Metochites on Ancient Authors and Philosophy: Semeioseis gnomikai 1–26 & 71. A Critical Edition with Introduction, Translation, Notes, and Indexes*, Studia Graeca et Latina Gothoburgensia 65 (Goteburg 2002).

Theodore Metochites (1270–1332) was one of the outstanding literary and political figures in the late Byzantine Empire. Among the vast number of his writings is the work Σημειώσεις γνωμικαί, translated by the author as *Sententious Notes*, a collection of 120 essays on various subjects and of varying length. The present edition gives an edition and translation of the first 26 essays, which contain a number on prominent ancient authors (to which is added no. 71 on Plutarch). Among these is no. 16 entitled 'On Philo' (pp. 150–157). The essay describes Philo first as a philosopher, regarding him as an adherent of Platonic philosophy, before turning to some intriguing comments on his style. The next essay also focuses on style, defending the thesis that all writers who were educated in Egypt, include-ing Philo, write in a rather harsh style. According to Theodore, although Philo 'bestows great care on his language, he does not strike the listeners' ears at all pleasantly or smoothly as regards the phrases he uses to disclose, shape and convey his thoughts' (p. 159). The translation is accompanied by a small number of elucidatory notes. (DTR)

N. Janowitz, "'You Are Gods': Multiple Divine Beings in Late Antique Jewish Theology,' in D. V. Arbel and A. A. Orlov (edd.), *With Letters of Light: Studies in the Dead Sea Scrolls, Early Jewish Apocalypticism, Magic, and Mysticism in Honor of Rachel Elior*, Ekstasis: Religious Experience from Antiquity to the Middle Ages 2 (Berlin 2010) 349–364.

In this chapter, part of a collection of essays in honor of Rachel Elior, the author takes her starting point from the latter's work on ancient Jewish texts dealing with numerous divine beings of various kinds. Part One is mainly devoted to Philo's ideas about where a being falls on the human/divine continuum; what it means to speak of 'divinity' in relation to the ascent of the soul, and specifically the soul of Moses; and, in contrast, Philo's view of false claims to divinity, exemplified by the emperor Gaius. Philo's conception of Moses as 'divine' is shaped by a late antique conceptual framework in which utopian figures are not limited by older definitions of the human as subject to death and the divine as immortal. Based on Philo's reading of the Pentateuch (cf. *Cher.* 40–47), he develops a 'theory of divine birth,' according to which all the matriarchs conceived semi-divine beings, and transmitted 'divine paternity' to their descendants, a theory with central importance for Philo's understanding of what is distinctive about Jewish identity (p. 355). Part Two, building on Frede's study of pagan monotheism, includes a brief treatment of Philo's thinking about the deity's role in the creation of matter. (SJKP)

C. Lévy, 'Breaking the Stoic Language: Philo's Attitude towards Assent (Sunkatathesis) and Comprehension (Katalepsis),' *Henoch* 32 (2010) 33–44.

The main focus of the article is on Philo's epistemology, but Cicero—who shares with Philo that he is not a true Greek philosopher—is used as a point of comparison. After some brief remarks on Stoicism as the dominant philosophy at this period, a comparison is presented of their use of the two Stoic concepts of assent (συγκατάθεσις) and comprehension (κατάληψις). Both undermine the Stoic view of a natural relation between representation and understanding of the objects of perception, Cicero from the viewpoint of academic suspension of assent (ἐποχή), Philo from the viewpoint of Mosaic philosophy. The author notes that the term for assent is rare in Philo, whereas the term for comprehension occurs frequently. He first examines the four passages where the former term and adjectives derived from it occur (*Mos.* 2.228, *Post.* 175, *Leg.* 2.65, *Deus* 100). Philo rejects the natural determinism between sensation and knowledge inherent in Stoic epistemology. The term for comprehension is much more common in Philo and at *Congr.* 141 he accurately gives the Stoic definition (but at *Her.* 132 it is used problematically, for which explanations are given). Here too Philo rejects the Stoic notion of a natural capacity of the human mind. The world is made to be known by human beings, but they have to recognize that God, the creator of the world, cannot be an object of comprehension. Philo thus disconnects knowledge and the autonomy of the self, and so introduces a new voice into the history of philosophy. The only possible hermeneutic is that of God's word. (DTR)

S. J. K. Pearce, 'Egypt on the Pentateuch's Map of Migration in the Writings of Philo of Alexandria,' in J. Jordan, T. Kushner and S. J. K. Pearce (edd.), *Jewish Journeys: from Philo to Hip Hop* (London 2010) 165–181.

Reprint of the article first published in 2009 in the context of a multi-disciplinary volume on the role of the journey in the construction of Jewish identities across time and place. See the summary in *SPhA* vol. 24, p. 212. (DTR)

M. K. M. Tso, *Ethics in the Qumran Community: an Interdisciplinary Investigation*, Wissenschaftliche Untersuchungen zum Neuen Testament 2.292 (Tübingen 2010), esp. chap. 3.

This revised Manchester University PhD includes a brief treatment of Philo in a chapter on 'The Language of Ethical Discourse' within a subsection on 'Greco-Roman Ethical Language in Second Temple Judaism' (pp. 38–42). The author aims to explore how Philo's account of Judaism, employing Greek philosophical-ethical concepts, raises issues and categories relevant to Qumran ethics. Focusing on Philo's role 'as a link between Greek and Jewish ethics,' he explores (1) Philo's concept of natural law and its relationship with Mosaic and Noachide laws (pp. 39–40), and (2) Philo's notions of virtue (pp. 40–42). He concludes that Philo's concepts of natural law and virtue raise questions about whether the Qumran authors appealed to natural law as a basis for their ethics and what the understanding of virtue was among the Qumranites. (SJKP)

M. Verman, 'Earthly and Heavenly Jerusalem in Philo and Paul: a Tale of Two Cities,' in D. V. Arbel and A. A. Orlov (edd.), *With Letters of Light; Studies in the Dead Sea Scrolls, Early Jewish Apocalypticism, Magic and Mysticism in Honor of Rachel Elior*, Ekstasis: Religious Experience from Antiquity to the Middle Ages 2 (Berlin 2010) 133–156.

The author explores a range of questions about the concept of a 'heavenly Jerusalem' in the Second Temple period: the extent to which the idea is rooted in biblical texts (no explicit references); whether it appears in the sectarian Dead Sea Scrolls (no); whether New Testament authors were influenced by their Jewish environment when writing on this subject; and how these issues relate to the thinking of Philo and Paul. With regard to these two authors it is concluded that 'each formulated the concept of heavenly Jerusalem independently and in a distinctive manner, as part of their larger intellectual enterprise' (p. 133). Philo (discussed on pp. 141–146) represents the earliest, datable references to the concept of a heavenly Jerusalem (focusing on *Somn.* 2.246–53). Philo's approach to this idea is bound up with his philosophically oriented biblical exegesis, whereby he associates the 'heavenly Jerusalem' with contemplation of the Divine. In Paul, however, the 'heavenly Jerusalem' functions polemically by way of contrast to its earthly counterpart as 'a potent weapon with which to counterattack his enemies' (p. 156). (SJKP)

O. WISCHMEYER, 'Cosmo e cosmologia in Paolo,' *Protestantesimo* 64 (2010) 163–179.

The article offers a reflection on Paul's cosmology, which it compares to Plato's cosmology in the *Timaeus* and to Philo's reading of the latter in *Opif.* The cosmology of Plato and Philo are not only reflections on the structure of the cosmos, but also on its origin and evolution as well as on humanity and history. The author notes Engberg-Pedersen's emphasis on the interrelatedness of Paul's cosmological and apocalyptic views; Paul's cosmology does not only refer to the creation of the universe, but also includes an apocalyptic vision of its end. According to the author Paul's understanding differs from Philo's and Plato's because he believes that perfection comes only at the end of the universe, not at its beginning. Paul's vision of the universe is thus subordinate to his Christology and eschatology, and entails a new anthropology which is no longer focussed on the 'first man'—as in Philo—but on the new creation in Christ. (HMK, based on the author's summary)

R. ZARZECZNY, 'Melchizedek i egzegeza Rdz 14, 18–20 w pismach Filona Aleksandryjskiego [Melchizedek and the exegesis of Gen 14:18–20 in the writings of Philo of Alexandria],' *Vox Patrum* 28/52 (2008) 209–268.

The article presents an analysis of Philonic texts which interpret the figure of Melchizedek in Gen 14. Not only does he receive an allegorical interpretation as symbol of mind, right reason and divine Logos, but he is also promoted to the rank of great high priest and given other features that are absent in the biblical text. Philo's interpretation had a profound influence on Patristic interpretation, especially in Ambrose, but perhaps also earlier in Hebrews. Philo's exegesis also stands at the beginning of a spiritual interpretation which was developed in heterodox and Gnostic circles. (DTR, based on the author's summary)

SUPPLEMENT

A Provisional Bibliography 2012–2014

The user of this supplemental Bibliography of the most recent articles on Philo is reminded that it will doubtless contain inaccuracies and red herrings because it is not in all cases based on autopsy. It is merely meant as a service to the reader. Scholars who are disappointed by omissions or are keen to have their own work on Philo listed are strongly encouraged to contact the Bibliography's compilers (addresses in the section 'Notes on Contributors').

2012

M. ALESSO, 'El sumo sacerdocio en Filón y la lectura de Clemente Alejandrino,' *Circe de clásicos y modernos* 16 (2012) 27–42.

M. ALEXANDRE, 'La culture grecque servante de la foi. De Philon d'Alexandrie aux Pères grecs,' in A. PERROT (ed.), *Les chrétiens et l'hellénisme. Identités religieuses et culture grecque dans l'Antiquité tardive*, Études de littérature ancienne 20 (Paris 2012).

Y. AMIR and M. R. NIEHOFF, *Philo of Alexandria Writings, part V, Allegorical Exegesis on Genesis 12-41* (Jerusalem 2012).

H. W. ATTRIDGE, 'Creation and Sacred Space: the Reuse of Key Pentateuchal Themes by Philo, the Fourth Evangelist, and the Epistle to the Hebrews,' in A. MORIYA and G. HATA (edd.), *Pentateuchal Traditions in the Late Second Temple Period: Proceedings of the International Workshop in Tokyo, August 28–31, 2007*, Supplements to the Journal for the Study of Judaism 158 (Leiden 2012) 243–255.

K. BERTHELOT, 'Philo and the Allegorical Interpretation of Homer in the Platonic tradition (with an Emphasis on Porphyry's *De Antro Nympharum*),' in M. R. NIEHOFF (ed.), *Homer and the Bible in the Eyes of Ancient Interpreters*, Jerusalem Studies in Religion and Culture 16 (Leiden 2012) 155–174.

M. BETTINI, *Vertere. Un'antropologia della traduzione nella cultura antica*, Piccola Bibliotheca Einaudi 573 (Turin 2012).

R. BLOCH, 'Alexandria in Pharaonic Egypt: Projections in *De Vita Mosis*,' *The Studia Philonica Annual* 24 (2012) 69–84.

F. BORCHARDT, 'The LXX Myth and the Rise of Textual Fixity,' *Journal for the Study of Judaism* 43 (2012) 1–21.

F. CALABI, 'Il giardino delle delizie e la storia delle origini secondo Filone di Alessandria,' in F. CALABI and S. GASTALDI (edd.), *Immagini delle origini*

— *la nascità della civiltà e delle culture nel pensiero antico,* Contributions to Classical Political Thought 5 (Sankt Augustin 2012) 173–194.

F. CALABI, 'La trasgressione di Adamo e la torre di Babele nella rilettura di Filone di Alessandria,' in E. MANICARDI and L. MAZZINGHI (edd.), *Genesi 1–11 e le sue interpretazioni canoniche: un caso di teologia biblica. XII Settimana Biblica Nazionale (Roma, 6-10 Settembre 2010),* Ricerche Storico-Bibliche (Bologna 2012) 155–170.

F. CALABI, 'Filone di Alessandria e l'*Epinomide,*' in F. ALESSE and F. FERRARI (edd.), *Epinomide: studi sull'opera e la sua ricezione,* Elenchos 60.1 (Naples 2012) 235–261.

M. CUTINO, 'Réemploi de Philon d'Alexandrie et typologies épistolaires dans la correspondance d'Ambroise de Milan,' in A. CANELLIS (ed.), *La correspondance d'Ambroise de Milan,* Centre Jean Palerne. Mémoires 33 (Saint-Étienne 2012) 201–236.

D. CREESE, 'Rhetorical Uses of Mathematical Harmonics in Philo and Plutarch,' *Studies in History and Philosophy of Science* 43 (2012) 258–269.

C. D'ANCONA, 'Plotin,' in R. GOULET (ed.), *Dictionnaire des philosophes antiques* (Paris 2012) 5.885–1070, esp. 966–969.

J. M. DILLON, *The Platonic Heritage. Further Studies in the History of Platonism and Early Christianity,* Variorum Collected Studies (Abingdon 2012).

L. DOERING, *Ancient Jewish Letters and the Beginnings of Christian Epistolography,* Wissenschaftliche Untersuchungen zum Neuen Testament 1.238 (Tübingen 2012).

C. FRAENKEL, *Philosophical Religions from Plato to Spinoza: Reason, Religion, and Autonomy* (Cambridge 2012), esp. 24–32, 100–122.

E. L. GALLAGHER, *Hebrew Scripture in Patristic Biblical Theory,* Supplements to Vigiliae Christianae 114 (Leiden 2012).

E. S. GRUEN, 'Caligula, the Imperial Cult, and Philo's *Legatio,*' *The Studia Philonica Annual* 24 (2012) 135–147.

M. HADAS-LEBEL, *Philo of Alexandria: a Thinker in the Jewish Diaspora,* Studies in Philo of Alexandria 7 (Leiden 2012).

H. HÄGG FISKÅ, 'Kunnskap og frelse i aleksandrinsk teologi og filosofi. Filon og Klemens [Danish: Knowledge and Salvation in Alexandrian Theology and Philosophy: Philo and Clement],' in B. EKMAN and H. RYDELL JOHNSÉN (edd.), *Soteria och gnosis. Frälsning och kunskap i den tidiga kyrkan. Föreläsningar hållna vid Nordiska patrisikermôtet i Lund 18–21 augusti 2010 [Swedish: Soteria and gnosis. Salvation and Knowledge in the Early Church. Papers given at the Nordic Patristi Conference in Lund 18–21 August 2010]* (Skellefteå 2012).

M. HILLAR, *From Logos to Trinity: The Evolution of Religious Beliefs from Pythagoras to Tertullian* (Cambridge 2012).

S. J. Joseph, *Jesus, Q, and the Dead Sea Scrolls: a Judaic Approach to Q (on Qumran and the Essenes)*, Wissenschaftliche Untersuchungen zum Neuen Testament 2.333 (Tübingen 2012), esp. 94–123.

J. L. Kugel, '*Jubilees*, Philo and the Problem of Genesis,' in N. Dávid, A. Lange, K. De Troyer and S. Tzoref (edd.), *The Hebrew Bible in Light of the Dead Sea Scrolls* (Göttingen 2012) 295–311.

J. L. Kugel, '*Jubilees*, Philo and the Problem of Genesis,' in *A Walk through Jubilees: Studies in the Book of Jubilees and the World of its Creation* (Leiden 2012) 391–405.

J. Leonhardt-Balzer, 'Priests and Priesthood in Philo: Could He Have Done without Them?,' in D. R. Schwartz and Z. Weiss (edd.), *Was 70 CE a Watershed in Jewish History? On Jews and Judaism Before and after the Destruction of the Second Temple*, Ancient Judaism and Early Christianity 78 (Leiden 2012) 121–147.

S. D. Mackie, 'Seeing God in Philo of Alexandria: Means, Methods, and Mysticism,' *Journal for the Study of Judaism* 43 (2012) 147–179.

P. W. Martens, *Origen and Scripture: the Contours of the Exegetical Life*, Oxford Early Christian Studies (Oxford 2012).

P. W. Martens, '*On the Confusion of Tongues* and Origen's Allegory of the Dispersion of Nations,' *The Studia Philonica Annual* 24 (2012) 107–127.

J. P. Martín (ed.), *Filón de Alejandría Obras Completas Volumen III* (Madrid 2012).

J. More, 'On Kingship in Philo and the Wisdom of Solomon,' in J. Cook and H.-J. Stipp (edd.), *Text-Critical and Hermeneutical Studies in the Septuagint*, Vetus Testamentum Supplements 157 (Leiden 2012) 499–525.

M. R. Niehoff (ed.), *Homer and the Bible in the Eyes of Ancient Interpreters*, Jerusalem Studies in Religion and Culture 16 (Leiden 2012).

M. R. Niehoff, 'Philo and Plutarch on Homer,' in Eadem (ed.), *Homer and the Bible in the Eyes of Ancient Interpreters*, Jerusalem Studies in Religion and Culture 16 (Leiden 2012) 128–153.

M. R. Niehoff, 'Philo and Plutarch as Biographers: Parallel Responses to Roman Stoicism,' *Greek, Roman, and Byzantine Studies* 52 (2012) 361–392.

C. S. O'Brien, 'The Middle Platonist Demiurge and Stoic Cosmobiology,' *Horizons: Seoul Journal of the Humanities* 3 (2012) 19–39, esp. 31–33.

P. A. Patterson, *Visions of Christ: The Anthropomorphite Controversy of 399 CE*, Studien und Texte zu Antike und Christentum 68 (Tübingen 2012).

S. J. K. Pearce, 'Philo and Roman Imperial Power: Introduction,' *The Studia Philonica Annual* 24 (2012) 129–133.

S. J. K. Pearce, 'Philo and the *Temple Scroll* on the Prohibition of Single Testimony,' in N. Dávid, A. Lange, K. De Troyer and S. Tzoref (edd.), *The Hebrew Bible in Light of the Dead Sea Scrolls*, Forschungen zur Religion und Literatur des Alten und Neuen Testaments 239 (Göttingen 2012) 321–336.

V. RABENS, 'Johannine Perspectives on Ethical Enabling in the Context of Stoic and Philonic Ethics,' in J. VAN DER WATT and R. ZIMMERMAN (edd.), *Rethinking the Ethics of John: "Implicit Ethics" in the Johannine Writings (Kontexte und Normen neutestamentlicher Ethik / Contexts and Norms of New Testament Ethics III),* Wissenschaftliche Untersuchungen zum Neuen Testament 1.291 (Tübingen 2012) 114–139.

I. L. E. RAMELLI 'Philo as Origen's Declared Model: Allegorical and Historical Exegesis of Scripture,' *Studies in Christian-Jewish Relations* 7 (2012) 1–17.

J. M. ROGERS, *Didymus the Blind and his Use of Philo of Alexandria in the Tura Commentary on Genesis* (diss. Hebrew Union College 2012).

T. A. ROGERS, 'Philo's Universalization of Sinai in *De Decalogo* 32–49,' *The Studia Philonica Annual* 24 (2012) 85–105.

J. R. ROYSE, 'Philo of Alexandria, *Quaestiones in Exodum* 2.62–68: Critical Edition,' *The Studia Philonica Annual* 24 (2012) 1–68.

D. T. RUNIA, 'Philon d'Alexandrie,' in R. GOULET (ed.), *Dictionnaire des philosophes antiques* (Paris 2012) 5.362–390.

D. T. RUNIA, 'Jewish Platonism (Ancient),' in G. A. PRESS (ed.), *The Continuum Companion to Plato* (London 2012) 267–269.

D. T. RUNIA, 'God the Creator as Demiurge in Philo of Alexandria,' *Horizons: Seoul Journal of the Humanities* 3 (2012) 41–59.

D. T. RUNIA and G. E. STERLING (edd.), *The Studia Philonica Annual,* Vol. 24 (Atlanta 2012).

D. T. RUNIA, K. BERTHELOT, A. C. GELJON, H. M. KEIZER, J. LEONHARDT BALZER, J. P. MARTÍN, M. R. NIEHOFF, S. J. K. PEARCE and T. SELAND, 'Philo of Alexandria: an Annotated Bibliography 2009,' *The Studia Philonica Annual* 24 (2012) 183–242.

K.-G. SANDELIN, *Attraction and Danger of Alien Religion: Studies in Early Judaism and Christianity,* Wissenschaftliche Untersuchungen zum Neuen Testament 1.290 (Tübingen 2012).

L. SAUDELLI, *Eraclito ad Alessandria. Studi e ricerche intorno alla testimonianza di Filone,* Monothéismes et Philosophie 16 (Turnhout 2012).

G. SCHÖLLGEN (ed.), *Reallexikon für Antike und Christentum Band 24* (Stuttgart 2012).

C. Tornau, art. Materie, 346–410, esp. 370–373 (Matter); M. Durst, R. Amedick, E. Enss, art. Meer 505–609, esp. 549–552 (Sea); S. Rebenich, art. Monarchie, 1112–1196, esp. 1164–1166 (Monarchy). (DTR)

D. R. SCHWARTZ, 'Philo and Josephus on the Violence in Alexandria in 38 C.E.' *The Studia Philonica Annual* 24 (2012) 149–166.

G. E. STERLING, 'The Interpreter of Moses: Philo of Alexandria and the Biblical Text,' in M. HENZE (ed.), *A Companion to Biblical Interpretation in Early Judaism* (Grand Rapids Mich. 2012) 415–435.

G. E. STERLING, 'When the Beginning is the End: the Place of Genesis in the Commentaries of Philo,' in C. A. EVANS, J. N. LOHR and D. L. PETERSEN (edd.), *The Book of Genesis: Composition, Reception, and Interpretation*, Vetus Testamentum Supplements 152 (Leiden 2012) 427–446.

G. E. STERLING, '"Prolific in Expression and Broad in Thought": Internal References to Philo's Allegorical Commentary and Exposition of the Law,' *Euphrosyne* 40 (2012) 55–76.

G. E. STERLING, M. R. NIEHOFF, A. VAN DEN HOEK and D. T. RUNIA, 'Philo,' in J. J. COLLINS and D. C. HARLOW (edd.), *Early Judaism: a Comprehensive Overview* (Grand Rapids Mich. 2012) 253–189.

G. J. STEYN, 'Can We Reconstruct an Early Text Form of the LXX from the Quotations of Philo of Alexandria and the New Testament: Torah Quotations Overlapping between Philo and Galatians as a Test Case,' in S. KREUZER, M. MEISER and M. SIGISMUND (edd.), *Die Septuagina — Entstehung, Sprache, Geschichte*, Wissenschaftliche Untersuchungen zum Neuen Testament 2.309 (Tübingen 2012) 444–464.

A. TIMOTIN, *La démonologie platonicienne. Histoire de la notion de daimôn de Platon aux derniers néoplatoniciennes*, Philosophia Antiqua 128 (Leiden 2012), esp. 100–112.

S. WEISSER, 'Why Does Philo Criticize the Stoic Ideal of Apatheia in *On Abraham* 257? Philo and Consolatory Literature,' *Classical Quarterly* 62 (2012) 242–259.

M. R. WHITENTON, 'Rewriting Abraham and Joseph: Stephen's speech (Acts 7:2–16) and Jewish Exegetical Traditions,' *Novum Testamentum* 54 (2012) 149–167.

B. WYSS, 'Philon und der Sophistendiskurs,' in M. HIRSCHBERGER (ed.), *Jüdisch-hellenistische Literatur in ihrem interkulturellen Kontext* (Frankfurt am Maim 2013) 89–105.

J. YODER, 'Sympathy for the Devil? Philo on Flaccus and Rome,' *The Studia Philonica Annual* 24 (2012) 167–182.

2013

A. AFTERMAN, 'From Philo to Plotinus: the Emergence of Mystical Union,' *Journal of Religion* 93 (2013) 177–196.

M. ALESSO, 'Filón como fuente de la identificacíon del sumo sacerdote con Jesús en Clemente Alejandrino,' in Á. HERNÁNDEZ, S. VILLALONGA and P. CINER (edd.), *La identidad de Jesús: unidad y diversidad en la época de la*

Patrística. Actas del I Congreso Internacional de Estudios Patrísticos, Universidad Católica de Cuyo (San Juan 2013) 167–198.

R. M. BERCHMAN, 'Arithmos and Kosmos: Arithmology as an Exegetical Tool in the *De Opificio Mundi* of Philo of Alexandria,' in K. CORRIGAN and T. RASIMUS (edd.), *Gnosticism, Platonism and the Late Antique World. Essays in Honour of John D. Turner* (Brill 2013) 167–198.

U. BITTRICH, 'Die drei Formen des Weisheitserwerbs bei Philo von Alexandrien und ihre Wurzeln in der aristotelischen Ethik,' in M. HIRSCHBERGER (ed.), *Jüdisch-hellenistische Literatur in ihrem interkulturellen Kontext* (Frankfurt am Maim 2013) 72–90.

M. BÖHM, 'Philo und die Frage nach den jüdischen Identitat in Alexandria,' in M. ÖHLER (ed.), *Religionsgemeinschaft und Identität. Prozesse jüdischer und christlicher Identitätsbildung im Rahmen der Antike,* Biblisch Theologische Studien 142 (Neukirchen-Vluyn 2013) 69–112.

S. C. BYERS, *Perception, Sensibility, and Moral Motivation in Augustine: a Stoic-Platonic Synthesis* (Cambridge 2013).

F. CALABI, *Filone di Alessandria,* Pensatori 32 (Roma 2013).

D. DE BRASI, '„Uno principe, pertanto, debbe consigliarsi sempre" (Machiavelli, Il Principe, XXIII): Fürstenspiegel in der jüdisch-hellenistischen politischen Philosophie?,' in M. HIRSCHBERGER (ed.), *Jüdisch-hellenistische Literatur in ihrem interkulturellen Kontext* (Frankfurt am Maim 2013) 51–71.

D. J. DEVORE, 'Eusebius' Un-Josephan History: Two Portraits of Philo of Alexandria and the Sources of Ecclesiastical Historiography,' in M. VINZENT (ed.), *Studia Patristica: Papers Presented at the Sixteenth Internaitonal Conference on Patristic Studies held in Oxford 2011* (Leuven 2013) 14.161–180.

M. J. EDWARDS, *Image, Word and God in the Early Christian Centuries,* Ashgate Studies in Philosophy and Theology in Late Antiquity (Farnham UK 2013), esp. 61–68.

C. FRAENKEL, 'Philo of Alexandria, Hasdai Crescas, and Spinoza on God's Body,' in R. S. BOUSTAN, K. HERRMANN, R. LEICHT, A. Y. REED and G. VELTRI (edd.), *Envisioning Judaism: Studies in Honor of Peter Schäfer on the Occasion of his Seventieth Birthday* (Tübingen 2013) 809–819.

P. FRICK, 'Monotheism and Philosophy: Notes on the Concept of God in Philo and Paul (Romans 1:18–21),' in S. E. PORTER and A. W. PITTS (edd.), *Christian Origins and Hellenistic Judaism: Social and Literary Contexts for the New Testament,* Texts and Editions for New Testament Study 10 (Leiden 2013) 237–258.

F. GARCÍA MARTÍNEZ, H. NAJMAN and E. TIGCHELAAR (edd.), *Between Philology and Theology: Contributions to the Study of Ancient Jewish Interpretation,* Supplements to the Journal for the Study of Judaism 162 (Leiden 2013).

A. C. Geljon and D. T. Runia, *Philo On Cultivation: Introduction, Translation and Commentary*, Philo of Alexandria Commentary Series 4 (Leiden 2013).

W. Helleman-Elgersma, 'Augustine and Philo of Alexandria's 'Sarah' as a Wisdom Figure (*De Civitate Dei* XV 2f.; XVI 25–32),' in M. Vinzent (ed.), *Studia Patristica: Papers Presented at the Sixteenth International Conference on Patristic Studies held in Oxford 2011* (Leuven 2013) 18.105–116.

W. Horbury, 'Biblical interpretation in Greek Jewish writings,' in J. Carleton Paget and J. Schaper (edd.), *The New Cambridge History of the Bible: From the Beginnings to 600* (Cambridge 2013) 289–320, esp. 311–316.

L. Kerns, 'Soul and Passions in Philo of Alexandria,' in M. Vinzent (ed.), *Studia Patristica: Papers Presented at the Sixteenth Internaitonal Conference on Patristic Studies held in Oxford 2011* (Leuven 2013) 11.141–154.

R. A. Layton, 'Moses the Pedagogue: Procopius, Philo, and Didymus on the Pedagogy of the Creation Account,' in L. Jenott and S. K. Gribetz (edd.), *Jewish and Christian Cosmogony in Late Antiquity*, Texts and Studies in Ancient Judaism 155 (Tübingen 2013) 167–192.

C. Lévy, 'L'étrange monsieur Aquilius,' *Bulletin de l'Association Guillaume Budé*, No.1 (2013) 202–213.

V. Limone, *Inizio e Trinità. Il neoplatonismo giovanneo nell'ultimo Schelling*, Philosophica 114 (Pisa 2013), esp. 99-104.

D. Lincicum, 'Aeschylus in Philo, *Anim.* 47 and *QE* 2.6,' *The Studia Philonica Annual* 25 (2013) 65–68.

D. Lincicum, 'A Preliminary Index to Philo's Non–Biblical Citations and Allusions,' *The Studia Philonica Annual* 25 (2013) 139–167.

W. Loader, *Making Sense of Sex: Attitudes Towards Sexuality in Early Jewish and Christian Literature* (Grand Rapids 2013).

J. P. Martín, 'Las esperanzas mesiánicas de Filón de Alejandría, un judío contemporáneo de Jesús,' in Á. Hernández, S. Villalonga and P. Ciner (edd.), *La identidad de Jesús: unidad y diversidad en la época de la Patrística*. Actas del I Congreso Internacional de Estudios Patrísticos, Universidad Católica de Cuyo (San Juan 2013).

O. Munnich, 'Δορυφορεῖν, δορυφόρος: l'image de la «garde» chez Philon d'Alexandrie,' *The Studia Philonica Annual* 25 (2013) 41–63.

M. R. Niehoff, 'A Jewish Critique of Christianity from Second-Century Alexandria: Revisiting the Jew Mentioned in *Contra Celsum*,' *Journal of Early Christian Studies* 21 (2013) 151–175.

M. R. Niehoff, 'Jüdische Bibelinterpretation zwischen Homerforschung und Christentum,' in T. Georges, F. Allbrecht and R. Feldmeier (edd.), *Alexandria*, Civitatum Orbis Mediteranei Studia 1 (Tübingen 2013) 341–360.

M. R. Niehoff, 'The Emergence of Monotheistic Creation Theology in Hellenistic Judaism,' in L. Jenott and S. K. Gribetz (edd.), *Jewish and Christian Cosmogony in Late Antiquity,* Texts and Studies in Ancient Judaism 155 (Tübingen 2013) 85–106.

M. R. Niehoff, 'Biographical Sketches in Genesis Rabbah,' in R. S. Boustan, K. Herrmann, R. Leicht, A. Y. Reed and G. Veltri (edd.), *Envisioning Judaism: Studies in Honor of Peter Schäfer on the Occasion of his Seventieth Birthday* (Tübingen 2013) 265–286.

J. Otto, 'Philo, Judaeus? A Re-evaluation of why Clement Calls Philo "the Pythagorean,"' *The Studia Philonica Annual* 25 (2013) 115–138.

A. Pasquier, 'Parole intérieure et parole proférée chez Philon d'Alexandrie et dans l'*Évangile de la Vérité* (NH I,3),' in K. Corrigan and T. Rasimus (edd.), *Gnosticism, Platonism and the Late Antique World. Essays in Honour of John D. Turner* (Brill 2013) 199–208.

S. Pearce, 'Rethinking the Other in Antiquity: Philo of Alexandria on Intermarriage,' *Antichthon* 47 (2013) 140–155.

S. J. K. Pearce, *The Words of Moses: Studies in the Reception of Deuteronomy in the Second Temple Period,* Texts and Studies in Ancient Judaism 152 (Tübingen 2013).

S. E. Porter and A. W. Pitts (edd.), *Christian Origins and Hellenistic Judaism: Social and Literary Contexts for the New Testament,* Texts and Editions for New Testament Study 10 (Leiden 2013).

V. Rabens, 'Philo's Attractive Ethics on the "Religious Market" of Ancient Alexandria,' in P. Wick and V. Rabens (edd.), *Religious Formation, Transformation and Cross-Cultural Exchange between East and West,* Dynamics in the History of Religions 5 (Leiden 2013) 333–356.

M. J. Reddoch, 'Enigmatic Dreams and Onirocritical Skill in *De Somniis* 2,' *The Studia Philonica Annual* 25 (2013) 1–16.

C. M. Rios, *O próprio e o comum: rastros de interculturalidade na escrita de Fílon de Alexandría* (diss. Universidade Federal de Minas Gerais 2013).

J. R. Royse, 'Did Philo Publish his Works?,' *The Studia Philonica Annual* 25 (2013) 75–100.

D. T. Runia, 'Philo and the Gentiles,' in D. S. Sim and J. S. McLaren (edd.), *Attitudes to Gentiles in Ancient Judaism and Early Christianity* (London 2013) 28–45.

D. T. Runia, K. Berthelot, E. Birnbaum, A. C. Geljon, H. M. Keizer, J. Leonhardt Balzer, J. P. Martín, M. R. Niehoff, S. J. K. Pearce, and T. Seland, 'Philo of Alexandria: an Annotated Bibliography 2010,' *The Studia Philonica Annual* 24 (2013) 169–224.

D. T. Runia and G. E. Sterling (edd.), *The Studia Philonica Annual,* Vol. 25 (Atlanta 2013).

G. Schöllgen (ed.), *Reallexikon für Antike und Christentum Band 25* (Stuttgart 2013).

> A. Lehnart, art. Mose I (literarisch), 58–102, esp. 74–75 (Moses); P. Mueller-Jourdan, art. Mystagogie, 404–422, esp. 414–415 (initiation); H. Crouzel and C. Mühlenkamp, art. Nachahmung Gottes, 525–565, esp. 538–541 (imitation of God); P. Terbuyken, art. Noe, 938–969, esp. 947–948 (Noah); K.-W. Niebuhr, art. Nomos, 978–1106, esp. 1025–1028 (Law). (DTR)

D. R. Schwartz, 'Humbly Second-Rate in the Diaspora? Philo and Stephen on the Tabernacle and the Temple,' in R. S. Boustan, K. Herrmann, R. Leicht, A. Y. Reed and G. Veltri (edd.), *Envisioning Judaism: Studies in Honor of Peter Schäfer on the Occasion of his Seventieth Birthday* (Tübingen 2013) 81–89.

T. Seland, 'Philo and the New Testament,' in J. B. Green and L. M. McDonald (edd.), *The World of the New Testament: Cultural, Social, and Historical Contexts* (Grand Rapids 2013) 405–412.

G. E. Sterling, 'Philo's Ancient Readers: an Introduction,' *The Studia Philonica Annual* 25 (2013) 69–73.

G. E. Sterling, '"A Man of the Highest Repute": Did Josephus Know the Writings of Philo?,' *The Studia Philonica Annual* 25 (2013) 101–113.

G. J. Steyn, 'A Comparison of the Septuagint Textual Form in the Torah Quotations Common to Philo of Alexandria and the Gospels of Mark and Matthew,' in *XIV Congress of the IOSCS. Helsinki 2010*, Septuagint and Cognate Studies 59 (Atlanta 2013) 605–623.

G. J. Steyn, 'The Text Form of the Torah Quotations Common to the Corpus Philonicum and Paul's Corinthian Correspondence,' in S. Moise and J. Verheyden (edd.), *The Scriptures of Israel in Jewish and Christian Tradition: Essays in Honour of Maarten J.J. Menken*, Supplements to Novum Testamentum 148 (Leiden 2013) 193–210.

G. J. Steyn, 'Torah Quotations Common to Philo of Alexandria and the Acts of the Apostles,' *Acta Theologica* 33 (2013) 164–181.

H. Svebakken, *Philo of Alexandria's Exposition on the Tenth Commandment*, Studia Philonica Monographs 6 (Atlanta 2013).

N. L. Tilford, '"After the Ways of Women": the Aged Virgin in Philo's Transformation of the Philosophical Soul,' *The Studia Philonica Annual* 25 (2013) 17–39.

L. Troiani, 'Filone di Alessandria nella *Storia Ecclesiastica* di Eusebio,' in O. Andrei (ed.), *Caesarea Maritima e la scuola orgieniana. Muticulturalità, forme di competizione culturale e identità cristiana*, Supplementi di Adamantius 3 (Brescia 2013) 211–215.

M. Vogel, 'Modelle jüdischer Identitätsbildung in hellenistisch-römischer Zeit,' in M. Öhler (ed.), *Religionsgemeinschaft und Identität. Prozesse jüdischer und christlicher Identitätsbildung im Rahmen der Antike,* Biblisch Theologische Studien 142 (Neukirchen-Vluyn 2013) 69–112.

B. Wyss, 'Philon und die Pentas. Arithmologie als exegetische Methode,' in T. Georges, F. Allbrecht and R. Feldmeier (edd.), *Alexandria,* Civitatum Orbis Mediterranei Studia 1 (Tübingen 2013) 361–379.

S. Yli-Karjanmaa, *Reincarnation in Philo of Alexandria* (diss. Åbo Akademi University 2013).

2014

P. Borgen, *The Gospel of John: More Light from Philo, Paul and Archaeology: The Scriptures, Tradition, Exposition, Settings, Meaning,* Novum Testamentum Supplements 154 (Leiden 2014).

L. Brisson, 'Alexandrie, berceau du néoplatonisme. Eudore, Philon, Ammonios et l'école d'Alexandrie,' in C. Méla and F. Möri (edd.), *Alexandrie la divine* (Geneva 2014) 354–363.

M. Hadas-Lebel, *Une histoire du Messie* (Paris 2014), esp. 136–138.

P. W. van der Horst, *Studies in Ancient Judaism and Early Christianity,* Ancient Judaism and Early Christianity (Leiden 2014).

C. Moreschini, 'Further Considerations on the Philosophical Background of *Contra Eunomium* III,' in J. Leemans and M. Cassin (edd.), *Gregory of Nyssa Contra Eunomium III: an English Translation with Commentary and Supporting Studies,* Supplements to Vigiliae Christianae 124 (Leiden 2014) 595–612, esp. 598–601.

M. R. Niehoff, 'Les juifs d'Alexandrie à l'école de la critique textuelle des païen,' in C. Méla and F. Möri (edd.), *Alexandrie la divine* (Geneva 2014) 733–740

V. Rabens, *The Holy Spirit and Ethics in Paul: Transformation and Empowering for Religious-Ethical Life,* 2nd ed (Minneapolis 2014).

L. Saudelli, 'Loi de Moïse et philosophies grecque: le judaïsme Alexandrie,' in C. Méla and F. Möri (edd.), *Alexandrie la divine* (Geneva 2014) 726–731.

G. Schöllgen (ed.), *Reallexikon für Antike und Christentum Lieferungen 203–205* (Stuttgart 2014).

R. J. Daly, Art. Opfer, 143–206, esp. 169–170 (sacrifice); C. Neuber, Art. Orakel, 206–350, esp. 312–313 (oracle); A. Fürst, Art. Origenes, 460–567, esp. 490–491 (Origen). (DTR)

The Studia Philonica Annual 26 (2014) 227–257

BOOK REVIEW SECTION

Sabrina Inowlocki and Badouin Decharneux, eds. *Philon d'Alex-andrie: un Penseur à l'Intersection des Cultures Gréco-Romaine, Orientale, Juive et Chrétienne*. Actes du colloque international organize par le Centre interdisciplinaire d'étude des religions et de la laïcité de l'université libre de Bruxelles (Bruxelles, 26–28 juin 2007). With the collaboration of B. Bertho. Monothéismes et Philosophie. Turnhout: Brepols, 2011. 526 pp. ISBN 978-2-503-52885-4. Price €95 (pb).

This volume of twenty-one essays takes its starting point from the complex reality of Philo's cultural and religious environment and the place of Philo's Alexandria as home to diverse traditions—Egyptian, Jewish, Greek, Roman and, after Philo's time, Christian. In their prefatory remarks, the editors underline the need to embrace a whole range of academic disciplines— philology, philosophy, theology, history, literature, and sociology—the better to illuminate Philo and the wider context of his thought. Most of the essays (five in English, the rest in French) are based on papers originally presented at an international colloquium at the Free University of Brussels in 2007. Reflecting that context, Part 1 of the collection begins with the colloquium's splendid keynote lecture, David Runia's "Why Philo of Alexandria Is an Important Writer and Thinker." Noting the relatively marginalized position of Philonic studies within Classics and Religious Studies, R. offers an eloquent account of the case for Philo's importance in seven fields of research: classics, ancient philosophy, New Testament studies, Gnosticism, Patristics, Judaism, and ancient history. As R. observes, the state of research on Philo varies widely between these disciplines and in several key areas—including Classics and Jewish Studies—"much remains to be done." In the second part of this excellent essay, R. illustrates the importance of each of these fields to the study of Philo through a close examination of cosmic religion and the cult of the heavenly bodies within Philo's thought and the wider Greco-Roman context. Overall, reflecting on Philo's importance in its own right, R. emphasizes two aspects that make Philo "distinct and special": his positive attitude to the Greek cultural heritage of Roman Alexandria and the Mediterranean world; and the spiritual depth and creativity of his allegorical commentaries.

The remainder of the volume includes essays which, taken together, touch on all the disciplines identified by R. as important to Philonic studies, though the larger part of them deals with interpreting Philo in the context of ancient philosophy or the reception of his work in Christian circles. The collection is divided into three parts, the first of which (Part 2, "Entre Jérusalem et Rome") considers Philo in different contexts, Jewish, Roman and Alexandrian. Martin Goodman ("Philo as Philosopher in Rome") explores the apparent—and usually unnoticed—oddness of Josephus's description of Philo as a "philosopher" in the Roman context of his role as leader of the Jewish embassy to Gaius Caligula. In "Grecs, Barbares et Juifs dans l'œuvre de Philon," Katell Berthelot looks at how Philo chooses to speak of humanity in general, of Jews in relation to the rest of humanity, and why Romans in particular are "curiously absent" from Philo's discourse. With the next essay, Ellen Birnbaum's "Who Celebrated on Pharos with the Jews? Conflicting Philonic Currents and Their Implications," we move directly to Alexandria and to Philo's account of contemporary Alexandrian Jewish practice and what it reveals—or does not reveal—about Jewish/non-Jewish relations in Philo's thought world. In her contribution, "Recherche homérique et exégèse biblique à Alexandrie: un fragment sur la Tour de Babel préservé par Philon," Maren Niehoff offers a valuable study of how to use Philo's works to shed light on the intellectual environment of Alexandria and the diversity of approaches to scriptural exegesis among the Alexandrian Jewish community (an English version of this essay is now incorporated into the author's 2011 monograph, *Jewish Exegesis and Homeric Scholarship in Alexandria*). Finally, Michèle Broze, in "L'Egypte de Philon d'Alexandrie: approches d'un discours ambigu," offers the only study in the collection focusing specifically on Philo in the context of traditional Egyptian religious thought, exploring the presentation of Moses as taught by Egyptian philosophers (in the *Life of Moses*), and reflections in Philo of traditions about Thoth as interpreter of language and the land of Egypt as image of the heavens.

Part 3, "Entre Athènes et Alexandrie," represents the largest section of the book, and comprises eight studies on Philo's works from the viewpoint of philology and the history of Greek philosophy. In "Monarchie divine et dieux des nations chez Philon d'Alexandrie," Monique Alexandre offers an analytical tour de force of Philo's treatment of the opposition between the divine monarchy of the God of Israel and polytheistic beliefs, stressing Philo's fundamental contribution to the history of thought in systematizing this opposition and in the field of semantic innovations relating to the language of polytheism and divine monarchy. The remaining contributions in this section represent a fine collection of detailed analyses by experts in the field, illustrating the complex interplay between the traditions of Scripture and Greek philosophy underpinning Philo's creativity. Carlos Lévy explores the neglected topic of Philo's innovative transformation, in philosophical terms, of the concept of "the sign" to articulate a theology of transcendence; Olivier Munnich examines Philo's reworking of traditional biblical and philosophical motifs, focusing on the idea of human life as a dream-world in the treatise *On Joseph* §§127–147; Francesca Calabi looks at Philo's thinking about divine rest vis à vis notions of divine activity within the Greek philosophical tradition; Francesca Alesse examines the uses of the term *prohairesis* in Philo's works, and the different traditions of thought that he exploits in the service of interpreting Scripture; Sharon Weisser studies the Philonic category of the *progressant* (προκόπτων), focusing on the figures of Hagar, Lot, and Aaron as representatives of this intermediate stage of the spiritual journey and the ethical attributes associated with it; Jérôme Moreau analyzes the exegetical process in Philo's *Her.* 90–101, and his innovative treatment of the idea of *pistis* as an act of the intellect, especially as applied to Abraham; while Lucia Saudelli studies examples of Frg 60 DK ("the way up and down is the same") of Heraclitus in Philo's works, with a view to demonstrating the contribution of Philo to knowledge of Heraclitus, and how far Philo's commentary on Scripture is informed by the philosophy of Heraclitus.

The fourth and final division of the collection deals with reception history ("Les temps des relectures"), and comprises seven essays dealing with Philo and the New Testament and the reception of Philo in Jewish and Christian tradition. With regard to New Testament traditions, both Fabien Nobilio and Baudouin Decharneux offer studies of Philo's works in relation to the Fourth Gospel, focusing on pneumatology and the doctrine of the Logos, respectively; and Peter Tomson presents a comparative analysis of the Letter to the Hebrews, probing the possible origins of its "Platonism" (or "Philonism") and its unusual association in the same document with apocalyptic ideology. In the realm of Patristics, Albert Geljon demonstrates the influence of Philo's interpretations of Genesis on the works of Didymus the Blind; while Sabrina Inowlocki shows the major role played by Philo and his writings in Eusebius's defence of Christianity, as set out in the *Praeparatio evangelica* and the *Demonstratio evangelica*. Attention to the Christian reception of Philo concludes with a provocative and stimulating contribution by Folker Siegert, in which he argues that Philo's hostility to Alexandrian exegesis (the endorsement of a historico-critical approach to the biblical text) leads, through its influence on Christian thinkers, to biblical fundamentalism. The last word in the volume is given to the Jewish reception of Philo in the renaissance period, with a welcome translation into French of Joanna Weinberg's pioneering article originally published in English in 1988, now presented under the title "La quête de Philon dans l'historiographie juive du XVIe siècle." Overall, the high quality of the volume reflects the careful attention of its editors and the rich cast of experts assembled for the purpose. Readers are well served by bibliography and indices covering citations from the works of Philo, other ancient authors, and Scripture. The balance of topics represented indicates the continued dominance of philosophy and New Testament/early Christian studies as disciplines within which Philo is treated as a figure of importance. In this respect, the collection confirms David Runia's conclusion that, in the fields of Jewish Studies and ancient history (particularly, in my view, as regards Alexandria, Egypt and the Jewish communities of the ancient Mediterranean world), much remains to be done.

Sarah Pearce
University of Southampton

SARAH J. K. PEARCE, *The Words of Moses. Studies on the Reception of Deuteronomy in the Second Temple Period*. Texts and Studies in Ancient Judaism 152. Tübingen: Mohr Siebeck, 2013. ISBN 978-3-16-150733-5. Xviii + 404 pages. Price €139 (hb).

The main part of this book is a revised version of Pearce's 1995 Oxford D.Phil. dissertation, supervised by Geza Vermes, to whose memory the book is dedicated. It is a detailed study of the interpretation of Deut 16:18–17:13 in Second Temple literature. It examines three themes, the establishment of local judiciaries, the need for more than one witness, and the higher court at "the place that the Lord your God will choose." The main sources examined are Chronicles, LXX Deuteronomy, the *Temple Scroll*, Philo, and Josephus, but other texts, from the Scrolls, New Testament, and Pseudepigrapha, are adduced on occasion. An "Introduction" sets out basic information about the textual forms of Deuteronomy current in the Second Temple period, and also about the main sources.

The "Introduction" also frames the study by reference to the modern discussion of Deuteronomy as a draft constitution—arguably, in the words of Bernard Levinson, "the first blueprint for a constitutional system of government." Pearce then asks: "To what extent were the laws of Deut. 16:18–17:13 already recognized in this period as laws for an ideal constitution? Did Jewish interpreters think that these laws should be put into practical effect, and if so how and by whom? How do the laws relate to existing judicial institutions? What aspects of these laws were seen as especially in need of explanation? What does the engagement of our interpreters with this material reveal about their distinctive concerns and their vision of the laws in Jewish society? " (p. 6)

The body of the work is divided into three chapters. The first addresses the establishment of local judiciaries in Deut 16:18–20. The first interpretation discussed is that of the Chronicler in the story of Jehoshaphat. This story is not deemed to reflect the actual judicial history of Judah either in the supposed time of Jehoshaphat or in that of the Chronicler, but is rather a utopian vision based on Deut 16:18–20. LXX Deut generally depends on a Hebrew text close to MT, with some elements close to the text reflected in the Temple Scroll. It has some substantial interpretive points, notably the coining of a new term, *grammatoeisagogeis*, as a plausible Hellenistic title for magistrates' assistants. In the case of the *Temple Scroll*, Pearce does not think that the Law of the King is a veiled critique of Hasmonean kingship. (She thinks the oldest core of T is pre-Hasmonean.) Rather she sees it as a development of the critique of kingship in 1 Samuel. "The Temple Scroll develops the law of Deut. 17:14–20 through the selective use of the prohibitions of Deut. 16:19, in association with the ambivalent traditions about kingship in the Book of Samuel" (p. 92). Philo subsumes laws for judges under the ninth commandment (false testimony) in *Spec.* 4.55–78. Pearce argues that Philo's view of justice is essentially Platonic, as can be seen by his comments on "the semi-villainous practice of taking bribes for good ends" (p. 104). Josephus reworks Deut 16:18–20 in *Ant.* 4.214–7, drawing on Pentateuchal narratives about Moses' appointment of judges. Notable here is the designation of "seven men" to rule in each city, although no such institution is known elsewhere in the Hebrew Bible. Pearce rejects the suggestion that Jewish towns were run by a council of seven in Josephus's own time, and sees rather a reflection of the seventy elders associated with Moses in Exod 24:1,9 and Num 11:16.

Chapter Two reviews the requirement of "two or three witnesses" for capital conviction in Deut 17:6. The LXX is close to the MT, with minor textual variants. The *Temple Scroll* also reflects both Deut 17:6–7 and Deut 19:15 with only minor variants from the MT. More interesting here is the *Damascus Document* which allows the combined testimony of three single witnesses to three separate transgressions of the Torah (CD 9.16–20). Philo's only explicit discussion of the prohibition of single testimony appears in *Spec.* 4.53–54. He focuses on the prohibition of single testimony without explicitly addressing the number of witnesses required. He sees the prohibition of single testimony as a matter of justice. He differs from other interpreters in seeing the prohibition as a precaution against the deceptions of the body, and he relates the special laws to the Ten Commandments.

Josephus (*Ant* 4.219) adds to the Deuteronomic law by specifying that the testimony of women and slaves may not be accepted. Pearce notes that "there is no certainty that he follows actual Jewish practice" and that he may be influenced by his Roman context (p. 197). Interesting variations on the law of witnesses are provided by the story of Susanna, where two witnesses prove unreliable, and the Testament of Abraham, which associates the requirement of three (not two) witnesses with the use of three tribunals at the Last Judgment. The law of witnesses is also reflected in several New Testament passages. The Gospel of Matthew provides the first example of a Christian community rule based on Deut 19:15, in the context of a procedure for reconciliation. First Tim 5:19 invokes the requirement of two or three witnesses in connection with charges against the elders.

Chapter Three considers the law that difficult cases be referred to "the place that the Lord your God will choose" (Deut 17:8–13). Here again the Chronicler's account of Jehoshaphat is part of the history of reception. The purpose, however, was not to describe a real court but to show the piety of Jehoshaphat in putting the Law into practice. LXX emphasizes that the cases in question are impossible for human judges (the verb is *adynateo*), and that the higher court functions by divine power. The *Temple Scroll* inserts a reference to "the book of the Torah" ("and you shall act according to the law/torah that they declare to you, and according to the word that they say to you from the book of the Law"). Pearce argues that "the book of the Torah" here is Deuteronomy. The royal council has a much wider function in the *Temple Scroll* than did the council of Jehoshaphat. It exercises control over all the activities of the monarch. Philo associates Deut 17:8–13 with the virtue of justice in *Spec.* 4.188–192. His presentation reflects very little of the language of LXX Deuteronomy, but it is shaped by that LXX passage nonetheless. He associates the need for a higher court with the limitations of the human intellect, and attributes the superiority of that court to the role of priests. Josephus (*Ant* 4.218) identifies the court in the holy city as "the chief priest and the prophet and the senate." Pearce rejects the view that Josephus based his description on the Sanhedrin, and sees it rather as a theoretical ideal. In *Against Apion* 2.187–94 he describes it as a court of priests, led by the High Priest.

The book concludes with an "Epilogue," which synthesizes the findings in relation to each of the main sources.

Pearce provides an excellent, detailed commentary on the passages in Second Temple literature that reflect the relevant sections of Deuteronomy. I have only minor quibbles with her treatment. I am not convinced that the paleographic evidence requires a pre-Hasmonean date for the *Temple Scroll* (or the Deuteronomic paraphrase that is one of its sources). A date in the second half of the second century BCE seems quite plausible. Neither am I convinced that "the book of the Torah" in the *Temple Scroll* is Deuteronomy. If so, how should the *Temple Scroll* itself, which is presented as direct divine revelation, be identified? Pearce is not necessarily wrong on these issues, but there are plausible alternatives to be considered. But on the whole, this is a rich and judicious discussion of the relevant passages.

The book is less successful in addressing the broader questions posed in the "Introduction": "To what extent were the laws of Deut. 16:18–17:13 already recognized in this period as laws for an ideal constitution? Did Jewish interpreters think that these laws should be put into practical effect, and if so how and by whom? How do the laws relate to existing judicial institutions?" Pearce is quite clear that these laws cannot be taken to reflect actual practice in any period. She does not, however, discuss the actual judicial practice of Second Temple Jews as revealed by the papyri. Such a discussion would be very helpful to put the theoretical literature in perspective. It would have been too much to attempt in this book, but it remains a desideratum for future research.

John J. Collins
Yale

FRED LEDEGANG, *Philo van Alexandrië Over de tien woorden, De Decalogo.* Budel, Netherlands: Damon, 2011. 149 pages. ISBN 978-94-6036-024-4. Price €22.90 (hb).

This book is only the second in modern times to present a translation of a complete work of Philo into the Dutch language. The first was the volume of G. H. de Vries, who in 1999 published translations of *Flacc.* and *Legat.* (reviewed in this journal in vol. 11 pp. 177–181). The author, a Dutch theologian and classical scholar, is best known for his research on Origen, publishing his dissertation under the title *Mysterium ecclesiae: Images of the Church and its Members in Origen* (Leuven 2001). It was not a great leap for him to turn to Origen's great Alexandrian predecessor and the source of so much of his exegetical techniques and themes.

The elegantly produced volume opens with an extensive introduction, which begins with an account of the arrival of Jews in Egypt and Alexandria and then moves on to an account of Philo and his "philosophy" before focusing on the content of the treatise that is being translated. The *De Decalogo* is an interesting choice, the movitation for which is not made explicit in the translator's preface. Ledegang points out that the Decalogue contains the main themes of the Law which are further explicated in the remaining laws (p. 7) and that Philo is the first author to write a separate treatise on it. It is striking, he notes elsewhere (p. 43), that the treatise only once makes use of the method of allegorical or symbolic interpretation (§49). The explanation he gives is that the Decalogue was given to the people by God himself and so was universally valid, whereas the particular laws needed allegorical interpretation in order to qualify for such universal application. It might be argued that for this reason the treatise is less suitable as a general introduction to Philo. On the other hand, it does illustrate well many Philonic themes, including the extensive use of concepts from Greek philosophy to explain biblical precepts.

The translation is based on the text in the Loeb Classical Library. It sensibly chooses a middle path between a literal rendering and a freer, more literary and modern style. Generally speaking it reads well. In one respect, however, I find its approach unusual. It systematically divides up Philo's long sentences into shorter units. There is nothing wrong with doing that. Most modern translators do the same. But this translation takes it to an extreme. In particular, it has numerous sentences starting with "Want" (the Dutch word for γάρ, that great bugbear for all translators of Greek). Sometimes there are also sentences starting with "Dat" (the Dutch word for "that") without being preceded by an introductory verb. A fine example of this method is the final paragraph of the work, §178. Philo's single lengthy Greek period is divided into four sentences, of which the first and last start with "Want," the second with "Maar dat" ("But that") and the third with "Dat." The effect is rather unusual and in my view not entirely satisfactory. The translator surprisingly does not avail himself of the Dutch word "immers" ("yet" in English, but with a causal sense), which is a fine way of dealing with the ubiquitous γάρ that is not available to the English translator.

The translation is accompanied by extensive footnotes which confirm that the author has thoroughly immersed himself in Philo and Philonic scholarship. The indices and bibliography are also very extensive, taking up a full twenty percent of the volume. Readers of Dutch will be grateful to the author and his publisher for undertaking this project and it is to be hoped that further Philonic treatises will follow. There are plenty to choose from.

David T. Runia
Queen's College
The University of Melbourne

TOBIAS GEORGES, FELIX ALBRECHTS and REINHARD FELDMEIER, eds., *Alexandria*. Civitatum Orbis Mediterranei Studia 1. Tübingen: Mohr Siebeck, 2013. xiv + 574 pages. ISBN 978-3-16-1516733. Price €139, $237 (hb).

The volume is based on an interdisciplinary symposion on Alexandria in 2010, the contributions of which were originally published in the series Biblische Notizen (BN 147/148). These contributions were extended and others added to create the first volume of the new series COMES, Civitatum Orbis Mediterranei Studia.

The book has five parts. The first focuses on the archaeology and history of Alexandria, the following parts on pagan, Jewish, Christian and Muslim Alexandria respectively. Thus it embraces roughly one-thousand five hundred years of the city's existence. The contributions (all in German) span a broad range of topics. They are introduced by a brief preface which summarises the contents and goes some way towards linking them.

The first part opens with a chapter by B. Bäbler on the archaeology of Alexandria, its foundation, the royal quarter, the lighthouse, public places, canals and cisterns, necropoleis, and the new city centre in late antiquity. Then D. Engler describes the scientific research and technological advances in mathematics, geography, astronomy, medicine, and mechanics developed in the city. H.-G. Nesselrath turns to what is known about the Museion and the Great Library, looking especially at their origin, the question of whether they were separate or the same institution, and outlining their history during Ptolemaic and Roman imperial times.

The part on pagan Alexandria begins with J. Zangenberg's observations on the social history of Greeks, Egyptians and Jews in Greco-Roman Alexandria which led to the pogrom of 38 C.E. I. Tanaseanu-Döbler studies philosophy in Alexandria, focusing on the circle around Ammonios Sakkas and his disciples. M. Bommas then looks into the theology and iconography of the Isis cult in Alexandria. And finally S. Schmidt researches the relevance of the statues of pagan idols, using the example of the fall of Serapis and the relevance of the Serapis cult for Alexandrian society in late antiquity.

The section on Jewish Alexandria is the largest and contains chapters on many important aspects of Jewish life in the city. The chapter by A.-M. Schwemer on the Greek and Jewish legends about the founding of the city compares them to other Greek foundation legends and the early Alexander traditions. Then R. G. Kratz develops a theory about a "biblical" and a "non-biblical" Judaism in Egypt, a contrast he sees in all aspects of Jewish life (origin, identity, political status, every-day life, religion, and literature) in Alexandria and Elephantine. F. Albrecht's contribution considers the

Septuagint's relevance, focusing on its origins, editions, as well as its tradition- and reception-history. F. V. Reiterer develops a contrast between Jerusalem and Alexandria focussing on OT faith in the context of Hellenistic politics and education. J. Dochorn problematizes the concept of Alexandrian Jewish literature and gives an overview of those texts that potentially originate in ancient Judaism (not just in Alexandria). K. Schöpflin studies the Hellenization of Jewish terms for God using the example of the book of Tobit. M. R. Niehoff looks into Jewish Bible interpretation between exegesis of Homer and later Christian exegesis, a short version of her recent book on the topic, *Jewish Exegesis and Homeric Scholarship in Alexandria* (Cambridge 2011). Philo not only plays a part in this chapter on allegory, but his arithmology of the number five receives discussion in B. Wyss' contribution. The section concludes with A.-M. Schwemer's overview of the Diaspora revolt under Trajan (115–117 CE), which effectively ended Jewish life in Alexandria.

The section on Christian Alexandria begins with the only known Christian Alexandrian of the movement's first generation, Apollos. J. Wehnert summarises what might be concluded about his life and teaching. W. Löhr then studies second cent. Christian "Gnostics" in Alexandria. The more "orthodox" side of Christianity is represented by R. Sedlak's chapter on the life and work of Clement, his criticism of false teachers and the composition of the *Stromateis*. P. Gemeinhardt then raises the issue of Christian attitudes toward pagan education, using the example of Origen and his reception.

Muslim Alexandria receives the shortest treatment in the book, with a single chapter by H. Biesterfeld on the transfer of Alexandrian education and knowledge to Baghdad over the centuries.

In spite of the limited scope of the last chapter, the volume as a whole does not restrict itself to a discussion of the intellectual influence of Alexandria. Its contributions are independent of each other, which means that sometimes the only connection between them is the occasional reference to "Alexandria." Not all of them even focus on the city itself, as can be seen in J. Dochorn's chapter, which rejects any attempt to identify specific "Alexandrian" texts.

Some chapters demonstrate that the authors are experts in their own area of expertise, but they do not draw on other, related issues. Thus I. Tanaseanu-Döbler neglects to relate Origen's views to his Jewish exegetical predecessor in Alexandria, Philo (p. 116–17), and S. Schmidt discusses the early Christian polemic against idols with recourse to Greek philosophers, whose opinions do not quite match (p. 166), but without recourse to OT idolatry criticism (such as Isa 2:8; Hos 14:1–3; Hab 2:5–20; Wisd 14:6) which matches the Christian views.

Occasionally the chapters present the authors' views rather than a consensus. Thus R. G. Kratz's contrasting of a later biblical and an earlier non-biblical Judaism in Egypt is highly debatable, especially when he writes about the Egyptian synagogue "according to the Palestinian model" in the second century B.C.E. At the time there were no synagogues in Judea and there is little evidence for synagogues in the rest of Palestine. The earliest *proseuchai* are found in Egypt at roughly the same time as the translation of the first books of the Septuagint, which indicates a relationship between the place and the study of Torah. On a less controversial but still relevant note, J. Dochorn's scepticism towards the possibility of the reconstruction of Alexandrian Jewish literature does not take into account that Philo, who undeniably is Alexandrian, is not a lone author and draws on a fertile literary tradition. Thus while it is not possible to prove Alexandrian provenance for a number of ancient Jewish texts, it is possible to point out probabilities.

Yet, while the contributions are individual and varied, it is precisely the independence and the special expertise of the authors that makes the volume so useful. The chapters are very well written and of a high scholarly standard. They relate to a wide range of topics, including Classics, ancient history, early Judaism, Christianity, as well as classical influence on Islam. Anyone working on these topics will find this book highly relevant for their research, and those readers merely interested in the city will find a stimulating overview of its versatile history and influence. It is the kind of book which makes learning German academically worthwhile.

Jutta Leonhardt-Balzer
University of Aberdeen

CARLOS FRAENKEL, *Philosophical Religions from Plato to Spinoza: Reason, Religion, and Autonomy*. Cambridge: Cambridge University Press, 2012. xxvii + 328 pages. ISBN 978-0-521-19457-0. Price $99 (hb), $33 (pb).

Though philosophy and religion often have been perceived as unlikely bedfellows, Fraenkel charts a lengthy tradition (from Plato to Spinoza!) in which they not only coexist, but one in which religious texts and traditions are harnessed and adapted by philosophers to legislate a rationally-oriented socio-political order. In his preface, Fraenkel posits a tidy relationship between the two entities, one that connects them through the exercise and fulfillment of reason: the "metaphysical foundation of a philosophical religion" is "the concept of God as Reason," and at its heart lies "the ideal of Godlikeness attained through the perfection of reason" (p. 6). This emphasis placed on reason by proponents of philosophical religion, as well as the pervasive presence of irrelevant and irrational religious beliefs and practices, however, leads inevitably to a tilted relationship, with religion serving as philosophy's "handmaid." Allegorical interpretation of religious texts and traditions is therefore necessary, since philosophical truths can "be located in, but not learned from, a religious tradition. As a consequence, the transition from the literal to the allegorical content can only be made by someone with prior philosophical training. This, in turn, implies that philosophy is not only the foundation and the goal of religion, but also holds the key to its true content" (p. 15).

At the head of this tradition stands Plato. Unfortunately, Fraenkel's forty-nine page treatment of Plato's philosophical-religious project is hard to follow, as its organization and progression are not readily apparent, and even with repeated readings they remain somewhat unclear. Additionally, the discussion is largely uninformed by recent scholarship, and a number of crucial topics are mishandled or ignored altogether. Plato's political theory is complex, and is perhaps most coherent when analyzed through the lens of the developmental approach, according to which Plato's ideas varied and/or were refined over time. The early Socratic dialogues, hobbled by epistemological and ethical *aporiae*, fail to offer a developed theory, while the *Republic*, from the middle period, benefits from the certain knowledge afforded by the Forms, and accordingly offers a detailed account of the ideal city and its political agenda. In that city, the two lower classes of citizens lack autonomy as well as access to true happiness and virtue. They must therefore be coercively ruled by an elite class of philosopher-rulers. In the *Laws*, from Plato's later period, the totalitarian program of the *Republic* is superseded by a more egalitarian "second best city," which educates its citizenry and attempts to persuade them to abide by social norms through appeals to reason. Coercion and constraint are less prominent, though notable exceptions involve atheists and religious mavericks (*Leg.* 907d–910d). Though the scope and scale of the legislation in the *Laws* is more extensive than that offered in the *Republic*, the *Laws* affords its populace, including women, a significant measure of autonomy, even allowing them to seek office. And while that autonomy is achieved through unconditional obedience to the laws of the city, the *Laws* prioritizes the attainment of a virtuous and happy life, at least to the extent possible for non-philosophers of varying levels of understanding and wisdom.

Though covering a wide range of texts, Fraenkel's analysis of Plato's political theory emphasizes the *Laws*, as this text is the closest Plato comes to offering a pedagogical-political program for non-philosophers (p. 63). Moreover, he contends that the *Laws* establishes the procedural precedent which all subsequent proponents of philosophical religion will follow. According to Plato's program, the "existing beliefs, practices, and institutions" of the ideal state, though initially "established by philosopher-rulers," are now largely misunderstood. The task of the philosopher-rulers presently in power is to engage in a "philosophical reinterpretation" of these "beliefs, practices, and institutions," and recover their latent intent (pp. 14, 84). Perhaps the best example of the aforementioned civic education in the *Laws* is evident in the explanatory and suasory preludes to the individual statutes and the law code itself (722c–723d; cf. Fraenkel, pp. 72–73).

As for other examples of a "pedagogical-political program for non-philosophers," Fraenkel appeals to the myths (e.g., the sun, line, and cave in the *Republic*, and the palinode in the *Phaedrus*), which he construes as poetic "images and parables" of "true doctrine" (pp. 67, 80). These myths, along with the "representation of God as a craftsman in the *Timaeus* and as a lawgiver in the *Laws*," are "likenesses which provide non-philosophers with an understanding (albeit imperfect in comparison to the philosopher's knowledge) of the metaphysical foundation of the natural and political order." Moreover, "these likenesses of true doctrines are part of the wisdom that makes self-rule possible for non-philosophers" (p. 80). Plato's myths have recently benefitted from a number of excellent treatments, and a recurring conviction, evident in many studies, is that no easy line of demarcation can be drawn between *mythos* and *logos*. As Kathryn Morgan observes, "by blurring the boundaries between *mythos* and *logos*, by tying myth so firmly into the philosophical context, by making it arise from and reflect dialectic, and finally, by sometimes labeling philosophical theory as *mythos*, Plato forces us to realize that all language is a story that interprets reality" (*Myth and Philosophy from the Presocratics to Plato*, Cambridge: Cambridge University Press, 2000, 287). Fraenkel's characterization of Plato's myths as "likenesses of true doctrines," offered for the guidance of non-philosophers, is therefore questionable. Furthermore, his claim that "Plato has no doctrine of allegorical interpretation" (p. 97) is apparently uninformed by *Phaedr.* 229c–230a, a text in which Plato's Socrates trivializes the allegorical interpretation of pre-existing myths (cf. Daniel S. Werner, *Myth and Philosophy in Plato's* Phaedrus, Cambridge: Cambridge University Press, 2012, 30–35).

Perhaps more egregious is Fraenkel's analysis of the role of religion in Plato's thought and practice, which is impoverished by its singular emphasis on reason. As has already been noted, Fraenkel considers "the center of a philosophical religion" to be "the ideal of Godlikeness," which is of course to be "attained through the perfection of reason" (p. 6). Moreover, a "visitor to Hellenistic Athens would find that all major philosophical schools—Platonists, Aristotelians, Epicureans, Stoics, and even Pyrrhonian skeptics—take Godlikeness to be the highest human perfection and promote their philosophy as the path to attain it" (p. 25). Leaving aside the imprecision of such a broad ascription of this particular *telos* to all philosophical schools, Fraenkel's exclusive emphasis on perfected reason in the *locus classicus* of the *homoiosis theoi* motif, *Theaet.* 176a–b, is particularly problematic (cf. pp. 52–53). At least two other aspects of this text, both of which are decidedly religious, are neglected: the ascetic "spirituality" evident in the "flight" from embodied existence, and the equation of "likeness to God" with becoming "holy." In his detailed study of this text, David Sedley attributes the surprising inclusion of "holiness" (ὁσιότης) in *Theaet.* 176b to Socrates' "religious convictions" ("The Ideal of Godlikeness," in *Plato 2: Ethics, Politics, Religion, and the Soul,* ed. Gail Fine; Oxford Readings in Philosophy. Oxford: Oxford University Press, 1999, 309–328, here 313). This text, a refutation of Protagoras' relativist doctrine that "humans are the measure of all things," does not offer the expected counter-proposal, i.e., a defense of divinely instituted moral standards. Instead, Plato's Socrates claims that the deity embodies the highest moral standards, thus providing humanity with the perfect exemplar of their instantiation (so Sedley, "The Ideal of Godlikeness," 314). The ascetic discipline underlying this text is also integral to Platonic piety, and is thoroughly imbued with a religious texture (cf. the recurring language of "purification" in *Phaed.* 66c–67d). Moreover, this praxis is organically tethered to Plato's religio-eschatological beliefs, as the philosopher who has freed him/herself from the passions of the non-rational aspects of his/her soul will enjoy a comparably blessed state in the hereafter (cf. *Phaed.* 80d–81e; *Gorg.* 524b–527e; and Harold Tarrant, "Literal and Deeper Meanings in Platonic Myths," in *Plato and Myth: Studies on the Use and Status of Platonic Myths,* ed. Catherine Collobert, Pierre Destrée, and Francisco J. Gonzalez; Mnemosyne Supplements 337; Leiden: Brill, 2012, 47–65, esp. 55–59). Though the rigors of this practice effectively restrict its applicability, even in the ideal city, it is nevertheless an integral aspect of Platonic philosophical piety. In his discussion of Plato's asceticism, Fraenkel fails to note both its religious texture, as well as its holistic connection with eschatology (pp. 54–60).

Fraenkel's consideration of Philo is preceded and followed by discussions of Clement, Origen, and Eusebius. According to these early Christian "philosophers," the historical priority of Moses helps establish Plato's dependence on Moses' "philosophy"; nevertheless, Plato often exerts the stronger influence. Plato's hierarchically oriented pedagogical-political scheme finds gainful employment in the interpretation of the sacred scriptures of Israel and the church, as the literal sense of these sacred texts is useful for guiding non-philosophers, while their hidden allegorical content discloses true philosophy for the initiate. Surfacing that philosophical content is problematic, however, since the "allegorical doctrines" of scripture "cannot be learned from Scripture but only disclosed through the interpreter who already knows them. Thus, Judaism and Christianity fail to provide the resources necessary to grasp their own truth" (p. 90). And in contrast to Philo, Origen believes the literal content can be discarded by those who have attained the "gospel of reason" (*Princ.* 3.6, 8; Fraenkel, p. 91).

Fraenkel's treatment of Philo's political-pedagogical program is some eighteen pages in length, and as with his discussion of Plato, interaction with contemporary scholarship is for the most part absent. He nevertheless commendably charts Philo's appreciation and adaptation of Moses' protreptic enterprise, with pedagogical guidance offered to "imperfectly rational members of the community" through "laws, stories, exhortations, and practices of worship," and "in proportion to the capacity of the recipient" (pp. 113–114; cf. pp. 118–122). And in a manner comparable to Plato's preludes in the *Laws*, Philo considers Moses' law to be essentially hortatory in nature, with persuasive "preludes and epilogues" that appeal to reason more prominently than bare commands or threats (*Mos.* 2.49–51; Fraenkel, pp. 118–122; cf. also the heuristic use of Philo's political-pedagogical effort in relation to Plato's *Laws*, in Julia Annas, "Virtue and Law in Plato," in *Plato's* Laws: *a Critical Guide,* ed. Christopher Bobonich; Cambridge Critical Guides; Cambridge: Cambridge University Press, 2010, 71–91). Furthermore, since Moses also "agrees with Plato that philosophy ought not to be taught to everyone," the law of Moses accordingly does not explicitly teach philosophy. It does, however, contain "true philosophical doctrines on the allegorical level" (p. 114). Anthropomorphic and anthropopathic representations of God, mythical depictions offered for the benefit of non-philosophers, are resolved on the allegorical level (p. 115). In all this, Fraenkel might have benefited from recent scholarship concerning the various intended audiences of the three different commentaries. Also unexamined are Philo's ubiquitous three stages of spiritual, moral, and philosophic development, which would have provided Fraenkel with a useful pedagogical model in depicting the progress and path from "non-philosopher," "not-yet-philosopher" (potential philosopher), to the adept philosopher.

Also of interest is Fraenkel's almost dispensational appraisal of Philo's self-understanding of his exegetical work. Socio-cultural advances and the gradual inculcation of the Mosaic law have contributed to the intellectual advancement of the Jewish people in Philo's time, thus obviating many of the primitive laws and practices in the law. Philo therefore sees himself as taking "the project of Moses one step further," elevating "the community as a whole to a higher level of perfection by partly disclosing Scripture's allegorical content" (p. 116). Fraenkel could have gained greater conceptual clarity for this assertion had he availed himself of David M. Hay's essay, "Philo's View of Himself as an Exegete: Inspired, but not Authoritative," *SPhA* 3 (1991): 40–52.

Certain to raise eyebrows are claims concerning the philosophic value of the Mosaic law and the relationship of exegesis to the practice of philosophy. Fraenkel insists that the Mosaic law "is not the kind of book whose study can lead to wisdom"; it therefore "plays no part" in Philo's own quest for wisdom and "philosophical inspiration" (p. 117). Though the autobiographical text of *Congr.* 74–76, with its singular focus on the encyclical studies, would seem to support the latter assertion, the other autobiographical text Fraenkel appeals to, *Spec.* 3.1, does not. Scriptural study frames *Spec.* 3.1–6: the "divine words and themes" (θείοις λόγοις ... καὶ δόγμασιν) that Philo identifies as playing an instrumental role in his philosophic praxis most likely represents a reference to sacred Scripture, and in 3.6 he exhorts the reader to "behold" him in his study, carefully scrutinizing and interpreting the "sacred words of Moses." The general claim that Moses' law "is not the kind of book whose study can lead to wisdom" is also easily refuted: (1) in a number of texts describing contemporary Jewish religious practice, the study of the law is defined as "philosophy," and portrayed as integral to a disciplined pursuit of wisdom (*Mos.* 2.214–215; *Spec.* 2.61–63; *Contempl.* 28, 67–78). (2) A comparable number of texts seem to indicate that the Mosaic law is a "faithful copy" of the law of nature (*Opif.* 3; *Mos.* 2.14, 48, 51), which further indicates a perceived conflation of wisdom/philosophy and scriptural exegesis. Accordingly, Philo's "contemplation of the cosmos" (θεωρία τοῦ κόσμου), recounted in *Spec.* 3.1, may actually reflect the study of Gen 1–2 rather than the heavens themselves. Fraenkel's distinction between exegesis and wisdom/philosophy is therefore completely foreign to Philo's thought and praxis (see, e.g., David T. Runia, *Philo of Alexandria and the Timaeus of Plato*, Philosophia Antiqua 44; Leiden: Brill, 1986, 535–42).

With regard to both Plato and Philo, Fraenkel's narrow, reason-centered construal of religion, with reason equated with revelation (p. 109), and religion assigned a subservient role as the "handmaid" to philosophy, is also subject to critique. Despite the valorization of reason in the thought of both ancient authors, a wealth of texts can be appealed to in support of a more holistic understanding, one in which a mutual relationship between religion and philosophy inheres. Thus, religion, as the handmaid to philosophy, is figured as leading to philosophic wisdom, but then the philosophic enterprise itself is accorded a religious texture, particularly in its highest expressions. In both Plato and Philo, the *telos* of philosophic achievement is occasionally depicted using the language and imagery of the mysteries, with ecstatic psychosomatic states accompanying a heightened state of knowledge (Plato, *Phaedr*. 244a–257b; *Symp*. 210a–212a; Philo, *Opif*. 69–71; *Migr*. 34–35; *Somn*. 1.164–165; *Spec*. 3.1–6). This inherent mutuality limits the applicability of a linear, one-sided model of their relationship, as well as an exclusive emphasis on rational states of knowledge. The emphasis on ecstatic states of knowledge also highlights the "givenness" of religio-philosophical experiential insight, representing as such a revelatory and divine gift of supra-rational and supernatural knowledge.

The last half of Fraenkel's book traces the development of religious philosophy in the thought of al-Fārābī, Averroes, Maimonides, and Spinoza. The optimistic epistemology of Aristotle may have contributed to al-Fārābī's belief that allegorical interpretations of sacred writ should be available to the general populace, philosopher and non-philosopher alike (p. 201). Motivating this decision is the conviction that the content of sacred writ is an "imitation of philosophy," which is "false if understood literally" (p. 161). In contrast, al-Fārābī's successor, Averroes, believed exposure to philosophy was likely to lead non-philosophers astray; he therefore restricted the use of allegory to philosophers (p. 169). Though Maimonides considered the Mosaic law in its entirety to be "perfectly rational," and "a perfect instantiation of the Divine Law," it is nevertheless an imitation of philosophy, "spoken in the language of cave dwellers" (pp. 176–78). Though it "contains wisdom, it is not possible to learn wisdom from it" (p. 178). Allegorical interpretation informed by Platonic philosophy is therefore required. This allegorical content should not be indiscriminately disseminated; the "pedagogical-political guidance" of religious leaders will instead gradually disclose its contents, thereby habituating and advancing non-philosophers to philosophical wisdom (pp. 182–83). This "step by step," gradual advancement is even evident in the Mosaic law, as its sacrificial laws, promises of rewards and punishments, and anthropomorphic portrayals of the deity all represent pedagogical "ruses," "false beliefs" that were "necessary only for a certain stage of the Jews' cultural religious development" (p. 189). Fraenkel's lengthy discussion of Spinoza chronologically follows the development of his thought, from apostate Jew, to his early attempts at philosophically reconciling scripture with reason, to the *Tractatus Theologico-Politicus*, which may well have laid the groundwork for the modern historical-critical method of biblical interpretation, as well as the radical Enlightenment's critique of religion.

The conclusion examines the legacy of Spinoza (in particular, Reimarus, Lessing, Kant, and Hegel) and questions whether secularization and the "paternalistic premise" of philosophical religions have rendered the whole enterprise obsolete (p. 297). Despite the aforementioned shortcomings in the sections on Plato and Philo, Fraenkel is to be commended for ably demonstrating the extent of their influence in subsequent thought, as well as strategically situating them in this long tradition.

Scott D. Mackie
Venice, California, U.S.A.

MARK EDWARDS. *Image, Word and God in the Early Christian Centuries.* Ashgate Studies in Philosophy & Theology in Late Antiquity. Surrey: Ashgate, 2013. 220 pages. ISBN 978-1-4094-0671-6. Price £19.99, $39.95 (pb).

The work under review is a survey of ancient attitudes toward images and words as they capture (or fail to capture) the nature of the divine. The tension between word and image is apparent in the Bible and early Christianity as well as in Platonic philosophy. Plato repudiates both word and image, but early Christian thinkers saw in Christ both the image of God in the flesh and the word of God in the scriptures. Nevertheless, for the church all extra-biblical images were to be eschewed until the early fourth century when the veneration of religious images becomes increasingly common.

Neoplatonists generally regarded images of the true Forms to have been impressed upon the human soul in the higher sphere. The task is to awaken the memory of those images through the study of texts, and those of Homer and Plato in particular. Only truths that were impressed in the higher realm can be accessed from the human soul. This stands in contrast to the early Christian view that all truth was located in Scripture and can be extracted by the skilled exegete.

Chapter one is a survey of Old Testament presentations of the deity, with the conclusion that words almost always accompany a theophany, indicating the superiority of words over images. In the second chapter, Edwards surveys the New Testament materials and highlights a much more intimate connection with God as visual image in the flesh. Jesus is "light" (John 8:12), and even intimates that he is the visual manifestation of the Father (John 14:9). An emphasis is placed on eyewitness testimony (2 Pet 1:16; 1 John 1:1) and on visual signs as confirmation of the Gospel (2 Cor 12:12; Heb 2:4).

Chapter three discusses the tension between word and image in classical Greek thought. On the whole the Greeks prefer the word to the image because of the tendency of images to deceive. Plato most prominently repudiates both word and image, but ironically represents both in the dialogue form. Aristotle prefers literature that evokes mental images, but warns that literature can deceive the mind (Homer and Hesiod in particular). The Stoics perhaps best harmonize word and image when they interpret literary scenes and even statues allegorically.

Chapter four covers thinkers from the early Roman era. Here Edwards discusses Philo most prominently. Philo, following the Second Commandment, rejects any plastic representation of God, and hence exalts the word as supreme. But he does not reject images altogether. For Philo hearing God and seeing God are virtually identical since we hear the word of God through the mind's eye. A biblical analogy can be found in Exod 20:18 which Philo interprets as a visible voice (cf. the Stoic understanding of voice as "struck air"). The human *logos endiathetos* alone is capable of "seeing God," an ethical state embodied in "Israel," etymologically understood as those who "see God." The next major thinker treated in this chapter, Plutarch, actually attempts a synthesis of word and image. Plutarch's awareness that Egyptian writing is pictographic leads him to regard images and words as essentially identical in their limitations.

The fifth chapter surveys Christian thinkers of the second century, all of whom reject the plastic image, and all of whom agree that Jesus as Word manifests the intellect of God in the scriptures. As guarantor of the written word, the Church is "the visible body of the Word" (p. 96). The human being is the only acceptable image since it was formed by God himself. The sixth chapter treats further thinkers from the second and third centuries. Tertullian believes that Christ pre-existed before the world as speech (*sermo*), manifested himself in angelic form to the patriarchs, took on human flesh, and inspired the apostles and prophets of the early church after his ascension. Clement adds to this idea the notion that Christ dwells in the hearts of his followers.

Origen adopts and extends the themes of his predecessors, arguing that Scripture is merely a continuation of the incarnate ministry of Christ, his *logos* being embedded no longer in human flesh but now in the written word. Scripture communicates to human beings at all levels, for the literal words of Scripture are "at once a veil and a vehicle to the deeper sense, as his flesh was at once the cloak and organ of his divinity" (p. 114).

Chapter seven discusses the Neoplatonists Plotinus, Porphyry and Iamblichus. Plotinus was willing to regard man-made images as imperfect representations of the eternal since the temporal cosmos was itself a diminished copy of the eternal Form. Porphyry continued these views even further, placing the image on par with the text. Rather than stressing the inadequacy of images to represent truth, Porphyry stresses the inadequacy of texts to do the same. Poets thus take license to "cheat the senses" because they are unable to represent the truth as it is. Artists do not have the same opportunity because they are confined to the plastic medium. Finally, Iamblichus "mentions images only to condemn them" (p. 133). He produces a number of commentaries, implying that words, at least in the dialogues of Plato, are legitimate approximations of truth, even if he also condemns both images and words as imperfect deformities of the true Forms.

Chapter eight surveys the fourth-century Christian attitude toward images. Prior to the fourth-century the church almost uniformly rejected the veneration of religious images. However, the attitude changes apparently during the reign of Constantine. Eusebius can boast of the church's possession of likenesses of Peter, Paul, and even of Jesus himself (*H.E.* 7.17). There is also a rise in the detailing of visionary experiences, such as Constantine's vision at the Milvian Bridge. Eusebius even treats "image" and "word" as complimentary terms in reference to Christ, the former referring to the paradigmatic human nature in which God made man, and the latter referring to Christ as the verbal expression of the divine intellect.

Chapter nine is devoted entirely to Proclus, who continues the focus of Iamblichus and even contemporary Christian thinkers in exalting the Platonic dialogues as repositories of cosmic truths. Nevertheless, they fall short of representing true Forms, which are present to the mind's eye only as images, albeit imperfect ones. The final chapter discusses the Christian Platonists Augustine and Dionysius the Areopagite. Both maintain the supremacy of text over image. Even when God communicates with the soul directly, Augustine says, he will do so through hearing rather than through seeing. The soul is led up to God by his grace, but proper exegesis of the biblical text is a *sine qua non* for contemplation of the divine.

Some criticisms of the book include numerous typographical errors, especially in the early chapters. For example, Edwards cites "Raifs" instead of "Rahlfs" (p. 5), 1 Cor instead of 2 Cor (p. 27), "Galations" instead of "Galatians" (p. 37). In addition, Edwards routinely fails to italicize consistently when he transliterates Greek letters, namely $\hat{e}$ and $\hat{o}$ (pp. 24–26, 36, 47, 55, 57, 90, 100, 118). He normally provides the English title *Creation* for Philo's *Opif.*, but in one instance titles it *Making* (p. 104; this passage is also absent from the index). One might also quibble over the title of the book, since entire chapters are devoted to the Old Testament and the Classical tradition, which hardly fall "in the early Christian centuries."

Despite these disappointments, Edwards fairly and effectively engages the polyvalent applications of "image" and "word" in the ancient world. From statues to mental impressions, the image in general fails to convey the clarity and poignancy of the word, whether spoken or written. An interfusion of the dichotomy between word and image occurs at the incarnation of Christ, and early Christians found both aspects of his nature useful in Christological discussions. Ultimately, image is subjected to word as an adequate representation of the divine in Christian thought. Neoplatonism was less uniform, but continued to acknowledge the validity of image either in addition to or over against word, even though both provide incomplete portraits of the divine.

Justin M. Rogers
Freed-Hardeman University
Henderson, Tennessee, U.S.A.

PAUL M. BLOWERS. *Drama of the Divine Economy: Creator and Creation in Early Christian Theology and Piety*. Oxford: Oxford University Press, 2012. 448 pages. ISBN: 978-01-99-66041-4. Price $150 (hb).

Blowers' book is a substantive survey of early Christian cosmology that, though acknowledging antecedent and contemporaneous Greco-Roman philosophical traditions as well as Hellenistic Jewish writings, seeks to highlight an internal coherence arising from distinctly Christian convictions that creation and redemption were "seamlessly entwined" (p. 12). Christian writers between the NT and the Middle Ages (the period Blowers surveys) "rarely, if ever, undertook straightforward expositions of cosmogony, metaphysics, physics, astronomy, etc. in isolation from ulterior theological and didactic concerns" (p. 3). They did not engage in cosmology for cosmology's sake but as part of an effort to present the world "in the mirror of the eschatological drama unfolded in Scripture" (p. 17), specifically the "end" of that drama, Jesus Christ, whose incarnation was already the drama's central plot even before the founding of the world.

Blowers' first chapter introduces this argument and sketches how the next eight chapters and epilogue will support it. Though his concern is the internal coherence of Christian understandings of cosmology, Blowers spends two chapters examining the Greco-Roman and then Hellenistic "legacies" that Christian authors received, reworked, and/or refuted. Chapter 2 presumes that the Greco-Roman cosmological legacy was not uniform but made up of traditions that were still rather fluid by the turn of the era. Blowers also notes that just as the biblical tradition had a philosophical aspect of sorts in its wisdom tradition, Greek natural philosophy had a connection with pagan theology and piety (see, e.g., Cleanthes' *Hymn to Zeus*). The chapter first looks at the divide between those who held to an infinite universe (such as the Atomists) and those to a closed world (Platonists, Peripatetics, and Stoics). The former claimed there was no "purposive beginning (*archē*) or end (*telos*)" (p. 22) to the cosmos, which comes about from randomly moving atoms in an infinite void. The latter more readily allowed that everything was the result of creation or at least some divinely determined design or end (though there was no uniformity, as seen in the contrast between Plato's *Timaeus* with its demiurgic myth and Aristotle's counter that the world had no beginning or end). It is this tension that Blowers explores next, looking at the spectrum of views about divine "creative" (or non-creative) cosmological activity. After a helpful review of Pre-Socratic approaches to "creationism," Blowers provides a thoughtful analysis of Plato's *Timaeus*. This inestimably influential myth would in very many ways come to serve as a "stimulating ideological" foil to early Christians' theology of creation. This is because the *Timaeus* was not a simple exercise in physics or metaphysics but, rather, Plato's espousal of "the cosmological matrix of the human story, and of human aspiration in politics, ethics, and more" (p. 29). The last part of chapter 2 looks at various philosophical views about "first principles" (*archai*). Whether as ontological principles or conceptual starting points, the different philosophical traditions gave these *archai* prominent roles not just in theology, teleology, physics, and metaphysics but also in ethics and morality.

Blowers' third chapter considers a second formative legacy of early Christian cosmology, Hellenistic Judaism. In particular, he examines the teleology, mediation of creation through Wisdom/Logos, and the scheme of God's creative activity in the two most important Hellenistic Jewish sources for Patristic theologians, namely Wisdom of Solomon and the writings of Philo of Alexandria. The treatment of Wisdom of Solomon concisely (four pages) shows how salvation history fulfills creation. The work of creation moves beyond cosmogony to include God's continuing involvement in the world as well as in the world's becoming, with Wisdom's guidance, an active player in God's redemptive work. Philo receives greater attention (seventeen pages). Acknowledging Philo's indebtedness to Middle Platonism, Blowers first looks at the Logos' role as bridging the "strict ontological divide" between the transcendent deity and material creation. Aware of the many difficulties in the source material and scholarly disagreements about Philo's Logos (such as whether the Logos is a metaphor or distinct entity), Blowers is careful not to overreach. He provides a duly cautious yet constructive presentation of the Logos' mediating role, emphasizing how the Logos guides both creation and individual souls to their ultimate perfection. For humans, this perfection is achieved through an "intimacy with the Logos that comes through ... stewardship of 'right reason,'" which includes "speculation into physics, contemplation (*theōria*) of the created world, and allegorical interpretation of Scripture"(p. 52). Blowers next brings to the fore themes in Philo's model of divine creation that he contends had the most influence on early Christian creationism: namely how creation came to have its beginning; whether creation from matter was *ex nihilo, aeterna*, or *continua*; and whether creation would eternally endure. In regards to the world's beginning, he explains how Philo finds in Gen 1–2 a "double creation" where the intelligible world arises 'simultaneously' as a perfect order and then occurs in time and space by the Creator's providential administration. In regards to creation from matter, Blowers is attracted to Winston's interpretation in terms of a *creatio aeterna*, but suggests it should be corrected in the direction of a theory of *creatio continua* or *simultanea* as proposed by Runia and Sterling. This view falls short by Patristic standards, however, since it did not sufficiently overcome the Platonic notion of matter as "an *archē* enjoying the Creator's pure eternity and priority" (p. 65; see below on chapter 6). As to the endurance of creation, Philo sides with Aristotle over the Stoics in holding the world to be without end or destruction.

Chapter four considers the process by which pre-Nicene self-consciously theological discourse about the Creator and creation took shape, especially given that the earliest Christian expressions (in the NT) were doxological and narratival in form and not systematic or consciously theological. Blowers first surveys the NT writings, showing that, though distinct from each other, they present compatible indications that the coming of Jesus Christ provides the key to both the history of creation and to the cosmos' eschatological fulfillment. Over the next couple of centuries, these indications were summarized and normativized for liturgical and didactic purposes through various renderings of the Rule of Faith as well as in the crucible of competing worldviews (such as Gnosticism). Speaking of the proto-Gnostic worldview rejected by the Pastoral Epistles, Blowers writes: "the friction involves not so much the cosmological presuppositions per se of these false teachers as their drawing of conclusions about the way of salvation and establishing their own 'congruence' between cosmology and moral or ascetical practices"(p. 79). Early theologians and apologists responded to Gnostic and Greco-Roman intellectual threats not with philosophical or theoretical cosmology but with a "consideration of creation within the context of soteriology, as woven into the very fabric of the Christian narrative of salvation in Jesus Christ" (p. 81). Irenaeus of course loomed large in the fight against Gnostics by "fighting plot (*hypothesis*) with plot, dramatic myth with dramatic myth" (p. 85). Irenaeus presents the scriptural economy of salvation as a single "grand creative and transforma- tive action of God in Jesus Christ" (p. 86). Furthermore, by making the incarnation the definitive act of cosmic recapitulation, Irenaeus "set[s] the standard" for Patristic teaching about creation generally. Blowers concludes this chapter by looking at two approaches that contrasted with Irenaeus, Origin's Platonic view (even if curtailed by the Rule of Faith) and Marcion's pitting of the "new god" against the OT creator. Still, both in their own ways held to a soteriologically-oriented view of creation.

The fifth chapter studies how early Christians interpreted the six days (Hexameron) of creation in Gen 1. The many and varied efforts of Patristic Hexameral interpretation defy easy categorization into spiritual or literal readings or into distinct genres. Blowers chooses to divide modes of read- ing Gen 1 between more analytical (textual, philosophical, and theological) and more devotional (inspiring wonder at creation and soliciting contem- plation of creation's purpose), though these are not mutually exclusive. He lists more than a dozen writers from the first millennium (including Theo- philus of Antioch, Origen, Didymus the Blind, Gregory of Nyssa, Ephrem, Jerome, Augustine, Theodoret, etc. up to Bede and John Scottus Eriugena, as well as some Syriac commentaries) who favor the analytical approach in their "desire to explain the peculiar textual features of Genesis, respecting the order, sequence, and character of divine creation of the world" (p. 110). But they also all take into account issues such as Trinitarian theology, ontology, metaphysics, theodicy, anthropogony, etc. Blowers draws from these writers as he considers analytical Hexameral interpretations in the light of three issues: how the contrast of "heaven and earth" (Gen 1) triggered "dialectical analysis of the potential and actual, intelligible and sensible, and incorporeal and corporeal dimensions of creation" (p. 138); how theological reasoning, not physical or metaphysical explanations, determined the exegesis of "hovering Spirit/wind" in Gen 1:2; and how the interpretation of "light" (Gen 1:3) and "luminaries" (1:14) shows that analytical commentators were pursuing soteriological and Christological understanding as much as they were an understanding of cosmogony and cosmology. Blowers then examines four devotional interpretations: Basil of Caesarea's *Homilies on the Hexameron*, Ambrose's *Hexameron*, the *Hexameron* of Anastasius of Sinai, and George of Pisidia's *Hexameron* (the latter two from the 7th century). In both analytical and devotional modes, Hexameral interpretation evinces what Blowers calls a "thick" approach; that is, for these readers Gen 1 was not simply about the origins of creation but about how "[b]eginning, middle, and end all came together already in the creation narrative as though it were a complex mosaic, which ... could point the church toward the destiny of creation in Jesus Christ under the abiding aegis of the Holy Spirit" (p. 138).

Chapter six is an excursus of sorts, where Blowers goes back through the Christian writings already assessed with an eye to how they treated three additional issues arising from Gen 1. First, determining the sense of *archē* in "in the beginning" (Gen 1:1) highlights how they navigated the general problem of the intersection of eternity and time, especially in the post-Nicene era where Christ is affirmed as uncreated Creator and true *archē* of the world, his incarnation defining the purpose and destiny of all creation. Second, many interpreters also embraced the notion of a dual creation, first "simultaneous" (ideal) and then actual, an exegetical move inherited from Philo but now taken over by Christian writers to demonstrate God's freedom, the providence of his creative action, and the ensuing stability of the cosmos. Worth mentioning in particular is Blowers' discussion of Patristic views about the unfolding of creation's providential structure, especially Augustine's *rationes seminales* and Maximus the Confessor's *logoi* and their role in the making actual what existed formally in the Divine Logos. Finally, and again with Philo in the background, Blowers examines what was and has remained a vexing issue for Christian theologians, namely: is creation *ex nihilo*, or is God's eternal nature somehow hedged in by a pre-existent material substrate since "nothing comes from nothing"? Blowers ably guides his readers through the different ways Christian writers answered this through the scriptures, which are themselves rather ambiguous on the matter. We find that ultimately what drove Christians to affirm creation as *ex nihilo*, or more positively, *ex Deo*, was not so much a desire to elucidate the beginning of the Cosmos as it was a conviction that the creation's "beginning" was tied up with its middle, and end, that "teleology ... commands protology in Patristic interpretation of Genesis and in the emerging Christian theology of creation" (p. 12).

In chapter seven Blowers returns to the trajectory of his study by examining how Patristic writers interpreted non-Genesis scriptural passages that speak of the Creator and creation. In the Old Testament, he looks at interpretations of the Psalms, Deutero-Isaiah, and the Wisdom Literature (especially Proverbs and Ecclesiastes); in the NT, he studies interpretations of Rom 8:19–23 (the groaning of creation), the seven texts that speak of a "cosmic Christ" (John 1:3, 10; Heb 1:1–2; Rom 11:36; 1 Cor 8:6; Col 1:15–20, Eph 1; and 1 Cor 15:28), and those passages that speak of the "new creation" in Christ (such as Gal 6:15, 2 Cor 5:17, 1 Cor 15:20ff., 2 Pet 3:12–13, and Rev 21:1). Blowers adeptly moves between the biblical source material and Patristic interpretations (there are many of them, from various times and places, with varied approaches). Despite this variety, Blowers makes the case (text by text, interpreter by interpreter) for a Patristic consensus that Scripture's witness to creation was not simply about cosmology per se but about how creation both pointed to and participated in the unfolding drama of salvation.

The subject of chapter 8 fleshes out the question that previous chapters begged, namely what precisely entwines creation and redemption? Here Blowers explores how Patristic interpreters, most taking their cue from Irenaeus that the incarnate Jesus Christ is the 'recapitulation' (Eph 1:10) of all things, discerned the cosmic plot summarized and brought to fruition in the different stages of Christ's life (his virgin birth, baptism, miracles and healings, passion and death, resurrection, and ascension). Blowers also investigates Patristic understandings of the place of the Holy Spirit in the origin and perfection of creation. After looking at the Patristic defense (especially by the Cappadocians) of the Spirit's place in the Trinity and what this meant for the divine economy, Blowers considers the animating, sanctifying, beautifying, and perfecting aspects of the Spirit's work in creation. Together, Patristic renderings of the ministry of Jesus and of the Spirit provide a "panoramic view" of the triune Creator's enacting of the new creation.

Blowers' final chapter looks at Patristic understandings of the church's involvement in the divine economical drama. This involvement came through contemplation of nature (which originated in monasticism but was made accessible to the larger Christian community by writers such as Basil and Ambrose); liturgical and sacramental practices (Sunday [the eighth day of creation], baptism, and the Eucharist form a nexus where believers and the created order come together in the *oikonomia*); and "stewardship" (or "use") of creation (this last issue is an apologia of Patristic theology against contemporary views that early Christians denigrated the environment and saw no positive human role therein). Though this chapter alone focuses on praxis, it is important to Blowers to include it as it provides further evidence that Patristic cosmological inquiry was not a theoretical exercise about natural beginnings but a pressing pastoral matter and, in itself, an encounter with both creation and the divine story that enfolds it. Blowers attaches an epilogue that brings the main themes of the book together and relates them to the contemporary theologians, Kevin Vanhoozer and Hans Urs von Bathasar. Both developed the category of *drama* as a means for expressing God's, and especially Christ's, salvific role in the doctrine of creation.

The *Drama of the Divine Economy* provides an excellent synthesis of Patristic scriptural interpretation and theology with regards to creation and its place in God's salvific activity. My few negative criticisms include the lack of a more substantive treatment of Wisdom of Solomon as well as the need for more discussion about Patristic approaches to God the Father's role in the divine economy. Given how much material Blowers covers and the innate complexity of much of it, the volume is very well edited and he demonstrates a sober enthusiasm and trustworthy method that sustains his reader throughout. Philonists may not find much new research about Philo but they will encounter a Patristic scholar who provides a diligent and careful presentation of the Alexandrian's work and related secondary scholarship and who appreciates its rich relevance to early Christian thinkers. Blower also tracks a diverse array of themes and exegetical moves in Philo as they are picked up and re-worked by Patristic writers. His study thus suggests many possibilities for further investigation of Philo's place in Greco-Roman philosophy, New Testament Studies, and (of course) Patristic writings, not to mention encouragement to (re-)engage Philo's teachings about creation in their own right.

Ronald R. Cox
Pepperdine University
Malibu, California, U.S.A.

SARAH CATHERINE BYERS, *Perception, Sensibility, and Moral Motivation in Augustine: a Stoic-Platonic Synthesis.* New York: Cambridge University Press, 2013. xviii + 248 pages. Hardcover. ISBN 978-1-107-01794-8. Price $99.

A comparison between the two great thinkers Philo and Augustine is an interesting exercise. Though the one is Jewish and the other Christian, they both stand squarely in the biblical tradition, recognising the scriptures as authoritative for life and thought. Both have an extensive knowledge of the ancient philosophical tradition, in Philo's case based on writings in Greek, in Augustine's case drawn mainly from Latin sources though supported by a limited knowledge of Greek material. Both used that knowledge in service of the understanding of scripture. There is the further question of the relationship between the two. Did Augustine have much, if any, acquaintance with Philo's works and thought, and if so, did it exercise any influence on the development of his thought?

Against this background, the book under review has much to offer Philonists. The author now teaches in the Department of Philosophy at Boston College, but did her research for this study at the Pontifical Institute in Toronto and the University of Notre Dame. The book takes its starting-point from the famous garden scene in the *Confessions*, when Augustine stands on the point of converting to the life of Christian virtue but is held back by attachment to "old loves" (8.26–27) before hearing the voice of a child telling him to "pick up and read" (8.29). The subject of the book is moral psychology. What motivates a person to act in the way he or she does, and what are the rational and emotional processes involved? In exploring these questions Byers turns to an under-exploited source, Augustine's sermons. In this genre of writing the bishop often discusses questions of moral behaviour and decision-making, showing his knowledge and use of philosophical doctrines from both the Stoic and the Platonist schools, though the utilization is often done in a subtle and non-technical way. The argument of the book proceeds in a sequence of seven logically connected chapters.

The first chapter focuses on perception and the language of the mind. Byers argues that when Augustine speaks of "the chaste dignity of continence appearing" to him (*Conf.* 8.27), he follows the Stoic view that all human perception includes mental language. Texts from sermons show him using ideas from Stoic epistemology, notably the doctrine of "sayables" (λεκτά). The kind that applies in this case is the dubitative, which expresses doubt in relation to impressions concerning personal happiness. The next chapter moves on to the topic of motivation. If according to Augustine perceptions involve linguistic content, then he will be sympathetic to the cognitive psychological theories developed by the Stoics. There are action-inducing impressions to which the subject assents with his rational soul (*animus*), resulting in a command to action in the self. Such imperatives are described by Augustine in the language of "suggestions" which can be followed for good or for ill. The Stoic element can be seen in the fact that it is not a conflict between rationality and a non-rational physical power (as in Platonism) that occurs, but rather a cognitive dissonance: should I or should I not adopt a new chaste life-style? But this does not mean that Platonism does not enter the picture. It is the beauty of chastity and the love that it inspires that makes it attractive and persuasive as a goal of action. This is recognised by the higher mental faculty of the mind (*mens*). And there is also a Christian element in his theory: the ability actually to perform virtuous actions is given by grace that has its origins in Christ. Augustine thus achieves a coherent synthesis of Stoicism, Platonism and Christianity.

Stoic doctrines are also relevant to Augustine's views on the emotions, which are treated in chapter three. Byers shows, drawing again on his sermons, that Augustine adheres to core Stoic psychological principles. Judgments are made on whether something is good or evil and so give rise to emotions, whether morally good (affections, εὐπάθειαι) or morally bad (passions, πάθη). But Augustine also recognises that he has to move beyond Stoicism. He cannot agree that everything that is not virtue must not be considered good. There are other goods not admitted by the Stoics, including eternal goods beyond this life. Byers also examines the concepts of "will" and "love"—so important for Augustine, with strong biblical and Platonic resonances—and how they relate to the emotions.

The next two chapters discuss "preliminaries to emotions" and here Philo makes an entrance. Chapter four focuses on Augustine's understanding and use of "preliminary passions" (προπάθειαι). As Margaret Graver has shown (RRS 9931), Philo uses the term and is in fact the first to record it, though it was clearly coined earlier. It denotes changes in the rational soul (*animus*) caused by false impressions, which make their impact because of assent given to previous impressions that caused damage to its thinking. He uses it, for example, to explain how panic comes over Abraham and a great fear takes hold of him (Gen 15:12). Byers shows how Augustine develops his own theory on what is involved in this process, using a fixed array of expressions and metaphors for it. In the next chapter the question is then asked whether there are corresponding preliminaries to good emotions, i.e. προευπάθειαι. The term is never found and there may be a gap in Stoic theory, but Augustine is able to fill the lacuna using the example of Sarah and Abraham's laughter in Gen 16. But how original is this interpretation? In fact his explanation of the incident shows close affinities to Philo's treatment in QG III and IV and in *Mut*. Philo is less precise and consistent in his use of the concept, but there are certainly striking parallels, in particular the association of "preliminary joy" with doubt. In addition, for the προπάθειαι Philo uses some of the same metaphors that we find in Augustine. These are not found in Origen or Ambrose, so that the conclusion that he draws on the Jewish exegete is warranted. But he also shows independence from Philo. The latter in QG 1.79 calls hope a προπάθειά τις, χαρὰ πρὸ χαρᾶς, ἀγαθῶν οὖσα προσδοκία. Byers notes that this usage is either a confusion or an extension of the term, since πρό must refer to the relatively distant future that one is expecting and not the almost immediate precursor to an emotion, i.e. joy. Her suggestion that Philo is aware of this and for this reason qualifies the term with τις must be seriously entertained. She concludes (p. 150) that Augustine developed some of the suggestions made by Philo into a consistent theory which complemented and completed the Stoic taxonomy of emotions and their preliminaries.

The final two chapters continue the examination of Augustine's moral psychology. The first examines his views on cognitive therapies, ways in which the emotions can be rehabilitated and the person can develop emotional health. In the second the question is asked as to how it happens that people are motivated to begin on that process through what is classically known as repentance or conversion. Augustine agrees with the commonplace notion that habituation influences perception. In addition he is profoundly persuaded of the doctrine of "original sin." He develops the theory of conversion through divine inspiration or grace. The final part of the book delves into some complex theological problems arising from the role that grace plays in this process. Augustine in fact develops two theories that have implications for the understanding of God's role and as theodicies are "unequally satisfying" (p. 212).

It has not proved easy to summarize in a few pages the rich content of this austere but highly instructive monograph. The author writes clearly and explains the philosophical concepts she is dealing with well. The reader who invests time in studying this book will learn much about ancient moral psychology as well as about Augustine's understanding and adapations of it. He or she will be left in no doubt about his brilliance and the exceptional clarity of his thinking, even in non-philosophical works such as sermons. Another great virtue of the book is that it consistently deals with both ideas and sources. Byers is able to show where Augustine obtained his know-ledge—very often Cicero or Seneca, but also Plotinus and on occasion Philo—and what he then does with that knowledge. It must be said, however, that from the viewpoint of presentation the book would be a lot more accessible if it contained both an introductory chapter introducing its subject and a concluding chapter drawing together and recapitulating its main themes.

Finally I would like to draw attention to some interesting remarks that Byers makes on the relation between philosophy and scripture. When discussing the theme of preliminary passions she claims that, although much of the material for Augustine's account comes from scripture, it is he who gives it the philosophical interpretation which it receives by discover-ing relations between various phrases in the scriptural text and developing them into a single psychological account (p. 106). The point is valid, but it is worth adding that Augustine, just like Philo, would understand that the theory was inherent in scripture and drawn from it rather than imposed on it. If the account can lay claim to truth, as Augustine would no doubt aver, and scripture is the repository of truth, then it will be present in scripture and not just "compatible" with it (ibid. n. 40). The relations between texts that he discovers are not just his work, but are due to the unity of scripture as guaranteed by divine inspiration. A difference between Philo and Augustine might be that the Christian bishop is more driven to find coherent theories in scripture than the Jewish exegete, who is inclined to a more piecemeal and probabilistic approach.

David T. Runia
Queen's College
The University of Melbourne

NEWS AND NOTES

The Philo of Alexandria Group of the Society for Biblical Literature

At the 2013 Annual Meeting of the Society for Biblical Literature in Baltimore, Maryland, the Philo of Alexandria Group met for three sessions: two on the theme of "Philo's Sources" and one, held jointly with the Midrash Section, on the theme of "Biblical Interpretation in Philo and Other Early Exegetes: Uses and Influences." On Sunday, November 24, in the first session on Philo's sources, presided over by Thomas H. Tobin, S.J. (Loyola University of Chicago), speakers and presentations included Michael B. Cover (University of Notre Dame), "The Sun and the Chariot: The *Respublica* and the *Phaedrus* as Rival Platonic Models of Psychic Vision and Transformation in Philo"; David Runia (University of Melbourne), "Philo and the Opinions of the Philosophers"; Carlos Lévy (Université Paris-Sorbonne [Paris IV]), "About Some Concepts of Philonian Epistemology"; and Jutta Leonhardt-Balzer (University of Aberdeen), "Philo's Sources for His Arithmology in the *Quaestiones*."

On Monday, November 25, in the second session on the same theme, presided over by Sarah Pearce (University of Southampton), speakers and presentations included David Lincicum (University of Oxford), "Philo's Library: The Scope and Shape of Philo's Indebtedness to Non-Biblical Texts"; Pura Nieto Hernández (Brown University), "Philo of Alexandria, Reader of Homer and the Archaic Poets"; Gregory E. Sterling (Yale Divinity School), "From the Thick Marshes of the Nile to the Throne of God: Moses in Ezekiel and Philo"; and Francis Borchardt (Lutheran Theological Seminary, Hong Kong), "Philo's Use of Aristeas and the Question of Authority." This session was followed by a Business Meeting at which it was announced that the SBL Annual Meeting Program Committee had approved the renewal of the Philo of Alexandria Group as a Seminar (see below). Because this was the last year of Sarah Pearce's term as program unit co-chair, she was warmly thanked for her six years of service to the Group. She will be succeeded by Ronald Cox (Pepperdine University) (again, see below).

Later that day Ronald Cox presided over the third and final session, on "Biblical Interpretation in Philo and Other Early Exegetes." Speakers and presentations included Ilaria L. E. Ramelli (Catholic University Milan and

Durham University), "Philo's Doctrine of Apokatastasis: Philosophical Sources, Exegetical Strategies, and Aftermath"; Jason Sturdevant (North Carolina State University), "God—'Not Like a Human' yet 'Like Humans': Divine Adaptability and the Logos in Philo of Alexandria"; and Deborah Forger (University of Michigan-Ann Arbor), "Divine Embodiment in the Gospel of John and Philo's *De Opificio Mundi*." A fourth speaker, Horacio Vela (University of Notre Dame), was scheduled to speak on "Stoic Interpretations of Gen 2:7 at Alexandria?" but was unable to attend.

The text of a number of the presentations has been taken up in the Special Section of the present volume of *The Studia Philonica Annual*.

Following a celebration, hosted by SBL, to commemorate twenty-five years of *The Studia Philonica Annual* (see below), members and friends of the Philo Group continued to enjoy each other's company over dinner at Watertable Restaurant in the Renaissance Baltimore Harborplace Hotel. Besides several of the meeting participants listed above, the group included Peder and Inger Borgen and Torrey and Anne-Margrete Seland, all of Norway.

Renewal of the Philo of Alexandria Group as a Seminar

In the Fall of 2013, the SBL Annual Program Committee approved the renewal of the Philo of Alexandria Group as a Seminar (the option to remain a Group was no longer available). Seminars are focused on long-range collaborative research projects and papers are made available prior to meetings, at which they are discussed but not read. Seminar Co-Chairs are Ellen Birnbaum (Cambridge, Massachusetts) and Ronald Cox (Pepperdine University) and the Steering Committee includes Sarah Pearce (University of Southampton) and David Runia (University of Melbourne).

In support of the renewal, Ellen Birnbaum, Ronald Cox, and Sarah Pearce, who collaborated in the effort, gratefully received letters of endorsement from the following six program units: Book of Hebrews in Context, Development of Early Christian Theology, Function of Apocryphal and Pseudepigraphical Writings in Early Judaism and Early Christianity, Hellenistic Judaism, Josephus, and Midrash.

Below is a statement, drafted by Ronald Cox, of the program unit's rationale, past accomplishments, and vision for the future:

> The works of Philo of Alexandria (c. 20 BCE–50 CE) are a nexus, a point of convergence, for many topics studied in the Society of Biblical Literature. One of the largest extant literary corpora from antiquity, Philo's writings include biblical commentaries, explanations about the Jews and their religion, and philosophical treatises. These works reflect Philo's familiarity with exegetical

and speculative traditions from several strands of Second Temple Judaism and Greco-Roman philosophical circles. Philo provides a window into much of the thought world of the nearly concurrent New Testament. His thinking anticipates many themes, concerns, and approaches of rabbinical writings and his works, methods, and theology were appropriated and adapted by several Christian authors of late antiquity. It is difficult to overstate Philo's importance or the need to continue scholarly inquiry into his writings, context, and influence.

The SBL Philo of Alexandria Group has established itself as the preeminent international body for this inquiry; it is the only SBL program unit devoted primarily to Philo and the only group on Philo in the world to convene annually. By this year's meeting, our group will have offered or co-sponsored 16 sessions since its renewal in 2007, with approximately 65 different participants and an average 50 attendees per session. Speakers at these sessions will have come from 13 countries in addition to the United States (Australia, Brazil, Canada, France, Great Britain, Hong Kong, Israel, Italy, Netherlands, New Zealand, Norway, Portugal, and Switzerland).

Philo Group sessions generally fit within two categories: (1) *Philo in Context* addresses the world that Philo reflects or influences and will have included sessions on the Bible as it existed textually and was read in turn-of-the-era Alexandria, Philo and the Roman world as seen through his writings and those of some contemporaries, Philo's Greco-Roman readers, and, finally, his sources. In addition, we will have conducted joint sessions with several other program units, including those on Midrash, Hellenistic Judaism, Moral Philosophy and Early Christianity, and Letters of James, Peter, and Jude. (2) *Interpreting Philo* sessions provide a venue for authors producing volumes in the Philo of Alexandria Commentary Series (PACS) to present translations of and commentaries on portions of Philo's treatises and to receive criticism and/or hear about related studies from invited scholars and session attendees in a wide array of disciplines. Treatises studied since 2007 include *De Vita Contemplativa, De Agricultura, De Confusione Linguarum,* and *Legum Allegoriae* 1-3. Of these, *On Cultivation (De Agricultura)*, by A. C. Geljon and D. T. Runia, has since appeared (2013), joining three other PACS volumes published already by both Brill and SBL. Especially important, papers presented in both categories, *Philo in Context* and *Interpreting Philo*, have been published in the peer-reviewed journal *The Studia Philonica Annual (SPhA)* as well as in other scholarly journals and books. Indeed because of our strong publishing record and continued commitment to publication, we are seeking renewal as a Seminar.

Though our group has accomplished much, especially in the last six years, there is much that remains. If renewed, the Philo of Alexandria Seminar would continue to serve as the world's only scholarly group given to annual study of this significant figure. We have a large base of international scholars dedicated to Philonic studies and an increasing number of interested scholars in related fields. With the continuing success of PACS and the *SPhA*, we are confident that we can continue to preserve and promote the results of our seminar's efforts for years to come. Through calls for papers and open sessions, we are cultivating younger scholars and providing ways for them meaningfully and substantively to engage in Philonic inquiry and to network with established scholars in our field. Indeed, the Philo group is sustained by a deep collegiality that unites scholars from very many backgrounds in the common cause of explicating this Alexandrian thinker's value to many realms of inquiry that concern the SBL.

The Co-Chairs and Steering Committee are delighted that SBL has renewed the Philo of Alexandria Seminar and we look forward to continuing, with the help of future participants and contributors, the work of the Seminar as outlined above.

Ellen Birnbaum
Ronald Cox

Celebration 25 years The Studia Philonica Annual

On Monday, 25 November 2014 at its annual meeting, the Society of Biblical Literature hosted a reception for authors and editors at which a celebration was held to commemorate that *The Studia Philonica Annual* has been published for twenty-five years. The first volume saw the light of day in 1989, following six earlier volumes of *Studia Philonica* published in 1971 to 1980. In a speech Bob Buller, the Director of Publications of SBL, praised the editorial team for their achievement. In response the inaugural editor David Runia warmly thanked the publishers the team had worked with, Brown Judaic Studies and SBL Publications, and the many scholars who had contributed in numerous ways to the success of the Annual over the past quarter of a century. A good number of these contributors were present at the ceremony, including the other members of the current editorial team, Greg Sterling, Sarah Pearce and Ronald Cox, and members of the Annual's Board. He ended his remarks by expressing the wish that the Annual would continue to serve as a fine instrument of research for Philonists all over the world.

David T. Runia

Bob Buller and David Runia

Editors and Board members present at the ceremony
From left to right: Tom Tobin, David Runia, Greg Sterling,
Torrey Seland, Ellen Birnbaum, Sarah Pearce, James Royce, Jutta
Leonhardt-Balzer, Ronald Cox

Philo conference at Yale

"Philo's Readers: Affinities, Reception, Transmission and Influence" brought faculty and graduate students from all over the world to Yale University from March 30 until April 1, 2014. Philo's life and work served as the center of the conference, but the diversity of expertise among the participants also allowed for an examination of Philo's affinities with earlier texts and the reception and influence of his work on later thinkers, especially Jewish and Christian readers. This conference brought together scholars in Ancient Judaism, Classics, New Testament, Ancient Christianity and Philosophy for interdisciplinary conversations about Philo in his intellectual and historical context. Scholars thus considered the potential for resemblances and divergences between Philo and Josephus, Numenius, Plutarch, and rabbinic literature. Conversations about reception and influence included a presentation on the transmission of Philo in Byzantium and discussions about readers of Philo, which included Ambrose and Eusebius and extended to Jewish mystical literature, Hegel, and Krochmal. Philo's own work also received significant attention, particularly his exegetical interactions with the Greek scriptures.

Special presentations included an introduction to ancient Alexandria by J. G. Manning, a session on the ongoing Hebrew translation of Philo's works by Maren Niehoff, an update on the *Studia Philonica Annual* by David Runia and Gregory E. Sterling, and a tour of the Dura Europos exhibit at the Yale University Art Gallery, led by Steven Fraade and Harold Attridge.

The conference complemented an ongoing seminar on Philo for faculty and graduate students in Ancient Judaism, New Testament, and Ancient Christianity during the spring semester at Yale, taught by Hindy Najman and Harold Attridge. In addition to participating in the conference, Maren Niehoff, David Runia, and Carlos Lévy also joined seminar discussions. Many graduate students from the seminar presented papers at the conference on topics such as Philo's writing and reading practices, gender in Philo, the nature of the logos, and the consequences of true/false belief in Philo. Other graduate papers situated Philo in a larger context, exploring his Egyptian environment and reading Philo alongside texts from Qumran. Further details and the titles of the papers presented can be found on the conference's website, www.philosreception.com.

The conference was sponsored by the William and Miriam Horowitz Fund, Yale's Judaic Studies Program, Yale Divinity School, the Department of Classics, the Department of Religious Studies, and the Yale Initiative for the Study of Antiquity and the Premodern World (YISAP).

Olivia Stewart

Vale Dieter Zeller (1939–2014)

The band of Philonists suffered another loss with the passing in February 2014 of the German scholar of New Testament and Ancient Religion, Dieter Zeller, at the age of 74 years.

Dieter Zeller was born in Freiburg im Bresgau, where he studied Philosophy, Theology and Biblical Studies. He continued his studies in Rome and was ordained as a priest in the Roman Catholic Church. His doctoral thesis completed in 1972 had as its subject "Jews and Heathen in the Mission of Paul." Four years later he completed his Habilitation thesis on the subject of sapiential monitory sayings in the Synoptic gospels. He was appointed Professor of New Testament in Luzern in 1980 and moved to the same chair in Mainz two years later. In 1984 he left the priesthood and was appointed Professor of Hellenistic Religions at the University of Mainz, a position which he retained until his retirement in 2004. His field of research was broad, with a particular focus on the writings and thought of Paul. He published widely, producing commentaries, monographs and a large number of articles. Sixteen of these were gathered together in the volume *Studien zu Philo und Paulus* published in Bonn in 2011 (see Bibliography elsewhere in this volume).

Dieter came to Philonic studies through his interest in Wisdom literature and Paul. In 1990 he published his important study on the concept of grace in Philo and Paul, in which he presented an insightful comparison of two thinkers who were near contemporaries and operated in a similar context, but through their differing loyalties developed distinct theological and anthropological views. His article, published in this Annual in 1995 on the life and death of the soul explored a key theme in Philo's allegorical system. From 1996 to 2003 he was a member of the International Philo Bibliography Project team, summarizing numerous articles written in German. Even after retiring from the project he remained involved, sending information on articles and even sometimes summaries. Dieter was a sharp-witted, well-trained scholar in the German tradition of biblical scholarship. Confident of his own views, he did not mind entering into lively exchanges with other scholars, but always remained courteous and open to other opinions. He was generous in his assistance to others, even when in the last period of his life he suffered from a debilitating illness. He will be missed, but his contribution to scholarship will live on. Vale, Dieter.

David T. Runia

The Studia Philonica Annual 26 (2014) 265–267

NOTES ON CONTRIBUTORS

KATELL BERTHELOT is currently appointed at the Centre Paul-Albert Février at the University of Aix-Marseille, Aix-en-Provence. Her postal address is Maison Méditerranéenne des Sciences de l'Homme, 5 rue du château de l'horloge, BP 647, 13094 Aix-en-Provence Cedex 2, FRANCE; her electronic address is katell.b@free.fr.

ELLEN BIRNBAUM has taught at several Boston-area institutions, including Boston University, Brandeis, and Harvard. Her postal address is 78 Porter Road, Cambridge, MA 02140, U.S.A.; her electronic address is ebirnbaum78@gmail.com.

FREDERICK E. BRENK, S.J. is Emeritus Professor at the Pontifical Biblical Institute in Rome, ITALY. His postal address is Arrupe House Jesuit Community, 831 North 13th Street, Milwaukee, WI 53233-1706, U.S.A.; his electronic address is fbrenk@jesuitswisprov.org.

JOHN J. COLLINS is Holmes Professor of Old Testament at Yale Divinity School. His postal address is Yale Divinity School, 409 Prospect, New Haven, CT 06511, U.S.A.; his electronic address is john.j.collins @yale.edu.

MICHAEL COVER is Assistant Professor of New Testament in the Department of Theology at Marquette University. His postal address is Marquette University-Theology, P.O. Box 1881, Milwaukee, WI, 53201-1881, U.S.A.; his electronic address is michael.cover@marquette.edu

RONALD COX, the Blanche E. Seaver Professor of Religion, is Associate Professor in the religion division at Pepperdine University. His postal address is Religion Division, Pepperdine University, Malibu, CA 90263-4352, U.S.A.; his electronic address is ronald.cox@pepperdine.edu.

ALBERT C. GELJON teaches classical languages at the Christelijke Gymnasium in Utrecht. His postal address is Gazellestraat 138, 3523 SZ Utrecht, THE NETHERLANDS; his electronic address is ageljon@xs4all.nl.

Heleen M. Keizer is Dean of Academic Affairs at the Istituto Superiore di Osteopatia in Milan, Italy. Her postal address is Via Guerrazzi 3, 20900 Monza (MB), Italy; her electronic address is h.m.keizer@virgilio.it.

Jutta Leonhardt-Balzer, Senior Lecturer for New Testament at the University of Aberdeen. Her postal address is School of Divinity, History and Philosophy, King's Quadrangle, University of Aberdeen, Aberdeen AB24 3UB, United Kingdom; her electronic address is j.leonhardt-balzer@abdn.ac.uk.

David Lincicum is University Lecturer in New Testament Studies at the University of Oxford and Caird Fellow in Theology at Mansfield College. His postal address is Mansfield College, Oxford OX1 3TF, United Kingdom; his electronic address is david.lincicum@theology.ox.ac.uk.

M. David Litwa is Lecturer in Classics at the University of Virginia. His postal address is University of Virginia, PO Box 400126, B006 Cocke Hall, Charlottesville VA 22903, U.S.A.; his electronic address is mdl2dj@virginia.edu

Scott D. Mackie has taught courses at Loyola Marymount University, Westmont College, and Fuller Theological Seminary. His postal address is 51 Rose Ave. #17, Venice CA 90291, U.S.A.; his electronic address is scottdmackie@gmail.com

José Pablo Martín is Professor Consultus at the Universidad Nacional de General Sarmiento, San Miguel, Argentina, and Senior Research fellow of the Argentinian Research Organization (CONICET). His postal address is Azcuenaga 1090, 1663 San Miguel, Argentina; his electronic address is philonis@fastmail.fm.

Maren R. Niehoff is Professor in the Department of Jewish Thought at the Hebrew University, Jerusalem. Her postal address is Department of Jewish Thought, Hebrew University, Mt. Scopus, Jerusalem 91905, Israel; her electronic address is msmaren@mscc.huji.ac.il.

Pura Nieto Hernández is Senior Lecturer in Classics at Brown University. Her postal address is Department of Classics. Box 1856 Brown University. Providence, RI 02912, U.S.A.; her electronic address is Pura_Nieto@ brown.edu

SARAH J. K. PEARCE is Ian Karten Professor of Jewish Studies at the University of Southampton. Her postal address is Department of History, Faculty of Humanities, Avenue Campus, Highfield, Southampton SO17 1BF, UNITED KINGDOM; her electronic address is sjp2@soton.ac.uk.

ILARIA L.E. RAMELLI is Professor of Theology and Bishop K. Britt Chair at the Graduate School of Theology, SHMS (Thomas Aquinas University "Angelicum"), and Senior Fellow in Religion at Erfurt University and in Ancient Philosophy at the Catholic University Milan. Her postal address is: Catholic University of the Sacred Heart, Philosophy Dept., Largo A. Gemelli 1, 20123 Milan, ITALY. Her electronic address is: ilaria.ramelli @unicatt.it & i.l.e.ramelli@durham.ac.uk

JUSTIN M. ROGERS is an Assistant Professor of Biblical Studies at Freed-Hardeman University. His postal address is FHU Box 2, Henderson TN 38340-2306, U.S.A. His electronic address is jrogers@fhu.edu

DAVID T. RUNIA is Master of Queen's College and Professorial Fellow in the School of Historical and Philosophical Studies at the University of Melbourne. His postal address is Queen's College, 1–17 College Crescent, Parkville 3052, AUSTRALIA; his electronic address is runia@queens.unimelb.edu.au.

TORREY SELAND is Professor Emeritus of The School of Mission and Theology, Stavanger, Norway. His postal address is Milorgveien 41, 3035 Drammen, NORWAY; his electronic address is torreys@gmail.com.

GREGORY E. STERLING is the Lillian Claus Professor of New Testament and the Reverend Henry L. Slack Dean of the Yale Divinity School. His postal address is 409 Prospect Street, New Haven, CT 06511, U.S.A.; his electronic address is gregory.sterling@yale.edu.

SHARON WEISSER is Lecturer at the Department of Philosophy, Tel Aviv University. Her postal address is The Department of Philosophy, Tel-Aviv University, P.O.B. 39040, Ramat Aviv, Tel-Aviv 69978, ISRAEL; her electronic address is weisser@post.tau.ac.i

The Studia Philonica Annual 26 (2014) 268–274

INSTRUCTIONS TO CONTRIBUTORS

Articles and Book reviews can only be considered for publication in *The Studia Philonica Annual* if they rigorously conform to the guidelines established by the editorial board. For further information see also the website of the Annual:

http://divinity.yale.edu/philo-alexandria

1. *The Studia Philonica Annual* accepts articles for publication in the area of Hellenistic Judaism, with special emphasis on Philo and his *Umwelt*. Articles on Josephus will be given consideration if they focus on his relation to Judaism and classical culture (and not on primarily historical subjects). The languages in which the articles may be published are English, French and German. Translations from Italian or Dutch into English can be arranged at a modest cost to the author.

2. Articles and reviews are to be sent to the editors in electronic form as email attachments. The preferred word processor is Microsoft Word. Users of other word processors are requested to submit a copy exported in a format compatible with Word, e.g. in RTF format. Manuscripts should be double-spaced, including the notes. Words should be italicized when required, not underlined. Quotes five lines or longer should be indented and may be single-spaced. For texts in Greek only Unicode fonts can be accepted. Authors are requested to use **a different font for Greek text**, e.g. SBL Greek (available at no cost from the SBL website), as compared to Roman text. For Hebrew the font provided on the SBL website is recommended. If the manuscript contains Greek or Hebrew text, a PDF version of the document must be sent together with the word processing file. No handwritten Greek or Hebrew can be accepted. Authors are requested not to vocalize their Hebrew (except when necessary) and to keep their use of this language to a reasonable minimum. It should always be borne in mind that not all readers of the Annual can be expected to read Greek or Hebrew. Transliteration is encouraged for incidental terms.

3. Authors are encouraged to use inclusive language wherever possible, avoiding terms such as "man" and "mankind" when referring to humanity in general.

4. For the preparation of articles and book reviews the Annual follows the guidelines of the *SBL Handbook of Style*, Second Edition, Atlanta: SBL Press, 2014. Here are examples of how a monograph, a monograph in a series, an edited volume, an article in an edited volume and a journal article are to be cited in notes (different conventions apply for bibliographies):

Joan E. Taylor, *Jewish Women Philosophers of First-Century Alexandria — Philo's 'Therapeutae' Reconsidered* (Oxford: Oxford University Press, 2003), 123.

Ellen Birnbaum, *The Place of Judaism in Philo's Thought: Israel, Jews, and Proselytes* (BJS 290; SPhM 2; Atlanta: Scholars Press, 1996), 134.

Gerard P. Luttikhuizen, ed., *Eve's Children: The Biblical Stories Retold and Interpreted in Jewish and Christian Traditions* (Themes in Biblical Narrative 5; Leiden: Brill, 2003), 145.

G. Bolognesi, "Marginal Notes on the Armenian Translation of the *Quaestiones et Solutiones in Genesim* by Philo," in *Studies on the Ancient Armenian Version of Philo's Works* (eds. Sara Mancini Lombardi and Paola Pontani; Studies in Philo of Alexandria 6; Leiden: Brill, 2011) 45–50.

James R. Royse, "Jeremiah Markland's Contribution to the Textual Criticism of Philo." *SPhA* 16 (2004): 50–60.

Note that abbreviations are used in the notes, but not in a bibliography. Numbers should be given in full for texts, e.g. *Aet.* 107–110; in references to modern publications the conventions of the *SBL Handbook of Style* should be followed (see p. 18). When joining up numbers in all textual and bibliographical references, the en dash should be used and not the hyphen, i.e. 50–60, not 50-60. For publishing houses only the first location is given. Submissions which do not conform to these guidelines will be returned to the authors for re-submission.

5. The following abbreviations are to be used in both articles and book reviews.

(a) Philonic treatises are to be abbreviated according to the following list. Numbering follows the edition of Cohn and Wendland, using Arabic numbers only and full stops rather than colons (e.g. *Spec.* 4.123). Note that *De Providentia* should be cited according to Aucher's edition, and not the LCL translation of the fragments by F. H. Colson.

Abr.	*De Abrahamo*
Aet.	*De aeternitate mundi*
Agr.	*De agricultura*
Anim.	*De animalibus*
Cher.	*De Cherubim*
Contempl.	*De vita contemplativa*
Conf.	*De confusione linguarum*
Congr.	*De congressu eruditionis gratia*
Decal.	*De Decalogo*
Deo	*De Deo*
Det.	*Quod deterius potiori insidiari soleat*

Deus	*Quod Deus sit immutabilis*
Ebr.	*De ebrietate*
Flacc.	*In Flaccum*
Fug.	*De fuga et inventione*
Gig.	*De gigantibus*
Her.	*Quis rerum divinarum heres sit*
Hypoth.	*Hypothetica*
Ios.	*De Iosepho*
Leg. 1–3	*Legum allegoriae* I, II, III
Legat.	*Legatio ad Gaium*
Migr.	*De migratione Abrahami*
Mos. 1–2	*De vita Moysis* I, II
Mut.	*De mutatione nominum*
Opif.	*De opificio mundi*
Plant.	*De plantatione*
Post.	*De posteritate Caini*
Praem.	*De praemiis et poenis, De exsecrationibus*
Prob.	*Quod omnis probus liber sit*
Prov. 1–2	*De Providentia* I, II
QE 1–2	*Quaestiones et solutiones in Exodum* I, II
QG 1–4	*Quaestiones et solutiones in Genesim* I, II, III, IV
Sacr.	*De sacrificiis Abelis et Caini*
Sobr.	*De sobrietate*
Somn. 1–2	*De somniis* I, II
Spec. 1–4	*De specialibus legibus* I, II, III, IV
Virt.	*De virtutibus*

(b) Standard works of Philonic scholarship are abbreviated as follows:

G-G   Howard L. Goodhart and Erwin R. Goodenough, "A General Bibliography of Philo Judaeus." In *The Politics of Philo Judaeus: Practice and Theory* (ed. Erwin R. Goodenough; New Haven: Yale University Press, 1938; repr. Georg Olms: Hildesheim, 1967), 125–321.

PCH   *Philo von Alexandria: die Werke in deutscher Übersetzung*, ed. Leopold Cohn, Isaac Heinemann *et al.*, 7 vols. (Breslau: M & H Marcus Verlag, Berlin: Walter de Gruyter, 1909–64).

PCW   *Philonis Alexandrini opera quae supersunt*, ed. Leopoldus Cohn, Paulus Wendland et Sigismundus Reiter, 6 vols. (Berlin: Georg Reimer, 1896–1915).

PLCL   *Philo in Ten Volumes (and Two Supplementary Volumes)*, English translation by F. H. Colson, G. H. Whitaker (and R. Marcus), 12 vols. (Loeb Classical Library; London: William Heinemann, Cambridge, Mass.: Harvard University Press, 1929–62).

PACS   Philo of Alexandria Commentary Series

PAPM   *Les œuvres de Philon d'Alexandrie*, French translation under the general editorship of Roger Arnaldez, Jean Pouilloux, and Claude Mondésert (Paris: Cerf, 1961–92).

R-R	Roberto Radice and David T. Runia, *Philo of Alexandria: an Anno-tated Bibliography 1937–1986* (VCSup 8; Leiden: Brill 1988).
RRS	David T. Runia, *Philo of Alexandria: an Annotated Bibliography 1987–1996* (VCSup 57; Leiden: Brill 2000).
RRS2	David T. Runia, *Philo of Alexandria: an Annotated Bibliography 1997–2006* (VCSup 109; Leiden: Brill 2012).
SPh	*Studia Philonica*
SPhA	*The Studia Philonica Annual*
SPhM	Studia Philonica Monographs

(c) References to biblical authors and texts and to ancient authors and writings are to be abbreviated as recommended in the *SBL Handbook of Style* §8.2–3. Note that biblical books are not italicized and that between chapter and verse a colon is placed (but for non-biblical references colons should not be used). Abbreviations should be used for biblical books when they are followed by chapter or chapter and verse unless the book is the first word in a sentence. Authors writing in German or French should follow their own conventions for biblical citations.

(d) For giving dates the abbreviations BCE and CE are preferred and should be printed in regular large caps.

(e) Journals, monograph series, source collections, and standard reference works are to be be abbreviated in accordance with the recommendations listed in *The SBL Handbook of Style* §8.4. The following list contains a selection of the more important abbreviations, along with a few abbreviations of classical and philosophical journals and standard reference books not furnished in the list.

ABD	*The Anchor Bible Dictionary*, 6 vols. New York, 1992
AC	*L'Antiquité Classique*
ACW	Ancient Christian Writers
AGJU	Arbeiten zur Geschichte des antiken Judentums und des Urchristentums
AJPh	*American Journal of Philology*
AJSL	*American Journal of Semitic Languages*
ALGHJ	Arbeiten zur Literatur und Geschichte des hellenistischen Judentums
ANRW	*Aufstieg und Niedergang der römischen Welt*
APh	*L'Année Philologique*
BDAG	Bauer, W., F. W. Danker, W. F. Arndt, and F. W. Gingrich. *A Greek-English Lexicon of the New Testament and Other Early Christian literature.* 3^d ed. Chicago: University of Chicago Press, 1999
BibOr	Bibliotheca Orientalis
BJRL	*Bulletin of the John Rylands Library*
BJS	Brown Judaic Studies
BMCR	*Bryn Mawr Classical Review* (electronic)
BZAW	Beihefte zur Zeitschrift für die alttestamentliche Wissenschaft

BZNW	Beihefte zur Zeitschrift für die neutestamentliche Wissenschaft
BZRGG	Beihefte zur Zeitschrift für Religions- und Geistesgeschichte
CBQ	*The Catholic Biblical Quarterly*
CBQMS	The Catholic Biblical Quarterly. Monograph Series
CC	Corpus Christianorum, Turnhout
CIG	*Corpus Inscriptionum Graecarum*. Edited by A. Boeckh, 4 vols. in 8. Berlin, 1828–77
CIJ	*Corpus Inscriptionum Judaicarum*. Edited by J. B. Frey, 2 vols. Rome, 1936–52
CIL	*Corpus Inscriptionum Latinarum*. Berlin, 1862–
CIS	*Corpus Inscriptionum Semiticarum*. Paris, 1881–1962
CPh	*Classical Philology*
CPJ	*Corpus Papyrorum Judaicarum*. Edited by V. Tcherikover and A. Fuks, 3 vols. Cambrige Mass., 1957–64
CQ	*The Classical Quarterly*
CR	*The Classical Review*
CRINT	Compendia Rerum Iudaicarum ad Novum Testamentum
CPG	*Clavis Patrum Graecorum*. Edited by M. Geerard, 5 vols. and suppl. vol. Turnhout, 1974–98
CPL	*Clavis Patrum Latinorum*. Edited by E. Dekkers. 3rd ed. Turnhout, 1995
CSCO	Corpus Scriptorum Christianorum Orientalium
CWS	Classics of Western Spirituality
DA	Dissertation Abstracts
DBSup	*Dictionnaire de la Bible*, Supplément. Paris, 1928–
DPhA	R. Goulet (ed.), *Dictionnaire des philosophes antiques*, Paris, 1989–
DSpir	*Dictionnaire de Spiritualité*, 17 vols. Paris, 1932–95
EncJud	*Encyclopaedia Judaica*, 16 vols. Jerusalem, 1972
EPRO	Études préliminaires aux religions orientales dans l'Empire romain
FrGH	*Fragmente der Griechische Historiker*. Edited by F. Jacoby et al. Leiden, 1954–
FRLANT	Forschungen zur Religion und Literatur des Alten und Neuen Testaments
GCS	Die griechischen christlichen Schriftsteller, Leipzig
GLAJJ	M. Stern, *Greek and Latin Authors on Jews and Judaism*, 3 vols. Jerusalem, 1974–84
GRBS	*Greek, Roman and Byzantine Studies*
HKNT	Handkommentar zum Neuen Testament, Tübingen
HNT	Handbuch zum Neuen Testament, Tübingen
HR	*History of Religions*
HThR	*Harvard Theological Review*
HUCA	*Hebrew Union College Annual*
JAAR	*Journal of the American Academy of Religion*
JAOS	*Journal of the American Oriental Society*
JAC	*Jahrbuch für Antike und Christentum*
JBL	*Journal of Biblical Literature*
JHI	*Journal of the History of Ideas*
JHS	*The Journal of Hellenic Studies*
JJS	*The Journal of Jewish Studies*
JQR	*The Jewish Quarterly Review*
JR	*The Journal of Religion*
JRS	*The Journal of Roman Studies*

JSHRZ	Jüdische Schriften aus hellenistisch-römischer Zeit
JSJ	*Journal for the Study of Judaism in the Persian, Hellenistic and Roman Periods*
JSJSup	Supplements to the Journal for the Study of Judaism
JSNT	*Journal for the Study of the New Testament*
JSNTSup	Journal for the Study of the New Testament. Supplement Series
JSOT	*Journal for the Study of the Old Testament*
JSOTSup	Journal for the Study of the Old Testament. Supplement Series
JSP	*Journal for the Study of the Pseudepigrapha and Related Literature*
JSSt	*Journal of Semitic Studies*
JThS	*The Journal of Theological Studies*
KBL	L. Koehler and W. Baumgartner, *Lexicon in Veteris Testamenti libros*, 3 vols. 3rd ed. Leiden, 1967–83
KJ	*Kirjath Sepher*
LCL	Loeb Classical Library
LSJ	*A Greek-English Lexicon*. Edited by H. G. Liddell, R. Scott, H. S. Jones. 9th ed. with revised suppl. Oxford, 1996
MGWJ	*Monatsschrift für Geschichte und Wissenschaft des Judentums*
Mnem	*Mnemosyne*
NCE	*New Catholic Encyclopedia*, 15 vols. New York, 1967
NETS	New English Translation of the Septuagint. Edited by Albert Pietersma and Ben Wright, New York: Oxford University Press, 2007
NHS	Nag Hammadi Studies
NT	*Novum Testamentum*
NTSup	Supplements to Novum Testamentum
NTA	*New Testament Abstracts*
NTOA	Novum Testamentum et Orbis Antiquus
NTS	*New Testament Studies*
ODJ	*The Oxford Dictionary of Judaism*. Edited by R.J.Z. Werblowsky and G. Wigoder, New York 1997
OGIS	*Orientis Graeci inscriptiones selectae*
OLD	*The Oxford Latin Dictionary*. Edited by P. G. W. Glare. Oxford, 1982
OTP	*The Old Testament Pseudepigrapha*. Edited by J. H. Charlesworth. 2 vols. New York–London, 1983–85
PAAJR	*Proceedings of the American Academy for Jewish Research*
PAL	*Philon d'Alexandrie: Lyon 11–15 Septembre 1966*. Éditions du CNRS, Paris, 1967
PG	Patrologiae cursus completus: series Graeca. Edited by J. P. Migne. 162 vols. Paris, 1857–1912
PGL	*A Patristic Greek Lexicon*. Edited by G. W. H. Lampe. Oxford, 1961
PhilAnt	Philosophia Antiqua
PL	Patrologiae cursus completus: series Latina. Edited by J. P. Migne. 221 vols. Paris, 1844–64
PW	Pauly-Wissowa-Kroll, *Real-Encyclopaedie der classischen Altertumswissenschaft*. 49 vols. Munich, 1980
PWSup	Supplement to PW
RAC	*Reallexikon für Antike und Christentum*
RB	*Revue Biblique*
REA	*Revue des Études Anciennes*
REArm	*Revue des Études Arméniennes*
REAug	*Revue des Études Augustiniennes*

REG	*Revue des Études Grecques*
REJ	*Revue des Études Juives*
REL	*Revue des Études Latines*
RGG	*Die Religion in Geschichte und Gegenwart*, 7 vols. 3rd edition Tübingen, 1957–65
RhM	*Rheinisches Museum für Philologie*
RHR	*Revue de l'histoire des religions*
RQ	*Revue de Qumran*
RSR	*Revue des Sciences Religieuses*
Str-B	H. L. Strack and P. Billerbeck, *Kommentar zum Neuen Testament aus Talmud und Midrasch*, 6 vols. Munich, 1922–61
SBLDS	Society of Biblical Literature Dissertation Series
SBLMS	Society of Biblical Literature Monograph Series
SBLSCS	Society of Biblical Studies Septuagint and Cognate Studies
SBLSPS	Society of Biblical Literature Seminar Papers Series
SC	Sources Chrétiennes
Sem	*Semitica*
SHJP	E. Schürer, *The History of the Jewish People in the Age of Jesus Christ.* Revised edition, 3 vols. in 4. Edinburgh, 1973–87
SJLA	Studies in Judaism in Late Antiquity
SNTSMS	Society for New Testament Studies. Monograph Series
SR	*Studies in Religion*
STAC	Studies and Texts in Antiquity and Judaism
SUNT	Studien zur Umwelt des Neuen Testaments
SVF	*Stoicorum veterum fragmenta*. Edited by J. von Arnim. 4 vols. Leipzig, 1903–24
TDNT	*Theological Dictionary of the New Testament*. 10 vols. Grand Rapids, 1964–76
THKNT	Theologischer Handkommentar zum Neuen Testament, Berlin
TRE	*Theologische Realenzyklopädie*, Berlin
TSAJ	Texte und Studien zum Antike Judentum
TU	Texte und Untersuchungen zur Geschichte der altchristlichen Literatur, Berlin
TWNT	*Theologisches Wörterbuch zum Neuen Testament*, 10 vols. Stuttgart 1933–79.
TZ	*Theologische Zeitschrift*
VC	*Vigiliae Christianae*
VCSup	Supplements to Vigiliae Christianae
VT	*Vetus Testamentum*
WMANT	Wissenschaftliche Monographien zum Alten und Neuen Testament
WUNT	Wissenschaftliche Untersuchungen zum Neuen Testament
YJS	*Yale Jewish Studies*
ZAW	*Zeitschrift für die alttestamentliche Wissenschaft*
ZKG	*Zeitschrift für Kirchengeschichte*
ZKTh	*Zeitschrift für Katholische Theologie*
ZNW	*Zeitschrift für die neutestamentliche Wissenschaft*
ZRGG	*Zeitschrift für Religions- und Geistesgeschichte*